IRELAND, ENLIGHTENMENT
AND THE ENGLISH STAGE, 1740–1820

The theatre was a crucial forum for the representation of Irish civility and culture to the eighteenth-century English audience. Irish actors and playwrights, operating both as individuals and within networks, were remarkably popular and potent during this period, especially in London. As ideas of Enlightenment percolated throughout Britain and Ireland, Irish theatrical practitioners – actors, managers, playwrights, critics and journalists – exploited a growing receptivity to Irish civility and advanced a patriot agenda of political and economic autonomy. Mobility, toleration and the capacity to negotiate multiple allegiances are marked features of this Irish theatrical Enlightenment whose ambitious participants saw little conflict between their twin loyalties to the Crown and to Ireland. This collection of essays responds to recent work in the areas of eighteenth-century theatre studies, Irish studies and Enlightenment studies. The volume's discussions of genre, colonialism, gender, race, music, slavery and dress open up new avenues of scholarship and research across disciplines.

DAVID O'SHAUGHNESSY is Associate Professor of English at Trinity College Dublin. He has published widely on eighteenth-century theatre studies, including *William Godwin and the Theatre* (2010). Most recently, he edited 'Networks of Aspiration: The London Irish of the Eighteenth Century', a special issue of *Eighteenth-Century Life* (2015) and co-edited *The Letters of Oliver Goldsmith* (2018).

IRELAND, ENLIGHTENMENT AND THE ENGLISH STAGE, 1740–1820

EDITED BY

DAVID O'SHAUGHNESSY

Trinity College Dublin

CAMBRIDGE
UNIVERSITY PRESS

University Printing House, Cambridge CB2 8BS, United Kingdom

One Liberty Plaza, 20th Floor, New York, NY 10006, USA

477 Williamstown Road, Port Melbourne, VIC 3207, Australia

314–321, 3rd Floor, Plot 3, Splendor Forum, Jasola District Centre,
New Delhi – 110025, India

79 Anson Road, #6–04/06, Singapore 079906

Cambridge University Press is part of the University of Cambridge.

It furthers the University's mission by disseminating knowledge in the pursuit of
education, learning, and research at the highest international levels of excellence.

www.cambridge.org
Information on this title: www.cambridge.org/9781108498142
DOI: 10.1017/9781108628747

© Cambridge University Press 2019

First published 2019

Printed in the United Kingdom by TJ International Ltd. Padstow Cornwall

A catalogue record for this publication is available from the British Library.

Library of Congress Cataloging-in-Publication Data
NAMES: O'Shaughnessy, David, 1976– editor of compilation.
TITLE: Ireland, Enlightenment and the English stage, 1740–1820 / edited by David
O'Shaughnessy, Trinity College, Dublin.
DESCRIPTION: Cambridge ; New York, NY : Cambridge University Press, 2019 | Includes
bibliographical references and index.
IDENTIFIERS: LCCN 2019005242 | ISBN 9781108498142 (alk. paper)
SUBJECTS: LCSH: Theater – Ireland–History – 18th century. | Theater – England – History –
18th century. | English drama – Irish authors – History and criticism. | English drama –
18th century – History and criticism. | Ireland – Intellectual life – 18th century. | Great
Britain – Intellectual life – 18th century. | Enlightenment – Ireland. | Enlightenment – England.
CLASSIFICATION: LCC PN601 .1745 2019 | DDC 792/.09415090/33–dc23
LC record available at https://lccn.loc.gov/2019005242

ISBN 978-1-108-49814-2 Hardback

Contents

Illustrations

Tables

Contributors

MICHAEL BURDEN is Professor in Opera Studies at Oxford University and Chair of the Board of the Faculty of Music; he is also Fellow in Music at New College, where he is Dean. His published research is on the stage music of Henry Purcell and on aspects of London dance and theatre in the seventeenth, eighteenth and nineteenth centuries. He is currently completing a volume on the staging of opera in London between 1660 and 1860; his publications include a collection of opera documents, the five-volume *London Opera Observed 1711–1843* (2013) and a study of the London years of the soprano Regina Mingotti (2013). A volume edited with Jennifer Thorp – *The Works of Monsieur Noverre Translated from the French: Noverre, His Circle, and the English* Lettres sur la Danse – appeared in 2014, and a jointly edited volume, *Staging History 1740–1840* in 2016.

HELEN BURKE is Professor Emerita of English at Florida State University. She is the author of *Riotous Performances: The Struggle for Hegemony in the Irish Theatre, 1712–1784* (2003) and numerous articles on eighteenth-century theatre. She is currently working on a book on the Irish diaspora and the eighteenth-century London stage. Recent publications relating to this topic have appeared in *Eighteenth-Century Fiction, Eighteenth-Century Life, Éire-Ireland* and the *Blackwell Companion to Irish Literature*.

JIM DAVIS is Professor of Theatre Studies at the University of Warwick. His major research interest is in nineteenth-century British theatre and his most recent books are *Comic Acting and Portraiture in Late-Georgian and Regency England* (Cambridge University Press, 2015), *Theatre & Entertainment* (2016) and Volume 2 of a two-volume edition of nineteenth-century dramatisations of Dickens (with Jacky Bratton) (2017). He is also joint-author of *Reflecting the Audience: London Theatre-going 1840–1880* (2001). Currently, he is working on an AHRC-funded project on theatre and visual culture in nineteenth-century Britain.

OSKAR COX JENSEN is Leverhulme Fellow in the Department of History, Queen Mary University of London, and until May 2017 was Research Fellow on 'Music in London, 1800–1851' at King's College London. He is the author of *Napoleon and British Song* (2015) and co-editor of *Charles Dibdin and Late Georgian Culture* (2018).

ROBERT W. JONES is Professor of Eighteenth-Century Studies at the University of Leeds, UK. His most recent book is *Literature, Gender and Politics in Britain during the War for America 1770–1785*, which was published by Cambridge University Press in 2011. He is the author of several essays and articles on Sheridan and is currently working a book entitled *The Theatre of Richard Brinsley Sheridan: Politics and Performance at Drury Lane*. With Martyn J. Powell, he is editing *The Political Works of Richard Brinsley Sheridan* in four volumes.

DECLAN MCCORMACK is a PhD candidate at the University of York, researching late eighteenth-century Northern British theatre with an emphasis on how actors used their theatrical identity to develop networks of association in the communities where they performed. His academic interests have grown out of prior experience working as a filmmaker in international development where he had many opportunities to see how civil society, government and external influences interact in local settings. He grew up in Richmond, North Yorkshire, home to the oldest Georgian theatre in its original form in Britain.

FELICITY NUSSBAUM is Distinguished Research Professor at the University of California, Los Angeles, and author most recently of *Rival Queens: Actresses, Performance, and the Eighteenth-Century British Theatre* (2013). Among her other books are *The Arabian Nights in Historical Context* (2009) with Saree Makdisi; *The Limits of the Human: Fictions of Anomaly, Race, and Gender* (Cambridge University Press, 2003); and *Torrid Zones: Maternity, Sexuality and Empire* (1995). Her essays on eighteenth-century drama have appeared recently in *PMLA, The Oxford Handbook of the Georgian Theatre* (2014), and *Charles Dibdin and Late Georgian Culture* (2018).

BRIDGET ORR is Associate Professor in the Department of English, Vanderbilt University. Her research and teaching interests are focused on theatre and empire in the long eighteenth century. In 2001, she published *Empire on the English Stage, 1660–1714* (Cambridge University Press), and she has recently completed *England's Enlightenment Theatre: Sentiment, Nation, Empire*. She is co-editor of *Voyages and Beaches: Cultural Encounter in the Pacific, 1769–1840* (1999). She has edited a special Pacific issue of *The Eighteenth Century: Theory and Interpretation* and has published essays on topics including Restoration erotica, Dryden's heroic plays, infanticide in voyage literature, localism in late Stuart drama, empire in Georgian drama, the *Arabian Nights* on the eighteenth-century stage, women in late Stuart theatre and early eighteenth-century theatrical sentiment.

DAVID O'SHAUGHNESSY is Associate Professor for Eighteenth-Century Studies at the School of English, Trinity College Dublin. He has published widely on William Godwin including *William Godwin and the Theatre* (2010). He edited 'Networks of Aspiration: The London Irish of the Eighteenth-Century', a special issue of *Eighteenth-Century Life* (2015). He edited *The Letters of Oliver Goldsmith* (Cambridge University Press, 2018) with Michael Griffin and is currently editing a new eight-volume edition of Goldsmith's works, also with Griffin, for Cambridge University Press. His essays have appeared in the *Journal for Eighteenth-Century Studies, Eighteenth-Century Life, Nineteenth-Century Literature, Huntington Library Quarterly* and in various volumes of essays on eighteenth-century theatre.

COLLEEN TAYLOR is a PhD candidate at Boston College. She has been the recipient of the Dalsimer Fellowship (2018–19), the IASIL Margaret MacCurtain Graduate Scholarship (2016) and winner of the ASECS Innovative Course Design Competition (2018). Her essays have appeared in *Éire-Ireland, Tulsa Studies in Women's Literature* and *Persuasions*. Her current research project is on Irish consumerism and novelistic representation at the turn of the nineteenth century.

Acknowledgements

This volume emerges from a conference held at the Long Room Hub, Trinity College Dublin in February 2017. I gratefully acknowledge the Marie Curie Career Integration Grant from the European Research Council that generously funded the conference. My thanks also to the Hub and its staff, especially Caitriona Curtis and Emily Johnson, for ensuring the smooth running of the event. I would also like to express my gratitude to all the conference speakers and delegates for generating such a lively discussion. A special acknowledgement to Colm Summers, Nick Johnson, Michael Stone and the cast and crew who produced a fantastic production of *Love à la Mode After Macklin* at Smock Alley Theatre to illuminate our academic discussion. I am grateful to my colleague Aileen Douglas for her staunch support of the conference and so many other aspects of my working life at Trinity.

I would also like to thank Kate Brett, Eilidh Burnett and Sharon McCann at Cambridge University Press for all their assistance on this book. The two anonymous readers were both enthusiastically supportive and very helpful with their various suggestions. My thanks to Linda Benson for her copyediting. I am very appreciative of the financial support provided by the School of English towards the cost of image reproduction.

Much of my own work on this volume was carried out while on a Marie Curie Global Fellowship at the Huntington Library in California. I would like to take this opportunity to thank the library and research division staff at the Huntington, especially Steve Hindle, Juan Gomez, Carolyn Powell and Catherine Wehry-Miller for their wonderful hospitality, as well as the cohort of Huntington fellows with whom I spent a very pleasant and stimulating year. My family and I were also made to feel extremely welcome during our time in sunny Southern California by Emily Anderson, Julie Carlson, Helen Deutsch, Bill Deverall, Kevin Gilmartin, Steve and Louise Hindle, Ray and Cinty Kepner, Felicity Nussbaum and Lindsay O'Neill.

I would also like to say a big thank you to all my former students on the MPhil in Irish Writing at Trinity College Dublin. Their enthusiastic seminar engagement with my work-in-progress on various dramatists featured in these pages has been rewarding in a number of ways. It is extremely gratifying to me – not to mention satisfyingly symbolic – that one of those students contributed a chapter to this volume.

My family, as always, bore the brunt of my exertions and it is a real pleasure to express my deep love and appreciation to Gobnait, Rory and Luke here as our little platoon continues its own rather eclectic Irish Enlightenment project.

INTRODUCTION

Staging an Irish Enlightenment

David O'Shaughnessy

I

Surveys of the Enlightenment have tended to focus on the major thinkers of the period; more recently though, attention has shifted to those accounts that emphasise the spaces and sociability of Enlightenment.[1] Despite this critical turn, the theatre historian is likely to remain disconsolate at the elision of theatre from many of these general studies, past and present. Theatre is certainly nodded to on occasion and listed as a metropolitan space where an expanding public sphere could assimilate and practise Enlightenment, but the treatment is typically superficial. One is left with the impression that theatre functions as a largely passive space for the circulation of externally sourced Enlightenment ideas and principles, with rather less attention paid to the notion that the theatre is also an agent of Enlightenment and that the actors, playwrights, managers and other associated people – hereafter collectively referred to as theatre practitioners – were fundamental to the generation of such ideas and principles.[2]

---

[1] Ernst Cassirer, *The Philosophy of the Enlightenment* (Princeton: Princeton University Press, 1951) and Peter Gay, *The Enlightenment: An Interpretation. The Rise of Modern Paganism* (London: Weidenfeld & Nicolson, 1967). But see also, for a more recent emphasis on Enlightenment thinkers, Anthony Gottlieb, *The Dream of Enlightenment: The Rise of Modern Philosophy* (London: Allen Lane, 2016). For more diffused accounts of Enlightenment with emphases on its spaces and places, see, for example, Peter Clark, *British Clubs and Societies 1580–1800* (Oxford: Oxford University Press, 2000); Jon Mee, *Conversable Worlds: Literature, Contention, and Community, 1762–1830* (Oxford: Oxford University Press, 2011); Roy Porter, *Enlightenment: Britain and the Creation of the Modern World* (London: Allen Lane, 2000); Gillian Russell, *Women, Sociability and Theatre in Georgian London* (Cambridge: Cambridge University Press, 2007); and Chad Wellmon, *Organizing Enlightenment: Information Overload and the Invention of the Modern Research University* (Baltimore: Johns Hopkins University Press, 2015).

[2] See, for instance, Porter's *Enlightenment* where theatre barely registers. A glance at the index is revealing. Significant eighteenth-century playwrights – Goldsmith, Holcroft, Inchbald, Steele – are listed but all citations relate to non-dramatic works. The Licensing Act 1695 appears a few times, but there is no mention of the 1737 Stage Licensing Act, a rather important piece of legislation that would persist in one form or other until 1968.

Theatre was a focal point in Georgian life. The playhouses of London and beyond were among the few spaces where people from almost all walks of life could gather together to engage with literary and performance culture. Theatre was central to political life and the display of – as well as resistance to – monarchical and aristocratic power; newspapers were heavily indebted to theatrical stories for the growth of their readership; the parliamentary and legal worlds aped its tropes and affective strategies in the pursuit of British liberty and justice; and it was the only literary sphere of Georgian life deemed sufficiently dangerous to be muzzled by state censorship due to its capacity to disseminate critique and channel ideas of societal change in a live participative environment. The political philosopher William Godwin, the leading reforming intellectual voice of the 1790s, believed strongly that theatre was pivotal to the mediation of Enlightenment ideas from educated persons (like himself) to others less privileged: theatre formed 'the link between the literary class of mankind & the uninstructed, the bridge by which the latter may pass over into the domains of the former'.[3] In short, theatre was a powerful, active cultural force in the eighteenth century, but it has been largely sidelined in the field of Enlightenment studies.[4]

This volume takes the case of Ireland's theatrical exports to Britain to showcase the possibilities of using an Enlightenment framework to bring together and interrogate a substantial body of staged cultural production.[5] The volume identifies London as a site of regional Irish Enlightenment activity; it treats this region as having commonalities and connections with the island of Ireland but also distinctive features; it argues that theatre has a particular force at this time for the eighteenth-century London Irish; and it adumbrates certain conditions of singularity that make this cultural output and its producers especially noteworthy. In brief, it suggests that

---

[3] Bodleian Library, Oxford. Abinger MS, c. 21, f. 57v. The manuscript is undated but probably dates from the mid-1790s.

[4] It is difficult to think of any English language general survey of the Enlightenment that engages properly with the theatre. Essay collections do occasionally make an effort although they have limited scope. See, for example, E. M. Dadlez, 'The Pleasures of Tragedy' in *The Oxford Handbook of British Philosophy in the Eighteenth Century*, ed. James Harris (Oxford: Oxford University Press, 2013), 450–67; and Peter Jones, 'Italian Operas and Their Audiences' in *The Enlightenment World*, ed. Martin Fitzpatrick, Peter Jones, Christa Knellwolf and Iain McCalman (London and New York: Routledge, 2004), 323–36.

[5] 'Theatre is a crucial medial hinge that provides a vantage point for considering a wide array of under-analyzed cultural and social phenomena', such as, for instance, the Irish Enlightenment. Daniel O'Quinn and Gillian Russell, 'Introduction' in 'Georgian Theatre in an Information Age: Media, Performance, Sociability', ed. O'Quinn and Russell. Special issue, *Eighteenth-Century Fiction*, 27.3–4 (2015): 337.

the presentation of Irish civility – understood in its broadest sense as being related more to civilisation than politeness – was a common desideratum of Irish theatre practitioners and one that was linked to new understandings of Irish history and culture emerging at this time.

These chapters will challenge Roy Porter's view that it was not until the 1790s that Irish grievances were 'directly coloured by enlightened (by then, also revolutionary) claims'.[6] Their publication is timely, coming in the wake of important reflections on Ireland and its Enlightenment, notably Michael Brown's door-stopping *The Irish Enlightenment* (2016).[7] Moreover, it responds to recent recognition from Irish historians, both social and intellectual, that theatre was a key facet of the Irish Enlightenment and more effort was required to determine its full importance.[8] On the British theatre history side, while work on the eighteenth century has been flourishing over the past couple of decades, the considerable Irish contribution made to the Georgian theatre, *pace* the notable exceptions of Helen Burke and Michael Ragussis, has not been adequately considered from an ethnic perspective.[9]

We will begin with a brief survey of the pervasive and sustained Irish theatrical activity in Britain of the long eighteenth century; this body of empirical evidence will establish a *prima facie* case for a study of this cultural phenomenon.[10] This introduction uses the remarkably successful

---

[6] Porter, *Enlightenment*, 241.

[7] See also the various volumes in the *Early Irish Fiction, c. 1680–1820* series, gen. ed. Aileen Douglas, Moyra Haslett and Ian Campbell Ross (Dublin: Four Courts Press, 2010–); Graham Gargett and Geraldine Sheridan, eds., *Ireland and the French Enlightenment, 1700–1800* (Basingstoke: Palgrave, 1999); Michael Griffin, *Enlightenment in Ruins: The Geographies of Oliver Goldsmith* (Lewisburg: Bucknell University Press, 2013); *The Letters of Oliver Goldsmith*, ed. Michael Griffin and David O'Shaughnessy (Cambridge and New York: Cambridge University Press, 2018); Máire Kennedy, *French Books in Eighteenth-Century Ireland* (Oxford: Voltaire Foundation, 2001); Ian McBride, *Eighteenth-Century Ireland* (Dublin: Gill & Macmillan, 2009); Sean D. Moore, ed., 'Ireland and Enlightenment'. Special issue, *Eighteenth-Century Studies* 45.3 (2012); David O'Shaughnessy, ed., 'Networks of Aspiration: The London Irish of the Eighteenth-Century'. Special issue, *Eighteenth-Century Life* 39.1 (2015); and, Amy Prendergast, *Literary Salons across Britain and Ireland in the Long Eighteenth Century* (Basingstoke: Palgrave, 2015).

[8] Craig Bailey, *Irish London: Middle-Class Migration in the Global Eighteenth Century* (Liverpool: Liverpool University Press, 2013), 219; and Ian McBride, 'The Edge of Enlightenment: Ireland and Scotland in the Eighteenth Century', *Modern Intellectual History* 10.1 (2013): 135–51; 148.

[9] See Michael Ragussis, *Theatrical Nation: Jews and Other Outlandish Englishmen in Georgian Britain* (Philadelphia: University of Pennsylvania Press, 2010) and a number of essays by Helen Burke (see Select Bibliography). The remarkable upsurge in work on Georgian theatre might be best summarised by pointing at Julia Swindells and David Taylor's excellent *Oxford Handbook of the Georgian Theatre, 1737–1832* (Oxford: Oxford University Press, 2014).

[10] Many important eighteenth-century figures will be outside the chronological remit of this volume, although they certainly merit further critical attention: playwright George Farquhar (Derry; 1676/

level of intense Irish activity in the London theatres at this time of relatively benign political conditions in London to argue that, seen in the context of patriotism and revisionist historiography, this activity can be usefully categorised as a regional strand of the Irish Enlightenment. The regional distinction is important as it allows us to connect these activities with the island of Ireland while allowing London some distinctive features and avoiding any totalising claims. The survey will be necessarily succinct and far from comprehensive, but the breadth and depth of the Irish theatrical community in London – the focus of our interest – across all dimensions of the theatrical public sphere will become apparent.[11] To be blunt, in this writer's experience, it is not unknown for eighteenth-century scholars to start in mild surprise when they learn that such and such a person was Irish, so the exercise seems worthwhile from that perspective as well. We will come to the question of the relevance of national identity for these practitioners shortly, but their previous assimilation as British or English writers has, at the very least, masked an important facet of their formative makeup.[12] I also note the county of origin when known to remind readers that Ireland, small country though it is, has its own regional diversity; having some sense of the geography of theatrical talent in Ireland opens up potential avenues of future scholarly enquiry.[13]

7–1707), playwright and novelist Mary Davys (Dublin?; 1674–1732), Richard Steele (Dublin; *bap.* 1672, *d.* 1729) and actor and playwright John Leigh (Dublin?; *c.* 1689–1726?) are only some examples. Helen Burke has also shown the forceful impact of visiting Irish actors in late seventeenth-century Oxford. Helen Burke, 'The Irish Joke, Migrant Networks, and the London Irish in the 1680s', *Eighteenth-Century Life* 39.1 (2015): 41–65.

[11] The conflation of Britain with London is, of course, problematic; it is freely conceded that the interplay between metropolis and centre should receive more attention as indeed the survey of Irish theatrical migrants to follow suggests. Declan McCormack's chapter is a substantive corrective to the volume's London-centrism and shows the rich possibilities of such work. Jane Moody has also shown that regional theatre had its own distinctive rhythms and idiosyncrasies. Nonetheless, it is fair to say, I think, that London theatre generally set the tone and repertoire even if the regions mediated and responded to those plays in distinctive fashions. Jane Moody, 'Dictating to the Empire: Performance and Theatrical Geography in Eighteenth-Century Britain', in *The Cambridge Companion to British Theatre, 1730–1830*, ed. Moody and Daniel O'Quinn (Cambridge: Cambridge University Press, 2007).

[12] There has been some important work on 'Irishing', to use James Chandler's term, some significant figures include Edmund Burke, Catherine Clive, Oliver Goldsmith, the Sheridan family and Margaret Woffington. But Chandler also warns of the dangers of narrow one-dimensional readings. See his discussion of Edgeworth in 'A Discipline in Shifting Perspectives: Why We Need Irish Studies', *Field Day Review* 2 (2006): 19–39; 30–39.

[13] On Irish regional theatre of the period, see Christopher Morash, *A History of Irish Theatre, 1601–2000* (Cambridge and New York: Cambridge University Press, 2002), 30–66.

2

Catherine Clive (?; 1711–85) and Margaret Woffington (Dublin; 1720?–60) were two of the leading female actors of our period.[14] Clive became the 'Darling of the Age' after being gifted the role of Polly in John Gay's *The Beggar's Opera* in 1732. Woffington's debut at Covent Garden was a royal command performance of Farquhar's *The Recruiting Officer* and made her an instant star. Both women would be at the centre of the Covent Garden and Drury Lane companies throughout the mid-century. Less familiar but substantial female actors include George Anne Bellamy (Dublin; 1731?–88), who had considerable success in the 1740s and 1750s, and Margaret Farren (Cork?; *d.* 1804) who started her career in London but who flourished in York. Eliza O'Neill (Louth; 1791–1872), admired by Hazlitt and Percy Shelley amongst others, was an extraordinary and immediate success at Covent Garden, hailed as the new Siddons.

Insofar as male actors go, James Quin (London; 1693–1766), Charles Macklin (Donegal; 1697?–1799) and John Henry Johnstone (Kilkenny; 1749–1828) are likely the most well-known names.[15] But we also have Spranger Barry (Dublin; *bap.* 1717, *d.* 1777), whose abilities, particularly in Shakespearean parts, made the handsome actor a bona fide star: Garrick never played Othello again after Barry's triumph in the role and their rival Romeos lit up the 1749–50 season. George Cooke (Dublin?; 1756?–1812) made his career as a provincial actor in the north of England before cracking London in 1800 with his Richard III. These names are known to theatre historians of the period, but there are others, much less well known, whose very longevity demands greater familiarity. William Havard (Dublin; 1710–78), for instance, acted for more than forty years in London; he was also author of the contentious tragedy *King Charles I* which drew big crowds at Lincoln's Inn Fields in 1737 and was identified by Lord Chesterfield, in his famous condemnation of the Stage Licensing Act, as a play that *should* be censored.[16] Alexander Pope (Cork; 1763–1835), no

---

[14] Much of the information that follows is readily available in various *ODNB* entries so I have eschewed individual references. The Select Bibliography will contain more detailed work on individuals where appropriate.

[15] Although Quin was born in London, he had considerable and heartfelt Irish roots. His grandfather was lord mayor of Dublin, and his father was educated at Trinity College Dublin. Quin himself went to school in Dublin from about 1700, he may also have attended Trinity, and it was in that city he began his acting career. Quin's Irish connections are manifold and his half-brother, Thomas Grinsell, was involved in the establishment of Irish freemasonry in London in the 1750s. Laurence Dermott, *Ahiman Rezon: Or A Help to All that Are, or Would Be Free and Accepted Masons*, 3rd edition (London: n.p., 1778), xxxv.

[16] Vincent J. Liesenfeld, *The Licensing Act of 1737* (Madison: University of Wisconsin Press, 1984), 83.

relation, acted at both Covent Garden and Drury Lane over five decades from 1786 to 1827: Ireland produced not only stars but many of the supporting cast that made up the human infrastructure of the London theatrical world.[17] As our knowledge of Georgian performance culture advances, we need to better assess the interactions, collaborations and interventions of this ensemble backdrop with Georgian stars to understand how celebrity was fashioned and cultural capital accrued.

Authoring plays was also an area of considerable strength. The comedies of Oliver Goldsmith (Westmeath; 1728–74), Richard Brinsley Sheridan (Dublin; 1751–1816) and 'the English Moliere' (according to Hazlitt) John O'Keeffe (Dublin; 1747–1833) are regularly anthologised and staged today. But there are a host of writers of considerable achievement: Isaac Bickerstaff (Dublin; b. 1733 – d. after 1808), Arthur Murphy (Roscommon; 1727–1805), Hugh Kelly (Kerry; 1739–77), Elizabeth Griffith (Glamorgan; 1727–93) and Frances Sheridan (Dublin; 1724–66) all achieved acclaim in the mid-century period. Indeed, a gnashing William Kenrick was so incensed by seemingly endless Irish theatrical success in the 1760s that he penned a mocking parody of Dryden's 'Epigram on Milton':

> What are your Britons, Romans, Grecians,
> Compar'd with thorough-bred Milesians?
> Step into G–ff–n's shop, he'll tell ye
> Of G–ds–th, B–k–rs–ff, and K–ll–:
> Three poets of one age and nation,
> Whose more than mortal reputation,
> Mounting in trio to the skies,
> O'er Milton's fame and Virgil's flies.[18]

Kenrick's disappointment in the wake of the failure of his own *The Widowed Wife* appears to have provoked this ethnic barb at Goldsmith, Bickerstaff and Kelly, all of whom were being published by the important London-based Irish publisher William Griffin. The 1770s and 1780s were also a period of remarkable Irish dominance in London's dramatic authorship: as well as Sheridan, Macklin and O'Keeffe, these decades saw considerable success for Leonard MacNally (Dublin; 1752–1820), Frederick Pilon (Cork; 1750–88) and Robert Jephson (Dublin; 1736/7–1803). MacNally had a number of Covent Garden

---

[17] More could also be said about Irish musicians and singers, scenographers and prompters based in Britain.

[18] William Kenrick, 'The Poetical Triumvirate. Written in the Year MDCCLXVII' in *Poems; Ludicrous, Satirical and Moral* (London: Printed for J. Fletcher [1768]), 269.

successes in the early 1780s such as *Robin Hood, or Sherwood Forest* (1784) and *Richard Coeur de Lion* (1786). Jephson's tragedy *Braganza* (1775) impressed the audience so much that it 'clapped, shouted, huzzaed, cried bravo, and thundered out applause'.[19] His *Count of Narbonne* (1781) was a dramatisation of Walpole's *Castle of Otranto* and also won much acclaim. Pilon's comedies were written rapidly to respond to the issues of the day, and he had a considerable reputation on this front: 'Mr. Pilon, in [*Aerostation* (1784)], has seized upon the subject uppermost in the public mind, and has introduced all the collateral topics of the day.'[20] One newspaper noted that Pilon and O'Keeffe received cash up front for their plays, while Richard Cumberland, an eminent playwright in his own right, had to make do with the uncertainty of a benefit night (*Morning Post and Daily Advertiser*, 18 November 1784). Irish playwrights in the 1780s then had a certain cultural force founded on their critical and commercial success which was, in turn, a function of a more general zeitgeist of Irish brio in late eighteenth-century London.

After the turn of the century, Irish playwrights continued to offer their wares to the British public with marked appreciation. James Kenney's (Limerick; 1780–1849) 1803 debut *Raising the Wind* had thirty-eight nights in its first season at Covent Garden. James Sheridan Knowles (Cork; 1784–1862) wrote a number of tragedies of sufficient quality that he was included in Hazlitt's *Spirit of the Age* (1825), *Virginius* (1820) probably considered his finest achievement. No less an ambition than a desire to 'do away any lingering prejudice that may still exist in England against the people of Ireland' was the objective of *The Sons of Erin*, a comedy by Alicia Le Fanu (Dublin; 1753–1817) which was staged to great applause in 1812.[21] Better known as a novelist today, Charles Maturin (Dublin; 1780–1824) captivated Byron with his tragedy *Bertram* (1816) which went through seven editions in the year after its tumultuous reception at Drury Lane. Before he became embroiled in the O'Connellite movement for Catholic Emancipation, Richard Lalor Sheil (Kilkenny; 1791–1851) wrote *Evadne, or, The Statue* (1819) which notched up thirty performances at Covent Garden. Although much lamented by many in the republic of letters, the Union does not appear to have impeded the persistent eastward flow of talent across the Irish Sea.

---

[19] Correspondence of Horace Walpole, cited in Jephson's *ODNB* entry.
[20] *General Evening Post*, 28–30 October 1784.
[21] Alicia Sheridan Le Fanu, *The Sons of Erin, or Modern Sentiment: A Comedy, in Five Acts Performed at the Lyceum Theatre* (London: J. Ridgway, 1812), iii.

Acting and playwriting are the most public of activities associated with the theatre – and are the focus of this volume – but the Irish theatrical contribution is not limited to these domains. David Taylor has reminded us that theatre managers are all too often elided from their proper place at the forefront of theatre history and how much we have to gain from paying proper attention to this instrumental figure.[22] In the Irish case, Richard Brinsley Sheridan leaps to mind, his near three decades in charge of Drury Lane Theatre constituting a substantial reign (although John Kemble did much of the day-to-day work). But Irish involvement in eighteenth-century theatre management was more extensive.

Owen Swiny (Wexford; 1676–1754) and Thomas Doggett (Dublin; c. 1670–1721) are notable figures from the early part of the century. Swiny managed the Queen's Theatre at Haymarket from 1706 before ending up managing Drury Lane in a consortium which included Doggett and Robert Wilks (Dublin; c. 1665–1732) in 1710. Swiny became an agent for the Italian opera in London and was based in Venice from 1721; he returned to London in the 1730s. Thomas Doggett, keen to make a public expression of his Whiggism, established a race on the Thames on 1 August 1716 to commemorate the second anniversary of George I's accession, a race that was still being run up to the end of the twentieth century. Although Richard Steele did not play much of an active part in the management of the theatre, we should also acknowledge that he held the governorship of Drury Lane from 1714 until his death in 1729. Charles Macklin operated as Charles Fleetwood's acting manager at times at Drury Lane.

But it is outside of London where Irish managers made their most significant mark during our period. Andrew Cherry (Limerick; 1762–1812), author of *The Soldier's Daughter* (1804), which went through more than thirty editions in Britain and America, also managed a theatre company in Wales. Francis Aickin (Dublin; c. 1735–1812) managed the Liverpool theatre, initially with John Kemble, before taking over at Edinburgh. The famous manager of Smock Alley Richard Daly (Westmeath; 1758–1813) cut his theatrical teeth on stage in London before turning to management back home. However, it is perhaps the name that is likely least known to theatre history that is the most striking from this list: John Boles Watson (Tipperary; 1748–1813), a friend of Roger Kemble (father of John), was a theatre manager at Cheltenham from 1779. Remarkably, Watson created a circuit of in excess of forty theatres: from

---

[22] David Francis Taylor, 'Theatre Managers and Theatre History' in *The Oxford Handbook of Georgian Theatre*, ed. Swindells and Taylor, 70–71.

Bristol it reached northwards to Holywell in Flintshire, and from Leicester it stretched across the midlands into Carmarthen in Wales. Outposts of Watson's empire could be found *inter alia* at Gloucester, Cirencester, Stroud, Hereford, Monmouth, Swansea, Oswestry, Evesham, Wolverhampton, Coventry, Birmingham, Daventry, Walsall and Tamworth.

The theatre was also central to the rapid growth of the readership of periodicals and newspapers over the century, and Irish writers here made a considerable contribution to 'the thickening traffic of theatrical intelligence' between playhouses and newspapers.[23] Former playwright Charles Molloy (Offaly; *d.* 1767) was editor of *Common-Sense*, the periodical in which the infamous *Vision of the Golden Rump* (the 1737 satiric print that helped provide the pretext for the introduction of the Stage Licensing Act) was published. Arthur Murphy contributed dramatic criticism to the *London Chronicle* from 1758. William Jackson (Dublin; 1737?–95), known as Scrutineer, became editor of the *Public Ledger* in mid-1770s (in whose pages he accused Samuel Foote of homosexuality), and he later acted as editor of the *Morning Post* (1784–86). Lapsed barrister Leonard MacNally also edited the *Public Ledger* for a period in the 1780s, a period in which his dramatic work was flourishing. Isaac Jackman (Dublin; 1752?–1831) edited the *Morning Post* (1791–95), while Frederick Pilon also worked on the *Morning Post* when he first landed in London. A fascinating piece of research awaits to be done on ethnic and political cooperation (collusion?) between the newspapers and theatres given the number of people who had a foot in both camps; certainly, Charles Dibdin, for one, was scathing:

> On the subject of the theatre, indeed, [newspapers] are all agreed; actors, authors, and musicians – though the first imitate, the second steal, and the third compile – are with them arrived to the highest pitch of perfection, when 'tis notorious the theatres have gradually declined for these last fifteen years. . . . But the inducement is evident; and while free admission, and now and then the reception of a farce, can insure the newspapers, trash must go down; and the new school, as it is called, impotent as it is, be palmed on the rising generation, as an improvement of the old one; though, Heaven knows! a spider's web may with as much propriety be instanced as an improvement on the labours of a silkworm.[24]

There is also a considerable body of more formal dramatic criticism. Samuel Derrick (Dublin; 1724–69) published *The Dramatic Censor;*

[23] Stuart Sherman, 'Garrick Among Media: The "*Now* Performer" Navigates the News', *PMLA* 126.4 (2011): 966–82; 970. See also Lucyle Werkmeister, *A Newspaper History of England 1792–1793* (Lincoln: University of Nebraska Press, 1967).
[24] *The Devil* 1 (1786), 8–9.

Being Remarks upon the Conduct, Characters, and Catastrophe of Our Most Celebrated Plays in 1752.[25]

His friend Goldsmith's *Essay on Theatre* (1773) was a powerful – if self-interested – indictment of sentimental comedy. Goldsmith's rival Hugh Kelly wrote an important imitation of Churchill's *Rosciad* in the narrative poem *Thespis: Or A Critical Examination into the Merits of All the Principal Performers Belonging to Drury-Lane Theatre* (1766–67). Francis Gentleman (Dublin; 1728–84) provided one of the most valuable accounts of Garrick's major roles in his two-volume *The Dramatic Censor* (1770). Edmond Malone (Westmeath; 1741–1812) was the most important eighteenth-century editor of Shakespeare.

Our definition of those Irish impacting the London theatre is capacious and is not confined simply to those born on the island of Ireland but extends to those who – insofar as we can tell – considered themselves to be, or were considered by others to be, Irish and/or were deeply marked by their association with the country and its inhabitants. People such as James Quin and Elizabeth Griffith are thus included. But as we consider this disparate group of people across the century, some questions should be posed: firstly, what difference does it make that they were Irish? How helpful is the marker of Irishness to the theatre historian attempting to recuperate the Georgian theatre scene? And is there any sense in which we can connect such a heterogeneous array of cultural producers, given their differences across gender, religion, politics and class? The claim in these pages is that Irishness mattered a great deal to these men and women as we can observe from their patterns of sociability, so much to the fore of current eighteenth-century studies.[26]

Irish migrants to England, particularly London, of the period found solace, opportunity and conviviality in networks that were sustained and strengthened by national ties.[27] As a large migrant community – and one that would flit regularly between Dublin and London – such links were arguably particularly important for theatre practitioners, a means to find one's bearings within the largest city in the Western world and its most

[25] See Norma Clarke's *Brothers of the Quill: Oliver Goldsmith in Grub Street* (Cambridge, MA: Harvard University Press, 2016) for a fascinating account of Goldsmith's circle of Irish writers.

[26] See, for instance, Clark, *British Clubs and Societies*; Jon Mee, ed., 'Networks of Improvement'. Special issue, *Journal for Eighteenth-Century Studies* 38.4 (2015); James Kelly and Martyn Powell, eds., *Clubs and Societies in Eighteenth-Century Ireland* (Dublin: Four Courts, 2010); Prendergast, *Literary Salons across Britain and Ireland*; and, Russell, *Women, Sociability and the Theatre*.

[27] Bailey, *Irish London*; Clarke, *Brothers of the Quill*; and, David O'Shaughnessy, '"Rip'ning Buds in Freedom's Field": Staging Irish Improvement in the 1780s', *Journal for Eighteenth-Century Studies* 38.4 (2015): 541–54.

celebrated theatrical scene. And there is a considerable body of anecdotal evidence that shows how established Irish actors and dramatists helped and supported new arrivals. Owen Swiny championed Woffington; Macklin helped get Spranger Barry and John Johnstone established; James Quin encouraged George Anne Bellamy and recommended Dennis Delane to Covent Garden; William Griffin gave Frederick Pilon his start at the *Morning Post* when he arrived in London; and Goldsmith was an obvious point of contact for Isaac Jackman when he travelled from Ireland: the accounts, letters and memoirs of actors and dramatists abound with manifold stories of interventions and encouragement.

Equally we can trace many diachronic and synchronic connections of literary influence and assistance. Goldsmith was thought to have based his lesser-known play *The Good Natur'd Man* (1768) on an anecdote about Richard Steele being visited by the bailiffs; in turn, Dennis O'Bryen founded the plot of his comedy satirising Charles James Fox on that of Goldsmith's (O'Bryen's play also pays homage to Macklin's Shylock with a vicious Irish moneylender character), giving us a multigenerational narrative thread to follow.[28] John O'Keeffe made his start by impressing George Colman with his dramatisation of the further adventures of Goldsmith's Tony Lumpkin (*Tony Lumpkin in Town* [1774]). He also reworked Robert Jephson's *The Campaign* (1784) – which featured a Stage Irishman drawn by Pilon – into a triumphant two-act afterpiece *Love and War* (1787). Leonard MacNally dedicated his *Sentimental Excursions to Windsor* (1781) to Macklin and explicitly acknowledged Sir Callaghan O'Brallaghan's importance to improving the stock of the London Irish. The omnipresent Macklin also did the recently arrived O'Keeffe's prospects little harm when he declared loudly in the pit that *The Agreeable Surprise* (1781) was 'the best farce in the English language, except the "Son in Law"'.[29] Often assistance took the form of a prologue or epilogue: Pilon wrote epilogues for Macklin and he also drew a Stage Irishman for Robert Jephson's *The Campaign*. Malone wrote the epilogue for Jephson's *The Count of Narbonne*. Alicia Le Fanu drew on her brother Richard Brinsley Sheridan, as Colleen Taylor discusses in her chapter. Arthur Murphy was involved in advising Macklin on early drafts. This list could be lengthened considerably although we should also note that Irish actors and writers, of course, did not depend exclusively on Irish connections,

[28] See David O'Shaughnessy, 'Making a Play for Patronage: Dennis O'Bryen's *A Friend in Need Is a Friend Indeed* (1783)', *Eighteenth-Century Life* 39.1 (2015): 183–211.
[29] *Recollections of the Life of John O'Keeffe: Written by Himself*, 2 vols. (London: Henry Colburn, 1826), 2: 5.

friendships and patronage for support: figures such as Samuel Johnson,
David Garrick and Thomas Harris were evidently of significant importance for many. But we can confidently say that Irish aid was generous and
forthcoming particularly at the outset of careers – at that moment when it
was most needed – and it tended to be sustained over longer periods. Irish
actors and writers looked to their own for help, inspiration and that all-
important 'in' when they attempted to forge a career in London.

   One must be careful to avoid suggesting that a shared Irishness collapsed
important distinctions within this rather heterogeneous group. Although
the overwhelming impression of conviviality and support is convincing,
there are well-documented cases of antagonism (e.g. Quin and Macklin,
Woffington and Clive, Goldsmith and Kelly). Nonetheless, the chapters in
this volume collectively make the argument that all of this cultural activity,
despite differences in politics, religion, gender, class or otherwise, all
contributed to an important strand of the Irish Enlightenment.

                                    3

It is probably safe to say now that the breezy sidelining of the notion of an
Irish Enlightenment is now well and truly in the past; however, questions
as to its extent and nature remain excitingly open.[30] While there have been
many noteworthy contributions to the discussion, Michael Brown's
The Irish Enlightenment is the most thorough and ambitious to date.
Brown's Irish Enlightenment unfolds over three thematic periods:
a religious Enlightenment (1688 – *c.* 1730), was followed by a social
Enlightenment (*c.* 1730–1760) and a political Enlightenment (*c.*
1760–98). A much simplified version of Brown's argument is that the
initial stages of the Irish Enlightenment are characterised by the confessional divides among Catholics, Anglicans and Presbyterians and their
respective modes of thought, scholasticism, empiricism and rationalism.
The middle period sees those divisions recede as a result of the convivial
sociability of the burgeoning public sphere, while the conflict between
empiricist loyalism and rationalist republicanism finally collapses around
the acrimonious nationalist question of 'who is Irish?', thus bringing about
sectarian rancour, rebellion and the end of the Irish Enlightenment.

---

[30] Roy Porter and Mikuláš Teich's *The Enlightenment in National Context* (Cambridge: Cambridge
   University Press, 1981) did not include an essay on Ireland although the names of Burke, Steele,
   Toland and Swift are all co-opted in the English Enlightenment. See also Porter's *Enlightenment*,
   xviii–xix for a flimsy conflation of the Irish in Britain with the 'English' (although he does make
   clear that his discussion is focused on the island of Britain).

While one can acknowledge the impressive scope of *The Irish Enlightenment*, like many general surveys noted at the outset, it has a theatre problem. Brown, to his credit, includes Goldsmith's *She Stoops to Conquer* (1773) and Macklin's *Love à la Mode* (1759) in his wide-ranging discussion of the sociable Enlightenment, but the texts are decontextualised, both from the authors' respective bodies of work and from their performance history and reception. Brown identifies the theatre as a 'barometer' for the sociable Enlightenment rather than considering it a catalyst for Enlightenment ideas.[31] There is a further geographical issue: the discussion co-opts these plays into a framework of the Irish Enlightenment, one concentrated on the island of Ireland, while leaving aside the fact that both plays were first staged in London and both men were, at the moments of these performances, long-term residents of London. Macklin moved there sometime in the mid-1720s and Goldsmith never once returned to Ireland after he arrived there in 1756. Certainly, the comedies were also staged at Dublin theatres, but these are substantive lacunae in his discussion insofar as the theatre historian might be concerned. As we know, Macklin's plays had very different receptions in Dublin and London, so the borders of Brown's Enlightenment, notionally the island of Ireland, are rather more porous than they seem to be presented.[32] And as we have seen from our survey, mobility of people is an essential component of our object of study.

There will be no advocacy for a hard border around the Irish Enlightenment here; rather, this volume will settle for the more modest assertion that Irish theatre practitioners in London consist of a distinctive and important facet of a broader and more diffuse Irish Enlightenment, one that is energised by its transnational kinesis and the cosmopolitan environs of London and epitomised by O'Keeffe's ebullient recollection of arriving in London:

> Oh joys of youth! from sight to sight I flew,
>> Now topp'd the Monument, now mounted Paul's,
>> No house five minutes kept me in its walls;
> My bunch of flowers held not one sprig of rue,
> The wax-work, Tower, and Abbey tombstones, all are *new*.[33]

---

[31] Brown, *Irish Enlightenment*, 241.
[32] On the varied reception of Macklin's plays, see Paul Goring '"John Bull, Pit, Box, and Gallery, Said No!": Charles Macklin and the Limits of Ethnic Resistance on the Eighteenth-Century London Stage', *Representations* 79.1 (2002): 61–81.
[33] *Recollections of John O'Keeffe*, 1:74.

The energising effect of O'Keeffe's move to London makes clear the problem identified by Charles W. J. Withers of seeing the nation as a 'container' for the Enlightenment. When it comes to the extraordinary and enriching free movement of labour, capital and entrepreneurship between Irish and British theatres, particularly between Dublin and London, it is surely impossible to do so. Withers's suggestion that we might rather consider 'regional manifestations' of Enlightenment ideas is a helpful way of considering the particularities of the voluminous Irish theatrical activity in the context of London's vibrant metropolitan environs: London is an important region of Irish Enlightenment but not one with a rigidly hermetic border.[34] Mobility between Ireland and England was crucial for the development of Irish theatre practitioners and equally to the richness of London theatres; mobility is also critical to our understanding of the Enlightenment; one might well say that it is fundamental to its spirit. Withers argues for the importance of showing how, where and the form in which ideas moved: 'translation', 'appropriation', 'reception' and 'mediation' are all key terms for explaining the Enlightenment, rather than simply describing it.[35]

'Mediation' is also the central term in the recent influential collection *This Is Enlightenment*. For its editors, the Enlightenment was an event in the history of mediation in which 'print took center stage'.[36] One does not have to dispute this claim to be discomfited by the near absence of theatre from the volume as a whole,[37] particularly when the production of plays in the period involved such a complex and scrutinised flow of mediations, from author(s) to theatre manager to copyist to examiner of plays to prompter to actors to audience, not to mention the 'complex intermedial relations endemic to theatrical culture' post-performance,[38] that is, the centrality of theatre to newspapers (whose Enlightenment credentials seem beyond reproach), caricature, painting and the novel, for instance. Theatre equally 'insinuat[ed] itself into other forms of mediation' just as print does.[39] Given the proliferation of Irish theatre practitioners, we might

[34] Charles W. J. Withers, *Placing the Enlightenment: Thinking Geographically about the Age of Reason* (Chicago: University of Chicago Press, 2007), 41.
[35] Ibid., 61.
[36] Clifford Siskin and William Warner, 'This Is Enlightenment: An Invitation in the Form of an Argument' in *This Is Enlightenment* (Chicago: University of Chicago Press, 2012), 10.
[37] Michael McKeon's essay 'Mediation as Primal Word: The Arts, the Sciences, and the Origins of the Aesthetic' is an honourable exception.
[38] 'Introduction' to *Georgian Theatre in an Information Age*, O'Quinn and Russell, 337. See also O'Quinn's, *Entertaining Crisis in the Atlantic Imperium, 1770–1790* (Baltimore: Johns Hopkins University Press, 2011), 1–39.
[39] *This Is Enlightenment*, 10.

proffer the Irish theatrical production of the period as, to take another Siskin and Warner term, a cardinal mediation, one that is not necessarily 'better' but one that is enabling – due to its multiplicity – in 'particular times and particular places'.[40]

London offered an enabling environment during our period: broad political conditions such as Scottophobia post 1745 and again during Bute's brief premiership in the early 1760s;[41] increased reliance on Irish troops during the Seven Years' War;[42] increased visibility of elite and articulate Irish (such as Burke and Goldsmith being members of Johnson's Club); and increasing Irish activity in middle-class professions in London[43] helped create an environment more receptive to the prominent actors and playwrights of the mid-eighteenth century. All of these conditions facilitated – to maintain our Siskin and Warner framework – the upward trajectory of Irish participation in the new theatrical infrastructure (gradual expansion of playhouses over the century); the new genres and formats of theatre, print and speech; new associational practices; and the new protocols of theatre (such as statutory censorship, introduced in 1737). The critical mass of Irish participants could flourish in the years subsequent to 1740.

What then might be the distinctive feature of the London Irish theatrical Enlightenment? As Dan Edelstein has pointed out, 'To locate the singularity of the Enlightenment, we must also consider *what* was mediated, not just *how* it was.'[44] The ideas, not just the means of transmission and modes of reception, matter. Edelstein champions a 'thin coherence' among Enlightenment thinkers and movements, rather than 'shattering [it] into a thousand little parts' as a pragmatic way of holding together a shared idea of Enlightenment.[45] This is helpful in terms of thinking about the commonalities and differences between this regional activity and Ireland; my suggestion is that the term 'civility' has a thin coherence for the London

[40] Siskin and Warner, 'This Is Enlightenment', 11.
[41] See John Brewer, 'The Misfortunes of Lord Bute', *The Historical Journal* 16.1 (1973): 3–43. The anti-Caledonian mood in London was noted by activists such as Charles O'Conor of the Catholic Committee who wrote opinion pieces for the London newspapers, often to compare the loyalism of Scottish Presbyterianism unfavourably with that of Irish Catholicism. See David O'Shaughnessy, '"Bit, by some mad whig": Charles Macklin and the Theater of Irish Enlightenment', *Huntington Library Quarterly* 80.4 (2017): 559–84; 568–69.
[42] Stephen Conway, *War, State, and Society in Mid-Eighteenth-Century Britain and Ireland* (Oxford: Oxford University Press, 2006), 57–66; Thomas Bartlett, *The Fall and Rise of the Irish Nation* (Dublin: Gill and Macmillan, 1992), 57–58.
[43] See the various essays in O'Shaughnessy, 'Networks of Aspiration'.
[44] Dan Edelstein, *The Enlightenment: A Genealogy* (Chicago: University of Chicago Press, 2010), 11.
[45] Ibid., 13–14.

Irish theatrical Enlightenment and that of the home nation but that there was a slightly more urgent register and emphasis for the London Irish, located as they were at the vanguard of mediating the Irish nation and people to their political masters.

Civility is also a central idea for Michael Brown's sociable Enlightenment:

> Civility offered a broad diagnosis of the ailments of the country and a means to ameliorate its condition, providing a varied and interlocking vocabulary for articulating the dilemmas of Irish life . . . forged a bond between private virtues and public benefits . . . civility supplied the Irish Enlightenment with a discourse for discussion and a project of activity that crossed the confessional divides . . . enabled Presbyterians, Anglicans, and Catholics to combine creatively in the development of their society. . . . It provided a discursive mode in which those committed to rational and empirical methodologies could collaborate in ameliorating the social environment.[46]

But for those Irish in London, on display to the English on and off stage, civility might be thought of as being not only to do with polite conduct, improvement and so on but also as being more specifically associated with the idea of civilisation itself. London, the ultimate jurisdiction of political power for Ireland, was the front line for the practical performance of civilisation, essential to the Irish patriot movement. The issue of Irish civility in this sense had been much in question – if not outright dismissed – in the wake of the Ulster Rebellion of 1641 and reports of Irish barbarism and savagery. Theatre and its writers and performers offered a very public and potent stage for the Irish to demonstrate their capacity for civility in this sense. Like Godwin, Irish dramatists saw theatre as offering a bridge to political justice; in the Irish case, this bridge involved shifting English perceptions of Ireland from barbarism to civilisation. Certainly, attitudes towards the Irish in London were often uncivil right through the century, and the theatre was also a rather raucous space to present civility; however, collectively, through their command of dramatic genres, technical craft, behaviour on and off stage and – crucially – their mediated selves across the mediascape of Georgian Britain, they could present a highly visible and cultured counter-narrative to centuries of historiographically rooted prejudice. And if we agree that the event of Enlightenment must involve a principle of singularity, our period of intense theatrical activity coincided with an enabling historiographical counter-narrative that validated the notion of Irish civilisation; this 'new' historiography was a response to the 1720 Declaratory Act which reaffirmed Westminster's right to legislate

---

[46] Brown, *Irish Enlightenment*, 209.

for Ireland. As this is a book about theatre, we shall attempt to unpack all of this and to move towards a conclusion by considering a performance event. Thus, with an ostentatious precision worthy of Archbishop Ussher himself, let us nominate 9 p.m.-ish on Saturday 14 February 1741 as the date of a performance singularity through which we can tie together the complex intermediation of patriotism, historiography and performance as they coalesce around the London Irish theatrical Enlightenment.

4

An expectant audience was in attendance that night at Drury Lane Theatre. It was to be the first performance of Shakespeare's *The Merchant of Venice* in more than forty years: George Granville's adaptation *The Jew of Venice*, believed to have improved on Shakespeare, had held the stage since 1701. Charles Fleetwood, then manager, was not enthusiastic, seeing little potential for the sort of financial success he required to fund his purse-draining gambling habit. But Macklin, then acting manager of the theatre, persisted and took the role of Shylock with the intention of playing it seriously despite strong scepticism: 'the laugh was universal. – His best friends shook their heads at the attempt; whilst his rivals chuckled in secret, and flattered him with ideas of success, the surer to work out his destruction.'[47] The performance, as we know, was an enormous success with Macklin receiving all sorts of rapturous plaudits from audience, colleagues and manager on the night.[48] The claim to Irish Enlightenment may seem strained at this point: as Emily Anderson has shown, Macklin's performance seems to have confirmed negative perceptions of his personal public character.[49] Indeed, far from Enlightenment, Macklin's snarling and vicious Shylock seems likelier to have re-invoked graphic descriptions of the cruel sectarian violence supposedly meted out by Irish Catholics in 1641. Yet Macklin's approach to Shylock has two central components that we might consider to offer an alternative view: the shift to a naturalist style of acting and the historical research that underpinned his interpretation of the character. Let us take each of those in turn as we focus more on Macklin the man, rather than the actor.

Paddy Bullard has shown how the Irish understanding of rhetoric differed significantly from that of the English, suspicious of its potential

---

[47] George Cooke, *Memoirs of Macklin*, 91.
[48] For a full account, see Cooke, 92–95 and Appleton, 47–55.
[49] Emily Anderson, 'Celebrity Shylock', *PMLA* 126.4 (2011): 935–49; 941–42.

for duplicity. Irish thinkers, such as Robert Molesworth, Samuel Madden and John Toland, saw rhetoric as an essential component of a civic education that would empower the patriot Irish to advocate for civil and economic rights. While this resulted in important publications on eloquence and oratory in the 1750s by academics John Lawson and Thomas Leland, not to mention actor-manager Thomas Sheridan, Bullard dates its roots to Molesworth in the 1690s and points to considerable discussion in the 1720s: it is a foundational precept of Irish patriotism.[50] Molesworth, like many eighteenth-century dramatists discussed earlier, was educated at Trinity College Dublin and Kirkman's account of Macklin's time at Trinity (as a servant) circa the same period suggests this is where Macklin's desire for self-improvement began.[51] It is probably here that he first encountered formal ideas of Irish patriotism. Macklin's later patriot credentials are certainly robust and his innovative natural style of acting, which offered the audience the sense of seeing the psychological truth of a character through the natural and affective delivery of his lines, might be read as emerging with – and emanating from – the Irish patriot emphasis on eloquence.[52] People, as Siskin and Warner have argued, have always required 'tools' for mediation; acting, where bodies are tools for the communication of refined or heightened emotions and ideals, is a particularly potent mode of mediation.[53] Macklin's triumphant radical reorientation of his embodied self opens up new possibilities and channels of dissemination and representation of Irish character, culture and history. The naturalistic mode, embodied in an Irish actor, challenged established perceptions of the Irish and facilitated the shift in the Stage Irishman from the devious Teague O'Divellys of the early century to the natural sincerity of Sir Callaghan O'Brallaghan and Major O'Flaherty of the later period. Even if Macklin's representation of Shylock evoked malevolence and fear in the moment, the public display of his technical ability to mediate Shakespeare, to embody ethnic character in a newly 'real' way, and display command of rhetorical eloquence – not to mention his restoration of Shakespeare's script to the stage – generated new possibilities of mediation. His appropriation and powerful re-engineering of Shakespeare – we might also consider *Love à la Mode* in this way – demonstrates the Irish capacity to assimilate 'high' British culture and reimagine it in a way that underlined

---

[50] Paddy Bullard, *Edmund Burke and the Art of Rhetoric* (Cambridge: Cambridge University Press, 2011), 52–78. See also Brown, *Irish Enlightenment*, 171–76.
[51] Kirkman, *Macklin*, I: 44–45.
[52] On Macklin's Irish patriotism, see O'Shaughnessy, 'Bit, by some mad whig'.
[53] Siskin and Warner, 'This Is Enlightenment', 4–5.

the value of cultural syncretism. John Hill, in the first serious British acting treatise to emphasize the emotional range of an actor, identified Macklin as a pioneering actor of the 'superior class' who could actually improve upon the authorial text:

> The author whose piece is to have the principal characters play'd by persons of this class may always attempt to venture to omit things, or to express himself but imperfectly . . . since he will be sure to have a supplement or a commentary as far as the nature of the passage will bear it in the performing.[54]

Hill recognised that Macklin's acting was an act of reading with intellectual and political implications. Macklin's eloquence and acting style provided an important supplement, one that publically transmitted his own intellectual accomplishments. And, at this time, in 1741, Macklin can be located within a critical mass of celebrated Irish acting. Margaret Woffington and Catherine Clive were also powerful agents for Irish theatrical prowess.[55] As for James Quin, although his classical style is understood as being eclipsed by Macklin, the evidence does not support this conclusion. Macklin and Quin played different roles in different styles but both were successful.[56] We might be better served by thinking of the quartet of Clive, Macklin, Quin and Woffington as representing the increasingly capacious rhetorical range of Irish acting, capable of confidently coding Irish civility for English audiences in a multiplicity of ways. For the eighteenth-century Irish actor, mastering verse or comic dialogue with eloquence and verve, coupled with innovative acting methods, the initial claim to Enlightenment was often simply the publically displayed act of performance.

Macklin's public success opened doors to participation in the sociable Enlightenment:

> A few days afterwards, Macklin received an invitation from Lord Bolingbroke to dine with him at Battersea. He attended the rendezvous, and there found Pope, and a select party, who complimented him very highly on the part of Shylock, and questioned him about many little particulars relative to his getting up the play, &c. Pope particularly asked him, why he wore a *red hat?* and he answered, because he had read that Jews in Italy, particularly in Venice, wore hats of that colour. 'And pray, Mr. Macklin', said Pope, 'do players in general take such pains?' – 'I do

---

[54] John Hill, *The Actor*, 249.
[55] Felicity Nussbaum, *Rival Queens: Actresses, Performance, and the Eighteenth-Century British Theater* (Philadelphia: University of Pennsylvania Press, 2010), 182–88, 190–224.
[56] See my discussion of Quin's Cato, pp. 171–72 and the 'league tables' of London acting in Nussbaum, Chapter 1, p. 51, this volume.

not know, Sir, that they do; but as I had staked my reputation on the character, I was determined to spare no trouble in getting at the best information.' Pope nodded, and said, 'it was very laudable.'[57]

Macklin's success in this particular role mediated his access to social circles previously out of reach, but this anecdote suggests that it was not only his delivery that facilitated his success but also that his performance was grounded in cognitive reflection that dared to know. The supplement he added to the Shakespearean text was historiographically founded. Macklin's triumph was based on his careful reading of his 'much-thumbed', as biographer Appleton claims, copy of Josephus's *History of the Jews*.[58] The sale catalogue of Macklin's library reveals a long-lasting interest in history, and he went on to write a history play as well as deliver lectures on British and Irish history at the British Inquisition.[59] Historiography was also central to Irish patriotism in the period as the Irish began to offer a counter-narrative to prejudice exemplified by John Temple's *History of the Irish Rebellion* (1646), reprinted frequently during the eighteenth century.[60]

When the Declaratory Act was debated in 1720, Richard Steele MP spoke against the bill. According to one report, he concluded by addressing the preamble to the bill and

> shew'd the severity of laying a whole Nation under the Imputation of attempting to Rebel; when nothing possibly could be shewn of that kind; but on the contrary, Numberless Instances might be given of their unparallel'd Zeal for the present Government, one of which he wou'd mention, Namely, the putting a price on the Pretenders Head, at a time when the People of England dar'd not do it.[61]

We can readily infer that the preamble raised the spectre of Ulster's bloody rebellion of 1641 but rehashing ideas of Irish Catholic barbarity, incivility and inability to self-govern would only galvanise Irish indignation.[62]

[57] Cooke, 94–95.   [58] Appleton, 46.
[59] Thomas King, *A Catalogue of the Library of the Late Mr. Charles Macklin, Deceased* [London, 1797]. The sale catalogue has now been digitised by Paul Goring and Rebecca Vollan and is searchable. www.librarything.com/profile/CharlesMacklin
[60] See Clare O'Halloran, *Golden Ages and Barbarous Nations: Antiquarian Debate and Cultural Politics in Ireland, c. 1750–1800* (Notre Dame and Cork: University of Notre Dame Press and Cork University Press, 2004) for a comprehensive discussion of the new Irish historiography of the period although the focus is very much on Ireland.
[61] *Several Speeches in the House of Commons in England, For and against the BILL for the better securing the Dependency of the Kingdom of* Ireland, *on the Crown of Gr.* Britain. In a *Letter from a* Gentleman *there to his* Friend *here* (Dublin, n.p., 1720), 5–6.
[62] See Joep Leerssen, *Mere Irish and Fíor Ghael: Studies in the Idea of Irish Nationality, Its Development and Literary Expression Prior to the Nineteenth Century* (Notre Dame and Cork: Cork University

Swift's Irish pamphlets of the 1720s, of course, are central here, but there was also an important London response with the publication of the English translation of Geoffrey Keating's *Foras Feasa ar Éirinn* published in 1723 in London.[63] Keating's history was described in the first *Dictionary of National Biography* as 'probably the last book of importance to circulate in manuscript in the British Isles', but the complicated and controversial story of its translation and publication need not detain us here.[64] Keating's fiery preface took British historians to task for acting like dung beetles who have 'ignored the "sweet Blossoms" and "fragrant Flowers" of Irish cultural history and instead directed by [their] sordid Inclination, [they] settle[d] [themselves] on some nauseous Excrement'. Keating's book, a complex mix of fact and fabulous fiction, offers a radically different account of the rich culture and traditions of Gaelic Ireland as well as tracing the genealogy of the nation back to Japhet, son of Noah, disputing the idea of the 'wild Irish' emerging quasi-organically from a bog, and its lengthy and eminent subscriber list indicates a London readership receptive to new ideas of Irish civility.[65] Later in the century, Charles O'Conor developed Keating's thinking for a post-Humean historiography in ways that were fundamental for the mediation of Irish civility to London and impressed, among others, Samuel Johnson. For both Keating and O'Conor, the reclamation and validation of Gaelic culture – language, music, writing – were central to their argument.

   The historical turn of 1720s Irish patriotism understood that empirical evidence needed to be mediated through persuasive channels to shift the public mood; the presentation of Irish civility and culture was critical to claims for political agency, and theatre practitioners in London were engaged with its mediation. John Quin was a subscriber to Hugh McCurtin's *A Brief Discourse in Vindication of the Antiquity of Ireland . . .* (1717), essentially an early and abridged translation of Keating published in Dublin. Macklin's library contained works by Toland, O'Conor and others on Irish history and culture and his *Love à la Mode* makes specific

Press and Field Day, 1986); and David Hayton, 'From Barbarian to Burlesque: English Images of the Irish *c.* 1660–1750', *Irish Economic and Social History* 15 (1988): 5–31.

[63] Geoffrey Keating, *The General History of Ireland . . . Collected by the Learned Jeoffry Keating, D.D.*, trans. and ed. Dermod O'Connor (London: Printed by J. Bettenham, 1723).

[64] Diarmuid Ó Catháin, 'Dermot O'Connor, translator of Keating', *Eighteenth-Century Ireland / Iris an Dá Chultúr* 2 (1987): 67–87.

[65] Subscribers who paid the 2 guinea cost of the book included the Prince of Wales, the archbishops of Canterbury and York, the Bodleian Library, the master of the Charter House school, Richard Steele, Hans Sloane, various members of the Irish and English peerage, and many of the London Irish diaspora, including names with patriot resonance such as Molyneux, Philpot and O'Conor.

reference to the importance of history writing to national narratives. Catherine Clive's *The Faithful Irishwoman* (1765) was boldly confident in Mrs OConner's insistence that they spoke better English in Ireland. Leonard MacNally's *The Claims of Ireland* (1782) seeks to legitimate Irish language and music, linking them to his appeal for Irish political autonomy; the pamphlet also points to the great similarities between Britain and Ireland and his play *Robin Hood* (1784) makes gestures towards cultural syncretism, the plot combining the English legend with Goldsmith's 'Edwin and Angelina' and with the music drawn from 'English and Irish ballads'.[66] The new historiography of Ireland had a galvanising influence on Irish theatre practitioners in London as they mediated their history, culture and national character to the London audiences.

5

The essays in this volume vary in their approaches to the Irish Enlightenment. But Macklin – appropriately, given the longevity of his London tenure – is a unifying presence for them all. His career and life touched on or cast a shadow over those of every significant person of interest in the chapters which follow. But when we reflect on how an Irish-speaking Catholic from the very rural Inisowen peninsula of Donegal, on the north-west coast of Ireland, travelled initially to Dublin, where he worked as a badge-man, or servant, at Trinity College Dublin, before overcoming initial racial prejudice in London and a criminal conviction to deliver one of the great Shakespearean performances of the century on 14 February 1741 and later writing one of the boldest political plays of the century, it is difficult think of anyone – within the theatre or without – who might be better thought to embody Enlightenment values of mobility, self-improvement and the public performance of 'daring to know'. Add to the mix his advocacy for actors' legal rights, his frequent brushes with the Examiner of Plays, his attempt to include women in his British Inquisition project and his emboldened speaking of the Irish language to the non-plussed Samuel Johnson, Enlightenment values of equality, the challenging of institutional authority, respect across genders and advocacy for minority cultures suffuse his extraordinary – and extraordinarily long – career.

Macklin was a combative figure, but the rude Macklin left to us in some accounts is, I suggest, largely irrelevant: what is essential here is what he

---

[66] *St. James's Chronicle*, 17 April 1784.

meant to those Irish who looked to him as a talisman of Irish improvement. In any case, his truculence has often been overstated and thus unfairly diminished his Enlightenment credentials.[67] Macklin is metonymic of a regional London Irish theatrical Enlightenment that was unified by a common objective of producing a counter-narrative of Irish civility to centuries of prejudice regarding Irish barbarism. There were particular conditions in place that allowed this counter-narrative to emerge in the decades between 1740 and 1800 and the large Irish population of the major London theatres of Covent Garden, Drury Lane and the Haymarket to flourish, onstage and offstage.

Michael Brown's Irish Enlightenment ends in failure with the bloody events of the 1798 Rebellion and the ensuing 1801 Union. But the regional London Irish theatrical Enlightenment did not fail in 1798. The eighteenth century had simply seen too much Irish success proliferating in the London playhouses, even for an event of this magnitude to knock it off course. The multigenerational proliferation of theatrical success exceeded the capacity of domestic turbulence and bloodshed – and its representation in newspapers, parliamentary speeches, caricature and elsewhere – to return stage stereotypes to the pernicious Teague O'Divelly. This was not for the want of trying in some quarters: there were certainly efforts to make the link between 1641 and 1798.[68] But the legacy of Clive, Woffington, Macklin and their peers lived on in the nineteenth century with O'Neill, Kenney, Sheridan Knowles and others. Oddly perhaps, the continuing success of the Stage Irishman and Irishwoman, problematic in many ways, also points to the resilience of the eighteenth-century's legacy into the nineteenth – there is no relapse to the bestial Irishman on stage, although the latter crops up in caricature and other forums. Rebellion and Union did not conclude this regional strand of the Irish Enlightenment; it merely slowed it down for a time.

* * * *

The emphasis of the first three chapters in this volume is on performance. Although discussions of Stage Irishmen are manifold in assessments of eighteenth-century Irish theatre, Felicity Nussbaum (Chapter 1) makes

---

[67] For a fuller version of this argument, see O'Shaughnessy, 'Bit, by some mad whig'.

[68] See, for instance, a reprinting of John Temple 'as the most Effectual Warning-Piece to keep them upon their Guard against the Encroachments of Popery' about Catholic Emancipation in 1812 which includes an account of 1798. *The Irish Rebellion: Or, An History of the Attempts of the Irish Papists to Extirpate the Protestants in the Kingdom of Ireland* ... (London: Printed for J. Brindley, J. Hodges, and M. Cooper, 1812).

a compelling argument that female actors are more agile and dynamic than their male counterparts in their capacity to scrutinise stereotypes and power relations between Britain and Ireland. Her emphasis on cross-dressing to explore origins and social class illuminates how actresses such as Catherine Clive, Margaret Woffington and Maria Macklin embodied the unsettled relations across the Irish sea. Crucially, Nussbaum detects a growing assertiveness among these women as the century progresses, a confidence that chimes with the increasing volume of Irish patriotism over the period.

This upbeat tone resonates with Jim Davis (Chapter 2), who assesses the career of John Johnstone, the quintessential Stage Irishman of the final quarter of the eighteenth century. For Davis, Johnstone's success was based on an adroit capacity to mediate Irishness in a manner alert both to the commercial demands of the London theatres and to the often febrile political backdrop of those years. Johnstone embodied tolerance and decency in an impressive swathe of roles that operated across the socio-economic spectrum, ensuring that Irishness was acceptable, even endearing to London audiences.

Oskar Cox Jensen (Chapter 3) is unconvinced. In his view, Johnstone's agency, not simply as an actor but also as a person, diminishes over his career. Johnstone's extraordinary popularity ensured that he was invoked in a proliferation of material and immaterial representations circulating in London. This is, Cox Jensen concedes, unremarkable in the burgeoning culture of theatrical celebrity, but, he argues, it takes on a special significance when the subject is seen to represent a nation. In the end, Johnstone is overwhelmed by stereotype, little more than an Irish 'dancing bear'. The differing views of Davis and Cox Jensen highlight the difficulty in deconstructing stereotypes and determining the parameters of success within a forum so enmeshed with other media, notably caricature, periodicals and song.

Thanks to the editorial efforts of John Greene, the work can begin proper on comparative studies of the Dublin and London theatres.[69] Although the relationship between the two cities is present throughout this volume, three essays take it as their particular focus, showing how such work might add to our understanding of Georgian culture and politics.

Music's importance to the representation of Irish civilisation is evident from Geoffrey Keating, Charles O'Conor and other cultural historians of

[69] *Theatre in Dublin 1745–1820: A Calendar of Performances*, ed. John C. Greene, 6 vols. (Bethlehem: Lehigh University Press, 2011).

the century: bards are perceived as keepers and embodiments of Gaelic culture, laws and history. When Goldsmith championed Turlough O'Carolan as 'the last Irish Bard', he recounted an anecdote of O'Carolan not only replaying a Vivaldi concerto he heard just once but instantly composing another in the same style; Irish culture then proves itself open to and capable of cultural synergies with European traditions.[70] Goldsmith was writing in 1760, at the moment, as Michael Burden (Chapter 4) shows us, the burletta was developing in London and Dublin. Burden's re-contextualisation of the burletta's history, based on detailed research of the Dublin and London calendars of the 1750s and 1760s, impresses on us the creative energies between the two cities as well as marking the involvement of figures such as Isaac Bickerstaff and John O'Keeffe in musical innovation.

Dissatisfied with a full-blooded Irish patriot take on Richard Brinsley Sheridan, Robert Jones (Chapter 5) calls for a more nuanced approach. He brings to attention the multiple political allegiances of Sheridan – Irishman, Foxite Whig and MP for Staffordshire – to dissolve impossibly coherent perceptions of man and playwright. Taking as his focus a single word in Sheridan's great comedy, *The School for Scandal*, Jones not only reaffirms that trade remained at the forefront of Irish patriot issues, as it was for Molyneux at the end of the seventeenth century, but also reminds us that Sheridan had duties and affiliations beyond Dublin or London that require further scholarly exploration. The mutability of personality that features in the play, argues Jones, shows how Sheridan worked through his Irish and English affiliations and has implications for how we understand other Irish writers negotiating these difficulties.

The ties that bind Dublin and London presented opportunity as well as difficulty. Colleen Taylor (Chapter 6) calls attention to Irish women playwrights of the late eighteenth and early nineteenth centuries, a cadre of writers, she points out, often overlooked due to Irish Romanticism's emphasis on female novelists. Taylor's careful reading of Sydney Owenson's *The First Attempt* (1807) and Alicia Sheridan Le Fanu's *The Sons of Erin* (1812) shows how politicised and Enlightened women could rewrite eighteenth-century theatrical tropes to refresh political discourse and make the case for female political agency. Glorvina's mantle (from *The Wild Irish Girl*), argues Taylor, was a powerful political symbol in both Dublin and London.

---

[70] Oliver Goldsmith, 'The History of Carolan, the last Irish Bard' in *The Collected Works of Oliver Goldsmith*, ed. Arthur Friedman, 5 vols. (Oxford: Clarendon Press, 1966), 3: 118–20.

The final quartet of chapters in the volume explores how writers took historical and geographical approaches to teasing out political stances on identity, ethnicity and Enlightenment ideas. I (Chapter 7) continue my interest in Macklin, taking as my subject his historical tragedy *King Henry the VII* (1746). Typically passed over in Macklin criticism (indeed, criticism of any kind), my reading of the play connects it to Addison's *Cato* (1713) and Irish theatrical antecedents to propose an alternative genealogy of eighteenth-century Irish theatre. Macklin's ambitious attempt to rewrite John Ford's *Perkin Warbeck* (1634), seen in an Irish patriot context, thus bolsters his claim to be an Enlightenment figure.

Bridget Orr (Chapter 8) also argues for the importance of eighteenth-century historical tragedy, a too often neglected genre. Orr takes the case of Arthur Murphy's *Alzuma* (1773), his favourite of his serious plays and shows what a rich reading can be produced when one acknowledges Murphy's multiple allegiances – Irish, Catholic and a pro-Bute propagandist in the 1760s when the play was written. Orr shows how *Alzuma* was shaped by – but did not ventriloquise – indigenous critiques of empire; Murphy's play is marked by a 'discourse of radical indigeneity' and provides a compelling argument for the further exploration of Murphy's serious plays – and indeed the eighteenth-century tragedy more generally.

James Field Stanfield will not be a name familiar to many, a point which underlines the value of Declan McCormack's (Chapter 9) archival work on the northern circuit of English theatre. As already noted, the volume is heavily London-centric, but McCormack shows the extraordinary stories that can be unearthed: Stanfield's life and career – slaver, actor, abolitionist, writer – unfolds not only across northern England and Scotland but also traverses the Atlantic. McCormack shows how Stanfield, clearly traumatised by his slaving past, used his theatrical success to fuel political and intellectual activism that established him as an important public reformer and a key participant in the 'Northern Enlightenment'. The chapter is a salutary reminder to theatre historians of the importance of looking beyond London and Dublin.

Helen Burke's chapter (Chapter 10) on John O'Keeffe, the most successful Irish playwright in London in the 1780s and 1790s, considers his work in terms of vernacular cosmopolitanism, that is, a mode of cosmopolitanism produced by migrants who travel due to compulsion or necessity. Looking at four of his major works that invoke the pastoral, Burke reveals how O'Keeffe drew on his Irish Catholic heritage – marked by dispossession and disenfranchisement – to extrapolate a 'paradigmatic story of modernity itself'. What Burke shows is how O'Keeffe combines his concern for toleration and hospitality with his enthusiasm for London to 'expand the ethical horizons of his drama': like so many Irish theatrical practitioners and patriots before him, O'Keeffe sought to demonstrate how Irish culture and thought could enrich Britain; there was no conflict between his allegiances to the Crown and the shamrock.

Like my portrait of Macklin, the Irish theatrical Enlightenment in London sketched out in this introduction may appear largely idealised: there were, of course, many objections to pretensions of Irish civility and manifold episodes of racial discrimination. But for those Irish that made it – and theatre was a success story, in the main – we cannot underestimate the confidence that participation in vibrant London metropolitan life engendered. We now know that domestic Irish theatre was a rich and distinctive endeavour – the cover image of this volume is intended partly tongue-in-cheek – but, for many in the theatrical professions, London was the goal.[71] Ambition and achievement unified these people, and there is a collective ebullient confidence that can be detected in their body of work and collaborations, energised by offstage Irish performative success and recognition, be it the wit of Laetitia Pilkington, the speeches of Sheridan, the conversational acumen of Burke or the growth in Irish participation in institutional and club life in eighteenth-century London. The London theatres had a critical mass of Irish migrants who supported and fed off one another's success. Enlightenment is concerned with individual and societal improvement, and the second half of the eighteenth century was critical to the dissemination of ideas of Irish Enlightenment in Britain by a group of remarkable people who operated increasingly with something of a swagger after 1745. The high point of this upbeat mood was the 1780s – when Irish playwrights were particularly dominant and buoyed by the public success of their predecessors, especially Macklin and Goldsmith – before the problems posed by the French Revolution and the United Irishmen intervened. Progression certainly stumbled then but by that stage, Irish civility had become a notion too entrenched to be toppled entirely.[72]

[71] See Helen Burke, *Riotous Performances: The Struggle for Hegemony in the Irish Theater, 1712–1784* (Notre Dame, IN: University of Notre Dame Press, 2003).

[72] This project has received funding from the European Union's 2020 research and innovation programme under the Marie Sklowdowska-Curie grant agreement No 745896. My sincere thanks to Emily Anderson, Michael Griffin, Felicity Nussbaum and Gillian Russell for taking the time to read this introduction and offer so many helpful comments.

PART I

Representations and Resistance

CHAPTER I

Straddling: London-Irish Actresses in Performance

Felicity Nussbaum

The careers of Irish actors and actresses itinerant between the London and Dublin theatres reflect the ongoing struggles to sustain their craft while straddling two cities. In particular, Irish actresses in character offered ways to embody the tensions between cities, ethnicities and sexes, and sometimes to resolve them.[1] Eighteenth-century London claimed the largest number of middling Irish men and women outside of Ireland, including perhaps fifty actors among those associated with the theatre.[2] Diasporic Irish actors played both Irish and English roles, while English actors accepted as many or more Irish roles. The Irish identity they portrayed, like the complicated relations between Ireland and England represented on the London stage, was often unstable and even unnerving. 'Irishness was never settled', as Helen Burke aptly observes: an 'untainted' Irishness simply does not exist, and the history of the internal struggles within the Irish diaspora 'moves us away from an English/Irish binary' towards multiple affiliations and alignments.[3] National identity in formation during the eighteenth century cannot, then, be simplified into an authentic essence. Toby Barnard similarly notes, 'A consistent, recognizable, metropolitan Irish identity had yet to stabilize within the capital's environs at this point in London's history.'[4] Straddling these various identities – ethnic, national and transnational – as Irish actors learned to do – can be perceived, as David O'Shaughnessy remarks, as enabling 'a more positive conception of

---

[1] As Colleen Taylor's discussion of Sydney Owenson's London persona in this volume demonstrates, women could also perform Irishness outside the theatre.

[2] Craig Bailey, *Irish London: Middle-Class Migration in the Global Eighteenth Century* (Liverpool: Liverpool University Press, 2013), 5.

[3] Helen Burke, 'Crossing Acts: Irish Drama from George Farquhar to Thomas Sheridan' in *A Companion to Irish Literature*, ed. Julia M. Wright, 2 vols. (Oxford: Wiley-Blackwell, 2010), 1: 136. Bailey, *Irish London*, similarly stresses 'fluid relationships and multidirectional flows of exchange', 8.

[4] David O'Shaughnessy, 'Introduction: "Tolerably Numerous": Recovering the London Irish of the Eighteenth Century', 7, thus characterises Toby Barnard's essay, 'The Irish in London and "The London Irish", c. 1660–1780', 14–40. Both essays appear in *Eighteenth-Century Life*, 39.1 (2015).

diaspora' to stress the enrichment such interaction allows.[5] London-Irish
theatrical relationships are characterised by thickening entanglements
rather than discrete loyalties, as Robert Jones (Chapter 5) and Bridget
Orr (Chapter 8) also discuss in this volume, and actors and actresses served
as performing agents who sometimes softened the differences, and sometimes exaggerated them.

Countering Michael Ragussis's view that ethnic difference, and particularly Irish stereotyping, becomes less entrenched after the 1750s, and that
'the theater exploded with new forms and strategies for portraying ethnic
difference', Paul Goring has contended that 'the ethnic voice gains only
limited legitimacy with eighteenth-century London and ... [that] traditional modes for representing Irishness on the London stage are not
radically overturned.'[6] Here I will ask how, specifically, does this controversy play out in relation to London-Irish actresses and Irish women
characters? Rather than supporting either view – that the onstage London-
Irish continued to be predictable and circumscribed (Goring) or became
more varied and less stereotypical (Ragussis) in the later part of the
century – I would like to calibrate more subtly the way Irish women
characters are portrayed, taking account of the social status, dramatic
context and gendering of those roles. My point is to stress the ways in
which Irish, Anglo-Irish and English actresses acting as Irish characters on
the eighteenth-century London stage add a fresh dimension to our com-
prehension of ethnicity in its actual performance. In this way, I hope to add
to the 'exciting new phase' in debating the importance of gender to modern
Irish history that Catriona Kennedy and others have identified,[7] especially
as we trace women's increasing access into the public sphere – a process also
traced by Colleen Taylor (Chapter 6, this volume) – during the Irish
Enlightenment.

'Irishness' in all its performative variety represented possibilities as well
as limits, range as well as restriction. Actor-playwrights such as Charles
Macklin, who anglicised his name, became Protestant and cultivated an

[5] O'Shaughnessy, 'Introduction,' *Eighteenth-Century Life*, 6. In David O'Shaughnessy, '"Rip'ning
  Buds in Freedom's Field": Staging Irish Improvement in the 1780s', *Journal of Eighteenth-Century
  Studies* 38.4 (2015): 541–54; 545, he argues that 'they were eager to take full advantage of the
  opportunities that metropolitan life offered without being shackled by their nationality'.
[6] Michael Ragussis, *Theatrical Nation: Jews and Other Outlandish Englishmen in Georgian Britain*
  (Philadelphia: University of Pennsylvania Press, 2010), 222 n119; and Paul Goring, '"John Bull, Pit,
  Box, and Gallery, Said No!": Charles Macklin and the Limits of Ethnic Resistance on the
  Eighteenth-Century London Stage', *Representations* 79.1 (2002): 61–81; 76.
[7] Catriona Kennedy, 'Woman and Gender in Modern Ireland' in *The Princeton History of Modern
  Ireland*, ed. Richard Burke and Ian McBride (Princeton: Princeton University Press, 2016), 361–62.

English accent for the London stage, straddled both worlds, as did his daughter Maria Macklin. He, like other such emigrants, felt 'neither fully assimilated as Englishmen nor fully at home in their native cultures'.[8] Irish dramatic characters often reflect this uneasy mix. In Macklin's *True-Born Irishman*, for example, the Anglophilic, social-climbing Mrs Diggerty comically attempts to affect an English accent and resists the stereotype of the brogue as a signal of Irish inferiority. In Garrick's 1772 farce *The Irish Widow*, Sir Patrick is puzzled when Whittle, who woos the eponymous Widow, doesn't understand him: 'I say, how can that be, when we both spake English?' (2.i).[9] If the London theatre was a site of both cosmopolitan ambition and Irish patriotism, we might remember that rural Ireland differed from urban Ireland, region from region, and neither Protestant nor Catholic Ireland was homogeneous. What passed for Irish in early America or in New South Wales differed from Irishness on the London stage. Macklin lamented the challenges of this variety after the Dublin success *True-Born Irishman* was panned in the London performance for its topical Irish allusions: 'There's a *geography* in *humour* [about national identities] as well as in *morals*, which I had not previously considered.'[10] We might then think of the Irish-London theatrical space for actors in performance as an unassimilated site in which the cultures meet but where neither is fully compatible with the other, nor thoroughly incorporated; for as in all contact zones, the dominant power prefers to make the asymmetrical relationship appear to be one of mutual exchange.[11]

Recent scholarly studies have explored the effects of Irish immigration on eighteenth-century London, but I know of no in-depth investigation of the importance of Irish *actresses* in the metropole, or of the Irish parts that women of both nations played.[12] For our purposes here, we may define Irish actresses as those born or raised in Ireland or those who had at least one Irish parent. Actresses and the Irish female characters they played frequently served as go-betweens or agents of assimilation across gender,

[8] Ragussis, *Theatrical Nation*, 53.
[9] David Garrick, *The Irish Widow* in *The Plays of David Garrick*, ed. Harry William Pedicord and Fredrick Louis Bergmann, 7 vols. (Carbondale: Southern Illinois University Press, 1980), 2: 151–84.
[10] William Cooke, *Memoirs of Charles Macklin, Comedian: With the Dramatic Characters, Manners, Anecdotes & c. of the Age in Which He Lived* (London: J. Asperne, 1806), 270.
[11] Susan Cannon Harris, 'Mixed Marriage: Sheridan, Macklin, and the Hybrid Audience' in *Players, Playwrights, Playhouses: Investigating Performance, 1660–1800*, ed. Michael Cordner and Peter Holland (Basingstoke: Palgrave Macmillan, 2007), 189–212, draws similarly upon Mary Louise Pratt's notion of the contact zone.
[12] On Irish immigration see Desmond Slowey, *The Radicalization of Irish Drama 1600–1900: The Rise and Fall of Ascendancy Theatre* (Dublin: Irish Academic Press, 2008); and Jeffrey H. Richards, *Drama, Theatre, and Identity in the American New Republic* (New York: Cambridge University Press, 2005).

class, national and religious lines. The parts Irish actresses took on ranged from peasant to aristocrat, fashionable fine ladies to cross-dressed women, rural to urban. Often perceived to be more malleable than their male counterparts, women players straddled these differences to a much greater degree than the male actors who seldom played cross-dressed or travestied roles.[13] As Pope reminds us in his much-cited lines from *Epistle to A Lady* (1735), women's identities were perceived to be more fluid than men's: 'Most women have no characters at all. . . . Matter too soft a lasting mark to bear.' Irish women frequently represented a mixed or diasporic identity. While sometimes taken as an index to the level of Irish civilisation, they often resisted such positioning. As is well known, the real women of eighteenth-century Ireland lacked political rights, and English common law limited their property and inheritance: 'Theirs was a subject[ed] and subsidiary role to the male, and . . . the nature and importance of these varying roles was, above all else, a function of class.'[14] Yet Irishwomen on the later eighteenth-century London stage, in contrast to the cult of domesticity dominating later periods, often reflect their empowerment in the economic and social spheres.[15]

A renewed emphasis on the actual *performance* of actresses in character animates issues of ethnicity and cultural tensions in ways that the scripting of the character alone, or the biography of the actress, does not do. Especially when character is enacted, gender becomes a powerful lens through which to navigate its overlapping with ethnicity and nationhood. Perhaps the best-known Irishwoman on the London stage in the mid-eighteenth century is actress-singer and playwright Catherine 'Kitty' Clive, who avoided stereotypes and evinced sympathy for both countries. She claimed an 'Irish-English' identity – a term she used in an afterpiece of her own composition – for the forceful, witty, independent and talented women characters she created on the page and on stage, in song and word.[16] Clive was immortalised in a striking porcelain miniature statue as Mrs Riot, the would-be English Fine Lady in Garrick's *Lethe* (1740). In the

---

[13] On women's military cross-dressing at public events in Ireland, see Padhraig Higgins, *A Nation of Politicians: Gender, Patriotism, and Political Culture in Late Eighteenth-Century Ireland* (Madison: University of Wisconsin Press, 2010), 192–201.

[14] Gearóid Ó Tuathaigh, 'The Role of Women in Ireland under the New English Order' in *Women in Irish Society: The Historical Dimension*, ed. Margaret MacCurtain and Donncha Ó Corráin (Westport, CT: Praeger, 1979), 26.

[15] Mary O'Dowd, *A History of Women in Ireland, 1500–1800* (Harlow: Pearson Longman, 2005), 142–43. Such opportunities began to disappear after 1800.

[16] See Felicity Nussbaum, *Rival Queens: Actresses, Performance, and the Eighteenth-Century British Theater* (Philadelphia: University of Pennsylvania Press, 2010) on Clive's career and writings, especially 182–88.

musical afterpiece she wrote and starred in, *The Faithful Irish Woman* (1765, originally called *A Sketch of a Fine Lady's Return from a Rout*, 1763), Clive plays the leading role of Mrs OConner. Her Irishwoman is neither a suffering mother nor a fortune hunter, nor someone who could be easily dominated. Instead, she personifies Ireland as a wealthy, propertied woman who generously assumes the debts of her lover, a suddenly destitute Englishman. Clive thus reversed the usual marriage of a fortune-hunting Irishman to an English heiress to allow an Irishwoman to elevate an Englishman by wedding her. She willingly shares his identity in marriage, while insisting that the English (implicating the London audience) are the ignorant ones in maintaining superstitions about the Irish.

While Charles Macklin's Irish Fine Lady spoke a mockable 'new kind of London English', Clive's Mrs OConner claims in her *Faithful Irish Woman* that the genteel Irish speak English without a brogue and that the purest English is spoken in Dublin. Instead of apologising for any linguistic markers, Mrs OConner taunts the English for their speech and promotes 'the Irish-English' language as a sign of the upper ranks in both countries. Clive, emphasising her Irishness in singing Irish airs, apparently counted herself among those who spoke such a language: she united both in her person and character a commoner with a lady of quality, and Irishness with an English affiliation. Clive benefitted mightily from her career on the English stage, but she hints in her afterpiece at the unequal economic and political conditions between the two countries. She cleverly deflates England's power as a nation into the character of an English sea captain who is a supplicant to the Irishwoman landowner.

The number of Irishwomen's dramatic roles in mid and late eighteenth-century plays was, however, surprisingly small, while the conventional stage Irish*man* appears everywhere, easily recognisable as a buffoonish fortune hunter, soldier, or footman who speaks roughly with a brogue and is known for his bulls and blunders (Figure 1.1).[17]

For both sexes, Irishness was frequently coded linguistically as speaking in dialect or involving the skewed use or abuse of the English language.[18] Depicted as unfamiliar with the bustling urban London society, such characters are naive, hard-drinking rustics, sometimes racialised, who

---

[17] Among the books discussing Irish male characters on the eighteenth-century stage is J. O. Bartley, *Teague, Shenkin and Sawney: Being an Historical Study of the Earliest Irish, Welsh, and Scottish Characters in English Plays* (Cork: Cork University Press, 1954).

[18] Jeffrey H. Richards, *Drama, Theatre, and Identity*, defines a *bull* as a 'metaphorical statement stressing apparent connections which are not real', and a *blunder* as the misapprehension or misapplication of English words, 188–89.

THE COMMITTEE.

M.ᴿ ROCK ᵃˢ TEAGUE
—A poor Irishman, Heaven save me.

London. Printed for J. Bell, British Library. Strand, July 28, 1792

Figure 1.1 J. Thornwaite (engraver) after J. Roberts, 'Mr. [Edward Anthony] Rock
as Teague in *The Committee, or, the Faithful Irishman*, Act I.i', *Bell's British Theatre*,
vol. 20 (London 1797). Call #: R682e-05. The University Library, University of
Illinois at Urbana-Champaign.

emerge from a barbaric past. At the same time, attempts to hide one's
Irishness became the object of stage satire. The wild, primitive Irishman
when imagined in the person of a woman evolves into a hard-drinking,
buxom, sexually loose, crude-talking woman delivering bulls and blunders
with a heavy brogue. For example, the Irish Widow quips, 'I wish the poor
young man dead with all my heart, as he thinks it will do him a grate dale of
good' (I.iii). But other Irish women of a certain status acted as cultural glue,
smoothing the roughness of Irishmen and drawing Irish and English
together in a womanhood sometimes not very distinct from English
womanhood. Attitudes to ethnicity could also be split between two
Irish male characters: one Irishman attempting to mask himself as
English might be paired with another who flouted his Irishness. In this
way, the theatre managed at once to question and to reproduce ethnic

abstractions.[19] What remains to be further explored is how this doubling sometimes occurred with paired Irish women, or in a relationship between a stereotypical Irish man and a pretentiously fine Irish-English lady, when one sex resisted assimilation while the other explored its possibilities. Or, alternatively, Irish theatrical identities were split between two women from different social classes, both Irish, or one Irish and the other English. Such doubling was sometimes personified in a cross-dressed actress shifting through disguise to explore social class and origin.

Cross-dressing – embodying the straddling of a character's defining sexual characteristics – served as a convenient shorthand to represent Irishness in all its variety in the period.[20] The cross-dressed woman represented a malleable 'mode of articulation, a way of describing a space of possibility', as Marjorie Garber has written, for 'the spectacle of trans-vestism often points towards other kinds of crises located elsewhere in the culture'.[21] Some of the most famous eighteenth-century Irish and Anglo-Irish actresses wore breeches, including Ann Barry, Kitty Clive, Margaret Doyle Kennedy, Elizabeth Farren, Dorothy Jordan and Maria Macklin, many of whom were known principally for their cross-dressed roles.

Peg Woffington, for example, was advertised as acting 'in the Irish manner' early in her career. Performing epilogues in breeches, she revealed an ability to embody national stereotypes without confining herself to one affiliation (Figure 1.2). In particular, cross-dressed Irish women characters were more closely aligned with Irish masculinity, even while encouraging audiences to turn the actresses' breech-bound bums and legs into erotic objects. In their male costumes, these women proved to be strong, spirited agents promoting their own interests as characters and as players.

Among the scant examples of female Irish characters on the London stage, clustered in the decades after the Seven Years' War,[22] are most

[19] Ragussis, *Theatrical Nation*, 44, posits that comedies such as Macklin's *Love à la Mode* featuring a heroic Irishman silenced ethnicities in part by encouraging the development of a proper, universal English accent on stage.
[20] Adele Dalsimer and Vera Kreilkamp, 'Re/Dressing Mother Ireland: Feminist Images in Art and Literature' in *Re/Dressing Cathleen: Contemporary Works from Irish Women Artists*, ed. Jennifer Grinnell and Alston Conley (Boston: McMullan Museum of Art, 1997), note that Mother Ireland was depicted in Celtic literature as a 'voracious warrior queen' or a 'female goddess' who 'haunts the battlefield', 37. Lisa M. Bitel, *Land of Women: Tales of Sex and Gender from Early Ireland* (Ithaca: Cornell University Press, 1998), similarly points to 'images of hostile and powerful women' prevalent within early allegories of Ireland, 204.
[21] Marjorie Garber, *Vested Interests: Cross-Dressing and Cultural Anxiety* (New York: Routledge, 1997), 11. See Nussbaum, *Rival Queens*, 193.
[22] Bartley, *Teague, Shenkin and Sawney*, attributes the increase in the appearance of Stage Irishmen from 1760 to 1800 to Ireland's population growth, 171.

Figure 1.2 Mrs. [Margaret] Woffington in the Habit of a Volunteer, *The Female Volunteer: Or, An Attempt to Make Our Men Stand* (London 1746).

famously Mrs O'Dougherty (alias Diggerty) in Macklin's aforementioned *The True-Born Irishman, or The Irish Fine Lady* (Dublin 1761, revised as *The Irish Fine Lady* in London 1767); the Widow Brady in David Garrick's frequently performed *The Irish Widow* (1772); Mrs OConner in Kitty Clive's burletta *The Faithful Irish Woman* (1765); Lady Fallal in Richard Griffith's *Variety; a Comedy in Five Acts* (1782); the cross-dressed Patrick in John O'Keeffe's *The Poor Soldier* (1783); Unah in Charles Dibdin's *Harvest Home; a Comic Opera* (1787); Irish mantua-maker Mrs Poplin in James Cobb's *English Readings* (1787); the cross-dressed Harriet in Thomas Holcroft's *Seduction* (1787); Sally Shamrock (Figure 1.3) in Samuel James Arnold's *The Shipwreck* (1796); and several Irishwomen in John O'Keeffe's comedies in the later decades.[23]

Though performative Irishness is usually comic, in William Philips's tragedy *Hibernia Freed* (1722), the commanding heroines Sabina and

---

[23] Bartley, *Teague, Shenkin and Sawney* identifies several of these female characters. Irishwomen also appear in O'Keeffe's *Love in a Camp; The Prisoner at Large* (1788); *The Toy, Or, The Lie of a Day* (1788); and *Wicklow Mountains* (1805).

Mrs. BLAND as SALLY.

Come buy Poor Sally's wooden ware.

Shipwreck

London Published by John Cawthorn, Nº 5, Catherine Street Strand Janᵞ 31. 1807.

Figure 1.3 Maria Theresa Bland (née Romanzini) as Sally Shamrock in *The Shipwreck* (London 1807). Call #: B642m-04. The University Library, University of Illinois at Urbana-Champaign.

Agnes inspire their lovesick men to patriotic valour against the usurping
Danes. Agnes asserts: 'I have a Soul wou'd urge me to the Field,/And on thy
Head revenge my Country's Wrongs' (II.i.19).

By my count – almost certainly not an exhaustive one – there are fewer
than twenty Irish women's roles over the course of the century; yet
paradoxically several are among the best-known and most popular comic
parts. In all of these plays, Irish women characters with their formulaic
representations helped establish the clichés of Irish identity; they also, by
contrast, helped solidify English femininity. These women are mannish,
unassimilable Irish peasants or tradeswomen, fine ladies suffering from
class envy hoping to be absorbed into Englishness, or feisty women acting
in breeches. The hard-drinking, pregnant peddler songstress Sally
Shamrock desperately searches for a husband; while Mrs Poplin, 'a walking
pincushion', struggles to be literate while hoping that the reading entertainments she sponsors will elevate the audience; and the aristocratic
Irishwoman, Lady Fallal, whose name means 'cheap trimmings', is 'a little
too bustling to be elegant'.[24] Resisting her husband's attempts 'to mod-
ulate, or soften off a little' her brogue (II.i.18) which she considers 'the
prettiest feather in my cap' (II.i.19), Lady Fallal proclaims, 'I would not
part with anything I brought from my own dear country upon any account
whatever' (II.i.18). These comic Irishwomen labourers and inept social
climbers invite a satiric response, unlike their cross-dressed fellow
Irishwomen who contest audience expectations to inspire admiration and
empathy.

Among the few scholars who mention Irish women characters,
Desmond Slowey remarks that 'the motif of the independent-minded
Irish female aristocrat runs through Irish plays, already emerging ... as
"your fine, gay, sprightly Irish Women."' He finds them to be 'more
practical than the men, who frequently behave idiotically, and they are
the engines of social change'.[25] Another kind of recurrent character is
instead my focus here – the Irish women cross-dressed as men who advance
the plot and break away from reigning conventional portrayals.
Particularly relevant are the frequently performed cross-dressed roles in

[24] Richard Griffith, *Variety; a Comedy in Five Acts* (London 1782), 5 (1.1).
[25] Slowey, *Radicalization of Irish Drama 1600–1900*, 97. Helen Burke, 'Country Matters: Irish
"Waggery" and the Irish and British Theatrical Traditions', in *Players, Playwrights, Playhouses:
Investigating Performance, 1660–1800*, suggests that 'the fashionably-dressed English female had been
a synecdoche for the British state that tried to impose its economic and political will on Ireland', 225.
Jeffrey H. Richards, *Drama, Theatre, and Identity*, discusses Irish female character in James Nelson
Barker's *The Indian Princess* (1808), 207–8.

The Irish Widow, The Poor Soldier and *The Shipwreck*. As is well-known, Garrick wrote *The Irish Widow; a Farce in Two Acts* (1772) as a vehicle for Ann Street Barry (1733–1801), second wife of actor Spranger Barry, to perform an Irish part.[26] The meaty breeches role, Garrick's innovation on Molière's farce *Le Mariage forcé* (1664), became a favourite of principal actresses until the 1820s, including Anglo-Irish actress Dorothy Jordan. As an Englishwoman acting the Irish Widow, both actress and character straddle two nationalities and sexes.

Though born in Bath, Ann Barry had followed her lover actor-manager Spranger Barry to Dublin. An English actress whose adopted Irish dialect rang true, she performed there from 1759 until about 1767, including as Mrs Diggerty in *The True-Born Irishman*, before returning to London. As the Widow Brady, she was reported to have 'spoke[n] the Irish accent in a most pleasing stile'.[27] That her real life bore some resemblance to the role may have enhanced the farce's popularity. While not actually an *Irish* widow, Ann Barry was the widow of her first husband, William Dancer, who, like the former husband of the Widow in the play, was something of a profligate. Her character is also self-referential when she remarks casually that she cares not how many husbands she buries: 'Indeed, I could dry up my tears for a dozen husbands when I were sure of having a tirteenth like Mr. *Whittol*. That's very natural, sure, both in England, and Dublin too' (I.iii.167). Offering a meta-theatrical *double entendre* – 'I shall make a very bad actress' (I.ii.163) – Barry as the Irish Widow (Figure 1.4) challenges the critics to 'laugh at me if they dare' (I.ii.163).

While critics did just that, largely panning *The Irish Widow*, London *audiences* loved the play, sustaining it through twenty performances in the first season and fifty-seven over the next five years.[28] Set in Scarborough, it features the aged dandy Whittle who seeks to woo the youthful Widow Brady away from his young nephew William but changes his mind when she affects to be an Irish harridan with a thick brogue. The Widow, unhappy about having 'to assume a character contrary to my disposition' (I.ii.162), pretends to be the conventionally loud, hyper-Irish woman but later drops that disguise to impersonate her soldier brother Lieutenant O'Neale. In her male persona, the cross-dressed Widow Brady challenges

[26] 23 October 1772, in William Hopkins, MS Diary, 1769–76, Folger Shakespeare Library, Washington, DC, cited in *Plays of David Garrick*, 2: 343.

[27] Arthur Murphy, *The Life of David Garrick, Esq.* 2 vols (London: J. Wright, 1801), 2: 95.

[28] 'Commentary and Notes', *The Irish Widow* in *Plays of David Garrick*, ed. Pedicord and Bergmann, 2: 343. Garrick notes in his dedication to Barry, 'some news-papers have criticized the farce, and the audiences have laugh'd heartily', 153.

Figure 1.4 Ann Barry as Widow Brady with Whittle in *The Irish Widow*, Act II.i,
Parson's Minor Theatre, vol. 3 (London 1794). Call #: Ib74 T794M 3. Beinecke Rare
Book and Manuscript Library, Yale University.

Whittle to a duel to defend her family's honour, defying the expectation
that women do not engage in swordplay.

For the Widow, exaggerated Irishness is performative, and performative with a bite. Typical of many Irish women characters, the Irish
Widow cross-dresses to avoid marrying against her will. Her sword-
and pistol-wielding manly Irish identity, she adamantly insists, is
preferable to Englishmen's class and gender confusions: 'These
[London] whipper-snappers look so much more like girls in breeches
than those I see in petticoats. . . . The fair sex in London here seem the
most masculine of the two' (II.i.176). She continues, 'women of all
qualities, are so mixt together, that you don't know one from t'other'
(II.i.177). Abandoning her sweet Irish lilt, Widow Brady offends her
aged would-be lover with her thick affected brogue that signals

a riotous coarseness: 'Fait and trot, if you will be after bringing me before the old Gentleman, if he loves music, I will trate his ears with a little of the brogue, and some dancing too into the bargain, if he loves capering' (I.ii.163). Whittle is appalled when she abandons her 'almost speechless reserve' to become an adventure-seeking 'wild, ranting, buxom widow' (I.ii.163). The cross-dressed Widow Brady quashes the national stereotype to charge that pretence and affectation are typical of the upper-class *English* elite of both sexes. The play concludes with an Irish tune as her father allows her marriage to the young English William, and the pair successfully trick old Whittle into parting with his nephew's inheritance.[29]

The Irish Widow, then, straddles the sexes, the social classes and the two countries. She slyly remarks ironically in dialect that every Irishwoman is fond of imitating her English betters: 'But I must know more of your English ways, and live more among the English Ladies, to learn how to be faitful [sic] to two at a time' (I.iii.165). Further, she defends the Irish against English double standards: 'An Englishman may look over the hedge, while an Irishman must not stale a horse' (I.iii.165). Her words apply to the English and the Irish, to men and women, noble and peasant. In short, cross-dressing for the Irish Widow – and for the actress playing her – enables her to challenge her second-sex status, criticise English attitudes, and direct her fate, unlike the English ladies for whom she expresses uncensored contempt.

Like *The Irish Widow*, Thomas Holcroft's very successful five-act sentimental comedy *Seduction* (1787) features a cross-dressed Irishwoman, Harriet (played on the London and Dublin stages by American-born Sarah Wilson), who similarly mocks the fashionable English elite.[30] Affecting a brogue as the Widow Brady had done, the cross-dressed Harriet in *Seduction* (Figure 1.5), 'that Irish, gentleman-like,

---

[29] David Garrick to George Faulkner, *The Letters of David Garrick*, ed. David Mason Little, George M. Kahrl and Phoebe de K. Wilson, 3 vols. (Cambridge, MA: Harvard University Press, 1963), 2: 833: 'If you see at yr return to Dublin any handsome Actress who can perform the part of the *Irish Widow* well, pray run away with her, & by that time you will be thoroughly sick of her, I will take her off yr hands & make her Fortune reviving the Widow–.' Garrick blamed Barry for bringing the run to a halt with her poor singing of the final Irish tune: 'for the Moment that Farce began to get ye managers profit & Credit, Mrs Barry found out ye Playing so late, & in her breeches would kill her, so the Irish Widow was destroy'd in ye midst of her Triumph'.

[30] Thomas Holcroft, *Seduction* [1787]: *A Critical Edition with Annotations*, ed. Joseph J. Latona (New York: Garland Publishing, 1987), 83. The play had three Dublin editions, ran nine nights in London and was produced successfully in New York and Boston. Quotations are from this edition.

Figure 1.5 Mrs. [Sarah] Wilson in the Character of Harriet in the Comedy of
Seduction, Act I.vii (London 1787). British Museum object: 1870,0514.2803.
©Trustees of the British Museum.

Lady' (III.v.234), unmasks the pretentious, untrustworthy Englishman.
Irishwomen in these comedies prove to be supple, resilient characters
who strongly contrast to weak Englishwomen, call out the licentiousness
of English men, reject the crudeness of hyper-masculine Irish men, and
turn men of fashion to men of feeling. They embody contact zones to
negotiate the layered complexities of cultural clash and exchange.

In another example, John O'Keeffe's *The Poor Soldier, A Comic Opera* (1783), 'a stock afterpiece for fifty years'[31] (followed by the sequel *Love in a Camp; or, Patrick in Prussia* [1785] in which Norah cross-dresses) is set in the rural Irish countryside of Carton, County Kildare. O'Keeffe thought of himself as something of a translator between the Irish and English in familiarising the English public with the traditional airs of Turlough O'Carolan, the harpist composer known as the Irish Orpheus.[32] The play furthered the association of national identity with sexual ambiguity through a male part successfully acted and sung by a woman. The London theatre was saturated with song, and the two-act opera, enriched by Irish country ballads, features three Irishwomen: a very manly Harriet juxtaposed to the sweet country girl Norah and to the feisty Kathleen. Margaret Doyle (Mrs Kennedy), of Irish ancestry but perhaps born in London, played Patrick in travesty dressed in a 'scarlet soldier's coat – white trousers – soldier's cap, and sword' (Figure 1.6).[33] Described variously as a counter-tenor or contralto, Doyle scored her greatest successes in male parts; she was not merely cross-dressed in *The Poor Soldier* but adopted a male role. As *Musical Memoirs* recounts, 'Notwithstanding the disadvantage of person with which she had to contend, her fine voice had almost the effect of fascinating the audience' (1:28). Her purported unattractiveness led to her 1777 debut in a male role as Captain Macheath (Figure 1.7) because of 'the plainness of her face, for she was by no means a Venus, and the badness of her figure, which displayed little of that symmetry so much admired in the graces' (1:28).

Like the Irish Widow Brady and *Seduction*'s Harriet, Margaret Doyle straddled gender definitions and nationalities as Patrick in a crowd-pleasing performance so beloved that she acted the role a hundred times between 1783 and 1789. *The Poor Soldier*, rumoured to be a favourite of George Washington, celebrates Irish Catholic soldiers who fought for the British in the American War.[34] Revised for its London premiere

[31] John O'Keeffe and William Shield, *The Poor Soldier* (1783), ed. William Brasmer and William Osborne, *Recent Researches in American Music Series*, vol. 6 (Madison: A-R Editions), vii.

[32] *Recollections of the Life of John O'Keeffe: Written by Himself*, 2 vols (London: H. Colburn, 1826), 2: 70–71.

[33] John O'Keeffe, 'The Poor Soldier' in *Cumberland's British Theatre: With Remarks Biographical and Critical*, 41 vols (London: J. Cumberland, 1828), 20: 8.

[34] O'Shaughnessy, 'Rip'ning buds in freedom's field', remarks 'The combination of an honest yet suitably deferential soldier with a demonstrably noble English superior was a formula that worked for theatre audiences', 551. See also Helen Burke, 'The Catholic Question, Print Media, and John O'Keeffe's *The Poor Soldier* (1783)', *Eighteenth-Century Fiction* 27.3–4 (2015): 419–48.

Figure 1.6 Margaret Doyle Kennedy as Patrick (behind Norah and the Captain) in
The Poor Soldier, II. v. (Paris 1783). British Museum object: 1890, 0415.318.
©Trustees of the British Museum.

in November 1783, the musical afterpiece first played as a show of nationalist sentiment in Dublin as *The Shamrock, or the anniversary of St. Patrick*
(April 1777), along with Macklin's *The Brave Irishman*, upon the opening
of the Fish-amble Street Theatre. Irishness in the opera buffa was signalled
with bulls, blunders, and rousingly sentimental Irish tunes. *The Universal
Magazine* remarked that Doyle as Patrick 'gave full scope to her

Figure 1.7 Margaret Ferrell [Kennedy] as Macheath in *The Beggar's Opera* (1777).

harmonious powers, and was encored twice', singing 'How happy the soldier who lives on his pay'.[35]

In *The Poor Soldier*, Patrick, returning after two years of military service in the American War, is forbidden to court his sweetheart Norah, Father Luke's ward.[36] The 'bounxious' country girl Norah fears that the Dublin lasses have stolen her dear Patrick: 'Tho' sattins, and ribbons, and laces are fine,/They hide not a heart with such feelings as mine.'[37] Patrick is fond of the benefits of military life but represents 'an injured though heroic Irish masculinity',[38] as Helen Burke has noted, made all the more poignant when played by a woman. Patrick had suffered a head injury in the American War while saving his captain, who is belatedly revealed to be Fitzroy, his rival for Norah. When Fitzroy in gratitude grants Patrick a commission and relinquishes his claim to Norah, the poor soldier, no

[35] *The Universal Magazine of Knowledge and Pleasure* 73 (November 1783), 259.
[36] The heavy-drinking priest threatens to send Norah to a French convent if she refuses to marry the English Protestant, Captain Fitzroy. See Burke, 'The Catholic Question', and O'Shaughnessy, 'Rip'ning buds'.
[37] John O'Keeffe, 'The Poor Soldier' in *The Dramatic Works of John O'Keeffe Esq. in Four Volumes*, ed. Frederick M. Link (New York: Garland, 1981), 2: I.ii.277.
[38] See Burke, 'The Catholic Question'.

longer impoverished, gains Father Luke's permission to marry Norah.[39] As played by Margaret Doyle in travesty, the physically compromised Patrick would have presented an Amazonian soldier's body, a maimed man-woman whose gender identification resisted easy categorisation. In addition, the Irish woman playing an impaired Irish man contradicts the stereotypic blundering Irishman. Patrick in performance, at once male and female, would also have queered the romantic scenes with Norah and complicated notions of what it means to be an Irish woman in love with an Irish man, overturning various national and gender stereotypes.

In all of these plays, the Irish actresses and characters jockey for status while recognising the hypocrisy of English elites and acknowledging their Irish heritage. At the same time, cross-dressed Irish female characters on the London stage, essential to the plots in exposing deceitful English men and women, bring into sharp relief the performative nature of an Irishness that resists being reduced to simplified formulas of sex, social class or nation.

Maria Macklin

Finally, I want to draw special attention to actress, singer, dancer and guitarist Maria Macklin (c. 1733–81) as a telling example of an Irish actress's successful career on the London stage. Maria was the daughter of Irish actress Ann Grace and playwright-actor Charles Macklin, though her parents never married.[40] The parts Macklin wrote specifically for his daughter take us to the centre of the gendered politics of Irish identity in the second half of the eighteenth century and were critical to her success. The women she plays – sometimes Irish, sometimes English, often cross-dressed – are witty, inventive characters who bring errant men of several nationalities into line with ingenious plots of her characters' designs (Figure 1.8).

As a child actor, Maria debuted in male roles, the first at Drury Lane as the Duke of York in *Richard III*. Charles Macklin's rigorous tutoring in

---

[39] Helen Burke, 'Acting in the Periphery: The Irish Theatre' in *The Cambridge Companion to British Theatre, 1730–1830*, ed. Jane Moody and Daniel O'Quinn (New York: Cambridge University Press, 2007), notes that Patrick's winning back his Irish sweetheart resonates with 'the Irish Catholic's longed-for recovery of his place in the Irish political nation', 225. In Charles Dibdin's two-act farce *Harvest Home* (1787), the rollicking countrywoman Unah, the 'little siren of the sod' sings 'wild Irish notes' and speaks with a 'comical brogue'.

[40] There is no record of Charles Macklin and Ann Grace having married, but Maria's mother acted as Mrs Macklin. It is unusual to find information about how an eighteenth-century actress learned her craft.

Figure 1.8 J. Thornwaite (engraver) after J. Roberts, Mrs. [Maria] Macklin in the Character of Camillo, *The Mistake*, Act II.i, *Bell's British Theatre*, vol. 25 (London 1797).

'natural acting', resembling David Garrick's method, demanded that his students perfect a phrase by repeating it as many as twenty times. (E.g., as Portia, Maria recited "Tis mightiest in the *mightiest*', but Charles insisted she emphasize the words differently: "Tis mightiest *in* the mightiest.'[41]) Disappointed in his daughter's early performances and ambitious for her, Charles insisted on providing more instruction before allowing her to appear in male parts as Prince Arthur in Garrick's *King John*, the eponymous Tom Thumb in Fielding's play, the Boy in Henry Carey's ballad opera *The Contrivances* and Brass in Vanbrugh's *City Wives' Confederacy*. In autumn 1748, she accompanied her parents to Smock Alley, Dublin, before resuming acting at Covent Garden in April 1751, to play her first female role as Athenais in Nathaniel Lee's *Theodosius* (1690).

---

[41] Sir Edmund Abbott Parry, *Charles Macklin* (New York: Longmans, Green, and Co., 1891), 92.

Investing a reported £1200 in his daughter's education, Charles Macklin sought to make her a fine London-Irish lady, according to biographer William Cooke, to entitle her 'to the first circles of life'. She mastered fluent French and Italian, 'nor was she less deficient in music, drawing, and a perfect knowledge of the *belles lettres*', which made her 'one of the most accomplished women in England'.[42] Believed to be the first musician to play the guitar (also called a pandola or cittern) on stage, she popularised its use. Though some found her acting to be 'politely cold, and languidly refined',[43] through six seasons at Drury Lane she attracted audiences in the title role of *Jane Shore*, as Lady Townly in *The Provok'd Husband,* Calista in *The Fair Penitent* and Monimia in *The Orphan.* She remained best known, however, for her comic breeches and travesty parts. *Gray's Inn Journal* reports, 'In Woman's Attire she is beautiful, [but] the Petticoat laid [aside], she is the very *Form* of *Beauty.* I do not remember to have seen any Actress wear the Breeches with so good a Grace ... she treads the Stage with the janty Air of a pretty Fellow.'[44]

It is clear that Maria Macklin, 'perhaps ... the only instance of a person's being regularly bred to the theatre',[45] was highly regarded in London. In the rankings on the 'Scale of Tragedians' of Drury Lane actresses published in *The Theatrical Review* (1757), while still early in her career Macklin fell just below celebrated actresses Susannah Cibber, George Anne Bellamy and Hannah Pritchard but ranked equal to Pritchard in voice, and higher in 'action'. On the 'Scale of Comedians' for the same year, she was ranked just below Kitty Clive and Pritchard, but above Mrs Green, Mrs Pitt and Peg Woffington (Figure 1.9).[46]

The Public Advertiser (1755) sang Maria's praises as the legitimate successor to Cibber:

---

[42] James Thomas Kirkman, *Memoirs of the Life of Charles Macklin*, 2 vols (London 1799), 1: 345. William Cooke, *Memoirs of Charles Macklin, Comedian* (London: James Asperne, 1804), 211, notes the amount spent on Maria's education.

[43] Hugh Kelly, *Thespis: Or a Critical Examination into the Merits of All the Principal Performers Belonging to Drury-Lane Theatre* (London: Printed for G. Kearsley, 1766–67), 40. Sir Nicholas Nipclose [Francis Gentleman], *The Theatres: A Poetical Dissection* (London: Printed for John Bell and C. Etherington, 1772), 76, charged that she was 'fetter'd with a father's rigid laws'.

[44] Charles Ranger [Arthur Murphy], *Gray's Inn Journal*, 21 (16 February 1754), 126.

[45] *Theatrical Biography, or Memoirs of the Principal Performers of the Three Theatres Royal*, 2 vols. (Dublin: Printed for H. Saunders et al., 1772), 2: 8.

[46] *The Theatrical Review: For the Year 1757, and Beginning of 1758* (London: Printed for J. Coote, 1758), 45–46.

(a)

The Scale of TRAGEDIANS.

	Genius.	Judgment.	Expression.	Action.	Voice.
Quin	15	17	14	15	17
Garrick	17	18	18	17	18
Barry	15	13	14	14	16
Moſſop	14	14	14	15	16
Smith	10	9	10	12	12
Havard	12	14	12	14	12
Roſs	10	11	10	9	11
Berry	9	13	11	7	5
Holland	10	9	10	8	13
Sheridan	12	16	15	10	7
Sparks	9	12	11	8	8
Mrs. Cibber	16	15	17	16	18
Mrs. Bellamy	13	12	14	14	14
Mrs. Pritchard	12	13	12	8	13
Miſs Macklin	11	11	12	9	13
Mrs. Woffington	12	13	14	14	(

(b)

The Scale of COMEDIANS.

	Genius.	Judgment.	Vis Comica.	Variety.
Quin	16	16	17	11
Theo. Cibber	12	8	13	10
Macklin	10	17	12	10
Garrick	18	16	18	18
Arthur	10	14	16	11
Woodward	15	12	13	13
Shuter	16	9	17	16
Yates	13	10	12	12
Berry	12	11	11	10
Palmer	12	13	9	11
Smith	11	10	9	10
Dyer	11	12	11	10
Taſwell	12	15	12	11
Mrs. Clive	11	16	17	15
Mrs. Pritchard	15	14	10	13
Miſs Macklin	12	13	11	12
Mrs. Green	14	10	12	13
Mrs. Pitt	13	12	12	13
Mrs. Woffington	13	12	13	13
* Mr. Foote	10	15	12	15

* This gentleman's talents are so much out of the common road, that I cannot at present settle what has excellence is in each particular, and will therefore leave every reader to rate his merit according to his own feeling.

Figure 1.9 'The Scale of Tragedians' and 'The Scale of Comedians'. *The Theatrical Review: For the Year 1757, and Beginning of 1758* (London 1758).

> Britannia spake: when lo! A Voice:
> 'Britain be happy, and rejoice,
> 'That, when your Cibber dies
> 'The Gods have yet in store for thee,
> 'A Macklin: and in her you'll see
> 'Another Cibber rise.'[47]

William Cooke concurs, if a bit grudgingly, 'Though Miss Macklin was not handsome, she was genteel in her person . . . She was, besides, a rising actress, and gave specimens of her singing and dancing in occasional entertainments, which made her a great favourite with the town.'[48]

Maria Macklin's career, most of which was in London, was intimately linked to that of her more famous father. Each of the plays in which they both appeared displayed the performance of kinship,[49] which added hints of incest or, at the least, unorthodox familial relations, to productions in which father and daughter were paired as potential lovers. In all the plays in which they starred, their actual relationship offstage also added complexity to their representation of London stage Irishness. The Macklins, including sometimes Maria's mother, acted together in any number of other plays, intensifying the performance of familial intimacies. Maria played Ophelia to Charles's Hamlet, Portia to his Shylock (Figure 1.10) and Violante to his Don Felix in Centlivre's *The Wonder*. Charles played an English suitor to Maria's Lucinda in Samuel Foote's popular two-act comedy *The Englishman in Paris* (1753). Reviews consistently praised Maria's 'elegance' in dancing, singing and playing the pandola.[50] After helping her father recover from bankruptcy, Maria joined the Covent Garden troupe in 1760 along with Charles, where she earned a substantial salary of £300 for the season. Father and daughter starred in the wildly popular productions of Macklin's *Love à la Mode* (Drury Lane 1759) and *The School for Husbands* (Covent Garden 1761), as well as *The Irish Fine Lady* (1767).

Maria never married. Her choice of a reclusive life, uncharacteristic of actresses and especially London-Irish actresses, inspired further gossip: 'Her qualifications producing her a very considerable salary, with a very genteel acquaintance, she humbly sat herself down to the quiet enjoyment of them, without hunting after new gratifications. She was unfashionable enough too, to be *religious*, and, in consequence, to contract a number of

---

[47] *Public Advertiser*, 22 March 1755.   [48] Cooke, *Memoirs of Charles Macklin*, 215.
[49] I am borrowing the term 'performance of kinship' from Vivian Davis who is engaged in a project on the topic.
[50] Francis Delaval to his brother [John Delaval], 23 March 1753, Delaval MSS in *The Manuscripts of Sir William Fitzherbert, Bart., and Others* (London: Eyre and Spottiswoode, 1893), 201.

Figure 1.10 Johan Zoffany (1733–1810), Charles Macklin as Shylock [and Maria Macklin in breeches], *The Merchant of Venice*, Act IV.i, oil painting on canvas (c. 1768). Call #: N06005. © Tate, London 2019.

out-of-the-way notions.'[51] Mocked for attending to her devotions more than rehearsals, we might conjecture that Maria's reclusiveness may have been because she quietly practised Catholicism in Protestant London. Accusing her of a flawed womanhood, Macklin's memoirist blamed her celibacy on 'a *coldness of constitution*' rather than a choice to be virtuous.[52] In a story much repeated but surely exaggerated, her death at age forty-eight was blamed on too-restrictive trousers because, in her frequent breeches parts, buckling her garter too tightly brought on a fatal tumour 'which, from motives of delicacy, she would not suffer to be examined, till it had increased to an alarming size. This fleshy excrescence was, however, cut off, and Miss Macklin underwent the operation with great firmness; but she never after regained her former strength'.[53] In short, while

[51] Kirkman, *Memoirs*, 2: 308.
[52] Though she was rumored to have entertained several proposals, her enraged father supposedly refused a baronet's proposition to keep Maria as a mistress (Cooke, *Memoirs*, 217).
[53] Kirkman, *Memoirs*, 2: 308.

audiences found her cross-dressed performances delightful, they judged the practice to be not only unfeminine, but also deadly.

In the first version of the prologue (A) to Macklin's *Love à la Mode*, Maria is a 'female Advocate' for a 'trembling Bard' who underscores the comedy's moral lesson. Professing filial gratitude, she alludes to her father's financial straits after his opening a tavern, a coffeehouse and a school to train orators, the British Inquisition. Though she seems to downplay Charles's Irishness, she nervously refers to the London theatre as '*this* precarious Soil' and appeals to the audience's magnanimity.[54] Although Charles had originally intended to play the successful Irish suitor to Maria's Charlotte,[55] he instead acted as the Scots Sir Archy Macsarcasm, a xenophobic knight. Set in London but accompanied by Irish tunes, the comedy arises from the contest between suitors' ethnicities for the English Charlotte, though ironically the motley group of suitors competes for the London-Irish actress. Charlotte/Maria good-naturedly interacts with these ethnic stereotypes and finally validates the awkwardly romantic Irishman who, while mocked for his brogue, proves counter-type to be the most honourable. A clever woman who outsmarts the hapless men by feigning that her fortune is lost, the Irishwoman acting as a London lady is, true to Enlightenment discourse, the barometer by which the suitors can test the depths of their ethnicity and claim the superiority of one country over another.

Charles and Maria together exemplify a London-Irish family's struggle to disrupt conventional notions of Irish identity even as they attempt to assimilate into Irish-English gentility; but *The True-Born Irishman* reflects, I think, the ability of the Irish woman of quality, more than the Irish man, to negotiate the relationship to Englishness. In the comedy, father and daughter play the married couple, Mr and Mrs O'Dogherty. The play suggests that urban Irishwomen suffer from 'The Irish Fine Lady delirium, or the London vertigo' when they venture to England's capital, for Mrs O'Dogherty longs to be English, or as she puts it in a comic malapropism, 'entitled' (II.i.106).

Most significant for our purposes, however, is Maria's cross-dressed role in Macklin's five-act comedy set in London, *The School for Husbands, or*

---

[54] The later version of the prologue (B) expresses Maria's anxiety about the play's reception but does not mention their relationship or Macklin's troubles. *The Prologues and Epilogues of the Eighteenth Century*, ed. Pierre Danchin, *The Third Part, 1737–1760* (Nancy: Presses universitaires de Nancy, 1990–), 6: 706, 707.

[55] 'Introduction', *Four Comedies by Charles Macklin*, ed. J. O. Bartley (London: Sidgwick and Jackson, 1968), 24. References to *Love à la Mode, The True-Born Irishman* and *The School for Husbands* are to this edition.

The Married Libertine (Covent Garden, 28 January 1761).[56] Her father acted as the rakish Lord Belville, and Maria played the heroine Angelica, in love with Belville's nephew, who disguises herself as a cross-dressed rival to Belville's wife. The principal characters in the play pretend to be someone else, creating a play within a play and reiterating the theme that the English aristocratic culture is rife with dissimulation and corruption. *School for Husbands* is Macklin's testament to the theatre's potential to reform the English nation while critiquing the unjust inscription of Irishmen in the cause of its imperial wars.

The play's women unite in the cause when Angelica's cousin Harriet, pretending to be a West Country rustic, accuses MP Lord Belville, who neglects the English nation's business to pursue his lascivious pleasures, of having been her lover: 'There is nothing shews the heart and latent spirit of these boasted lords of creation, so well as woman', charges Angelica (III.i. 156–57). A disguised Belville had promised to marry Harriet with a bogus contract in spite of already being married. Harriet and her cross-dressed cousin Angelica hatch a plot to 'hold a council of matrimonial and female revenge' (II.i.154). Wearing 'her brother's regimentals' and organising the women in military fashion to defend Harriet's honour, Angelica invokes 'The Magna Charta of our sex against the falsehood and tyranny of yours' (III.i.156). She insists, 'Not only your cause, but the cause of every injured wife in Great Britain, is vindicated up to the most wicked revenge, that ridicule can inflict' (IV.i.169). A brave cross-dressed woman schools the husband and saves the women of England from errant men.

The real London-Irish daughter upends the plots of her London-Irish father. Maria Macklin in breeches, claiming she cannot think as a woman when dressed as a man, pretends to make love to Lady Belville, who wants to inspire her philandering husband's jealousy. As the cross-dressed Angelica, Maria gets to draw a sword on her real father acting as Lord Belville and give him his comeuppance. Bound and gagged, the disguised Belville is refused special treatment with a dig against Irishmen's inscription: 'for if you was the lord leeftenant of Ireland you must go when you are commanded' (III.i.168). Justifying the need for harsh satire to effect reform, much laughter ensues at Lord Belville's expense as the London-Irish Macklin, playing an irresponsible member of Parliament in the play he has written, ironically stands accused of weakening the sovereignty of the British nation and its empire.

---

[56] Both Macklin and Maria moved from Drury Lane to Covent Garden in 1760 to perform *The School for Husbands* for nine nights.

Being a London-Irish actress was all about attempting to make a living, of course, but it was also an attempt to rise in social standing so that Irishness could be incorporated into the fashionable yet flawed English genteel class. Irishwomen roles and their performance were, as I have argued, often representative of the unsettled relationship between the two countries. These clever Irish actresses and their characters bring men into line with chameleon-like ability to vary their linguistic markers of class and nation, and to embody both sexes to mock the weak English elite. Employing Irishness and its alignment with gender elasticity, they take on agency to make use of stereotypes but also to empty them of their force.

Conventional modes of Stage Irishness continued to be performed in the late eighteenth century, but London-Irish actresses and their characters, especially those that impersonated men, afforded a way to dart in and out of stereotypes, playing to London audience expectations while also scuttling them. As we have seen, English and Irish actresses played Irish parts, and Irish actresses played Irish and English parts from fine ladies to soldiers to middling upstarts and country peasants. Their very willingness to reimagine themselves afforded the Irish in London the potential for assimilation as well as retaining their difference. Though the sample is necessarily small, there appears to be a growing assertiveness among these actresses and their roles in the later eighteenth century. Strong and eccentric Irish women characters, though often the butt of satire in conventional ways, unfailingly mock English affectation and venery even as they puncture the bluster of their fellow countrymen. To be a London-Irish woman in the theatre, performing Ireland's struggles, was, as is the case for immigrants everywhere, to remain malleable, even as that very willingness to accommodate signalled resistance to a fixed ethnicity and stereotypes of otherness.

CHAPTER 2

John Johnstone and the Possibilities of Irishness, 1783–1820

Jim Davis

In a study of some of the more prosperous middle-class Irish migrants to London in the eighteenth century, Craig Bailey has argued that it is important to emphasise 'the possibilities rather than the limits of Irishness' and that 'Irish identity was far too important for most middle-class Irish to jettison'.[1] The largest population of middle-class Irishmen outside of Ireland was resident in London in the eighteenth century, but, says Bailey, 'scholars have mistaken the identity of middle-class migrants by making poverty the touchstone of Irishness, and by presuming that visible Irish characteristics such as language, accent and name necessarily had negative meanings'.[2] To investigate further 'the possibilities of . . . Irishness' in late eighteenth– and early nineteenth–century London, this chapter will focus on John Johnstone, a London-based Irish actor, who mixed privately in fashionable society, but whose stage repertoire encompassed both the Irish gentleman and his low comedy counterpart.

In England, Johnstone was identified as 'Irish Johnstone', whereas some actors who left Ireland earlier in the eighteenth century to make a career on the English stage sought to 'pass' as Englishmen. This seems to have been true of Charles Macklin, whose struggles to lose his Irish accent are well documented and, at least initially, of Michael Kelly.[3] Moreover, Bailey suggests that whether or not middle-class Irishmen kept their accent was more a matter of taste and of personal preference than of status.[4] On the stage, however, the Irish accent and dialect were often used for comic effect, whatever a character's social background, suggesting that the

---

[1] Craig Bailey, *Irish London: Middle-Class Migration in the Global Eighteenth Century* (Liverpool: Liverpool University Press, 2013), 5.
[2] Bailey, *Irish London*, 11.
[3] See James Thomas Kirkman, *Memoirs of the Life of Charles Macklin Esq.*, 2 vols. (London: Lackington, Allen and Co., 1799), 1: 62–64, 69–70 and Bailey, *Irish London*, 2
[4] Bailey, *Irish London*, 13–14.

convention of stereotyping through language and dialect was still maintained in the theatre.

Language and how it was spoken, however, mattered outside as well as within the theatre. According to Michael Ragussis, 'actors on the Georgian stage . . . were keenly aware of their own ethnicity, of the ethnic mixes of their audiences, of the place of dialect in the roles they played.'[5] Thus we might assume an awareness by actors and audiences of the issues being played out via performances of ethnic identity and dialect. If, on one level, Irishmen were comical because of their brogue, on another level there was an underlying plea for tolerance and acceptance of their difference or 'otherness'. Further, Ragussis argues, the pressure to assimilate, to speak the English language rather than the Irish brogue, to pass as English, is caricatured in such plays as Macklin's *Love à la Mode* and *The True-Born Irishman* so that 'the trope of the failed ethnic imposter became a way of authenticating minority cultures'.[6] Such a tendency was enhanced by an actor like Johnstone, who brought ethnic and linguistic authenticity to his performances.

The more gentlemanly Irishman, whom Johnstone played with even greater ease than his low comedy roles, was also a stereotype, but one who had been freed from earlier, more negative conventions, such as fortune hunting and dishonesty. Both Charles Macklin and Richard Cumberland had developed Irish characterisations undercharged with tolerance and humanity, embodying aspects of what has come to be called the Irish Enlightenment. Michael Brown's recent study of the Irish Enlightenment suggests dramatists such as Macklin and Goldsmith contributed to a greater understanding of social order and social function and of the need for tolerance, civility and true sentiment in Irish society.[7] Brown sees the eventual failure of the Irish Enlightenment as represented by the 1798 rebellion and the Act of Union in 1801, which in turn led to a greater emphasis on nationalism and sectarianism.

Nevertheless, the impact of the Irish Enlightenment on the representation of the Irish on the English stage is arguably significant, a factor implicit in an essay on the Stage Irishman by Richard Cave. Cave suggests that during this period, both Irish dramatists and Irish actors attempted to create a more positive image of the Irishman on stage:

[5] Michael Ragussis, *Theatrical Nation: Jews and Other Outlandish Englishmen in Georgian Britain* (Philadelphia: University of Pennsylvania Press, 2010), 77.
[6] Ibid., 69.
[7] See Michael Brown, *The Irish Enlightenment* (Cambridge, MA: Harvard University Press, 2016), 557.

The tendency, as one might expect from the prevailing social situation, was to promote a marked class division in respect of methods of characterisation. Servant-figures remained close to the stereotypes; upper-class Irish figures began . . . to appeal for acceptance as persons of sense and sensibility while still being distinguished from the English characters amongst which they moved. As Irish these figures were Other, but grounds were being found on which their Otherness might be deemed admissible. What is noticeable in this is that Irish Otherness is often characterised by preserving features of the stereotype while redeeming them from pejorative judgement.[8]

This is true of both the low comedy and more gentlemanly roles Johnstone played: he was adept at making the Irish gentleman credible, while also transcending the vulgar low comedy associated with other performers of comic Irishmen, perhaps because, as Walter Donaldson claims, he was the only comedian 'who could delineate the refined Irish gentleman and enter into the genuine unsophisticated humour of a son of the Emerald Isle with equal talent'.[9] Donaldson adds:

> There is not much difficulty in creating laughter, like the clown in the ring, by uttering the usual number of jokes put into the mouth of the bogtrotter, or skipping about the stage as the Irish valet, displaying all the vagaries of a merry-andrew; but the task of the Irish actor to realise the accomplished gentleman – such as Sir Lucius O'Trigger or Major O'Flaherty – is not so facile, as ease, deportment, and address are all indispensable in the embodiment of those two finished specimens of Irish character. . . . Jack Johnstone, then, may be named as the only actor that has ever appeared in any theatre capable of sustaining the high and low *role* of his native country with ability.[10]

However, the Irish judge Jonah Barrington distinguished between these two types, claiming that Johnstone 'was a truly excellent performer of the more refined species of Irish characters, but Nature had not given him enough of that *shoulder-twist* and what they call the "*potheen-twang*", which so strongly characterise the genuine "*vis comica*" of the lower

---

[8] Richard Allen Cave, 'Staging the Irishman' in *Acts of Supremacy: The British Empire and the Stage, 1790–1930*, ed. J. S. Bratton et al. (Manchester: Manchester University Press, 1991), 69.
[9] Walter Donaldson, *Recollections of an Actor* (London: John Maxwell & Co, 1865), 29.
[10] Ibid., 29. A memoir in the *Dublin University Magazine* 43 (1854), 393, seems to endorse this view:

> Whether in or out of his stage-clothes, Johnstone was a remarkably handsome man, with a bearing so innately gentleman-like, that it was impossible, by any external travesty, to change him into a clown. But his constitutional humour made up for that strange deficiency in his rustics, a want of natural vulgarity. His acting was ease personified, without the slightest appearance of art or labour. In a military character, or a travelled gentleman, he stood above all rivalry.

orders'.[11] There seems to have been a general view that in low comedy roles, Johnstone adapted Irishness and the Irish brogue into a form that made them accessible to English audiences. In effect, he anglicised Irishness.

Leigh Hunt suggested that an actor like Johnstone, 'whose business it is to mimic into ridicule the peculiarities of his birth-place, must literally be one of those who have no honour in their own country'.[12] He indirectly draws attention to the ambiguity of Johnstone's position on the London stage and the complex discourses around ethnicity, language, dialect and oppression that must underline any discussion of the theatrical representation of Irishness and the Stage Irishman in late eighteenth– and early nineteenth–century England. It may be the case that stereotypical elements of Irishness were often preserved through the use of the Irish dialect or brogue across all classes in the plays of the period, most effectively perhaps by native-born Irish actors such as Johnstone. The Irish dramatist John O'Keeffe (perhaps self-servingly) considered that only an Irishman could play Irish characters and only an Irishman could write them,[13] but the end result may still be a construction or a modification. This is certainly one of the issues that needs to be addressed in considering the career of John Johnstone and his contribution to English perceptions of Irish national identity. Another, however, is the extent to which Johnstone enabled a change in perception of Irish low comedy characters.

Johnstone the Actor

Johnstone was born around 1749, probably in Kilkenny. His father had reputedly been a riding, quarter and paymaster in an Irish regiment and had intended a military career for his son, but he had died when Johnstone was a child. Johnstone is said to have been apprenticed to a lawyer but left after a dispute; subsequently, he joined the army, possibly a cavalry regiment in Clonmel, as a cadet. A dispute with a fellow soldier almost led to a court martial, but the intervention of a colonel, who had been impressed by his singing, led to a recommendation to one of the Dublin theatres. Evidence for all of this is somewhat insubstantial, but if Johnstone had served as a soldier, it is quite possible that this experience contributed to his ease in military roles later in his career.

---

[11] Jonah Barrington, *Personal Sketches of His Own Times*, 2 vols. (London: Henry Colburn, 1827), 2: 210.
[12] Leigh Hunt, *Critical Essays on the Performers of the London Theatres* (London: Printed by and for John Hunt, 1807), 121.
[13] John O'Keeffe, *Recollections of the Life of John O'Keeffe*, 2 vols. (London: Henry Colburn, 1826), 2: 310.

Johnstone commenced his theatrical career at the Smock Alley Theatre
in Dublin in 1775, building a reputation for himself based on his singing
voice; he was then engaged at Covent Garden Theatre in London, allegedly
on the recommendation of Charles Macklin, making his debut as Lionel in
Bickerstaff's *Lionel and Clarissa* in 1783. His first original role there was
Dermot in John O'Keeffe's *The Poor Soldier* (1783), and he subsequently
performed a series of Irish roles in opera, comedy and farce and became
particularly identified with some such as Sir Lucius O'Trigger in
Sheridan's *The Rivals* (1775). He also appeared at the Haymarket
Theatre, toured the provinces (which included return visits to Ireland)
and spent the last seventeen years of his career as a member of the Drury
Lane company. According to the *Gentleman's Magazine:*

> After remaining several years at Covent Garden, and finding his voice not
> improving with time, he formed the admirable policy of taking to Irish
> parts, which were then but very inadequately filled. His success was beyond
> example: his native humour, rich brogue, and fine voice for Irish ditties,
> carried all before him. In fact, he was the only actor who could personate
> with the utmost effect both the patrician and plebeian Irishman.[14]

According to Donaldson, 'Johnstone's figure was above the middle
size, and well-formed; his face was handsome, and indicative of the spark-
ling humour inherent in him – in fact, he was Kilkenny
itself.'[15] *Oxberry's Dramatic Biography* described his appearance as 'manly
and handsome', adding that 'he possesses tolerable merit as an actor; his
deportment is easy and genteel; and his readings are the result of a good
natural understanding. In the character of an Irish gentleman, such as *Sir
Callaghan O'Brallaghan,* or *Major O'Flaherty,* he is extremely happy.'[16]
In the opinion of the dramatist John O'Keeffe, it was his physique that
enabled him to play the 'grand and bold Irishman',[17] as well as other types
of Irish characters. James Boaden also referred to Johnstone's capacity to
play the more refined Irishman and to the way in which he made the
Irishman 'sparkle with humour, and in either blunder or mischance, anger
or jest, uniformly delightful'.[18]

---

[14] *Gentleman's Magazine* 99.1 (February 1829), 184.
[15] Donaldson, *Recollections of an Actor*, 29–30.
[16] Quoted in *Oxberry's Dramatic Biography and Histrionic Anecdotes*, 5 vols (London: George Virtue,
1825–26), 4: 78.
[17] *Recollections of the Life of John O'Keeffe*, 2: 310.
[18] James Boaden, *The Life of Mr Jordan Including Original Private Correspondence and Numerous
Anecdotes of Her Contemporaries*, 2 vols. (London: Edward Bull, 1831), 2: 58.

Critical testimony to Johnstone's skills as an actor was prolific. William Hazlitt considered that Johnstone 'has a great deal of "the milk of human kindness" in all his acting. There is a rich genial anxiety of manner, a laughing confidence, a fine oily impudence about him, which must operate as a saving grace to any character he is concerned in, and would make it difficult to hiss him off the stage'.[19] The *New Monthly Magazine* claimed that in the records of the stage, no actor ever approached Johnstone in Irish characters,[20] while Oxberry's memoir of Johnstone proclaimed him 'the best actor of Irish characters that the stage ever possessed'.[21] The *Monthly Mirror* referred to his 'admirable performance of *Hibernian* characters, of which he is avowedly and decisively the most finished representative that has ever appeared on the stage. His humour is the richest and most natural that can be imagined, and never fails to convulse the audience.'[22] Johnstone made many of his low comedy Irish characters very likeable. In so doing, he may have endeared them to his audiences, countering the clichéd view of the Irish as ignorant and unintelligent. This tendency may of course have served an ideological function by the 1790s when both the French Revolution and dissent in Ireland (particularly the threat of Irish uprisings supported by the French) were perceived as a danger to England. Johnstone's Irishmen presented a more positive image of the Irish, underlining perhaps the need for unity between the two nations. Meanwhile, Johnstone himself lived as an Irishman in London, mixing in high society, while assuming very different personae on stage, all of which highlighted 'the possibilities of ... Irishness'.

Throughout Johnstone's London career, dramatists continued to include the low comedy Irishman in comedies and farces, while the more gentlemanly Irishman was also gaining ground. The low comedy Irishman is often defined by his use of the brogue and his blunders, while Hazlitt refers in 1815 to 'the ease, the ignorance, the impudence, the simplicity, the cunning, the lying, the good-nature, the absurdity and the wit of the common character of the Irish' in a review of *My wife! What wife?* Hazlitt also notes the use of the brogue in this play, describing how it 'floated up and down, and twisted round, and rose and fell, and started off or rattled on, just as the gusts of passion led' and how 'the words ...

---

[19] *London Magazine* (January 1820) in William Hazlitt, *The Complete Works of William Hazlitt*, ed. P. P. Howe, 21 vols. (London: J. M. Dent & Sons Ltd., 1930–34), 18: 276.
[20] *New Monthly Magazine* (April 1829), 173.
[21] *Oxberry's Dramatic Biography and Histrionic Anecdotes*, 4: 74.
[22] *Monthly Mirror* 13 (April 1802), 229.

tumbled out together'.[23] He uses this review to compare the Irish and Scottish characters, defining the Irish as 'impetuous', depending on 'extreme unconsciousness', 'animal spirits' and 'the feeling of the moment'. The Irish character, in Hazlitt's view, is much more adapted for the stage because 'it presents more heterogeneous materials, and it is only unconscious absurdity that excites laughter.' As a result, the Irishman is 'a standing dish' that is regularly served up in contemporary farce.[24] In fact, this standing dish is not so much the Irishman as the low comedy Stage Irishman. Hazlitt's definitions derive from the theatre rather than from life: his comments may appear relatively benign, but they accentuate a tendency, already implicit in some contemporary plays, to portray the Irish as simple-minded and impulsive. The popularity of such characters was due to the actors who played them, particularly so in the case of John Johnstone, who used his own charm and personality to legitimate and make attractive the low comic Irishman to contemporary London audiences. He mediated the negative stereotype in a way that seems to have generated laughter based on tolerance rather than on contempt. Further, in some of the roles written for him, he modified the excesses of the Stage Irishman.

The Brogue

Not everyone found Johnstone's Irishmen totally authentic. Anne Mathews (widow of Charles Mathews the Elder) states that John Philpot Curran, the Irish Master of the Rolls, 'did not altogether approve of Johnstone's stage-Irishmen, exquisite as they were to every other person'. While he admired Johnstone as a comedian, 'whether as the humorous *gentleman* or the broader characters of Irish life, both of which he made effective and delightful', he was disappointed in Johnstone's failure to deliver the 'genuine brogue': 'He *translates* it', said he, 'for the English ear. And', he added, perhaps speaking in political metaphor, 'he is perhaps right; for it is very difficult to represent a *genuine* Irishman to the satisfaction of a British audience. In truth, the Irish brogue is a very sweet liquid

---

[23] Hazlitt, *Complete Works*, 5: 238 (*Examiner*, 30 July 1815). Ironically, the Irish character in this play was performed by Tokely, an English actor. Elsewhere Hazlitt refers to Johnstone's use of the brogue, drawing attention to 'Johnstone's lubricated brogue, curling round the ear like a well-oiled moustachio' (Hazlitt, *Complete Works*, 18: 276 [*London Magazine*, January 1820]) and to his blundering 'in his own beautiful brogue' in a production of *Henri Quatre* (Hazlitt, *Complete Works*, 18: 330 [*London Magazine*, May 1820]).

[24] Hazlitt, *Complete Works*, 5: 238.

but it won't bear to be put into English bottles.'[25] The singer Michael Kelly
tells another version of this anecdote: he says he encountered Curran the
night after he had been to see *The West Indian* at Drury Lane. '"Well", said
I, "did you think that my friend Jack Johnstone was an inimitable Major
O'Flaherty?" – "Why, indeed", said he, "I thought it was an able representation of the Irish gentleman, but not of the Irish brogue – our friend
Jack Johnstone does not *give* us the brogue, Sir, he *translates* it."'[26] As Craig
Bailey suggests, perhaps Johnstone's authenticity was lost in translation,
although he quite probably had to moderate his accent for English ears.[27]
In so doing, in the eyes of Irish patriots such as Curran, he may have
betrayed his kinsmen by providing a deliberately watered-down version of
the Irishman, adulterated to comply with English tastes and perceptions.
A more benign reading would be that Johnstone mediated the genuine
Irish character in a way that was alert to the political and commercial
strictures of the London theatres, particularly at times of national anxieties
and tensions.

Although accounts of Johnstone's use of the brogue tend to be descriptive, the brogue itself has a long and controversial history. It has often been
considered to denote ignorance and an incapacity for articulate speech.
Jonathan Swift declared that 'what we call the Irish brogue is no sooner
discovered, than it makes the deliverer, in the last degree, ridiculous and
despised.'[28] Richard and Maria Edgeworth are more discriminating: even if
the Irish brogue is 'a great and shameful defect', they argue, it is no
different in impact from the many regional dialects existing among the
English. They trace the contempt for the brogue back to the Irish 'bulls' or
spoken blunders that are uttered in the brogue. The tone is so powerful
that the brogue itself becomes, rightly or wrongly, associated with blunders. Thus, the Irish brogue not only signifies authenticity: it raises
negative expectations and creates stereotypes as well.[29] It was also what
made Irish characters so popular on stage. Leigh Hunt considered that for
the Englishman, 'it is enough in fact that the Irishman has a different sort

---

[25] Anne Mathews, *Anecdotes of Actors: With Other Desultory Recollections* (London: T. C. Newby,
    1844), 234.
[26] Michael Kelly, *Reminiscences*, ed. Roger Fiske (London: Oxford University Press, 1975), 108. Kelly
    also recalls unsuccessfully attempting to acquire the Irish brogue for a character he had to play under
    instruction from Johnstone (*Reminiscences*, 217).
[27] Bailey, *Irish London*, 13.
[28] Jonathan Swift, 'On Barbarous Denominations in Ireland', *The Works of Jonathan Swift*, 19 vols.
    (Edinburgh: Archibald Constable and Co, 1824), 7: 148.
[29] Richard Lovell Edgeworth and Maria Edgeworth, *Essay on Irish Bulls* (New York: Printed by
    J. Swaine, 1803), 152–62.

of pronunciation and manner from his own, and the English stage must exhibit a set of Hibernian characters for his amusement.' This was why Johnstone was so useful, as an 'actor who is a native of Ireland and not overweeningly proud of his country's pure dialect and logical reasoning'. There is nothing very special about Johnstone's use of the brogue suggests Leigh Hunt: he speaks it because he is unable to do anything else.[30]

Leigh Hunt considered the basis of Johnstone's humour to be his dialect, but that it was also the cause of his limitations. Consequently, his verdict on Johnstone was ambivalent:

> These national peculiarities, while they hinder his success in any other character, give him that exclusive and prominent situation on the stage, which he maintains by the assistance of an original humour; and Mr Johnstone will always preserve a considerable and deserved reputation ... His range of character ... though it is very wide in his own country, is nothing elsewhere and his effect therefore is very local, while it is not likely to be half so strong where he is even most understood as where he is not, for what drollery will Irishmen find in their own dialect?[31]

Yet, despite this critique, Leigh Hunt praises 'the pleasantry with which Mr Johnstone enlivens this brogue' through 'his open manner, his simplicity of attitude and gesture, and his variety of emphatic tone'. 'His performance of Sir Callaghan', he writes, 'is an excellent specimen ... of his skill in preserving our respect under those defects of dialect and speech which generally give the actor a kind of familiar inferiority to his audience'.[32]

Other critics and commentators found Johnstone's brogue far less problematic. William Robson, the Old Playgoer, considered it perfectly acceptable, writing that 'it has been doubted whether the use of *brogue* in a dramatic representation be a legitimate means of provoking laughter; but if we could have Johnstone to deliver it, the critics who set their faces against it would be sadly in the minority.'[33] Robson expands on these perceptions, adding that 'directly a man attempts to speak the Irish brogue, he becomes coarse and blackguardly. Such was not Jack Johnstone: if the character was coarse, his style of humour softened down and took off its asperities; if it was exalted or pathetic, it lost nothing in his hands.'[34] Robson considered Johnstone able to adapt and modify the brogue according to character, ranging from the broad, yet natural *patois* of a character like Brulgruddery to the Irish officer with 'his brogue so delicate, so fine, so

[30] Leigh Hunt, *Critical Essays on the Performers of the London Theatres*, 118. [31] Ibid., 121.
[32] Ibid., 119. [33] William Robson, *The Old Playgoer* (Fontwell: Centaur Press Ltd., 1969), 68.
[34] Ibid., 67.

scarcely perceptible, that you would declare the gentleman and the soldier merely retained it to give music to his discourse, and to add power to the insinuation of the Irishman's all-persuasive tongue'.[35] Ragussis suggests that '[s]peaking ethnic dialects with accuracy upon the stage began to do battle with speaking a kind of uniform ethnic jargon meant only as caricature' and encouraged the notion that authenticity was to be found in actors who performed their own ethnicity on stage.[36] Even if the brogue was partially lost in translation, Johnstone's own ethnicity gave authority to his representations.

Johnstone's Roles

Johnstone was so popular in Irish roles on the London stage that they were regularly interpolated into new plays, often with a song or two, even when this was quite inappropriate.[37] Charles Edward Horn recalls how he had to recompose some Irish songs for Johnstone to sing when he appeared in Thomas Dibdin's *The Ninth Statue, or, The Irishman in Baghdad* (Drury Lane, 1814). 'So old and great a favourite was Johnstone', he writes, 'that every farce to be brought out must have an Irishman in it – as in Baghdad, Persia or France, wherever the scene was, an Irishman was the principal feature'.[38] Horn is not particularly sympathetic to these demands, but, according to John Adolphus, biographer of the actor John Bannister:

> Johnstone's appearance . . . was really an epoch in the drama. A good, well-accomplished Irishman was greatly wanted. . . . Johnstone, therefore, flashed upon the town, the blaze of new luminary. His perfect brogue, his exquisitely comic manner, and his agreeable voice in singing, formed an irresistible charm, which was much enhanced by his handsome person and free military address. His ballads in 'Love-à-la-mode' . . . added to his other qualifications, excited the ambition of dramatists and song-writers. Many a part was produced with little pretension to wit or humour, but its success

---

[35] Ibid., 65.   [36] Ragussis, *Theatrical Nation*, 74–75.

[37] John Genest quotes Thomas Dutton's excoriating comments on Johnstone's role of Sligo in Thomas Morton's *The Blind Girl, or the Receipt for Beauty* (1801). Dutton describes the role as 'one of the species of *dramatic monsters*' indebted to the fact that modern dramatists have to adapt their characters to the performers, whether or not appropriate to the play. Thus, 'because Johnstone has deservedly acquired celebrity for his apt personation of Irish characters – they must needs lug an Irishman into the list of D. P. . . . If a list were to be made of all the pieces in which an Irishman is pressed into the service, merely for the sake of Johnstone, it would not be a short one.' John Genest, *Some Account of the English Stage*, 10 vols. (Bath: H. E. Carrington, 1832), 7: 516.

[38] *Charles Edward Horn's Memoirs of His Father and Himself*, ed. Michael Kassler (London: Society for Theatre Research/Aldershot: Ashgate Publishing Ltd., 2003), 5.

was deemed certain if Johnstone talked about the crature, shilelahs, and petticoats, and sung smaalilou, bubberoo, whack, or gramachree.[39]

Irish characters were therefore *de rigueur* in new plays presented at any theatre where Johnstone was engaged.[40] In effect, without Johnstone, there would have been far fewer Irish characters in the plays of the period.

Johnstone's Irish characters were much in demand, as Adolphus testifies:

> A play, a farce, an interlude, a pantomime, or any other piece, let the scene be laid where, and the time fixed when, the author pleased, could hardly at that period be brought on the stage without an Irishman. This was a severe task upon Jack Johnstone, but it was entirely his own doing: he played, he looked, he sung the character so admirably; he exhibited so much true feeling, and such spontaneous fun, that it seemed almost a fraud upon the audience, in any house where he was engaged, to exclude him from a piece in which there could be a pretence for introducing him. ... Place an Irishman in India, in Calais, in Granada, or the Sierra de Ronda, if Johnstone were that Irishman, the criticism of the audience ... forgot all difficulties of place and climate; and, if he had made his entrance on an uninhabitable island, he would have been cordially welcome.[41]

In Adolphus's view, it was Johnstone's skills as actor that not only made his performance of Irish characters so effective but also created further demand for them. His roles also highlighted a reassuring – as far as an English audience was concerned – Irish presence in a wide range of geographical locations, demonstrating the complicity of the Irish in Britain's global agenda. While we might base an analysis of the representation of Irishness on the London stage in this period on an analysis of dramatic texts, Johnstone is the key to unlocking the impact and significance of so many of them in performance.

---

[39] John Adolphus, *Memoirs of John Bannister, Comedian*, 2 vols. (London: Richard Bentley, 1839), 2: 107. Johnstone's impact on the drama is confirmed by the *Monthly Mirror* 13 (April 1802), 229:

> He may be said to have given a new direction to the English comedy, since his unprecedented excellence in this species of character has induced our modern dramatists to consult their own interest, by framing opportunities for the exhibition of his *unique* talents, to which in many instances they have been entirely indebted for the success of their productions; and of late years few of our popular plays and farces are without his powerful name among the *Dramatis Personae*.

[40] Johnstone personified the Irishman through his skills as an actor and singer. Yet, when a collection of so-called Irish ballads was published under the title *The Shamrock* in 1830, edited by a Mr Weekes of the Drury Lane Theatre, it was lambasted by *Fraser's Magazine* 3 (June 1831), 538, in an article on the 'National Song of Ireland'. The types of Irish songs sung by Johnstone, who was mentioned by name in the article and wrongly attributed English nationality, were castigated as examples of the 'spurious trash which passes current in this country [England] for Irish song'.

[41] Adolphus, *Memoirs of John Bannister, Comedian*, 1: 312.

His popularity and economic value to the managements that employed him, plus his facility at singing 'Irish' songs, rendered his presence increasingly essential in new productions. This also meant that by the end of the eighteenth century, he shared responsibility with contemporary dramatists for the proliferation of Irish characters on the London stage and how they were written. From his arrival in London in 1783, Johnstone undertook roles already in the repertoire, such as Major O'Flaherty and Sir Callaghan O'Brallaghan, as well as roles especially written for him. From the start, John O'Keeffe, often in collaboration with the composer William Shield, created a number of singing roles for Johnstone at Covent Garden Theatre, not all of which required that he play Irish characters. From the early 1790s, however, there is a greater emphasis on Irish roles, further enhanced by his summer engagements in 1791 and 1793–1800 at the Haymarket Theatre, managed by George Colman the Younger, one of Britain's leading dramatists in this period. Colman cerainly recognised Johnstone's talent and wrote a series of Irish roles for him, ranging from the idiotic, blundering Looney Mactwolter in the farce *The Review; or The Ways of Windsor* (1800) to more nuanced roles – what John Taylor defined as parts that 'occupied a middle rank and were neither low nor high' – such as Kenrick, a kind and loyal servant, in *The Heir at Law* (1797), in which he 'displayed a touching and affected sensibility'.[42] In Colman's *The Surrender of Calais* (1791), he played O'Carroll, a faithful and kindly Irish retainer in the service of the governor of Calais; in *The Mountaineers* (1793) he was Captain Kilmallock, an Irishman in the Spanish service caught up in the siege of Granada around 1490. In the last two pieces and *The Review*, Johnstone's characters were also provided with a conventional Irish ditty to sing. Whether Colman's plays were historical or contemporary, and whatever their location, Johnstone's roles introduced an Irish element, invariably affirming the decency and good-heartedness of the Irishman alongside (in some cases) a celebration of English honour and patriotism.

Space is insufficient here to consider Johnstone's full repertoire. Four particularly successful and representative parts, however, were Sir Callaghan O'Brallaghan in Charles Macklin's farce *Love à la Mode* (1759), Major O'Flaherty in Richard Cumberland's *The West Indian* (1771), Murtoch Delany in William Macready's *An Irishman in London or, The Happy African* (1792) and Dennis Brulgruddery in George Colman the Younger's *John Bull* (1803). In his second season at Covent Garden, Johnstone was cast by Macklin as Sir Callaghan in *Love à la Mode*, one of

---

[42] John Taylor, *Records of My Life*, 2 vols. (London: Edward Bull, 1832), I: 423.

four suitors for the hand of Charlotte (Figure 2.1). The others are a Scot, Sir Archy MacSarcasm (the role played by Macklin), a Jew and an English squire. When Charlotte's father announces he has lost his fortune (a ploy to test the sincerity of the suitors), all but Sir Callaghan lose interest. Sir Callaghan was one of the first roles in which Johnstone played the military Irishman, but *The West Indian* provided him with a further role as a kind-hearted Irish soldier, Major O'Flaherty, who unravels all manner of plotting and chicanery and ensures a just outcome to the play (Figure 2.2). Bridget Orr notes how early nineteenth-century commentators saw O'Flaherty as 'a humanising *reprise* of the stock character', but that contemporary reviewers were 'less conscious of any deviation from the stereotyped impression of good nature, fortune-hunting, impetuousness, bravery and the unconscious humour occasioned by dialect'.[43] Johnstone was not the original O'Flaherty, but it subsequently became one of his regular roles at Covent Garden. Arguably it was his capacity to play the part more effectively and more subtly than his predecessors in Irish roles which may well have been accountable for the early nineteenth-century shift in attitude towards the role.[44]

Johnstone also played numerous low comedy characters. For his benefit in April 1792, he first played the role of Murtoch Delany in *The Irishman in London* (Figure 2.3). Murtoch is visiting London with his master Colloony, but he is much less enamoured of the city. On his first appearance, we learn that his pocket has been picked and that with all the pushing and shoving, he has been 'tumbled about bravely; for the people here walk the streets as if they couldn't see', so that 'I was going backward every step I went forward.' Unlike Colloony, who is impressed by how much better everything is in England, Murtoch defends his native country: 'Och! Maister Pat, don't be running down our country; myself can't bear it; you know the roads are a thousand times better in Ireland.'

In *John Bull* (1803), which is in many ways a state-of-the-nation play, Johnstone's character of the Irish landlord, Dennis Brulgruddery, provides a very positive perspective on Irishness in relation to Englishness (Figure 2.4). His kindness to the heroine, Mary, leads another character, Peregrine, to state:

---

[43] Bridget Orr, 'Empire, Sentiment and Theatre' in *The Oxford Handbook of the Georgian Theatre, 1737–1832*, ed. Julia Swindells and David Francis Taylor (New York: Oxford University Press, 2014), 633.
[44] Sir Walter Scott admired Johnstone in this role. See his *Biographical Memoirs of Eminent Novelists and Other Distinguished Persons*, 3 vols (Edinburgh: Robert Cadell, 1834), 1: 200.

Figure 2.1 W. Ward (engraver) after Martin Arthur Shee, 'Mr Johnstone as Sir Callaghan in *Love à la Mode*', mezzotint (1803). Call #: S.218-1997. Theatre Collection, Victoria and Albert Museum.

Figure 2.2 James Thomson, 'Mr Johnstone as Major O'Flaherty', engraved for Oxberry's New English Drama (London 1818). Call #: ART File J73.5 no.5. Used by permission of the Folger Shakespeare Library.

> 'Tis national in him to blend eccentricity with kindness. John Bull exhibits a plain, undecorated dish of solid benevolence, but Pat has a gay garnish of whim around his good nature; and if now and then 'tis sprinkled in a little confusion, they must have vitiated stomachs who are not pleased with the embellishment.

In the play's epilogue (which was sung by Johnstone), Colman suggests that however hackneyed the blunders of the Stage Irishman are, the charm of Johnstone's acting makes them acceptable. For Thomas Gilliland, Johnstone as Brulgruddery was unique and inimitable:

> [H]is style of painting the passions and native oddities of honest Dennis, exceeds description; his beauties are to be seen and felt with delight, but cannot be minutely illustrated; they are like the masterly touches of a fine picture, the more the observer points out its perfections, the more his eye will discover for gratification and praise.[45]

---

[45] Thomas Gilliland, *The Dramatic Mirror*, 2 vols. (London: C. Chapple, 1808), 2: 793.

MR JOHNSTONE.
as Murtock Delany in the Irishman in London

Figure 2.3 T. Warburton (engraver) after W. Wellings, 'Mr Johnstone as Murtock Delany in The Irishman in London', stipple and etching (1797). British Museum number: 1870,0514.1914. ©Trustees of the British Museum.

The *Monthly Mirror* considered that Brulgruddery was 'drawn with infinite humour . . . and keeps the audience in an uninterrupted roar of laughter whenever he is before them. It is national with him to blend eccentricity with kindness. This is his character. The goodness of his heart is as conspicuous as the whimsicality of his behaviour'. The review added that 'Johnstone displayed all that prodigality of humour, and rich characteristic expression, for which he is so remarkable, and in which we can never hope to find his equal.'[46] Colman's script (and doubtless Johnstone's performance) places an Irish landlord (together with a Yorkshire waiter) in a Cornish inn without any sense of incongruity. Equally, despite his drinking and whimsicality, Brulgruddery does more than provide comic relief; in a play about Englishness, he exemplifies (albeit from an Irish perspective) exactly those qualities of decency and fairness also embodied by Job Thornberry, the English brazier whom spectators and critics identified as the play's representative John Bull.

---

[46] *Monthly Mirror* 15 (March 1803), 188–90.

Figure 2.4 Samuel De Wilde, 'John Johnstone as Dennis Brulgruddery', water-colour (c. 1803). Call #: G0334. The Garrick Club.

Private Life

In private life, Johnstone was very much the sociable Irish gentleman. 'He is favoured by the countenance and esteem of many persons of the first distinction in the UNITED KINGDOM', wrote the *Monthly Mirror*, 'and is happy in the society of a number of the most respectable families'.[47] The *Dublin University Magazine* recalls him as

> one of the most agreeable table companions that ever enlivened society; and, for an after-supper song, unrivalled; – convivial, and at the same time prudent and saving in his worldly affairs, qualities not often blended in the thoughtless sons of Hibernia. He was a remarkably handsome man, of elegant manners and deportment; and in personal appearance, presented an exact beau ideal of the travelled Irish gentleman and officer.[48]

The newspaper editor John Taylor describes how he often met Johnstone at the hospitable table of his old friend Mr Const, the chairman of the Middlesex Sessions, 'where Johnstone's humour, high spirits, and musical talents, rendered him at all times the life of the company'.[49] Taylor also alludes to Johnstone's association with the Prince of Wales and suggests another reason for his ease in high society:

> His accuracy in representing the higher order of Irish, was the effect of his intercourse with persons of high rank in this country and in Ireland. He had been frequently honoured with the countenance of his late Majesty, when Prince of Wales, and invited to the royal parties: a proof that he must have been a well-bred man, or he never could have been in the company of a Prince distinguished by a union of ease, affability, and dignity, of which there are perhaps few parallels in the civilized world. . . . His companionable qualities, as well as his musical talents, rendered him an attractive object, and though there was a familiar spirit in his manner, he was always well bred.[50]

Oxberry's memoir, which referred to Johnstone's 'dignified and gentlemanly appearance' states that Johnstone 'is, we believe, a very good companion; and is frequently invited to the Prince of Wales's parties, but that honour we must attribute rather to the melody of his voice, than the sprightliness of his conversation'.[51] Nevertheless, the *Thespian Dictionary* makes clear that Johnstone, whom it claims was 'on terms of intimacy with persons of the first distinction', always sang willingly at

[47] *Monthly Mirror*, 13 (April 1802), 229.   [48] *Dublin University Magazine*, 40 (1851), 561.
[49] Taylor, *Records of My Life*, 1: 423.   [50] Ibid., 424.
[51] *Oxberry's Dramatic Biography and Histrionic Anecdotes*, 4: 78.

social occasions and 'never disgraced his profession', unlike those who would only sing at social events if they had been hired to do so.[52]

In the late eighteenth century, Johnstone was a regular performer at the anniversary dinners of London's Benevolent Society of St Patrick (BSSP), which, bolstered by a combination of singing and drinking, served to encourage charitable contributions to support the Irish but also aimed to cement social harmony between the English and Irish.[53] Johnstone's presence is hardly surprising, given his skills as a singer, his social situation and his ethnicity. David O'Shaughnessy suggests that the BSSP included a number of Irish playwrights based in London who shared 'a pragmatic cosmopolitanism that tempered patriotic fervour'.[54] He pays particular attention to John O'Keeffe, particularly focusing on O'Keeffe's play *The Shamrock*, subsequently revised as *The Poor Soldier* (1783), stating that 'it is only by placing it in the political and historical context of the BSSP's establishment that we can fully tease out its value as a cultural artefact that has much to tell us about Anglo-Irish relations in London at the time.'[55] Significantly, Johnstone's first original role when he joined Covent Garden Theatre was Dermot in *The Poor Soldier*, a rival suitor with Darby (a low comedy Irish role especially written for the English comedian John Edwin) for the hand of Kathleen. Johnstone arguably brought a sense of authentic Irishness to this small role and over time played many more roles created by O'Keeffe. In O'Keeffe's *Patrick in Prussia; or, Love in a Camp*, a sequel to *The Poor Soldier*, he was cast as Captain Patrick, an Irish role played by the English actor John Bannister in the earlier play. If, as O'Shaughnessy suggests, in relation to plays such as *The Poor Soldier*, '[t]he associational world of the London stage was an important locus of Irish political, cultural and commercial aspiration',[56] then we need look not only at the dramatists but also at actors such as Johnstone who embodied such aspiration on stage.

Johnstone not only performed at the anniversary dinners of the BSSP. He also belonged to a glee club meeting at the Garrick Head Coffee House in Bow Street and to the Anacreontic Society, a club for amateur musicians frequented by professional gentlemen. He reputedly belonged to the

---

[52] *The Thespian Dictionary or Dramatic Biography of the Present Age* (London: James Cundee, 1805), n.p.

[53] Craig Bailey, 'From Innovation to Emulation: London's Benevolent Society of St Patrick, 1783–1800', *Eighteenth-Century Ireland*, 27 (2012): 162–84; 176.

[54] David O'Shaughnessy, '"Rip'ning Buds in Freedom's Field": Staging Irish Improvement in the 1780s', *Journal for Eighteenth-Century Studies*, 38.4 (2015): 541–54; 542.

[55] Ibid., 550. [56] Ibid., 551.

Westminster Cavalry Association and he supported charitable causes, returning for one night at Drury Lane, 18 May 1822, when he volunteered his services as Dennis Brulgruddery for the benefit of his distressed countrymen. Johnstone appears to have played the Irish gentleman offstage and on, mixing effectively within English society while maintaining a distinct sense of national identity and demonstrating 'the possibilities of . . . Irishness'.[57]

Conclusion

From the 1780s through to the early years of the nineteenth century Johnstone represented Irishness on the London stage in all its gradations: whether or not he was authentic, whether his brogue was 'translated' into a form suitable for English consumption, was immaterial. For London audiences he personified Irishness. There were of course other Irish actors on the London stage: Edward Rock in low comedy roles and latterly Tyrone Power, whom some preferred to Johnstone. Johnstone however was able to play a very wide range of Irish characters, to modify the brogue according to the role and to distinguish between the different social classes he represented. There is little evidence of extreme stereotyping or of caricature. In fact, in performance he arguably effected what Michael Ragussis suggests the character of Sir Callaghan achieved in *Love à la Mode*, the deconstruction of the Irish stereotype. In league with Sir Archy, Charlotte agrees to allow Sir Callaghan to woo her while observed by other suitors from behind a screen. The assumption is that Sir Callaghan will make a fool of himself, but this does not in fact happen. In Ragussis's view, 'the discrepancy between his actual behaviour and the expected blunders of the stereotypical Irishman exposes the stage Irishman as a theatrical construct.'[58] Johnstone played this role early in his career and, arguably, in his own performances also deconstructed the stereotypical Irishman through the roles specially written for him by dramatists such as Colman the Younger. Inevitably his characters spoke in some form of Irish brogue and identified as Irish rather than attempting to pass as the sort of 'outlandish Englishman' that Sir Callaghan excoriates in *Love à la Mode*. Certainly, Johnstone may have presented a form of modified Irishness to his London audiences, as Curran's comment (quoted earlier) implied. Yet, if we are fully to understand the representation of Irish national identity, as mediated by the London stage, then it is to actors

[57] Bailey, *Irish London*, 5.   [58] Ragussis, *Theatrical Nation*, 48.

such as Johnstone we must look as much as to the dramatists who created Irish roles. We must also question Leigh Hunt's rather immature notion that Johnstone mimicked 'into ridicule the peculiarities of his birth-place', a generalisation not borne out by most contemporary accounts of his acting.

Johnstone's function in mediating Irish national identity on the English stage is complex. In his enactment of more gentlemanly roles, he arguably embodied characters who were, in some cases, products of the Irish Enlightenment. His low comedy roles send out contradictory signals, but characters such as Kenrick and Dennis Brulgruddery suggest that tolerance and decency are national Irish characteristics indistinguishable across class. During and beyond the Irish rebellion of 1798, Johnstone's Irish characters remained as popular and prominent as ever. In James Boaden's *Cambro-Britons*, staged in July 1798 at the Haymarket Theatre, a play based on ancient Anglo-Welsh hostilities and focusing on issues of patriotism and loyalty, Johnstone played the comic role of O'Turloch, an Irish minstrel; some years earlier in *British Gratitude and Hibernian Friendship, or An Escape from France* (J. C. Cross, Covent Garden, 29 April 1794), a play in which an Irish character counters fears of a possible French-Irish alliance against England, he created for his benefit the role of Captain O'Leary, who upholds 'true Liberty and old England'. Johnstone is arguably the Englishman's Irishman, providing onstage a non-rebellious and unthreatening portrayal of his countrymen, almost as if Irish popular resistance in the early 1790s, the later rebellion and the 1801 Act of Union had never taken place. His Irishmen offered the reassuring sense that the Irish provided the psychological supporting infrastructure for the maintenance of English liberty and, by association, implicated themselves in Enlightenment possibilities. Through the 1790s and early 1800s, in low comedy and more gentlemanly roles, as well as in his offstage persona as an Irish gentleman in London, Johnstone demonstrated 'the possibilities of . . . Irishness' to both his audiences and acquaintances.

Not only did Johnstone encapsulate Irish national identity for contemporary London audiences but even for native Irish audiences he also seems to have preserved a sense of authenticity, despite long periods of absence. Almost twenty years after making his debut on the London stage, he was acclaimed, on a return visit to Dublin, as the genuine Irishman.[59] Subsequently, the *Illustrated Dublin Journal* stated the following:

[59] *A Biographical Dictionary of Actors, Actresses, Musicians, Dancers, Managers, & Other Stage Personnel in London*, ed. Philip H. Highfill et al., 16 vols. (Carbondale and Edwardsville: Southern Illinois University Press, 1973–93), 8: 212.

It can never be questioned that he was the truest painter of Irish character that ever lived. There was no trait to be found throughout its extensive range, from the accomplished gentleman to the unlettered peasant, that he was not equally master of, and which he did not depict with equal spirit and vividness; and this always in such a way as to make us pleased with the picture of ourselves, and acknowledge its truth, while we laughed at its strange and often ludicrous peculiarities. There was nothing in Jack Johnstone's personation that Irishmen would ever feel ashamed of, or that they would not willingly allow to go forth to the world at large as faithful delineations of their eccentricities and faults, as well as of their drolleries and virtues.[60]

This account was written posthumously, but it does suggest many of the reasons why Johnstone so effectively represented Irish characters in the theatre of his time with an exuberance tempered by restraint and a heightened truthfulness unimpeded by caricature.

[60] *Dublin Penny Journal*, 1 (1841), 39.

CHAPTER 3

The Diminution of 'Irish' Johnstone

Oskar Cox Jensen

'If a gentleman happens to be born in a stable, it does not follow that he should be called a horse.' So runs the disavowal of Irishness long attributed to Wellington.[1] Of course, today's academics know better: surely the phrase originates with the radical Irish politician Daniel O'Connell, who, in a speech of 16 October 1843, is recorded as remarking in court: 'The poor old Duke! what shall I say of him? To be sure he was born in Ireland, but being born in a stable does not make a man a horse.'[2] O'Connell's jest 'was received with great laughter' in the court room and transforms our understanding of the analogy, from a pretty nasty racial slur to a confident, jocular assertion of identity. But what does it do to our appreciation of Irishness and identity politics, not to mention horses, when we learn that O'Connell had – consciously or otherwise – borrowed his joke from James C. Cross, a minor London lyricist, responsible for the words to 'A Man An't A Horse! An Irish Song Sung by Mr. Johnstone, at the Readings & Music, Theatre Royal, Haymarket', back in 1795?[3] The song begins:

> Of a great well known Family near Tipperary
> Who trotted a Pole or who shoulder'd a Hod,
> I was sprung & so thinking the prospect to vary
> Left my Old Antient Ancestors Home and the Sod.
> I'd a twist of the brogue I determin'd to alter,
> And spake native English jonteely of course
> If bred up a foreigner why should I faulter!
> Tho' born in a Stable a Man an't a Horse.

---

[1] This attribution is still given in Craig Bailey, *Irish London: Middle-Class Migration in the Global Eighteenth Century* (Liverpool: Liverpool University Press, 2013), 11.
[2] Shaw's *Authenticated Report of the Irish State Trials* (Dublin, 1844), 93.
[3] British Library, shelfmark G.367 (9). Similarly, the expression 'Like a bull in a china shop', dated by the OED to 1839, seems to originate with a Charles Dibdin the Younger/William Reeve song of 1808: see British Museum, object no. 1861,0518.1198.

Three subsequent verses belie the sentiment that concludes the third verse – "'Bout pronuncification, then why make a bother?' – as the song's protagonist endures discrimination from employers and innkeepers on the grounds of his accent, the concluding joke being that the deluded narrator believes himself to have mastered 'native' English and can only assume that 'I've the brogue on my Face' – that is, 'my plump Irish Features betray me' – whereas the dialect lyrics make clear that the brogue remains upon his tongue.

Set to highly generic music by the jobbing composer William Reeve, 'A Man An't A Horse' is not an easy song to decipher. Ostensibly, its humour inheres in this bathetic ironising of the singer's protestations that he has learnt to talk 'English so native and easy'. Yet it admits of a more egalitarian hearing, whereby we side with the plain-speaking, intrepid Irishman against the hypocrisy and prejudice of great men and innkeepers and agree – in a universalist rather than nationalist sense – with his vehement refrain, 'Tho' born in a Stable, a Man an't a Horse'. It is unclear whether Cross, the lyricist, was simply fulfilling a brief to deliver a generic comic Irish number, or flirting with a dangerously fraternal message as war with Revolutionary France raged, emboldened by the acquittals and the subsequent short-lived possibility for free speech in the recent 1794 Treason Trials. More promising is the song's relation to its initial singer at the Haymarket: the Irish actor John Henry Johnstone. Celebrated in London and across Britain as the Stage Irishman *par excellence*, Johnstone's career – though on the face of it a long and successful one – ran uncomfortably close to the experience of the song's narrator. In this chapter, I will look at certain aspects of that career, in which – to stretch the equine analogy to its limits – a man who began his race as a thoroughbred had become by its end a one-trick pony. Rather than concentrate on his most famous roles or the principal sources for his biography, aspects amply and expertly covered by Jim Davis (Chapter 2, this volume), I will present an argument in three acts. First, *where is Johnstone?* and second, *who is Johnstone?*, as it is my contention that the *who* is heavily mediated by the *where*. Finally, *wherefore 'Irish' Johnstone?*, as I would like to suggest that in fact, there is a lot in a name, and that this particular sobriquet was emblematic, not of Johnstone's undoubted success, but of the cost of that success: namely, his diminution as an actor and still more so as an individual, increasingly reduced in agency and complexity by a proliferation of monolithic intermedial representations that operated beyond his personal control.

Where Is Johnstone?

I might reasonably be expected to begin by stating that John Henry Johnstone was born in Kilkenny in 1749 – or, as some sources have it, Dublin in 1755 – and continue with an overview of his career. The essentials are swiftly dealt with, besides being handled more deftly and extensively by Davis: Johnstone was, in brief, one of the great London Irish actors and singers, the pioneer of the Regency Stage Irishman, a staple comedian of Covent Garden, Drury Lane and the Haymarket, a long-lived, twice-married, chequered-past figure of anecdote and legend. It seems more to my purpose to pursue the proliferation of these biographical details, corroborated, disputed, apocryphal, than to attempt to sift through them for anything so unlikely as the truth. More profitable, surely, to take seriously than to dismiss the error in the *Gentleman's Magazine*'s 1829 obituary which states that 'He was born at Tipperary, the son of a small but respectable farmer, having a large family', when we recall that the first lines of 'A Man An't A Horse' state that the singer is born 'Of a great well known Family near Tipperary who trotted a Pole or who shoulder'd a Hod'.[4] The tantalising possibility that the magazine's contributor con-flated one of Johnstone's stage roles with the man himself is not so remote, when we ask *where is Johnstone?* and repeatedly encounter his simulacra far beyond the reach of his corporeal reality.

That bodily presence was itself subject to a certain degree of mobility. Johnstone's London debut was on 2 October 1783 at Covent Garden, in the role he had previously made his own in Dublin, that of Lionel in *Lionel and Clarissa*. During the winter seasons, he remained at Covent Garden until 1803, through success and controversy, before transferring to Drury Lane, where he remained until 1820. In the 1780s, 1792 and 1803, he also returned to Ireland, playing Dublin's Smock Alley and Crow Street as well as Waterford, Limerick, Cork and Newry. From 1791, he spent the summers at the Haymarket; in 1797, he visited Birmingham; in the 1810s, he played Edinburgh in the summer, and for his first farewell in 1820 he made it as far as Liverpool. In 1791–92, he indulged the Earl of Barrymore's request to appear in private theatricals at Wargrave; socially, we also discover him on the Continent with Michael Kelly in 1790, and with the Prince Regent's set at Carlton House and in Brighton, where in 1801 he played a notorious hoax; nor did he miss many gatherings of the Anacreontics when in London, so we must place him in venues such as the Crown and Anchor

---

4 'Mr. Johnstone', *Gentleman's Magazine* 145 (1829), 183.

tavern, a favourite landmark of the City of London. Already there is the sense that Johnstone's identity must have been somewhat mutable, as a Dubliner in London, a metropolitan in the provinces, an actor at the opera, a professional on the amateur stage, a working performer among the titled indolent. The bulk of his time, however, was spent between the adjacent west-central parishes of St Giles in the Fields and St Paul Covent Garden: though he was more than once kept by wealthy women, his own residences were at Great Russell Street in the early 1790s, then at number 19 in the Covent Garden Piazza itself during his busiest professional period, and, from 1810, back north a little into what is now Bloomsbury, at 5 Tavistock Row. He socialised as well as slept, breakfasted and worked in the area; besides being a member of the Sublime Society of Beef Steaks which met at Covent Garden, from 1793 he was a founder-member of the Glee Club, which met at the Garrick's Head, Bow Street, and also frequented the nearby Brown Bear, described by William Parke as 'a public house of the lowest class', and he even repented his headaches on the other side of the piazza, at St Paul's Church, where he was eventually buried.[5]

This micro-geography mattered, particularly later in his career: as shall be seen later, the benefits of a geographically proximate set of social and professional networks were offset by a less salubrious set of associations that would compound the ultimate reduction of his character. At this stage, it is at least clear that Johnstone got about, though rather less than some contemporaries, and both occupied and moved between spaces marked by widely different social and even racial identities. Yet this corporeal mobility was as nothing compared to the spaces – and I do not mean to suggest that this is anything other than typical for the period – wherein Johnstone was represented. While the man himself appeared upon various stages, his avatars spread across those stages' material productions and the piracies thereof: on the playbills jostling for space on exterior walls, bidding for pedestrian perusal; in the published playtexts retailed to a monied market of readers and amateur thespians; in full-length operatic reductions

[5] For this paragraph, see the entry for 'Johnstone, John Henry, 1749?–1828, actor, singer', in *A Biographical Dictionary of Actors, Actresses, Musicians, Dancers, Managers, & Other Stage Personnel in London, 1660–1800*, ed. Philip H. Highfill et al., 16 vols (Carbondale and Edwardsville: Southern Illinois University Press, 1973–93), 8: 208–15; L. M. Middleton, 'Johnstone, John Henry (1749–1828)', rev. K. D. Reynolds, *Oxford Dictionary of National Biography* (Oxford, 2004), at oxforddnb.com/view/article/14969; William Oxberry, 'Memoir of John Johnstone', in *Oxberry's Dramatic Biography and Histrionic Anecdotes*, 5 vols. (London, 1825–26), 4: 73–83; William T. Parke, *Musical Memoirs; Comprising an Account of the General State of Music in England*, 2 vols. (London: Henry Colburn and Richard Bentley, 1830), 1: 175–76, 294, 322–23; ' Tyrone Power; A Biography. – Part II', *Dublin University Magazine, A Literary and Political Journal* 40 (July–December 1852), 561.

and the scores of single songs, ranging in price between one and twelve
shillings in London, though a song's music could be had for as little as
sixpence in Dublin; in the lyrics of those songs as reproduced in songbooks,
chapbooks and garlands, or upon single slips and broadsides, sold at
bookstalls or hawked and sung around Ireland and Britain by pedlars,
flying-stationers and ballad-singers; in the illustrations produced to accompany those song lyrics, operating at different aesthetic and economic
registers, from the idiosyncratic selection of woodcuts, sometimes
a century old, used by the ballad press, to the custom hand-coloured prints
commissioned by the firm of Laurie and Whittle at 53 Fleet Street, to which
last I shall return below. Stand-alone visual legacies of productions in
which Johnstone starred, in the form of character portraits, compare
with the twenty-nine known portraits of Johnstone, and their many
reproductions, which were often reprinted in the theatrical biographies,
memoirs and miscellanies that devoted numerous pages to Johnstone both
during his career and after his death. Some of these drew upon manuscript
sources such as letters and diaries to compile their notices, an attention
replicated in numerous periodicals, while a plethora of works on other
subjects thought it proper to mention him tangentially.[6] Less tangibly, we
might place these material spaces in discourse with the immaterial: with the
conversations, rumours, anecdotes and fancies conceived by his contemporaries, his theatre audiences and the far greater number of consumers
whose only contact with Johnstone was through forms of print media.
Some of these forms – such as ballads, scores and playtexts – would often
have been performed in their turn within the context of domestic

[6] See Highfill et al., *Biographical Dictionary*, for the list of portraits. Character portraits range from
collectable prints to lottery tickets: see respectively F. Warburton after W. Wellings,
'Mr. Johnstone as Murtock Delany in the Irishman in London' (London, 1797), British
Museum 1870,0514.1914; and 'Dennis Brulgruddery' (London, 1816), British Museum
1862,1217.143. Prose works (from memoirs to periodicals) with an explicit focus on Johnstone as
a titular figure include 'Biographical Sketch of Mr. Johnstone', *Monthly Mirror* 14 (1802), 227–30;
'Mr Johnstone', *Gentleman's Magazine*; and Oxberry, 'Memoir of John Johnstone'. He also features
largely in such works as John Adolphus, *Memoirs of John Bannister, Comedian*, 2 vols. (London,
1839); 'Macklin-ana', *Monthly Mirror* 4 (1797), 296; William Macready, *Macready's Reminiscences,
and Selections from His Diaries and Letters*, ed. Frederick Pollock (New York: Harper and Brothers,
1875); Anne Mathews, *Anecdotes of Actors: With Other Desultory Recollections* (London, 1844);
Parke, *Musical Memoirs*; 'Tyrone Power', *Dublin University Magazine*; Lester Wallack, *Memories
of Fifty Years* (New York, 1889); and James Winston, *Drury Lane Journal: Selections from James
Winston's Diaries, 1819–1827*, ed. Alfred L. Nelson and Gilbert B. Cross (London: Society for
Theatre Research, 1974). Works in which reference is made to Johnstone range from 'Aleph'
(William Harvey), *London Scenes and London People* (London, 1863) to John Wilson et al., *Noctes
Ambrosianae*, 2 vols. (Nov 1824–July 1827, originally published in *Blackwood's Edinburgh
Magazine*, reprinted Redfield, New York, 1859).

consumption, so that to a great number of people across the Anglophone world, Johnstone was a person only experienced at a vicarious double remove. Johnstone, in short, was more or less everywhere, in sound, word, image and imagination, even while the well-fed and watered body of John Henry Johnstone slumbered in St Giles's. There was nothing exceptional about this, especially in the first great age of celebrity – yet it takes on especial significance when the perception of one man's identity was so bound up with the representation of an entire nation.

Who Is Johnstone?

Spread across so many forms, Johnstone the man becomes a peg to hang identities upon: he simply did not have the agency to control either the shaping or the reception of his total image. Over the course of his career, each success took him further from a position of influence over this image, as a new wave of cross-media representations issued forth from the pens of critics, diarists, songwriters, artists, caricaturists: representations that tended to coalesce rather than diverge, consolidating a consensual persona for Johnstone, particularly within the imaginary of southern England, centring on London. To take up a central thread, Johnstone began as an Irish actor of promise and potential, yet he became simply an actor of Irishmen – indeed, *the* actor of Irishmen, though never *the* Irish actor. His 1783 London debut at Covent Garden was in his favourite role as the titular Lionel, a romantic hero down from Oxford, one of many love interests he had specialised in at Dublin, Cork and Kilkenny.[7] A stellar notice in the *Theatrical Review* was effusive in praise of his 'person, voice, and action', without ever hinting at his national identity; on the back of this success, Johnstone was soon playing the best roles available, from Macheath, to Aimworth in *Maid of the Mill*, and some critics opined that he might make a great tragedian, such were his powers.[8] Yet twenty years later, his debut at Drury Lane was in the public's favourite role for the man they had made him into: the comic Irish servant Murtock Delaney in William Macready's *Irishman in London*.[9] While the role was considered a good one and supports a complex and even radical interpretation, the change from leading man, free of racialised characteristics, to that of comic Irishman is symptomatic of the essential *diminution* of Johnstone across his career – a phenomenon that entangled an individual with a set of roles and

[7] Highfill et al., *Biographical Dictionary*, 8: 209.
[8] Ibid., 209; Adolphus, *Memoirs of John Bannister*, 2: 105–6.   [9] Ibid., 212.

a broader collection of national prejudices, in the course of which the talent and versatility of a highly regarded actor were ultimately subsumed and reduced within one particular English conception of the foolish, libidinous, alcoholic Irishman. This argument may itself appear reductive, deaf to the revisionist trend that has sought out subtlety and subversion within the performance of stock characters; certainly, Davis draws very different and altogether more optimistic conclusions from Johnstone's career. Yet it is a case I shall attempt to make.

I would like to begin by suggesting that this diminution was largely effected in the years between the start of the 1790s, and Johnstone's 1803 transfer to Drury Lane: years in which events both great and small, yet all equally beyond Johnstone's control, had a significant impact upon his career and public character. Most obviously, the turbulent politics of this decade and the repressive actions of the British state led first to the Irish rebellion of 1798 and subsequently to the Act of Union, in a few short years that had enormous implications for Anglo-Irish relations and perceptions. Certainly in the short term and at least until Waterloo, the more positive eighteenth-century interpretations of the Stage Irishman took a palpable hit. This new theatrical climate was most evident in the return of the slang distortion of the English language used to signify Irishness in stage lyrics of around 1800, so that, for example, 'the' became 'de' – a linguistic register used to suggest mental inferiority that was swiftly redeployed for blackface representations.[10] These were the only songs remaining for Johnstone to sing, for the decade's epochal politics were preceded by three developments rather closer to home: the first decline in Johnstone's celebrated tenor voice, resulting in a loss of both tone and range;[11] the replacement of William Shield, the house composer at Covent Garden, by the less-talented serial plagiarist William Reeve in 1791;[12] and the blossoming out, from the tutelage of the celebrated vocal pedagogue Venanzio Rauzzini, of the tenor John Braham, who would almost singlehandedly redefine the ideal of a leading male singer on the London stage.[13] Taken

---

[10] 'National Song of Ireland', *Fraser's Magazine* 3/17 (June 1831), 537–56, 543 inc. *fn*; for the latter development, see e.g. Derek Scott, *The Singing Bourgeois: Songs of the Victorian Drawing Room and Parlour*, (2nd edn, Farnham: Ashgate, 2001), 81; and Richard Middleton, *Voicing the Popular: On the Subjects of Popular Music* (New York: Routledge, 2006), 11–13.

[11] Highfill et al. summarise that 'his failing singing voice caused his gradual abandonment of musical roles', *Biographical Dictionary*, 8: 212. The link between this failing and his specialisation is made in Wilson et al., *Noctes Ambrosianae*, 2: 264 n, and 'Mr. Johnstone', *Gentleman's Magazine*, 183–84.

[12] Victoria Halliwell, 'Reeve, William (1757–1815)', *Oxford Dictionary of National Biography* (*ODNB*) www.oxforddnb.com/view/article/23304.

[13] 'Tyrone Power', *Dublin University Magazine*, 559–62, 560 notes that 'During several seasons he [Johnstone] flourished as a leading vocalist; but Braham rose, and soon distanced competition.' His

together, these three factors dramatically curtailed Johnstone's performative options; while he had taken on Stage Irish parts as early as his first season in London, when he played Dermot in John O'Keeffe and Shield's *Poor Soldier*,[14] they now became his defining roles. Whether Johnstone jumped or whether he was pushed is both unknowable and, ultimately, unimportant: for even if the decision to specialise was his, it was taken in the absence of a viable alternative.

It is Braham's counterexample that, above all else, inclines me to read Johnstone's career change as a diminution: as a development that undoubtedly enriched the English theatregoer's experience, as Davis makes clear, yet at the expense of Johnstone's own identity, both individual and national. Braham stands as the victorious rival: a tenor similarly subject to racial prejudice, in his case anti-Semitic, yet one who – though he disavowed his origins, dropping the 'A' of Abraham from his name and ultimately converting to Christianity, in clear distinction from Johnstone's adoption of the 'Irish' moniker – managed in his professional life to transcend such prejudices, by means of both his enormous (and highly cultivated) musical talent and his self-fashioning as an icon of Britishness, most notably in his spectacularly successful composition 'The Death of Nelson'.[15] Considered as singers, Braham's science and skill took him – exceptionally for a Briton – to the Italian opera and the greatest stages of Europe and the United States, with free rein over his repertoire, whereas Johnstone's limitations saw him reduced from a wide range of songs to a narrow set of comic genre pieces. It is in these songs that the changing nature of the Stage Irishman in the 1790s is most readily perceived.

In his second London season, Johnstone obtained the excellent part of Captain Henry – the first of many captains – in the new comic opera *Fontainbleau [sic]; or, Our Way in France*, written by his compatriot O'Keeffe with music by Shield.[16] The part was a showcase for his voice, whether in the Siciliana 'My morning of life ah how tranquil' or in the opera's chief hit 'Let Fame Sound the Trumpet'. The latter is a remarkable, complex composition spanning two octaves in the vocal part, with an extended hold on high G and a coloratura passage from bars 70 to 84

---

eclipse by not only Braham, but Kelly and Incledon, is also asserted in *Oxberry's Dramatic Biography, and Histrionic Anecdotes*, 5 vols (London 1825–26), 4: 78–79.

[14] Highfill et al., *Biographical Dictionary*, 8: 209.

[15] See Scott, *Singing Bourgeois*, 8–10, for a brief discussion of this song. Ironically, where national identity is concerned, Braham's verses are clearly indebted to the melody of Étienne Nicolas Méhul's 1794 'Chant du Départ', which Napoleon adopted as a national anthem in preference to the 'Marseillaise'.

[16] British Library W87/5971.

ending with a fermata on high C.[17] The principal oboist of the company recalled this, many years later, as 'an original and beautiful composition, well sung by Johnstone'.[18] Just as significant were the song's patriotic, martial overtones, embellished by lyrical reference both to the classics and to India, in praise of the flourishing of the British Empire. As O'Keeffe recalled:

> The opera came out, and went off the first, and every night after, with the most brilliant *éclat* . . . . The King commanded it on the ninth night. Mr. Sarjant, one of the band, was very excellent on the trumpet, and was heard to great advantage in my song of 'Let Fame sound her Trumpet,' set by Shield, and sung by Johnstone. . . . Johnny Beard, the famous manager, and first singer of his time, pronounced it to be the best trumpet-song he had ever heard.[19]

In its music, lyrics and associations, this was as creditable a song as any British actor might hope to perform and indeed, in later years, both Charles Incledon and Braham himself counted it among their successes.[20] By that time, Johnstone was scraping the bottom of the barrel, yet his earliest songs in Irish parts, from 1784 to 1790, were by no means poor fare. His two solos in his debut Irish role of Dermot, again co-written by O'Keeffe and Shield, were the elegant 'Dear Sir, This Brown Jug', which became a staple of songbooks for two generations, and the serenade 'Sleep On, Sleep On', the melody of which is perhaps the most convincing imitation of an 'authentic Irish' tune in Johnstone's London repertoire.[21]

By 1790, Johnstone was at the height of his powers. For that year's *The Picture of Paris*, he played an Irish officer in what was little more than a cameo – essentially an excuse to air Shield's two new compositions, 'None Can Love Like An Irishman' and 'There Was An Irish Lad', both extravagantly amorous in theme.[22] The latter, which features perhaps the last airing of Johnstone's high C, is an accomplished tune with a silly lyric concerning the farcical courtship of a nun by the titular Irish lad. The shape of things to come is audible in the final line of its chorus – 'he sung sweetly Smalilou, Gramacchree and Paddywhack' – a foreshadowing of the nonsense refrains that would soon become his stock-in-trade. As with 'A Man An't A Horse', one also wonders whether the song did

---

[17] Ibid., 50–52.   [18] Parke, *Musical Memoirs*, 1: 44.
[19] John O'Keeffe, 'Recollections of the Life of John O'Keeffe', as serialised in *New Monthly Magazine* 16 (1826), 468.
[20] *A Select Collection of Songs; or, an Appendage to the Piano-Forte* (Newcastle, 1806), 30; *The New Evergreen, being A Select Collection of the Most Celebrated Songs* (London, 1818), 46.
[21] British Library E.108.e (3), 6, 24.   [22] British Library E.91.c (2), 10–11, 24–25.

not affect the obituary writer for the *Gentleman's Magazine*, who, some thirty years later, would describe Johnstone's youthful wooing in terms remarkably similar to this narrative. 'None Can Love Like An Irishman', meanwhile, comes across as a bold, chauvinistic boast of Irish virility, neither undercut nor contradicted by stage action, its words conceivably penned by the radical author Robert Merry,[23] and beginning as follows:

> The turban'd Turk who scorns the World
> May strut about with his Whiskers curl'd,
> Keep a hundred Wives under Lock and Key,
> For nobody else but himself to see,
> Yet long may he pray with his ALCORAN
> Before he can love like an Irishman.

The deployment of Orientalist prejudice to bolster pride in an otherwise subaltern Irish identity is a rhetorical strategy that was soon to be repeated in Macready's *The Irishman in London; or, The Happy African*, when Johnstone's character, Murtoch Delaney, asserts his masculine potency in a series of exchanges with the servant Cubba, played in blackface.[24] Yet the song goes further still in its national politics, for though the playtext published at London features a third verse disparaging 'The Finikin Fops', the edition of the song sold in Dublin 'As Sung by Johnstone' instead makes fun of 'The London Folks', adding at least some of the English to the list of nationalities (Turkish, French, Spanish, Italian, Dutch, Russian, Prussian, Swedish) less virile than the Irish.[25] Considered as verse, such lyrics might easily appear absurd – yet it is hard to deny the force of Shield's music, which lends the words a swaggering potency. Set in B minor and spanning a thirteenth, it is a sophisticated and memorable tune that allows Johnstone as singer considerable space to demonstrate the virtuosity of his upper range. The sparse accompaniment of the Dublin edition, where the convention was to reduce the score to a single page, nonetheless suggests the skill of Shield's accompaniment, from dramatic shifts in the harmonic interval at key phrases to the infectious instrumental flourish that follows each verse. Both the singer on stage and the product sold in Dublin proclaimed a national identity that was masculine, patriotic and self-assured.

[23] Corinna Russell, 'Merry, Robert (1755–1798)', *ODNB*, at oxforddnb.com/view/article/18611.
[24] William Macready, *The Irishman in London; or, The Happy African: A Farce. In Two Acts* (3rd edn, London, 1806), 30–32.
[25] British Library H.1601.g (9).

Nonetheless, both songs in *The Picture of Paris* conformed to the stereotype of Irishman as incorrigible lover: the scope of Johnstone's roles was already contracting. After Shield's departure from Covent Garden, he lost even the redeeming potential of the music, as Reeve, Shield's replacement, seemed content to peddle an endless series of highly generic, almost indistinguishable compositions in 6/8 time, of a narrow melodic compass, all based on the same pattern of a 16-bar fiddle tune. This is not to say they were 'bad' music; they were in many ways fit for their purpose, which was to enable a light, comic narrative, leaving the singer more or less free to concentrate on the word play and the articulation of his celebrated brogue. Rarely did they span more than an octave – 'A Man An't A Horse' exceptionally ranges an eleventh – and it was just as rare for their lyrics to transcend the typical 'bulls' and blunders of the turn-of-the-century Stage Irish caricature. They are full of sweethearts, pigs, potatoes, whiskey, comic misunderstandings and nonsense choruses, the titles alone proving sufficiently synecdochal: 'The Tight Irish Boy', 'The Tipsy Hibernian', 'The Land of Potatoes', 'O'Whack's Journey to Paris' and so on. Reeve was far from the only factor in this development: for not only did he collaborate with numerous lyricists, but the songs written for Johnstone at other venues at this and subsequent stages of his career conformed to the same model. Those composed by Samuel Arnold might feature more memorable, though equally restricted, music, as in the case of 'Corporal Casey', 'Looney McTwalter' or the still-famous 'Oh Dear, What Can the Matter Be?'; yet their range and their lyrics were uniformly reductive, presenting the loquacious fool; the unaware Irish rogue and simpleton; the butt, not the coiner, of one unvarying English joke. It was one thing for a performer to specialise in roles where he might make use of natural or cultural advantages, or turn the prejudices of his audience to his own ends; quite another to be given a long succession of songs that afforded so little scope for artistic expression, while setting up a series of laughs at the expense of his own people. In relation to writers and audiences, this was Johnstone, not as autonomous wit, but as dancing bear.

Wherefore 'Irish' Johnstone?

Johnstone's career of course admits of a more positive interpretation: of the line taken by Helen Burke in relation to Robert Owenson, who, she demonstrates, inserted various signifiers into his performances that

subverted the Stage Irish stereotype,[26] or that of Craig Bailey, who might
point to the entrepreneurial networks of Irish migrants that launched and,
to a point, sustained Johnstone's undoubtedly profitable London career:[27]
migrants ranging from the veteran playwright Charles Macklin who is
credited with introducing him to Covent Garden Theatre,[28] to O'Keeffe
and Kelly, to Macready. On his death, Johnstone left twelve thousand
tangible signs of success in his will, and perhaps as many positive memories
in the minds of those who would recall and often write of him.[29] And yet
I would demur from amplifying this quite valid revisionist perspective,
largely on account of the increasing loadedness of Johnstone's nickname,
'Irish', which grew from a convenient means of distinguishing him from
other Johnstones and Johnsons in an early theatrical company to
a prohibitive millstone, obscuring and hobbling the man who wore it.[30]

In part, this was a sign of the times. In a climate of war and revolution,
attitudes towards expressions of Irish identity became increasingly con-
flicted throughout the 1790s and especially from 1798, while onstage
representations of all national types, including John Bull, tended towards
crudeness. As the British army and indeed navy became ever more reliant
upon Irish manpower, Johnstone found himself playing an endless succession of captains and corporals – yet it was politically essential that these
figures were subservient: loyal soldiers, rough around the edges, but always
hard-fighting followers in the ranks of King George. In this highly conservative new orthodoxy, it was inconceivable that 'Irish' Johnstone could
be given a song such as 'Let Fame Sound the Trumpet': an emblem of
subaltern Irishness could no longer be allowed to voice the dispassionate,
grandiose perspective of imperial authority. Thus he found playing for
laughs to be not merely personally expedient, but politically necessary.

To return to the question 'where is Johnstone?' we might observe this
loss of agency by following Johnstone's later songs beyond the site of their
first performance. The British Museum holds six of the Laurie and Whittle
sheets based upon his Drury Lane repertoire and sold to a middling
audience, in all of which a custom etching occupying half the sheet

[26] Helen M. Burke, *Riotous Performances: The Struggle for Hegemony in the Irish Theatre, 1712–1784* (Notre Dame, IN: University of Notre Dame Press, 2003), 263–65.
[27] See Bailey, *Irish London*, 2–3, 8–10.
[28] The assistance is recorded in a letter of Macklin's, subsequently published, by which means it became part of the public narratives around Johnstone. 'Macklin-ana', *Monthly Mirror*, 296. This letter, though not cited, clearly influenced the accounts given in: Oxberry, 'Memoir of John Johnstone', 75; Adolphus, *Memoirs of John Bannister*, 2: 105–6; 'Mr. Johnstone', *Gentleman's Magazine*, 183.
[29] Middleton, 'Johnstone'.   [30] I am indebted to John Greene for this information.

surmounts the song's lyrics. In all save one of these, Johnstone himself is effaced from the image, replaced by a caricatured Irishman whose features are given varying degrees of idiocy. The image accompanying 'Paddy M'Shane's Seven Ages' from 1807, drawn by Isaac Cruikshank and reproduced in Figure 3.1, is arguably the most travestied. Johnstone's avatar is a heavily racialised figure, his face a simpleton's, shillelagh shouldered and trailing shamrocks, with a pig snuffling at his heels. He is depicted in an impoverished Irish hovel, where bed, kitchen and cow share the same room. The verses, attributed variously to George Colman (presumably the Younger) or to a Major Downs, are a parody of Shakespeare, in which the conceit is that if the bard had been born Irish, his life would have been a succession of drunkenness, violence, stupidity, cuckoldry, war, service, theft and ultimate poverty, all rendered farcical by the language and presumed delivery. Such sentiments were by now Johnstone's meat and drink – yet even he may have baulked at his depiction by Cruikshank.

Print publication of songs labelled as being 'sung with unbounded applause' by Johnstone demonstrably reduced his capacity to self-fashion, instead implicating him within the prejudicial rhetoric of metropolitan caricature. Yet these songs were also sung and sold in the street as broadsides and slips, introducing a still more invidious register of associations. As the journalist William Harvey recalled around 1812, quoting from verse two of 'The Yorkshire Irishman':

> Irish Johnstone was then the chief attraction, as funny man, at the theatres, and many a street comedian strove to imitate his brogue, in such jokes as these:–
>
> > Single misfortunes, they say,
> > To Irishmen ne'er come alone –
> > My father, poor man, was first drowned,
> > Then shipwrecked in coming from Cork;
> > But my mother she got safe to land,
> > And a whisky-shop [*sic*] set up in York.[31]

Of course, all successful stage singers had their songs pirated and performed in the street. Yet more was at stake for Johnstone than for most. According to the first Mendicity Report, conducted in 1818, more than a quarter of all mendicants on the London streets – which included ballad-

---

[31] 'Aleph', *London Scenes and London People*, 349.

Figure 3.1 Isaac Cruikshank, 'Paddy M'Shane's Seven Ages', letterpress and etching (1807). Charles Peirce Collection, Folder 21. Courtesy, American Antiquarian Society.

singers – were of Irish origin, a figure that, despite excluding second-generation immigrants, was twice the sum total of all non-English nationalities.[32] Johnstone, as the epitome of the performing Irishman, would have been constantly subject to parallels, conscious or otherwise, with street entertainers such as Thomas McConwick, an immigrant interviewed and sketched by John Thomas Smith, who 'sings many of the old Irish songs with excellent effect, but more particularly that of the "Sprig of Shillelah and Shamrock so green" [a comic-Irish song first performed and popularised by Johnstone], dances to the tunes, and seldom fails of affording amusement to a crowde[d] auditory'. Smith reports McConwick's testimony:

> [T]he English populace were taken with novelty, and that by either moving his feet, snapping his fingers, or passing a joke upon some one of the surrounding crowd, he was sure of gaining money. He carries matches as an article of sale, and thereby does not come under the denomination of a pauper. Now and then, to please his benefactors, he will sport a bull or two, and when the laugh is increasing a little too much against him, will, in a low tone, remind them that bulls are not confined to the lower orders of Irish.[33]

For many Londoners, this disreputable, patronised singer of Johnstone's songs, depicted in Figure 3.2, must have been on some level synonymous with the on-stage original.

So prevalent were imitators such as McConwick that the figure of the foolish Irish street-singer swiftly became a literary type. In John Badcock's response to Pierce Egan's *Life in London*, an encounter with 'an Irish paddy' is played for laughs, wherein a Johnstone-esque song is 'sung with an Irish accent, to the tune of "Morgan Rattler," accompanied with a snapping of his fingers, and concluded with a something in imitation of an Irish jilt . . . altogether so truly characteristic of the nation to which he belonged, as to afford our Heroes considerable amusement'.[34] Even a decade after Johnstone's death, in William Thomas Moncrieff's stage adaptation of Dickens's *Sam Weller*, the titular character has a comic turn where he impersonates the archetypal Irish ballad-singer, dancing

---

[32] *The First Report of the Society Established in London for the Suppression of Mendicity* (London: J. W. Whiteley, 1819), 14–16.

[33] John Thomas Smith, *The Cries of London: Exhibiting Several of the Itinerant Traders of Antient and Modern Times* (London: J. B. Nichols, 1839), 67.

[34] John Badcock, *Real Life in London; or, the Rambles and Adventures of Bob Tallyho, Esq. and His Cousin, the Hon. Tom Dashall, through the Metropolis*, 2 vols (London: Printed for Jones & Co., 1821), 1: 124.

Figure 3.2 John Thomas Smith, 'The Dancing Ballad-Singer with his Sprig of Sillelah [*sic*] and Shamrock so green', plate 22 of idem, *The Cries of London*, etching. Author's collection.

'grotesquely', and singing another of Johnstone's signature pieces, 'Oh Dear, What Can the Matter Be?'[35] Yet it is perhaps most indicative of this collapsing of boundaries between the distinguished actor and the ignominious stereotype that the song Harvey quotes above, 'The Yorkshire Irishman', was famously sung, not by Johnstone at all, but by his contemporary John Emery.[36] Due no doubt to its generic lyrical bulls, and perhaps its melody – which pastiches the tune known as 'Brian Boru's March' – Harvey conflated the song with Johnstone, his memory mixing the two in the promiscuous imagined space of the street.

---

[35] William Thomas Moncrieff, *Sam Weller, or, The Pickwickians. A Drama, in Three Acts* (London: Printed by T. Stagg, 1837), 99.
[36] British Library G.425.ss (25) [1804].

This street was at once a conceptual and a physical space, and while the former exerted a certain potency in the diminution of Johnstone, it was scarcely extricable from the latter. I have already observed that Johnstone's activities were centred on Covent Garden, while his residences at either end of his career were in the northern part of St Giles, this entire parish being closely associated with the Irish poor.[37] His daily commute skirted Seven Dials itself, the first-ever slum, known in the nineteenth century as 'Little Dublin'.[38] That is, the district of London in which, according to gossip and rumour, Johnstone gambled, drank to excess, played practical jokes, indulged in affairs and elopements – in other words, exhibited any number of the vices associated with the Stage Irishman – was also the region in which the Irish poor begged on the streets and sold Johnstone's songs.[39] If the networks of the Irish diaspora explored by Bailey and David O'Shaughnessy are all about transcending a stock image of poverty and disorder, then Johnstone, entangled as he was in the centre of that stock image, was making a very poor fist of things indeed, to the detriment of his own and his country's reputation.[40] The decades of his career had been unkind to the London Irish: whereas the Napoleonic Wars helped rehabilitate the Scottish, offering a romanticised framework of the loyal soldier in place of the Jacobite rebel, the same years, centred on the fraught process of uneven unification, ensured that the dominant metropolitan context for Irishness was not the burgeoning, Enlightenment culture of the 1780s that had so recently beguiled the town but rather one of rebellion across the water and inglorious poverty in London itself. Just as the stage was preparing to receive Sir Walter Scott's noble Highlanders, it enshrined the Stage Irishman as crude stereotype – a process in which Johnstone himself had been, willingly or no, complicit.

A final objection might be raised here, for why should Johnstone shoulder the burden of a supposed patriotism? Who are we to censure a career founded upon the exploitation and perpetuation of a stereotype: is this not simply a man making capital out of the resources available to him? Yet Johnstone himself seems, in the last analysis, to have been consumed by

---

[37] This indelible link persisted well into the century, the journalist James Greenwood remarking in his history of the district that 'St. Giles's and the Irish are identical'. James Greenwood, *Unsentimental Journeys: Or, Byways of the Modern Babylon* (London: Ward, Lock & Tyler, 1867), 127.

[38] Lesley Shepard, *John Pitts, Ballad Printer of Seven Dials, London, 1765–1844* (London: Private Libraries Association, 1969), 39.

[39] For these allegations, see Highfill et al., *Biographical Dictionary*, 8: 209–13, and Parke, *Musical Memoirs*, 1: 117, 294, 333.

[40] See especially David O'Shaughnessy, ed., 'Networks of Aspiration: The London Irish of the Eighteenth Century'. Special issue, *Eighteenth-Century Life* 39.1 (2015).

the nebulous accretions of his 'Irish' appellation. On Saturday 18 May 1822, aged around seventy, Johnstone made his final stage appearance in a benefit at Drury Lane, held on behalf of the 'Irish Distress districts' – a move indicative of fellow feeling with his poor compatriots both in London and in Ireland, and acknowledgement perhaps of the reciprocal influence of the reputation of each.[41] Reports differ over the attendance, his reception and the calibre of his performance. Yet it is striking that according to one account: 'He was announced as follows: – Dennis Brulgruddery (with the epilogue song), Mr. John Johnstone, who, on this occasion, although retired from his public duties, has, unsolicited, allowed himself to be announced for that character.'[42] He did not take the stage under his own name but opened the entire evening *in character* as the most famous of his Stage-Irish parts. This appearance was apparently 'the signal for unanimous shouts'.[43] Yet his reprise of the role at the end of the night went off less successfully:

> At the close of it, Johnstone sang the misfortunes of *Dennis Brulgruddery*, and tacked to it three verses applicable to his situation; one of which ran as follows: –
>> 'Though I've blundered thro' many an Irishman's part,
>> No blunder, I trust, will be found in this heart,
>> Which, bursting with gratitude, bids you adieu,
>> And sinks as it sighs out its farewell to you.'
> The bad taste of stepping from the blunders of *Dennis*, to the farewell of JOHNSTONE, was inexcusable; and our readers will conceive the bad effect[.][44]

To the reviewer at least, the distinction was clear. Posterity did not want Johnstone, but Dennis: it was the immortal buffoon, not the superannuated actor, that commanded column inches and the appreciation of the periodical's imagined readership. Johnstone, it would seem, had spent the past quarter-century collaborating in his own usurpation. In an age when theatregoers were at all times aware of both actor and role, one man at least had been generally diminished to the latter dimension alone, by his own hand, by political will, by pen, by etcher's needle, by the associative power of St Giles.

Three months before this 1822 farewell, the theatrical critic for the *New Monthly Magazine* had taken exception to a new production at Drury

---

[41] Winston, *James Winston's Diaries*, 51. It was later recorded that this was 'a cause in which he feels a deep interest' – 'Tyrone Power', 560.

[42] 'Tyrone Power', 560. Dennis Brulgruddery is an innkeeper in the George Colman the Younger play, *John Bull; or, The Englishman's Fireside*, first performed in 1805.

[43] *Oxberry's Dramatic Biography*, 4: 81.   [44] Ibid., 82.

Lane, *Giovanni in Ireland*. Among the many accusations levelled at the play was the complaint that 'A number of characters from the best Irish novels were introduced ... but they retained nothing but their names.'[45] Once again, the London stage had stripped away all markers of intellect and individuality from Irish cultural endeavours, leaving only one-dimensional names. By the same token, 'Irish' Johnstone signified everything that could be poured into the first word, and precious little of the second. It is an obvious point to end on, but that name itself clearly meant something to those who used it: something agreed upon, something significant and something that would have been superfluous if that English public counted numerous Irish men and women among their own social circle, as opposed to the world of 'low-lifes' whom they observed on the streets. This nickname was no marker of intimacy, but one of difference, an eternal brand upon the man who had come to London as a lead actor of non-racialised parts. His real friends, and fellow actors, never thought of him as 'Irish' Johnstone. They all called him 'Jack'.[46]

---

[45] 'The Drama', *New Monthly Magazine and Literary Journal* 6.14 (1 Feb 1822), 58.
[46] Highfill et al., *Biographical Dictionary*, 8: 214; Parke, *Musical Memoirs*, 1: 333; Wilson, *Noctes Ambrosianae*, 2: 264; 'Tyrone Power', 559, 561; Adolphus, *Memoirs*, 1: 266; 2: 105, 115; 'National Song of Ireland', *Fraser's Magazine*, 538 n; John Philpot Curran in Bailey, *Irish London*, 13.

PART II

Symbiotic Stages: Dublin and London

Midas, *Kane O'Hara and the Italians: An Interplay of Comedy between London and Dublin*

Michael Burden

The Irish actor and playwright John O'Keeffe recorded in his *Recollections* of 1826 that in about 1760,

> A wish to encourage native talent induced Lord Mornington to prevail on Kane O'Hara to write *Midas* for Crow-street, in opposition to the Italian burlettas at Smock-alley. I was at Kane O'Hara's in King-street, Stephen's-green, one morning, at a meeting with Lord Mornington, [and] Mr Brownlow, M. P., a musical amateur and fine player on the harpsichord, when they were settling the music for *Midas*.[1]

Whether O'Keeffe's short paragraph is entirely accurate is unclear, but it does introduce the two Irishmen who were instrumental in the writing of *Midas* – the key work in the genre and its key musical characteristic.

The Irishmen are Lord Mornington and Kane O'Hara, co-founders in 1757 of the Musical Academy of Dublin. Lord Mornington, Garret Wellesley (1735–81), was educated at Trinity College Dublin; in 1764, he was appointed the institution's first professor of music. A composer and a violinist, he is known today mainly as a composer of glees, which appear in most collections published in Britain and Ireland. Kane O'Hara (1711/12–82) was also a product of Trinity, graduating in 1735. *Midas* was his first publicly performed work; after its success, he moved to London where his other burlettas – *The Golden Pippin*, *The Two Misers* and *April-Day* were written, performed and published.

Midas, the key work, was first performed in Dublin on 22 January 1762 (see no. 45 in tables that follow), but it is recorded as being staged at the private theatre belonging to William Brownlow in April 1760. As O'Keeffe's narrative suggests, the idea was to work up O'Hara's 'slight

---

[1] John O'Keeffe, *Recollections of the Life of John O'Keeffe*, 2 vols. (London: Henry Colburn, 1826), 1: 53.

pastoral' into a piece that would compete with the Italian opera troupe that was visiting Dublin, with a view to providing competition for the Italian burlettas which, wrote the author of the preface to the London edition, 'had been blended with the exhibitions of the Theatre, and almost triumphed over the best productions in our language'.[2] O'Hara's contribution to the project was the text, a take-off of the mythological character of Midas, best known for having a touch that turned everything to gold. However, according to Ovid, Midas was present at the musical competition in which Pan competed with Apollo and found 'his ears transformed into long, shaggy grey ones for his foolishness in preferring Pan's rustic notes to Apollo's ethereal harmonies.'[3] The latter story is the one O'Hara uses as his point of departure.

The scenes of *Midas*, it was claimed, were 'written in the true spirit of the mock-heroic':

> BURLESQUE, in all times, for the stage of ATHENS down to the DRAGON of WANTLEY, has been esteemed one of the provinces of the Drama. Its humour principally consists in making dignified personages raise in our minds trite and ordinary ideas, or else in giving trivial objects a serious air of gravity and importance.[4]

As indeed we find in O'Hara's text, which opens as Apollo is drummed out of heaven by Jupiter, having been detected in an amour; falling to earth, he disguises himself as a shepherd, Pol, and immediately makes advances to Farmer Sileno's two daughters. Midas, already in love with one of them, organises a singing contest between Pol and Pan, awarding the first prize to Pan. Pol reveals himself to be Apollo and claps a pair of ass's ears on the unfortunate Midas.

The text has been panned by Pat O'Connell, who has remarked that O'Hara's 'verse rarely rises above clever doggerel'; it was, though, clearly doggerel that the public liked.[5] At least up to a point: David Erskine, writing in his 1764 *Companion to the Play-house*, goes to the heart of the problem believing that the function of burlesque in turning '*great* Things to Farce' is lost here, because the 'Heathen Deities' are 'ridiculous enough in themselves, and too absurd for burlesque'.[6] *Midas* was O'Hara's one big

---

[2] Kane O'Hara, *Midas: An English Burletta* (London: G. Kearsley et al., 1764), 'To the Reader'.

[3] Commentary on Melchior Meier's Apollo and Marsyas and the Judgment of Midas. Engraving, 1581. Metropolitan Museum of Art, New York, 41.1.210.

[4] O'Hara, 'To the Reader'.

[5] Pat O'Connell, 'O'Hara, Kane [Kean]' in *The Encyclopaedia of Music in Ireland*, ed. Harry White and B. Boydell, 2 vols. (Dublin: University College Dublin Press, 2013), 2: 765–66.

[6] David Erskine Baker, *The Companion to the Play-house: Or, An Historical Account of All the Dramatic Writers (and Their Works) that Have Appeared in Great Britain and Ireland, from the Commencement*

hit; although it had a poor reception when first performed in London in 1764, it did (when cut from a full three acter) turn into a successful two-act afterpiece (no. 42). The popularity of this two-act version was long lived. Performed all over the country, it had reached Boston, Massachusetts, by at least 1791, and in a final flourish, it was – of all things – performed in 1857 in New York.

The genre's key characteristic, nailed by O'Keeffe, was that the score was largely *assembled* rather than newly *composed*, a procedure that not only allowed the use of old favourites but also made possible textual and musical substitutions. One characteristic of the numbers is that they had elaborate Italian introductions, a characteristic which was emphasised by the simplicity of the tunes that accompanied the texts. The use of Italian music and classical plots has caused the burletta to be described as a satire on opera seria,[7] but in truth, it has the characteristics of the English masque.[8] These references have led to the claim that the work was a stylistic bridge between ballad and comic opera, although it is not clear why such a bridge might be considered important. O'Hara himself was later to nod to some further kinship with the Italian intermezzo; in the introduction to his *April-Day*, he wrote:

> I adopt the laconic Dialogue of Italian Burletta in order to comprise my fable within the narrow limits of late prescribed by the taste of your audiences. This is short enough to admit their being indulged with some popular Petite Piece after it.[9]

The French 'petite piece' was, of course, the English afterpiece, which could be any work of a shortish nature used after the main event of the evening, a slot in which not only *April Day* but *Midas* too would have the greatest success.[10] In whatever length it was, though, it was sung throughout, a characteristic that would become vital during discussions of the form during the Regency, as we shall see later.

---

    of Our Theatrical Exhibitions, Down to the Present Year 1764, 2 vols. (London: Printed for T. Becket and P.A. Dehondt, 1764), 1: 'Additional Plays'.

[7] Nicholas Temperley, 'Burletta', in *The New Grove Dictionary of Music and Musicians*, ed. Stanley Sadie, 29 vols. (London: Macmillan, 2001), 4: 634.

[8] Roger Fiske, *English Theatre Music in the Eighteenth Century* (Oxford: Clarendon Press, 1986), 318, and Michael Burden, 'The English Theatre Masque 1690–1800', 2 vols. (PhD diss, University of Edinburgh, 1991), 1.

[9] Kane O'Hara, *April-Day, a Burletta* (London: G. Kearsley, 1777), 'Extract of a Letter from the Author … ', vi–vii.

[10] Michael Burden, 'Afterpiece' in *The New Grove Dictionary of Opera*, ed. Stanley Sadie, 4 vols. (London: Macmillan, 1992), 1: 33–4; and also 'Mainpiece', 3: 156.

O'Keeffe also gives an account of the Italian burlettas to which Mornington's patronage is said to have been a response, and which are thought to be the first Italian operas sung in Dublin.[11] The general characteristics of the form were described convincingly by Edward Wright, who on visiting the theatre in Venice noted the following:

> The *Intermezzi* (or intermediate Performances) which they have in some of their smaller Theatres between the Acts, are very comical in their way, which is somewhat low, not much unlike the Farces we see sometimes on our Stage. They laugh, scold, imitate other Sounds, as the cracking of a Whip, the rumbling of Chariot Wheels, and all to Musick.[12]

These were the sorts of lively pieces that the Italian company brought to the city in 1761.[13] The troupe was managed by the singer Antonio Minelli and consisted mainly of the D'Amici family, an arrangement that would last until the performances beginning on 29 January 1762.[14] The company performed those works found at nos 43 to 51, with the competing *Midas* at no. 45. The season was supported by subscription 'for performing Burlettas or Italian Comic Operas at the Theatre in Smock Alley for the ensuing Season. There shall be forty Representations during the Season.' The subscription – 'without which this undertaking cannot possibly be carried on' – allowed for places to be kept in boxes, pit or lattices, and those wishing to 'encourage the subscription' were 'desired to send their Names to Latouche's Bank'.[15] The uptake was not fast, and the company had arrived before it was filled; there must have been a period of worry for all concerned, since the burlettas could not begin until there were sufficient subscribers on the books.[16] However, the season did get underway, and the announcements make it clear that the programme also included two brackets of dancing by named performers: John Tioli, Giuseppe Genovisi, Marianna Ricci and Vincenza Lucchi.[17] The presence of dancing confirms the notion that this season was a serious effort not just to perform the small burlettas or 'intermezzi' but also to promote a season organised in the Continental manner; they did later appear occasionally as afterpieces.[18]

---

[11] T. J. Walsh, *Opera in Dublin 1705–1797: The Social Scene* (Dublin: A. Figgis, 1973), 126.

[12] Edward Wright, *Some Observations Made in Travelling Through France, Italy, &c. In the Years 1720, 1721, and 1722*, 2 vols. (London: Tho. Ward and E. Wicksteed, 1730), 1: 85.

[13] 1760, according to O'Keeffe, *Recollections*, 1: 52.

[14] *Faulkner's Dublin Journal*, 26–30 January 1762.   [15] Ibid., 6–10 October 1761.

[16] Ibid., 5–8 December 1761.

[17] John C. Greene, ed., *Theatre in Dublin 1745–1820: A Calendar of Performances*, 6 vols (Bethlehem: Lehigh University Press, 2011), 1: 752; 19 December 1761.

[18] See, for example, Smock Alley's performance of *Cymbeline* on 3 May 1762, which included La *Cascina* as an afterpiece.

The company's most important members were Signora Domenico D'Amici, who 'was most captivating in the song where the ring is held over her head by the Squire', and her father, who, O'Keeffe declared, was

> the best comedian I have ever seen before, or since. His acting in a burletta, where he personated a physician, a beau, and a terrified blacksmith, the latter in a night scene with a lantern, was wonderfully fine in the diversity of character.[19]

As this suggests, the quality of the acting appears to have carried the drama, rather than any intrinsic merit of plot or music. When it was all over, the company departed after giving two performances on 22 and 26 May 1762 of *La Partenza; or The Farewell*, a work whose title nodded to Metastasio's famous text,[20] but whose content consisted of 'the favourite Airs in the [season's] Burlettas'.[21]

The context outlined here has, however, led to an emphasis on O'Hara's contribution, a narrative in which his 'musical and lyrical genius brought the English burletta into being in 1762'.[22] However, the genre's form and style we now attribute to O'Hara seem to have existed in London in the late 1750s. On 4 February 1758, the publication of a collection called *The Polite Songster* – 'Pieces of Wit and Humour … entirely free from the general and too just Complaint of Immodesty' – was announced in the press, which included an extract of a 'humouresque Burlesque Burletta'.[23] The extract that appeared in the *Songster* was headed '*Sung at* COMUS'S COURT *by the Choice Spirits*'. According to Thomas Busby, Comus's Court, a vocal club, was inspired by the 'simply and manly music' Thomas Arne wrote for his popular setting of *Comus*, the performance of which 'gave rise to a variety of convivial and vocal associations, several of which were dignified with the appellation of *Comus's Court*'.[24] Another of these associations was apparently The Choice Spirits; the formulation of the heading used in the *Songster* suggests some inter-club event. The author of the 'Burlesque Burletta', who was named in the press but not in the *Songster*, was the polymath George Alexander Stevens (1710–84), who, according to Baker's

---

[19] O'Keeffe, *Recollections*, 1: 52–53.

[20] For some discussion of Metastasio's text, see Gillen D'Arcy Wood, *Romanticism and Music Culture in Britain, 1770–1840: Virtue and Virtuosity* (Cambridge: Cambridge University Press, 2010), chap. 3.

[21] *Faulkner's Dublin Journal*, 11–15 and 22–25 May 1762.

[22] Phyllis T. Dircks, *The Eighteenth-Century English Burletta* (Victoria, BC: English Literary Studies, 1999), 40; see also Margaret F. Maxwell, 'Olympus at Billingsgate: The Burlettas of Kane O'Hara', *Educational Theatre Journal*, 15.2 (1963): 130–35.

[23] *Whitehall Evening Post or London Intelligencer*, 2–4 February 1758.

[24] Thomas Busby, *Concert Room and Orchestra Anecdotes of Music and Musicians, Ancient and Modern*, 3 vols. (London: Clementi and Co., 1825), 3: 9.

Biographia Dramatica, counted Comus's Court among the convivial societies to which he belonged.[25] Stevens was an 'actor, lecturer, author,
manager, [and] puppeteer',[26] with his early acting career spent in the
provinces and in London. He is now best known for *The Lecture on
Heads*, a remarkable one-man show which he premiered on 26 April 1764
at the Haymarket.[27]

But from 1751 to 1753, Stevens worked in Dublin, where he acted at the
Smock Alley Theatre and founded a club with Isaac Sparks, 'The Lord
Chief Joker', called the Nassau Court. The club's meetings were held in the
Inn in Nassau Street and seem to have discussed subjects of humour in a
mock-heroic manner.[28] It was part of the proliferation of convivial (and
other) clubs in the second half of the eighteenth century which offered
both intellectual engagement and 'a chance to converse and carouse';[29]
they reflected a number of changes in Irish society including an increase in
the number of newspapers, the rise of the coffee-house culture and 'the
intellectual justification provided by the Enlightenment for indulging in
sensual, and most importantly, natural, pleasures of the table and the
flesh'.[30] Stevens also produced a range of small comic satires from about
1751, including the 1753 *Distress upon Distress*, an 'Heroi-Comi-Parodi-
Tragedi-Farcical Burlesque'; it was not intended for the stage, but it
exhibits Stevens's sound understanding of theatrical genres and an ability
to manipulate them for his own agenda. Stevens's skills are evident in the
fragment of the apparently tautologically titled 'burlesque burletta'.
Dircks, in *The Eighteenth-Century English Burletta*, suggests four main
characteristics of the genre: a plot relying on a single joke; stock plots
and type characters; a reliance on what in other contexts was considered
exaggerated acting; and an all-sung, operatic-style score, the use of which
automatically attracted ridicule through the juxtaposition of operatic
music to the low plots.[31] But as *Midas* exemplifies, the 'stock plots' in the
early years were classical stories, so much so that Fiske refers to this group

[25] David Erskine Baker, *Biographia Dramatica; or, A Companion to the Playhouse*, 2 vols. (London: Longman, Hurst et al., 1812), 1: 629.

[26] 'George Alexander Stevens' in *A Biographical Dictionary of Actors, Actresses, Musicians, Dancers, Managers and Other Stage Personnel in London, 1660–1800*, ed. Philip H. Highfill et al., 16 vols. (Carbondale: Southern Illinois University Press, 1973–93), 14: 220.

[27] For a full account of the lecture, including bibliographical details, see Gerald Kahn, *George Alexander Stevens and The Lecture on Heads* (Athens: University of Georgia Press, 1984).

[28] *Pennsylvania Packet*, 20 April 1785.

[29] Martyn J. Powell, '"Beef, Claret and Communication": Convivial Clubs in the Public Sphere, 1750–1800', in *Clubs and Societies in Eighteenth-Century Ireland*, ed. James Kelly and Martyn J. Powell (Dublin: Four Courts Press, 2010), 353–71, 354.

[30] Powell, 'Beef, Claret and Communication', 353.   [31] Dircks, *English Burletta*, 80–81.

of works as 'classical' burlettas.[32] And as already mentioned, the work has two characteristics in common with O'Hara's later burletta, the notion of a classical parody and an all-sung structure.[33] Further, the principal number in the extract, the duet, is a da capo number in doggerel Italian. The defining characteristics of the burletta, then, defined it before O'Hara was on the scene, and they appear to have come via Stevens's omnivorous approach to the genres that he encountered and his avid interest in satire.

In this relaxed approach to plot and genre, we can see the coming together of some strands of the Enlightenment, as mentioned above by Powell. The stories were definitely realistic and bourgeois, the characters when not themselves bourgeois, embodied bourgeois themes and motivations, and whatever lessons were advanced, it was very much in the notion of 'instruction with delight.' There was not room in the genre for the convoluted stories of earlier opera, and when the tales of the superstitious appeared only to be mocked and parodied in works such *Le Devin du Village*, or, indeed, *Midas*. The simplicity of the text in the vernacular, and the simplicity of the music in an uncomplicated gallant style, combined to produce a 'natural' genre which, while it never reached the aesthetic heights of true opera buffa, was nevertheless accessible and entertaining.

With these possibilities in mind, we can return to the burletta with a somewhat modified view of its origins and influences. There have been other scholarly considerations in a variety of contexts including those by Dircks, Fiske and Joseph O'Donohue,[34] and while covering some of the same ground, the direction of this chapter is to look particularly at the interplay between the Italian and English repertories in the two capitals of Dublin and London; it is evident that the story of the burletta suggests that the history of the evolution of theatrical genre more generally in the eighteenth century must pay attention to the interplay, in some ways symbiotic, of these two important cities of theatrical production.

The Burletta in London before *Midas*

The Italian burletta in London before *Midas* came in three groups. One group at the end of the 1740s was staged by the company of John Francis

---

[32] Fiske, *English Theatre Music*, 318–22.   [33] *The Polite Songster* (London: J. Ross, 1758), 256.
[34] Joseph Donohue, 'Burletta and the Early Nineteenth-Century English Theatre', *Nineteenth Century Theatre Research*, 1 (1973): 29–51.

Crosa; these constituted some of the first comic operas in London (nos 1–
10).[35] The second group consists of those works performed in the early
1750s at Covent Garden by Giuseppe Giordani's company (nos 13–17, and
22–23), and by a second anonymous company (nos 18–21). The third group
consists of those works performed in English translation at the Marylebone
Gardens in the late 1750s, mostly in translations by the composer Storace
and John Trusler, junior, the son of the Gardens' proprietor (nos 24–28).

The Crosa company, brought in from abroad by the then impresario of
the King's Theatre, Francesco Vanneschi, undertook two seasons, those of
1748–49 and 1749–50, both of which consisted entirely of burlettas.
Towards the end of his second season, he did stage two *opere serie* 'to
endeavour to please the quality' (nos 11–12), a euphemism for an 'attempt
to stave off bankruptcy', but Crosa's insolvency, from which he escaped in
his socks, saw him eventually apprehended in Amsterdam and brought
back to London. After Crosa's departure from the scene, the burletta
disappeared from the programmes of the Opera House, which also then
closed until the 1753–54 season. Crosa's programmes were remembered by
Horace Walpole as 'a good set … which did not take at all', confirming
what is clear from the performance statistics and the collapse of the
season.[36]

The second group of Italian burlettas that appeared in London (nos 3–7)
was staged at Covent Garden; Walpole also saw these and commented,
'We abound in diversions, which flourish exceedingly on the demise of
politics. There are no less than five operas every week, three of which are
burlettas.' The staging of these at Covent Garden was somewhat unexpected, since the theatre was then a playhouse with a mixed programme of
works in English. And there was clearly some expectation, based on Crosa's
failure, that these burlettas might have a negative reception: '[B]ut these
being at the playhouse and at play prices, the people instead of resenting it
as was expected, are transported with them, call them their own operas, and
I will not swear that they do not take them for English operas.'[37]

[35] See Richard G. King and Saskia Willaert, 'Giovanni Francesco Crosa and the First Italian Comic
Operas in London, Brussels, and Amsterdam, 1748–50', *Journal of the Royal Musical Association*, 118.2
(1993): 246–75, and Michael Burden, *Impresario and Diva: Regina Mingotti's Years at the King's
Theatre, London* (Farnham: Ashgate, 2013), for some account of Crosa's activities.
[36] Walpole to Horace Mann, 28 January 1754; W. S. Lewis, Warren Hunting Smith and George L.
Lam, eds., *Horace Walpole's Correspondence*, 48 vols. (London: Oxford University Press, 1960),
20: 410.
[37] Ibid.

The performance of the pieces in the playhouse context seems to have engendered a completely different appreciation of the operas, suggesting yet again that the perception of the opera was that it was not a place of frivolity, but a place for serious, if not learned, entertainment. The opera, trying to establish itself for the first season after the Crosa company 'In Homage to Majesty, let the KING'S THEATRE in the *Hay-Market* take the Lead, where the foreign Representations of NERONE, a Medley; ENRICO, the Story of *Tancrede* and *Sigismunda*: and *Didone Abandonnata*, complain that neither the Receipts nor Applause have been violent.'[38]

As with the D'Amici family company, the success of the performances relied on the acting skills of the players, in particular those of Nicolina Giordani, also known as La Spiletta, a name derived from her role in *Gli amanti gelosi*. Walpole described her as having 'veracity and variety of humour',[39] while Arthur Murphy concluded she was 'an excellent comic actress'.[40] But it is Paul Hiffernan – Irish journalist and friend of Goldsmith – who has left us the clearest description of her acting style with all its quirks and affectations:

> *Burlettas (Italian* musical Absurdities) at Covent-Garden have pleas'd, and chiefly thro' the Performance of one Actress. She plays off with inexhaustable Spirits all musical Evolutions of the Face and Brows; while in her Eye wantons a studied Archness, and pleasing Malignity. Her Voice has Strength and Scope sufficient; has neither too much of the feminine, nor an Inclining to the male. Her gestures are very varying; her Transitions quick and easy. Some over-nice-Critics, forgetting, or not knowing the Meaning of the Word Burletta, cry that her Manner is outré. Wou'd she not be faulty were it otherwise? The Thing chargeable to her is (perhaps) too great a Luxuriance of comic Tricks; which (an austere Censor wou'd say) border on unlaced Lasciviousness, and extravagant Petulance of Action.[41]

This is echoed by Thomas Gray, who claimed that when 'her first air ravish'd everybody; they forgot their prejudices; they forgot that they did not understand a word of the language; they enter'd into all the humour of the part, made her repeat all her songs, & continued their transports, their laughter, & applause to the end of the piece.'[42]

---

[38] Paul Hiffernan, *The Tuner* 1 (1754): 16.
[39] Walpole to Richard Bentley, 19 December 1753; *Horace Walpole's Correspondence* (1973), 35: 410.
[40] *Gray's Inn Journal*, 22 December 1753.   [41] Paul Hiffernan, *The Tuner* 1 (1754), 17.
[42] Gray to Francesco Algarotti, 9 September 1763, in *The Works of Thomas Gray*, ed. John Mitford (London: J. Mawman, 1816), 2: 420.

As Walpole had remarked in jest (but only half), 'I will not swear that they do not take them for English operas.' The Giordani troupe departed at the end of the 1753–54 season, but Covent Garden appears then to have imported some Italian singers who undertook three burlettas in the next season (nos 18–20). The performers included the newly arrived Francesco Baratti (*fl.* 1754–55) and the Crosa Company singer Eugenia Mellini (*fl.* 1748–55), both of whom took the named roles in *La serva padrona* in a performance staged '*For the Benefit of the MANAGERS of the Italian Company, which play'd the BURLETTAS at Covent-Garden Theatre, this Season*'.[43] In fact, it was claimed that the management of the company had been seduced into bringing it over, only to have the still-anonymous promoter abandon them in a welter of debts and difficulties. At the beginning of February 1755, the Giordani company returned for two shows at the Haymarket Theatre, and again in January 1756, with two performances at Covent Garden (nos 22–23). And that was the end, for the moment, of the Italian burletta in the London theatres.

The third group consists of the small clutch of pieces performed between 1758 and 1761 by Dominica Seratina (or Saratina) and Frederick Charles Reinhold, mostly at the Marylebone Gardens (nos 24–28). All the works were of Italian origin, and all were translated into English by Stephen Storace, advertising himself as Stefano Storace,[44] and John Trusler, junior. John Trusler, senior, was the owner of the gardens, and also the father of Elizabeth, his eldest daughter who was married to Storace. Trusler, senior, records that he 'translated, from the Italian, several burlettas, and adapted them to the English stage' and that he 'had the profit of the printed books there sold'.[45] As we might expect, *La serva padrona* was the most successful of these:

> Sga Seratina and Mr Reinhold have distinguished themselves surprisingly; and though this entertainment is performed in the English language, clearly proves that it is in the Power of an Englishman to excel even the Italians in that kind of performance; Sga Seratina (though an Italian) expresses the English Dialect with all the Graces, and proper Expressions which that kind of performance requires.[46]

[43] *Public Advertiser*, 22 January 1755.
[44] Mollie Sands, *The Eighteenth-Century Pleasure Gardens of Marylebone* (London: Society for Theatre Research, 1987), 37–41.
[45] John Trusler, *Memoirs of the Life of Rev. Dr. Trusler* (Bath: John Browne, 1806), 567.
[46] *Public Advertiser*, 27 June 1758.

The Favourite Songs from the burletta were published with the Italian underlaid beneath the English. The volume was brought out by James Oswald, the Scottish composer whose publishing career is still ill understood, but who in the 1750s seems to have subverted John Walsh's grip on the *Favourite Songs* label to publish a number of Italian aria collections from the opera. An attempt was made to perform the work elsewhere, and a new version was prepared that claimed to have a new act, a new character, and 'be as it was when it was performed in Naples'. However, Marylebone Gardens moved to protect its property; the first performance, due to be given on 12 January 1759, was 'stopp'd by particular desire of the Lord Chamberlain'. But the same announcement continued 'but as a great many of the Nobility and Quality are very desirous to see this entertainment, it will soon be presented at another theatre'.[47] Those who wanted to see it clearly had some influence and managed to prevail on the owners to be allowed to give performances 'By Authority, for three nights only'.[48]

The outstanding success of the English *La serva padrona* at Marylebone was followed by *Il cisebeo alla moda; or, The Modish Coquet* in the setting by Baldassare Galuppi, and another work attributed to Pergolesi, *La strateggemma; or The Stratagem*. The performances of these burlettas took place out of doors, 'on a small stage in the garden with applause';[49] we discover that despite that the fact that 'the weather has been bad', the performances were 'generally to numerous and polite Company'.[50] As the weather became colder, the performances moved into the ballroom 'being elegantly fitted up for that Purpose'.[51] And although it was an exceptional event – Prince Edward and Princess Amelia were visiting – there are reports that the burletta, which started at 7 p.m. and was over by 8 p.m., was performed a second time.[52] The works, then, were short enough to be repeated should the company be enthusiastic enough or grand enough to justify the management's organising a repeat.

A further performance by the same cast was given at Drury Lane of a version of J. A. Hasse's setting of *Il tutore* (*Lucilla e Pandolfo*), written for Naples in 1730; this was unsuccessful, but some comment was offered on the issue of translation:

---

[47] Ibid., 12 January 1759.   [48] *The London Stage 1660–1800*, 4: 2, 718.
[49] Trusler, *Memoirs of the Life of Rev. Dr. Trusler*, 567.   [50] *Public Advertiser*, 2 August 1758.
[51] Ibid., 12 September 1758.   [52] Ibid., 6 July 1758.

> Those who understand musical Compositions, and the Nature of such an Undertaking, will be sensible of the Difficulty of finding such *English* Words as would not prove too stubborn for Musick, originally adapted to the *Italian* Language. ... The Designer, who's an *Italian* [hopes] that the *English* Language is not altogether incompatible with *Italian* Harmony.[53]

These sentiments of apologia were frequently expressed in the eighteenth century, but this is the only time they appear in relation to these early 'Englished' burlettas, perhaps because the performance was for a grander playhouse, rather than one for the pleasure gardens.[54] But the text included the remark that what the translation required 'was not so much as Elegance of Stile, as a Finesse of Syllables', a comment that acknowledged that the essence of the work was not high flown sentiments, but entertaining patter. The same cast went on perform the Marylebone Gardens stagings of *La serva padrona* and *La stratagemma* with two more new works – *The Ridiculous Guardian*, with music by Hasse, and *The Cocquette*, with music by Galuppi – at the Haymarket in the summer of 1761 (nos 29–32); however, after this, works of this type translated from the Italian (other than versions of *La serva padrona*) seemed to fall from favour.

But something called an Italian 'burletta' did make a return. The following season, against all the odds, the Opera House once more managed to rise phoenix-like from the ashes of financial mismanagement; by 1760, it was in the hands of the singer Colomba Mattei. And when her season was announced later that month, Mattei produced one of the most elaborate opera advertisements yet placed in the eighteenth-century press, for it not only laid out the repertory but also matched the singers to the genres. She announced her undertaking direction of the Italian serious operas and burlettas for the ensuing winter, promised the performance of them for the best advantage of the public, and listed the members of the company she had engaged:

> *For Serious Operas*: herself, Philippo Elisi (the first singer in Italy), Gaetano Quilice (tenor), Angiola Calori (second woman), Giovanni Sorbelloni (second man), and a new singer for the lowest character. For the Burlettas: Sga Paganini (the first female character and the foremost in Italy), Gaetano Quilici (the first man), Sga Eleradi (second woman), Paganini (second man), Signor N. N. (third man), Angiola Caroli and Sorbelloni (to perform the serious parts in the Burlettas). Dancers: Mlle Asselin (first woman dancer), Gheradi (first dancer of the men, and ballet

---

[53] *Il tutore; or, The Tutor* (London: G. Woodfall, 1759), 2: 'Advertisement'.

[54] The claimed 'designer' was not Italian, but Hasse himself, with his Christian name Italianised as 'Adolfo' on the title page; he did not, however, visit London, and the attribution seems fictitious.

master), famed both in the serious and comic as well as for his invention as for exercises in dancing. There will also be other comic dancers, and figures both for the serious operas and burlettas.[55]

And as can be seen at the top of the advertisement, Mattei reintroduced what she called 'the burletta' (nos 33–38). Her use of the term 'burletta' in her advertisements may have been a desire to use a genre description that her potential audience would understand, and Walpole again used it: 'We have at present a rage for burlettas. … If pleasures can tempt people to stay in town, there will be a harvest all summer; operas at the little theatre in the Haymarket, and plays at Drury Lane.'[56] But he should have known better, for what Mattei in fact promoted were largely full-length Italian comic operas; the burletta (in Italian) did not return to the Opera House.[57]

Codas – London and Dublin

There are codas to this sequence of events in both London and Dublin, codas that illustrate the cross-over in performances and repertory between the two capitals. And if the present example is taken as a case study of possible theatrical interactions, those codas also suggest that much might be learned from extended studies of this kind. In London, in the 1762–63 season, two of the Amicis arrived from Dublin; these were the singers whose performances inspired the development of *Midas* for public consumption. Mattei employed both of them, and both sang in the four comic operas promoted that season. But as O'Keeffe himself mentioned, Anna D'Amicis also made her mark in *opera seria*, and as her arrival coincided with that of J. C. Bach, she played roles in his first two London operas, *Zanaida* and *Orione; o sia, Diana vendicata*. Both singers appear to have then departed the London scene, possibly because when Mattei's management gave way to that of Giardini, the programme then consisted entirely of *opera seria*. Meanwhile in Dublin, Minelli, who had formerly managed the D'Amicis, reappeared. He seems to have spent the intervening year in Edinburgh where he teamed up with Mauro and Rosa Guerini or Guirini, and now he promoted the Guerinis in a number of performances of five burlettas at the Crow Street Theatre at the end of the 1763–64 season (nos

[55] *London Evening Post*, 26–28 August 1760.
[56] Walpole to Horace Mann, 14 May 1761. *Horace Walpole's Correspondence*, ed. Lewis et al., 21: 506.
[57] See Saskia Willaert, 'Italian Comic Opera at the King's Theatre in the 1760s: The Role of the Buffi', in *Music in Eighteenth-Century Britain*, ed. David Wyn-Jones (Aldershot: Ashgate, 2000), 17–71, for some account of Mattei's seasons.

52–56).[58] The company, recorded in Edinburgh and Newcastle in 1762–63 season, and then in York and Manchester before Christmas 1763, disappears before its appearance in Dublin. But by June of 1764, the company advertised it had run out of money for in promoting what was in effect a benefit performance (no. 56), the Guerinis asked for 'the Protection and assistance of the Nobility and Gentry to raise a Little Money to enable them to undertake their Voyage and Journey'.[59] Minelli disappeared, but the Guerinis were still in Dublin the next season, when they sang with the newly arrived Giordani burletta troupe. The Giordanis had disappeared from the scene after their performances in London in January 1756 but now appeared in Dublin, where on 23 November 1764 they performed *Gli amanti gelosi* and *Don Fulmione* at the Smock Alley Theatre (nos 57–58). The company also appeared in the 1765–66 season, and then again, they, too, disappeared. One member of the family, the son Tomasso, stayed behind in Ireland and, to quote Highfill, was prominent in Dublin musical circles.[60]

And O'Hara's almost unwitting influence – one neither particularly English nor Irish in character – on the history of drama came about by accident. In 1780, Henry Fielding's burlesque tragedy *Tom Thumb* was, apparently, revived at Covent Garden. However, it was not Fielding's burlesque that was staged, but a version by O'Hara, one announced as a 'burletta'. As discussed earlier, the burletta consisted of pre-written tunes linked together by recitative; that is, they were all-sung works, a different process and resultant genre entirely from Fielding's. George Colman the Younger, dramatist, manager, and later John Larpent's successor as Examiner of Plays, claimed that O'Hara's burlesque had been 'inadvertently announced by the managers … as a burletta', presumably because of O'Hara's association with what were then being promoted as burlettas.[61] It was now open season; rather than commissioning new works, the minor theatres added music to existing works on almost any comic subject.

The definition of a burletta became unexpectedly important in the Regency, for it was a circumstance that gave the minor theatres a precedent for a way around the 1737 Licensing Act, which had restricted their repertory to pieces with music. In 1824, Colman told the Lord

[58] Sybil Rosenfeld, *Foreign Theatrical Companies in Great Britain in the 17th and 18th Centuries* (London: Society for Theatre Research, 1955), 37–38.
[59] *Faulkner's Dublin Journal*, 9–12 June 1764.
[60] 'Tommaso Giordani', in Highfill et al., *A Biographical Dictionary*, 6: 220.
[61] Richard Brinsley Peake, *Memoirs of the Colman Family, Including Their Correspondence*, 2 vols. (London: Richard Bentley, 1841), 2: 398–99.

Chamberlain that a burletta must have at least five or six songs 'where the songs make a natural part of the piece, *and not forced into an acting piece*, to qualify it as a burletta': 'A drama in rhyme, and which is entirely musical; a short comic piece, consisting of recitative and singing, wholly accompanied, more or less, by the Orchestra.'[62] Colman follows this with a list of works that includes all of O'Hara's outputs, plus Arnold's *The Portrait*. All these, he claimed, came 'under the description of rhyme, recitative, vocal and instrumental music, with nothing spoken'. His only exception is *Tom Thumb*, the mistakenly announced revision, to which just a few songs had been added while Charles Dibdin wrote:

> Burletta, properly speaking, consist only of recitative and air, and should be performed only by a small number of Characters, without change of Scene; although *Midas*, and some other pieces of that description have been styled Burlettas; but I think as Dramatic Dialogue, and Change of Scene, being used in them, disqualifies them from being so termed.[63]

Colman's commentary, however, also gives some indication of the way the definition and performance changed over time:

> They first performed it according to the definition I have just given. Then they made their recitative appear just prose, but the actor running one line into another, and slurring over the rhyme; soon after, a harpsichord was touched now and then, as an accompaniment to the actor; sometimes once in a minute; then once in five minutes; at last not at all; till the process of time, musical and rhyming dialogue has now been abandoned; and a burletta now, if it be one, is certainly an old friend with quite a new face.[64]

According to Colman, the matter was put to the lawyers – whether one can believe that the Privy Council and the Crown lawyers were involved as claimed is another matter – who replied that 'they could not tell', and although Colman assumed that they would consult the 'veterans of the stage', they seem to have worked themselves into a knot of difficulty over the whole matter and ended up in the position of the ancient philosopher who said 'all I know is that I know nothing'.[65] However, the minor theatres persisted, to the (claimed) detriment of original work, the income of the patent houses, and the overall quality of the dramatic works produced in London during this period, and the issue was raised during the hearings

[62] Peake, 2: 398.
[63] Charles Dibdin, *Professional and Literary Memoirs of Charles Dibdin the Younger* (London: Society for Theatre Research, 1956).
[64] Peake, 2: 399.   [65] Ibid., 398.

under of the Select Committee on Dramatic Literature, during which
seven different witnesses were asked to define the term, and did so, with
a variety of results.

Conclusion

Thus far, things seem relatively clear. On one hand, there were the Italian
burlettas performed by Italians in Italian companies. Although the works
have the size and character of Italian intermezzos, they are usually performed on their own on the bill. On the other hand, there are clear claims
for both English and Irish responses to their success. The first claimed
English response was one of translation and repackaging; in this process, *La
serva padrona* became *The Servant Mistress* (no. 24). The first Irish response
was, of course, *Midas*, O'Hara's challenge to the Amici Company's performances. This spawned the new but limited genre of the classical burlesque as its subject, an exemplar for O'Hara's subsequent works.

However, this supposed interplay is troubling in its neatness. The translation of *La serva padrona*, for example, was precipitated not by the desire to
create an English form but was also an attempt to exploit a popular
performance in Italian from the Opera House by taking it to the populace
at Marylebone Gardens. A columnist in the *Public Advertiser* noted that 'the
Uncommon Applause of the new Entertainment … has excited the curiosity
of a great many of the Nobility and Gentry that had never seen Marybone
before.'[66] And it further occupies a position of quite different significance to
that given to it by Dircks, for it was the first complete Italian opera to make
this move from the elite Opera House to the pleasure gardens. Once there,
the opera continued to appear on the bills at Marylebone, with performances
of a new version arranged by Samuel Arnold from 1770 to 1774 (no. 61). It
was also briefly the subject of some competition with Ranelagh Gardens,
which in 1770 concurrently promoted a version by Charles Dibdin (no. 60).
There were also two more English versions, both prepared in London by
Irishmen; Isaac Bickerstaff prepared a version titled *He Wou'd If He Cou'd;
or, An Old Fool Worse Than Any* for Drury Lane in 1771 (no. 62), while John
O'Keeffe worked up another as *The Maid's the Mistress*, for Dominica
Seratina's benefit at Covent Garden (no. 64).

What does emerge is that the burletta as an all-sung Italian form does
not survive either the arrival of fully fledged Italian comic opera in 1760 or
of the burletta in English exemplified by *Midas* in 1764. After Mattei's

---

[66] *Public Advertiser*, 27 June 1758.

season, almost the only performances of any Italian burletta (in Italian) in London were those of *La serva padrona* (nos 63, 65 and 66), once as a Royal Command performance, and twice in the setting by Paisiello. What stops the genre gaining traction in London in the form of the Continental intermezzo is the structure of the programme at the King's Theatre, which had a ballet at the end of the evening, something that the audiences would not do without. There was no appetite whatsoever for an evening of *opera seria* interspersed with comic scenes.

And contrary to what is usually stated, the large claims made for *Midas* as a new genre both by its creators and subsequent criticism seem to be both open to question in terms of its origin and unrealised in its influence. Looking at the table again, we can see the premiere of Midas (no. 45) surrounded by performances of the Italian burlettas at the other house. So far, so good, but there were no Dublin spin-offs of O'Hara's work, so the notion that a new and competitive native genre had suddenly emerged (one that appears not to have been either new or native) as planned by O'Hara, Mornington and Brownlow is misplaced. It is true, though, that it has historical importance in the codification of the genre as it came to be understood later in the century,[67] and it also illustrates the ease with which the genre – or at least, *Midas* – circulated between London and Dublin. This question of generic intervention and modification is also taken up in Helen Burke's (Chapter 10) and David O'Shaughnessy's (Chapter 7) chapters in this volume.

The reasons that *Midas* remained in the repertory at all seem to be down to two factors. Firstly, the compositional structure – if it can be called that – allowed the replacement of tunes and, indeed, song texts, suggesting that the work could easily be adapted to different casts. Moreover, both the words and tunes could reflect the current political climate, as happened with performances in London and Dublin during the Regency crisis. The songs in the *Improved Edition of ... Midas* of 1789 were billed as being 'adapted to the times', while another edition claimed to be a 'parody of the songs in the burletta of Midas' and sung by Her Majesty, the Prince of Wales, Mr Fox, Mr Pitt and others. The greatest number of performances of the work is clustered after this date, suggesting that this new-found popularity was based on the work's use as a vehicle for political satire. Secondly, the roles, particularly that of Apollo, seem to have unaccountably attracted a number of singers. In the eighteenth century, the role was played almost invariably by George Mattocks

---

[67] Frederick Elliott Warner, 'The Burletta in London's Minor Theatres During the Nineteenth Century, with a Handlist of Burlettas' (PhD diss., The Ohio State University, 1972), 20.

Figure 4.1 George Mattocks as Apollo in *Midas* 'Ah, happy Hours how fleeting',
engraving, (1778). Call #: M444 g-04. The University Library, University of Illinois
at Urbana-Champaign.

(Figure 4.1), who was a renowned player of comedy parts and crossed-dressed
roles, such as that of Achilles in *Achilles in Petticoats*. After 1800, Apollo began
to be played by women, in particular by Madame Vestris (Figure 4.2), also
known for her cross-dressing and elegant legs.[68] More surprisingly, it was sung
by the conservative English soprano Louisa Pyne, who chose it for her
farewell concert in New York in 1857.[69] And the desire to be pictured in
'character' – and one played by a major figure at that – seems to have been
responsible for the same portrait being used to represent both Miss Bartolozzi
(Madame Vestris) and Miss Featherstone in the role (Figures 4.3 and 4.4).
Perhaps the 'vigorously anti-traditional' nature of the genre's roles for women
noted by Suzanne Aspden[70] was made possible because the genre itself was so
'anti-traditional' and allowed even these grand performers to appear as a
burlesque Apollo carrying a harp.

[68] Rachel Cowgill, 'Re-Gendering the Libertine, or, the Taming of the Rake: Lucy Vestris as Don Giovanni
on the Early Nineteenth-Century London Stage', *Cambridge Opera Journal*, 10.1 (1998): 45–66.
[69] George Clinton Odell, *Annals of the New York Stage* (New York: Columbia University Press, 1931),
vol. 6.
[70] Suzanne Aspden, 'Review: *The Eighteenth-Century English Burletta* by Phyllis T. Dircks', *Music &
Letters*, 82.1 (2001): 112.

Figure 4.2 Madame Vestris as Apollo, etching, published in 'Fairburn's Portraits' by John Fairburn (early 19th century). Call #: S.2680–2009. Harry R. Beard Collection, Victoria & Albert Museum.

Figure 4.3 Miss Bartolozzi (Madame Vestris) as Apollo in *Midas* 'The Airs of a God she gives with delight/But who wouldn't wish her a woman by night', hand coloured etching (*c.* 1820). Call #: S.2566–2009. Harry R. Beard Collection, Victoria & Albert Museum.

Figure 4.4 Miss Featherstone as Apollo in *Midas*. Anonymous, engraving. Call #: F288ta-01. The University Library, University of Illinois at Urbana-Champaign.

Appendix

Tables: Interplay of comic operas and burlettas between London and Dublin, 1748–1800

CG   London: Theatre Royal Covent Garden
CHR   London: China Hall, Rotherhithe
CS   Dublin: Crow Street Theatre
DL   London:Theatre Royal, Drury Lane
HAMM   London: Windsor Castle Inn, Hammersmith
HAY   London: The Little Theatre in Haymarket
KT   London: King's Theatre, or the Opera House
MG   London: Marylebone Gardens
RG   London: Ranelagh Gardens
SA   Dublin: Smock Alley Theatre

These tables have been compiled using the following sources: Michael Burden and Christopher Chowrimoottoo, http://italianaria.bodleian.ox.ac.uk/; the *English Short Title Catalogue*, http://estc.bl.uk/; *Theatre in Dublin, 1745–1820: A Calendar of Performances*, ed. John C. Greene, 6 vols. (Lenham: Rowman & Littlefield, 2011); *A Biographical Dictionary of Actors, Actresses, Musicians, Dancers, Managers and Other stage personnel in London, 1660–1800*, ed. Philip H. Highfill, Kalman A. Burnim and Edward A. Langhans, 16 vols. (Carbondale: Southern Illinois University Press, 1973–93); *The London Stage 1660–1800*, ed. Emmett L. Avery, Charles Beecher Hogan, William Van Lennep, Arthur Hawley Scouten and George Winchester Stone, 5 parts, 11 vols. (Carbondale: Southern Illinois University Press, 1960–68), parts 4 and 5; Dougald MacMillan, *Catalogue of the Larpent Plays in the Huntington Library* (San Marino, CA: Huntington Library Press, 1939); Claudio Sartori, *I libretti Italiani a stampa dalle origin al 1800*, 6 vols. (Milan: Locatelli, 1990–94); and T. J. Walsh, *Opera in Dublin, 1705–1797: The Social Scene* (Dublin: A. Figgis, 1973).

Table 4.1 *London, 1748–1757*

No	Opera	Advertised Genre	City/Theatre/Seasons/Performances
John Crosa's troupe			
1	*La comedia in comedia*	Dramma Giocoso per Musica	**London KT 1748:** November 8, 12, 15, 26. **1749:** January 3, 7, 10, March 11, June 3.
2	*Orazio*	Dramma Giocoso per Musica	**London KT 1748:** November 29, December 3, 6, 10, 13, 17. **1749:** January 14, 17, February 21, March 7, June 3.
3	*La finta frascatana*	Dramma Giocoso per Musica	**London KT 1748:** December 31.
4	*La maestra*	Dramma Giocoso per Musica	**London KT 1749:** February 28.
5	*Li tre cicisbei ridicoli*	Dramma Giocoso per Musica	**London KT 1749:** March 14, 18, April 1, May 11, 27.
6	*La Pace in Europa*	Serenata	**London KT 1749:** April 29.
7	*Il negligente*	Dramma Giocoso per Musica	**London HAY 1749:** November 21, 25, 28, December 2, 5, 9, 12, 16. **KT 1750:** March 20, 24.
8	*Madama Ciana*	Dramma Giocoso per Musica	**London HAY 1750:** January 13, 16, February 3, April 18, 19, 21.
9	*Don Calascione*	Comic Opera	**London KT 1750:** February 10, 17, April 28.
10	*La serva padrona*	'Comic Interludes'	**London KT 1750:** March 27.
11	*Adriano in Siria*	Opera	London **KT 1750:** February 20, 24, March 3, 6, 10, 13, 27, April 3.
12	*Il trionfo di Camilla*	Dramma	**London KT 1750:** March 31, April 7.

Giordani's troupe

13	Gli amanti gelosi	Dramma. Comico per Musica.	**London CG 1753:** December 17, 20, 31. **1754:** January 2, 4, 7, 9, 11, 14, 16, 28, March 11.
14	Lo studente alla moda	Dramma Comico-Giocoso.	**London CG 1754:** January 18, 21, 26, February 6.
15	L'amor costante	Dramma Giocoso per Musica	**London CG 1754:** February 11, 13, 15, 18, 20.
16	La cameriera accorta	Opera comica.	**London CG 1754:** March 4.
17	Gli amanti gelosi	Pantomimical Burletta	**London SI 1754:** September 3, 4, 5, 6.

Another company

18	La moglie a forza	Intermezzo	**London CG 1754:** [NR]
19	L'arcadia in Brenta	Opera comica	**London CG 1754:** November 18, 22.
20	Bertoldo, Bertoldino	Italian Burletta	**London CG 1754:** December 9, 16, 19, 23, **1755:** January 3.
21	La serva padrona	Burletta	**London HAY 1755:** January 22, 29, February 7.

Giordani's troupe

22	L'albergatrice	Italian Comic Opera	**London HAY[a] 1755:** February 3, 17, 20.
23	La comediante fatta cantatrice	Burletta	**London CG 1756:** January 12, 16.

Giordani departs?

---

[a] Lord Chamberlain's Office: 'License to Nicolina Giordani for *Burlettas* or *Italian Comedies* at the Little Theatre in Hay. during this season'. BDA, VI, 219.

Table 4.2 *London Marylebone Gardens, 1757–1760*

No	Opera	Advertised Genre	City/Theatre/Seasons/Performances
24	*La serva padrona; or, The Servant Mistress*	Burletta	**London MG 1758:** June 8, 10, 13, 14, 15, 17, 20, 21, 22, 23, 24, 26, 27, 28, 30, July 1, 3, 4, 5, 7, 8, 10, 11, 12, 13, 15, 17, 18, 19, 20, 21, 22, 24, 25, 28, 29, 31, August 2, 4, 7, 10, 11, 12, 14, 16, 17, 21, 22, 25, 28, 29, 30, September 2, 4, 5, 6, 7, 8, 9, 11, 13, 14, 15, 18, 19. **1759:** April 17, May 19, 21, 22, 23, 24, 25, 26, 28, 29, June 4, 6, 7, 8, 19, 20, 22, 25, 26, 29, July 3, 5, 7, 10, 12, 14, 17, 19, 21, 24, August 16. **1760:** June 3, 4, 5, 6, 7, 9, 10, 11, 12, 13, 13, 14, 16, 17, July 9, 19, 24, 25, 26, 28, 29, 30, August 11, 13, 14, 16, 20.
25	*La serva padrona; or, The Servant Mistress*	Burletta	**London HAY 1759:** March 29, April 5.
26	*Il cisebeo alla moda; or, The Modish Coquet*	Burletta	**London MG 1759:** May (10, 11, 12, 13, 14, 15, 16, 17, 18, 19, 20, 21, 22, 23, 24, 25, 26, 27, 28, 29, 30, 31, June 1, 2, 3, 4, 5, 6, 7, 8), 9, 13, 21, 22, 23, 26, 27, 30, July 2, 4, 8, 11, 12, 13, 16, 18, 20, 23, 25. **1760:** July 10, 11, 14, 15, 16, 17, 18, 21, 22, 23,
27	*La stratagemma; or, The Stratagem*	A tragical-comical burletta	**London MG 1759:** July 26, 27, 28, 30, 31, August 1, 2, 3, 4, 6, 7, 8, 9, 10, 11, 13, 14, 15, 17, 18, 20, 21, 22, 23, 24, 25, 27, 28, 29, 30, 31, September 1, 3, 5, 6, 7, 8, 10, 11, 12, 13. **1760:** June 18, 19, 20, 21, 23, 24, 27, July 2, 3, 4, 5, 7, 8, 31, August 1, 2, 25, 26.
28	*Il tutore; or The Tutor*	Comic burletta	**London DL 1759:** December 14.

Table 4.3 *London Haymarket, 1761*

No	Opera	Advertised Genre	City/Theatre/Seasons/Performances
29	*La serva padrona; or, The Servant Mistress*	Burletta	**London HAY 1761:** May 29, July 14, 15, 16, 17, 18, 20, 22, 23, 24, 25, August 1, 4, 6, 7, 8, 11, 12, 25, 27, 29.
30	*La strattagemma; or, The Stratagem*	A tragical-comical burletta	**London HAY 1761:** June 23, 27, 30, July 2, 4, 6, 7, 8, 9, 11, 13, 21, August 5.
31	*The Ridiculous Guardian*	A comic burletta	**London HAY 1761:** July 28, 29, 30, 31, August 1, 2, 3, 4, 5, 6, 7.
32	*The Coquette*	A comic burletta	**London HAY 1761:** August 13, 14, 15.

Table 4.4 *London and Dublin, 1761–1765*

Colomba Mattei arrives

No.	Title	Genre	Performances
33	Il mercato di Malmantile	Opera comica	London KT 1761: November 10, 17, 23, December 2, 7, 14, 21. 1762: January 4, 25, April 14.
34	Bertoldo, Bertoldino	Opera comica	London KT 1762: January 11, 19.
35	Le nozze di Dorina	Opera comica	London KT 1762: February 1, 8, March 22.
36	Il filosofo di campagna	Comic opera	London KT 1762: February 15, 22, March 15, April 29.
37	La famiglia in scompiglio	Dramma giocoso	London KT 1762: April 3, 12, 19, 26, May 1, 18.
38	Il tutore e la pupilla	Comic opera	London KT 1762: November 13, 20, 27, 29, December 6, 13, 20. 1763: January 1, 15, 24, February 14, March 14, 24, May 9.
39	La cascina	Dramma giocoso	London KT 1763: January 8, 10.
40	La serva padrona	Interlude	London KT 1763: March 24, April 21, May 9.
41	La finta sposa	Dramma comico.	London KT 1763: April 14, 28.

Midas arrives in London

No.	Title	Genre	Performances
42	Midas (in three acts)	An English burletta	London CG 1764: February 22, 23, 24, 25, 27, 28, 29, March 1, 2, 3, DL 1764: March 16.

Amicis in Dublin

No.	Title	Genre	Performances
43	La cascina	Burletta; or Italian comic opera	Dublin SA 1761: December 19, 21, 22, 26, 29. 1762: January 2, 16, 19, April 3, May 3, 15.
44	La finta sposa	Burletta	Dublin SA 1762: January 5, 9, 12, 23,
45	Midas	English burletta	Dublin CS 1762: January 22, 25, 29, February 6, 11, 22, April 3.
46	Gl'intrighi per amore	Burletta	Dublin SA 1762: January 29, February 3, 6, 10, 13, 17, March 24, April 14, 28, May 15.
47	Il filosofo di campagna	Dramma giocoso	Dublin SA 1762: February 20, 23, March 3, 10, 13, April 21, 24, May 12.
48	La creanza	Burletta	Dublin SA 1762: February 27, March 6, April 17.
49	Il mercato di Malanatile	Burletta	Dublin SA 1762: March 17, 20, 27, 31, May 19.
50	La serva padrona	Burletta	Dublin SA 1762: March 24, April 17.
51	Li due rivali	Burletta	Dublin SA 1762: May 1, 5, 8.

Giordani troupe arrives

No.	Title	Genre	Performances
52	La serva padrona	Burletta	Dublin CS 1764: April 28, June 14.
53	La zingara	Burletta	Dublin CS 1764: May 3, 5, June 14.
54	Livietta e Tracollo	Burletta	Dublin CS 1764: May 12.
55	Il maestro di musica	Burletta	Dublin CS 1764: May 19.
56	Li tre cicisbei rivali	Burletta	Dublin CS 1764: June 2.

Giordani troupe arrives

No.	Title	Genre	Performances
57	Gli amanti gelosi	Burletta	Dublin SA 1764: November 23, 28, December 3, 10, 17, 31. 1765: January 19, 24, April 9.
58	Don Fulminone (L'amante di due donne)	Dramma comico	Dublin SA 1765: January 7, 12, 31.

Giordani troupe departs

Table 4.5 *London, later performances of the Italian and English versions of* La serva padrona, *with the two-act version of* Midas, *1766–1800*

No	Opera	Advertised Genre	City/Theatre/Seasons/Performances
59	*Midas (in two acts)*	Burletta	**London CG 1766:** February 5, 6, 10, 11, 15, 17, 20, 22, 24, 27, March 1, 4, 6, 8, 120, 13, 18, 31, April 4, 9, 15, 16, 28, 30 May 7, 15, October 14, 16, November 7, 13. **1767:** February 10, 12, 28, March 5, 12, 19, April 4, 12, 28, May 4, 6, 11, October 27, 31, November 5, 6, 24, 27, December 5, 9, 11. **1768:** January 2, 19, 28, February, 9, 18, March 21, April 4, June 4, September 30, October 15, 29, November 5, 12, 16, 24, December 1, 9, 16. **1769:** February 11, 16, 23, March 2, 9, 30, April 4, 24, 28, May 4, 6, 11, October 27, 31, November 5, 12, 16, 24, December 9, 19. **1770:** January 3, 20, March 10, 12. **HAY:** August 1, 3, 6, 16. **CG:** September 26, October 10, 11, 13, 30, November 13, December 7, 15. **CG 1771:** March 7, May 9, 16, September 25, October 2, 7, 14, 23, 25, December 19. **CG 1772:** March 28. **CG 1773:** February 6, September 24, 27, October 4, 9, 12, 15, 18, 25, November 8, 15, 19, 22, December 21. **CG 1774:** January 24, February 3, 21, 26, March 10, 15, 24, May 5, 26. **CG 1775:** January 21, November 13, 14, 17, 20. **CG 1776:** May 6, 7. **HAY:** September 18. **CHR:** September 23. **CG 1777:** March 31, April 2, 8, 10, 12, 21, May 2. **HAY:** June 9, 13, 18, July 1, 14, 16, August 22, 23, September 4, 8, 10, 11. **CG 1778:** January 29. April 25, May 5. **HAY:** June 12, 16, 17, 23, July 17, 20, 25, August 7, 24. **CG 1779:** March 27, April 6, 16, 20, May 1, 18. **HAY:** June 17, 19, 24, 26, July 17, 19, 30, August 12. **CG:** September 24, October 4, 13, 23. **HAY 1780:** May 30, August 2. **CG:** October 3. **CG 1781:** April 2, 23, May 24. **HAY:** August 15. **CG:** October 19. **CG 1782:** February 18, 19. **HAY 1783:** August 26. **CG 1784:** April 26, 28, May 18. **HAY:** July 24, 26, August 3. **CG:** October 18, December 13, 15. **CG 1785:** March 12, 19, May 16.

	Title	Genre	Performances
60	*The Maid Mistress*	Serenata	**HAMM:** July 15. **CG:** November 2, 4, 28. **CG 1786:** April 21, December 5. **CG 1787:** May 10. **HAY:** August 10. **CG:** September 24. **CG 1788:** February 16. April 28. May 11. June 16. HAY: July 29. CG 23. **CG 1791:** May 6. **CG 1794:** November 7, 10. **CG 1795:** February 13, November.
61	*La serva padrona; or, The Servant Mistress*	Entertainment of Music	**London RG** 1770: May 28. June 27. July 4. 13. **London MB** 1770: June 16, 19, 23, 26, 30, July 3, 5, 7, 10, 12, 14, 24, 31, August 7, 14, 16, 18, 23, 25, September 4, 6, 11, 15, 18, 20. **1771:** May 23, June 4, 6, 11, 13, 18, 20, 25, July 18, 23, 25, 30, August 1, 8, September 3. **1772:** August 20, 25. **1773:** July 22, 27, August 12, September 16. **1774:** 23, 28, August 1, 11, 16, 31, September 5, 7, 13.
62	*He Wou'd If He Cou'd; or, An Old Fool Worse Than Any*	Burletta	**London DL** 1771: April 12.
63	*La serva padrona*	Intermezzo	**London KT** 1776: April 23.
64	*The Maid's the Mistress*	Burletta	**London CG** 1783: February 14. 17.
65	*La serva padrona*	Comic opera	**London KT** 1794: May 29, June 3, 23, 24, July 1, 3, 5.
66	*La serva padrona*	Comic opera	**London KT** 1799: June 25, 29, July 6, 9, 16, 20, August 3.

CHAPTER 5

Trading Loyalties: Sheridan, The School for Scandal *and the Irish Propositions*

Robert W. Jones

Richard Brinsley Sheridan's place as an Irishman on the London stage has never been entirely assured. He has never seemed quite Irish enough nor to have fitted comfortably into postcolonial paradigms of alterity or exclusion. Sheridan does not appear in the usual roster of Irish dramatists: Goldsmith, Wilde, Shaw, Synge and Beckett. He is perhaps rather too successful, and too comfortably inserted into the Foxite *beau monde*.[1] Nor does he seem to say enough about Ireland. This is not to say that there have not been attempts to make Sheridan more Irish. Fintan O'Toole's biography, which did so much to reinvigorate Sheridan studies, advocated his Irishness unequivocally though at the cost of creating an unduly coherent identity and implausibly consistent set of loyalties.[2] Twenty years after the publication of *A Traitor's Kiss*, there is a need for a more subtle appraisal, one that acknowledges how Sheridan might have been pulled in different directions. Negotiating such multiple loyalties was typical for many Irish writers, as Bridget Orr's discussion of Arthur Murphy (Chapter 8, this volume) also makes clear. The early triumph of his comedies, enabled Sheridan to purchase Drury Lane in 1776, granting him control of his repertoire. Success was not limited to the theatrical world: in 1780, Sheridan became MP for Stafford, a prosperous manufacturing borough, which boasted around 320 independent-minded voters. He soon needed to please this audience as much as those who paid to see his plays and consequently promised his electors that he would always defend their interests.[3] At Westminster, Sheridan's oratorical skills secured his prominence in almost all parliamentary reports, while his connection with the

---

[1] See Leslie Mitchell, *The Whig World, 1760–1837* (London: Hambledon Continuum, 2005).
[2] Fintan O'Toole, *A Traitor's Kiss: The Life of Richard Brinsley Sheridan* (London: Granta, 1998).
[3] Richard Brinsley Sheridan, 'To the Electors of Stafford', *Letters of Richard Brinsley Sheridan*, ed. Cecil Price, 3 vols. (Oxford: Clarendon Press, 1966), I: 134.

Whigs meant that he became a figure through which many contemporaries made sense of the political scene. The issue should not be Sheridan's great successes or his immersion into English society but the uses he made of those connections and how they, in turn, reveal his complex identity.

These concerns are central to the new ways in which Sheridan and his family are being understood by scholars. The whole family demand increasing amounts of critical attention. Although Richard Brinsley Sheridan remains the prime focus and regularly assumes his place in assessments of the period's culture and politics, his pre-eminence is not unrivalled.[4] His mother, Frances (*née* Chamberlain), has been reappraised as a novelist and playwright sensitive to national and colonial crises.[5] The contribution to Irish and British culture made by Sheridan's multi-talented but difficult father, Thomas, has been freshly appreciated, as actor, theatre manager, and elocutionist.[6] Neither are Sheridan's siblings neglected. His sister Alicia Le Fanu was a playwright and her mother's canny biographer and remains a source for her brother's career.[7] His youngest sister Elizabeth, long dismissed as a mere letter writer, has been rediscovered as a novelist. Her epistolary novel *The Triumph of Prudence over Passion* is a tale of romantic crisis, sharp in its assessment of contemporary Irish politics. The reappraisal of Elizabeth Sheridan marks a shift in Sheridan studies: the Irishness of the family is now centre stage.[8] The re-conceptualisation of the family as sympathetic to Irish causes and conscious of their Irish identity is still to have its full effect in work on Richard

---

[4] See David Francis Taylor, *Theatres of Opposition: Empire, Revolution, and Richard Brinsley Sheridan* (New York: Oxford University Press, 2012). Gillian Russell, *Women, Sociability and Theatre in Georgian London* (Cambridge: Cambridge University Press, 2007), 178–225; and Daniel O'Quinn, *Staging Governance: Theatrical Imperialism in London 1770–1800* (Baltimore: Johns Hopkins University Press, 2005), 204–13.

[5] See Sonja Lawrenson, 'Frances Sheridan, "The History of Nourjahad" and the Sultan of Smock Alley', *Eighteenth-Century Ireland* 26 (2011): 24–50; Kathleen M. Oliver, 'Frances Sheridan's Faulkland, the Silenced, Emasculated, Ideal, Male', *Studies in English Literature 1500–1900* 43 (2003): 683–700; and Betty A. Schellenberg, 'Frances Sheridan Reads John Home: Placing *Sidney Bidulph* in the Republic of Letters', *Eighteenth-Century Fiction* 13 (2001): 561–77.

[6] See Conrad Brunström, *Thomas Sheridan's Career and Influence: An Actor in Earnest* (Lewisburg: Bucknell University Press, 2011); and Madeleine Forrel Marshall, 'Late Eighteenth-Century Public Reading, with Particular Attention to *Sheridan's Strictures on Reading the Church-Service* (1789)', *Studies in Eighteenth-Century Culture* 36 (2007): 35–54.

[7] See Colleen Taylor, Chapter 6, this volume, and Anna M. Fitzer, 'Relating a Life: Alicia LeFanu's *Memoirs of the Life and Writings of Mrs Frances Sheridan*', *Women's Writing* 15 (2008): 32–54.

[8] Elizabeth Sheridan, *The Triumph of Prudence over Passion*, ed. Aileen Douglas and Ian Campbell Ross (Dublin: Four Courts Press, 2011). See also Anna M. Fitzer, 'Revealing Influence: The Forgotten Daughters of Frances Sheridan', *Women's Writing* 20 (2013): 64–81.

Brinsley Sheridan. Yet Sheridan was marked by his Irishness. It set him apart from other Foxites, as it did Dennis O'Bryen.[9] Sheridan's Irish connection also impelled him. Writing to her sister in June 1785, Elizabeth Sheridan reported: 'Dick is a very warm friend to the Irish, Mrs S. cannot conceive the violent attachment he has to that country, but from her I found he acts on this occasion from his own feelings, totally independent of any wish his party may have to harass the Minister.'[10] Alicia might have paused over her sister's distancing deixis: '*the* Irish ... *that* country ... *this* occasion'. Elizabeth appears not to accept either her brother's participation in or his claims to *that* identity. Nor perhaps does she accept her own, revealing the painful paradox of the migrant, who is never quite at home. Neither Sheridan nor his sisters and brother have been considered in terms of an Irish diaspora, Irish migration and remigration or as playing a part in the London Irish community.[11] Their omission from these emerging scholarly debates underplays the extent to which the Sheridans were obliged, like other Irish men and women working in England to negotiate multiple loyalties, while maintaining identities of some suppleness.

Sheridan's political position required considerable deftness to maintain, not least because London's political stages, like those of its theatres, required shifting, mobile performances. Party opinions could be cherished but parliamentarians, then, as now, needed to respond flexibly to unfolding events. In this context, Sheridan's Irishness, like his theatrical past, was both hindrance and help. A significant crisis came in 1785 when William Pitt's government attempted to create a new trading arrangement between Ireland and Britain. It is to the controversy generated by Pitt's proposals that Elizabeth Sheridan is referring. The measure was intended as a 'final adjustment' to Anglo-Irish relations following the forced concession of legislative independence in 1782. Irish public opinion was initially favourable, and Sheridan seems to have been hopeful that some good would come from what were referred to as the 'Irish propositions'. The emergence of

[9] David O'Shaughnessy, 'Making a Play for Patronage: Dennis O'Bryen's *A Friend in Need Is a Friend Indeed* (1783)', *Eighteenth-Century Life* 39 (2015): 183–211.
[10] Elizabeth Sheridan, *Betsy Sheridan's Journal: Letters from Sheridan's Sister 1784–1786 & 1788–1790*, ed. William Le Fanu (London: Eyre & Spottiswoode, 1960), 58.
[11] See David O'Shaughnessy, '"Tolerably Numerous": Recovering the London Irish of the Eighteenth Century'; and Toby Barnard, 'The Irish in London and the "London Irish"' in David O'Shaughnessy, ed., 'Networks of Aspiration: The London Irish of the Eighteeenth Century'. Special issue, *Eighteenth-Century Life* 39.1 (2015). See also Craig Bailey, *Irish London: Middle-Class Migration in the Global Eighteenth Century* (Liverpool: Liverpool University Press, 2013).

British protest, especially in the manufacturing counties of England, including Staffordshire, forced Pitt's government to make amendments. The revised propositions made new and seemingly onerous demands on the Irish legislature. Sheridan opposed the new propositions in a series of brilliant speeches, but his rhetorical success cannot disguise the awkwardness of his predicament as the Irish-born MP for Stafford. This chapter examines this critical moment to explore how Sheridan, in seeking to balance or at least hold onto more than one set of loyalties – to Ireland, to his place amidst the English Whigs and with his Staffordshire electors – came under pressure. Analysis of Sheridan's triangulation takes its impetus from the strange appearance of the 'Mayor of Manchester' in *The School for Scandal*, or, since Sheridan had a profound aversion to publication, the place of 'Manchester' in a distinct manuscript transmission of the play.[12] Exploration of this evolving aspect of *The School for Scandal* exposes not only the play's sensitivity to the many contradictions of empire but also reveals Sheridan's multiple involvements, as playwright, Irish patriot, critic of empire and English Whig politician.

I

Some of the pressures placed on Sheridan, as not quite English, for being, as it were, *really* Irish, reverberate in his comedies, where characters whose identities are doubled, disguised or otherwise duplicitous abound. Sir Lucius O'Trigger in *The Rivals* is the clearest example, but he is, in truth, an all-too-obvious Stage Irishman. His ardent recollections of '*Blunderbuss-Hall*' and the 'dirty acres' that have slipped from his grasp cannot hide his dishonest intentions.[13] He is what he is: an Irishman on the make. Something more suggestive because more self-consciously performed occurs at the end of *St Patrick's Day* when, in opposition to his soon-to-be father-in-law, Lieutenant O'Connor refuses to renounce either his 'Country' or the army. The audience knows that he is an officer in the 'Royal Inniskillins', a British regiment, albeit raised in Ireland (*DW*, I: 193, 163). O'Connor's dual identification, coming after he and his men have

12 Frank Donoghue, 'Avoiding the "Cooler Tribunal of the Study": Richard Brinsley Sheridan's Writer's Block and Late Eighteenth-Century Print Culture', *ELH* 68 (2001): 831–56.
13 Richard Brinsley Sheridan, *The Dramatic Works of Richard Brinsley Sheridan* ed. Cecil Price, 2 vols. (Oxford: Clarendon Press, 1973), I: 116. Subsequent references appear in the text. See also David Haley, 'The Literary Origins of Sir Lucius O'Trigger' in *Richard Brinsley Sheridan: The Impresario in Political and Cultural Context*, ed. Jack E. DeRochi and Daniel J. Ennis (Lewisburg: Bucknell University Press, 2013), 61–82.

exhausted the hospitality of the English village in which they are quartered, points to a more migratory or diasporic performance: bi-locational, two loyalties, almost two identities. Sheridan's canon contains many such episodes of disguise and dissembling. Most characters in *The Rivals* are trying to appear as they are not, and deceptions, including self-deceptions, abound, underscoring the ways in which identity might continue to be performed rather than inherited.[14] Jack Absolute presents himself as Ensign Beverly, hoping to woo Lydia Languish. His scheme nearly works, but it collapses when she discovers his 'unmanly imposition' (*DW*, 1: 126). More pertinently, Absolute's scheme brings him into conflict with his father who threatens to 'unget' him. 'Upon my credit', says Fag afterwards, 'were I in your place, and found my father such very bad company, I should certainly drop his acquaintance' (*DW*, 1: 99). Family relations are placed, consequently, under some pressure. For his part Absolute prefers to evade his father's ire with a 'penitential face', but the presumption proves all too effective; unnerved by his compliance Sir Anthony wonders if he has not been 'playing the hypocrite' all along (*DW*, 1: 103, 105). As elsewhere in *The Rivals*, it is performance rather than inheritance that underwrites character, which seems only ever to be the semblance of an unwanted original. How Sheridan's father, Thomas, a proud and irascible Irishman, understood this disavowal is not clear.

Drawing still more explicitly on Restoration precursors (notably Congreve), *The School for Scandal* offers a complex version of these disjunctions and disavowals.[15] Similarly concerned with loosened or disguised connections, *The School for Scandal* lacks the reassuring sense that 'real' identities lie behind guises. This occurs most clearly in relation to the character of Joseph Surface, who, if played right, possesses a heroic capacity for hypocrisy.[16] His extravagant deceptions occur in a context dominated by strained marital relations; financial and familial negligence; and, most significantly, empire. Empire appears in the genial form of the returning

---

[14] Dror Wahrman, *The Making of the Modern Self: Identity and Culture in Eighteenth-Century England* (New Haven: Yale University Press, 2004). See also Paul Goring, '"John Bull, Pit, Box, and Gallery, Said No!": Charles Macklin and the Limits of Ethnic Resistance on the Eighteenth-Century London Stage', *Representations* 79 (2002): 61–81; and Michael Ragussis, 'Jews and Other "Outlandish Englishmen": Ethnic Performance and the Invention of British Identity under the Georges', *Critical Inquiry* 26 (2000): 773–97.

[15] See Eric S. Rump 'Sheridan, Congreve and *The School for Scandal*' in *Sheridan Studies* ed. James Morwood and David Crane (New York: Cambridge University Press, 1995), 59–70; and Christine S. Wiesenthal, 'Representation and Experimentation in the Major Comedies of Richard Brinsley Sheridan', *Eighteenth-Century Studies* 25 (1992): 309–30.

[16] Charles Lamb, 'On Some of the Old Actors' in *Works of Charles and Mary Lamb*, ed. E. V. Lucas, 7 vols. (London: Methuen, 1905), 2: 140.

nabob Sir Oliver Surface, who, to test his nephews, disguises himself as the money lender Mr Premium. The conventions of eighteenth-century stage comedy suggest that Sir Oliver's shape shifting, like that of Absolute or O'Connor, takes the form of an excessive facility – something which can be achieved with surprising ease, rather than, as for many colonial subjects, something required. The credulous acceptance of claimed or performed characters forms a key part of the play's mockery of the contemporary moment. Sir Peter's faith in Joseph's sentiments, the confidence with which Sir Oliver assumes he can impersonate a Jewish money lender, only to be told that 'the principal is a Christian' (*DW*, 1: 372, 389). These are only the most striking instances: the play abounds in false identities, false reports of character. Sir Oliver's disguise plot runs alongside a sense that parentage and inheritance, the often labile markers of identity or loyalty, are disavowed. *The School for Scandal* reveals the lack of values at the heart of upper-class society. Relationships are negotiated, eschewed and monetised: Joseph, characteristically, has sold his parental home; although his younger brother, Charles, has bought it from him, he lacks the funds and the will to preserve it, making his acquisition a hollow gesture (*DW*, 1: 394–95).

Avoidance and disavowal structure the play's famous picture scene. Sir Oliver has arrived at Charles Surface's home to test his nephew and if possible to provide him with the funds necessary to recover his profligacy. The expedient of selling, by auction, the family portraits, as a means to both objectives, is immediately hit upon. The sale begins with mockery of Sir Joshua Reynolds, whose portraits, Charles explains, exist 'independent' of their sitters. By contrast, the pictures Charles wishes to sell are an 'Inveterate likeness – all Stiff and Aukward as the Originals' (*DW*, 1: 404). So, even as the canvases are held up, there is a question of their relation to the sitters and to the owner-vendor. The first lot to go is Sir Richard Raviline, then old Aunt Deborah, a couple of be-wigged 'Beaux', a judge, two parliamentary brothers and a provincial mayor. Sir Oliver buys them all. Eventually there is but one picture left, Sir Oliver's own portrait, featuring not only his pre-Eastern face but also 'an Unforgiving Eye, and a damn'd disinheriting Countenance'. Despite the physiognomic threat posed by his ancestor's image, Charles will not sell and promises to keep 'poor Noll . . . while I've a Room to put it in'. Sir Oliver, gratified, instantly acknowledges that the 'rogue's my nephew after all'. Charles's money problems are at a stroke resolved; his debts will be cleared and his dependants all cared for (*DW*, 1: 405–7, 410). His restitution is too quick and too easy. Supported by his tremendous 'eastern liberality', Sir Oliver has succumbed to sentimental desire for a homecoming, disregarding all sense of right or wrong. His nephew's actions are equally problematic: the reward is too well anticipated; inheritance becomes not duty or steward-ship but is reduced to great expectations and, ultimately, cash. Despite his self-proclaimed 'domestic Character' and his uncle's effusions, Charles has gained the money he always believed he was entitled to. A flood tide of imperial gain has swept the derelictions of the metropolis away, but perhaps all too obviously (*DW*, 1: 372, 405).

The monetisation of sentiment is the crux of the scene, just as money will enable the reconciliation of the Teazles later in the play. Connection, especially by inheritance and bequest, is relentlessly devalued.[17] The sale of the family pictures makes this plain. Everyone is for sale. The Blunt brothers – 'William and Walter' – exemplify this realisation: both were 'Members of Parliament' and, surprisingly, 'this is the first time they were either bought or sold.' If this is political satire, it is frankly tame. However, the business becomes more pointed almost immediately. Holding up the next picture to go, Charles exclaims mockingly: 'Here's a Jolly Fellow – I don't know what Relation – But he was Mayor of Manchester' (*DW*, 1: 406). This, at least, is how the line reads in most editions, including the current Oxford, Penguin and New Mermaid paperbacks. Why Manchester? Perhaps because along with Leeds, Sheffield and Birmingham, Manchester was one of the fastest-growing industrial towns in England, fast matching ports such as Liverpool, Hull and Portsmouth. Despite Manchester's rapid growth, little attempt was made to renew its civic structures and the town remained under the archaic governance of a manorial court. Manchester did not gain a mayor until the 1830s.[18] Nor was Manchester Sheridan's first choice. Early manuscripts, including the licensing copy submitted to the Lord Chamberlain's office in May 1777, have the mayor as Bristolian. Manuscripts produced during the next few years specified Norwich.[19] Bristol and Norwich were the second- and third-ranking cities in the country (with mayors to boot). So again: why Manchester? The explanation offered by Cecil Price is that Mancunians

---

[17] See Susan Staves, 'Resentment or Resignation: Dividing Spoils among Daughters and Younger Sons' in *Early Modern Conceptions of Property*, ed. John Brewer and Susan Staves (London: Routledge, 1995), 194–218.

[18] Frank O'Gorman, *The Long Eighteenth Century: British Political and Social History 1688–1832*, 2nd ed. (London: Bloomsbury, 2016), 123, 147, 296. For more detailed discussion, see Arthur Rackham, with the assistance of Ina Stafford Russell, *The History of Local Government in Manchester*, 3 vols. (London: Longmans Green, 1939–40).

[19] The earliest surviving manuscript is the Frampton Court MS, reprinted in W. Fraser Rae, *Sheridan's Plays Now Printed as He Wrote Them* (London: David Nutt, 1902), 188.

had been rapturous when the play was performed in the town during the summer of 1778. This production was reported in the *Morning Chronicle*, which Price took as confirmation of his conjecture, adding, plausibly enough, that touring theatre companies might always introduce the name of the town to please local audiences (*DW*, 1: 406 n).[20]

There are some flies in this soup. No documentary evidence supports the claim that other towns ever appeared in the script. Norwich remains the object of mockery in theatrical manuscripts produced after 1778, notably a copy created for a production in Portsmouth in 1779.[21] Norwich continued to appear in manuscript presentation copies created for Sheridan's elite circle, notably the *Second Crewe, Buckinghamshire* and *Banbury* manuscripts. Later Drury Lane prompt books, such as Fawcett and Cumberland, retain Norwich.[22] More: the Dublin pirated edition of 1780 has Norwich, as does the semi-official 1799 printing that derives from the manuscript given by Sheridan to his sister Alicia Le Fanu and which she sold on return to Ireland.[23] Manchester only appears in three versions of the text: the *Georgetown* manuscript, given to Frances Anne Crewe in the 1780s. Crewe, with whom Sheridan had an affair, was a significant figure amongst the Foxite Whigs, both in London and at her home, Crewe Hall, in Cheshire. Thomas Moore thought that *Georgetown* contained Sheridan's last revisions, and it has had considerable status ever since.[24] Manchester appears in the *Tickell* manuscript, owned by Sheridan's niece Elizabeth Anne Tickell, produced around 1808. *Tickell* seems to have a close connection to the *Georgetown* text, as it includes the poem 'Addressed to a Lady', which Sheridan had written for Crewe to accompany the manuscript.[25] Finally, when John Murray printed the text in 1821, the Mayor was also from Manchester.[26] These three versions, which provide the copy texts for most

---

[20] *Morning Chronicle*, 19 June 1778.

[21] See Robert W. Jones, 'Texts, Tools and Things: An Approach to Manuscripts of Richard Brinsley Sheridan's The School for Scandal', *Review of English Studies* 66 (2015): 723–43.

[22] For an overview of the MSS of *The School for Scandal*, see F. W. Bateson's introduction and notes to Richard Brinsley Sheridan, *The School for Scandal*, ed. F. W. Bateson (London: New Mermaids, 1979).

[23] [Richard Brinsley Sheridan], *The School for Scandal. A Comedy as it is performed at the Theatre-Royal in London and Dublin* (Dublin, 1780); and Richard Brinsley Sheridan, *The School for Scandal. Taken from a Correction Copy, Performed at the Theatres, London and Dublin* (Dublin: n.p., 1799).

[24] Thomas Moore, *Memoirs of the Life of the Right Honourable Richard Brinsley Sheridan*, 2 vols. (London: Longman, Hurst, Rees, Orme, Brown and Green, 1825), 1: 260–1.

[25] On the *Tickell* manuscript and its relationship to *Georgetown*, see Ann Blake, 'Introduction' to *Richard Brinsley Sheridan The School for Scandal*, ed. Ann Blake (London: New Mermaids, 2004), 27–29.

[26] See Richard Brinsley Sheridan, *Works of the Late Right Honourable Richard Brinsley Sheridan*, ed. Thomas Moore, 2 vols. (London: John Murray, 1821).

modern editions of the play, are not the responsive, locally adjusted texts
that Price had in mind. They are, more convincingly, private versions of
the text, held within families, which may have overlapped with the prompt
copies held at the only theatre entitled to produce it. *Georgetown* is
a distinctly private, enclaved version, offered as a flirtatious gift, and not
a response to any local situation, save for the fact that Crewe Hall, where
the manuscript resided for much of its existence, is forty miles from
Manchester and about the same distance from Stafford. Crewe Hall is
also where Sheridan participated in the political, cultural and sexual
intrigues of Whig society.

   These connections might explain the insertion and subsequent retention
of Manchester, but not really. Manchester is better understood as a specific
reference to the politics of Anglo-Irish trade in 1785. Viewed in this light,
the altered name becomes a declaration of filiation, of Irish loyalty and
specifically Irish concerns, an association expressed as an anxious and
complex allusion to Manchester, its civic life and, especially, its commerce.
It is in connection with Manchester that the relationship between Sheridan
and Ireland, and between Stafford's citizens and their MP, threatened to
come unstuck. This is a lot to claim on the basis of a single word, albeit
a now famous name. But Manchester means more than the city that now
bears that name. Sheridan deploys 'Manchester' as both shared local
reference and shorthand for something greater. There is no need to dismiss
the methodological assumption, relied on by others that play texts are, at
certain points, highly mutable, adapted by players and playwrights in
response to changed conditions.[27] They then get settled and the process
of revision and amendment ceases. It is in precisely this way that
Manchester enters *The School for Scandal*, and stays there. The changed
text operates in a different context from the original play, one that it helps
create, offering differing claims to Irish filiation as a result. The reference to
Manchester intensifies the picture scene's address to the ambiguities of
empire. This argument rests on the contention that the *Georgetown* manuscript was produced in the mid-1780s (later than is commonly suggested),
and that the *Tickell* manuscript and Murray's edition derive either from it
(which is unlikely) or from another now lost manuscript copy. Unlike
manuscripts which retained Norwich, the *Georgetown* manuscript and its

---

[27] F. W. Bateson, 'The Application of Thought to an Eighteenth-Century Text: *The School for
Scandal*' in *Evidence in Literary Scholarship: Essays in Memory of James Marshall Osborn*, ed.
René Wellek and Alvaro Ribeiro (Oxford: Clarendon Press, 1979). See also Shirley Sturm Kenny,
'The Playhouse and the Printing Shop: Editing Restoration and Eighteenth-Century Plays', *Modern
Philology* 85 (1988): 408–19.

decedents are reserved texts, reflecting Sheridan's private concerns, even if, save for some precise amendments, they are in the hand of a professional scribe rather than Sheridan's own characteristic scrawl.

2

By the mid-1780s, Sheridan was secure within the ranks of the Foxites, though the party seemed remote from power, not least because its leadership was depressed by George III's defeat of Fox's India Bill.[28] However, by early 1785 they were resurgent. Pitt's taxes on coal, bricks and cotton, introduced the previous year were proving unpopular, while the Westminster election controversy gave their satirists abundant opportunities to exploit the government's embarrassment.[29] The principal bones of contention in 1785, however, were the Irish propositions, introduced to the Irish parliament in February 1785 by Thomas Orde, chief secretary to the Lord Lieutenant, the Duke of Rutland. The propositions rested on the Smithean assumption that free trade would bind Britain and Ireland more effectively than any other measure.[30] Orde claimed that the propositions would encourage a stable and liberal commerce between Britain and Ireland. This principle was enshrined in the first proposition: 'That it is highly important to the general interests of the British empire, that the intercourse and commerce between Great Britain and Ireland should be finally regulated on permanent and equitable principles, for the mutual benefit of both countries'. Orde presented nine further propositions to the Irish Commons, these announced that duties would be lowered as trade was regularised to the advantage, it was claimed, of Irish agriculture, manufacture and commerce. In return, Ireland would provide a secure supply of funds to Britain in years of surplus; these requisitions were intended to cover the necessary expenses of empire. Presenting the propositions in London some weeks later, Pitt stressed this financial dimension, contained in the second proposition. He also placed far greater emphasis on the regulatory controls set out in the remaining propositions.

---

[28] See Boyd Hilton, *A Mad, Bad, and Dangerous People? England 1783–1846* (New York: Oxford University Press, 2006); and L. G. Mitchell, *Charles James Fox* (New York: Oxford University Press, 1992).

[29] [Richard Tickell and Joseph Richardson], *Probationary Odes for the Laureatship with a Preliminary Discourse by Sir John Hawkins* (London: J. Ridgway, 1785). See also Robert W. Jones, 'Foxite Satire: Politics, Print, and Celebrity' in *The Oxford Handbook of Eighteenth-Century Satire*, ed. Paddy Bullard (Oxford University Press, 2019).

[30] See James Livesey, 'Free trade and Empire in the Anglo-Irish Commercial Propositions of 1785', *Journal of British Studies* 52 (2013): 103–27.

The difference between Pitt's and Orde's versions provoked almost immediate dispute.[31]

Sheridan's first intervention in what would prove a long and fractious process came on 14 March, when a petition against the propositions was presented from several manufacturing towns. The petitioners, who were supported by several MPs, were animated by what seemed a clear disparity between what Orde had promised in the Irish parliament and what Pitt had said at Westminster. Sheridan exploited this distinction, lamenting the disquiet given to the manufacturers. To make his point, he drew upon a recent newspaper advert, signed by Josiah Wedgwood, which raised concerns as to the effect on English manufacturers if Ireland became, as Orde had promised, 'the *emporium of trade*'. Pitt, Sheridan noted, had said nothing of the kind. Nor had he since allayed the fears of Wedgwood and his friends, indeed he had been dismissive of them.[32] Sheridan reflected with some candour on his own position, and here accounts of his speech differ noticeably. Shorter reports record Sheridan reflecting that 'if he gave credit to Mr. Orde's assertions, as an English member of Parliament, he could not vote for the propositions: and were he to assent to all that [Pitt] advanced, as a well-wisher to Ireland, he most certainly rejected his proffers.'[33] Other newspapers suggest that Sheridan's good wishes towards Ireland encouraged him to look favourably on the first proposition and possibly some others, even as he dismissed the remainder. According to the *Morning Chronicle*, Sheridan requested 'more information respecting the propositions, because as a friend to Ireland he wished to vote for several of them'.[34] In a similar vein, the *Public Advertiser* reported that 'as friend both to this country and Ireland', Sheridan 'wished to see a permanent system established to the mutual interest and advantage of both countries'. What is clear is that Sheridan, rejected emphatically the idea, advanced in the debate by Pitt, that to accept the first proposition was to accept them all. This clear distinction, which would prove crucial later, reveals that throughout the

[31] James Kelly, *Prelude to Union: Anglo-Irish Politics in the 1780s* (Cork: Cork University Press, 1992). See also Douglas Kanter, *The Making of British Unionism, 1740–1848: Politics, Government, and the Anglo-Irish Constitutional Relationship* (Dublin: Four Courts, 2009); and David R. Schweitzer, 'The Failure of William Pitt's Irish Trade Propositions', *Parliamentary History* 3 (1984): 129–45.

[32] *Morning Post*, 15 March 1785. See also Richard Brinsley Sheridan, *Speeches of the Late Right Honourable Richard Brinsley Sheridan: Several Corrected by Himself and Edited by a Constitutional Friend*, 5 vols. (London: Patrick Martin, 1816), 1: 146. Subsequent references appear in the text.

[33] *The Parliamentary Register: Or, History of the Proceedings and Debates of the House of Commons*, 45 vols. (London: J. Debrett, 1781–96), 18: 405. See also *Gazetteer and New Daily Advertiser*, 15 March 1785; and *Morning Herald*, 15 March 1785.

[34] *Morning Chronicle*, 15 March 1785.

debate, Irish legislative freedom was an article of faith for Sheridan, and not, as has sometimes been claimed, a mere parliamentary tactic.[35]

Responses in Ireland were similarly positive. Pitt's proposals, if carefully introduced, would provide a boost to Irish exports. With some caveats, this favourable view of the propositions prevailed even amongst patriots. Henry Grattan, to take but one example, was muted in his response, though he remained alive to the constitutional implications of what Pitt proposed.[36] British public opinion remained hostile. Animated by what was perceived to be a repeal of the Navigation Acts, with consequent implications for the security of their businesses, protest from merchants and manufacturers were extensive and well organised. Numerous petitions were canvassed and submitted to Parliament, some fifty-six in March and April alone.[37] The manufacturing counties, especially Lancashire, played a central role in a well-organised and vociferous campaign. British manufacturers were surprisingly wary of free trade. None more so than Wedgwood, who, as a prominent Staffordshire manufacturers, took a significant role in the General Chamber of Manufacturers. A crucial meeting was held in Manchester in April 1785, when the town's merchants were particularly prominent, though it was Wedgwood who led the event. While Wedgwood had always been worried by perceived threats to the security of British manufacturing, the Irish propositions excited his worst fears.[38] Wedgwood did not share Pitt's belief that trade could achieve amity between nations. Ireland, he contended, would benefit unduly as its low taxes and low costs would allow it to 'outstrip' British trade. The proposed arrangement would promote, he claimed, not trade and amity but 'perpetual jealousies, & irreconcilable animosities'. Wedgwood and his companions would prove effective campaigners, successfully mobilising protest in much of the north of England.[39]

Facing opposition within and without Parliament, Pitt withdrew and amended his proposals in late April. Some of the initial propositions were revised, while new ones were inserted to appease manufacturing interests and specifically East and West India merchants. It was consequently necessary to renumber the propositions, eventually there would be

---

[35] *Public Advertiser*, 15 March 1785; *Whitehall Evening Post*, 12–15 March 1785. See also Martyn J. Powell, 'Charles James Fox and Ireland', *Irish Historical Studies* 33 (2002): 169–90.

[36] Kelly, *Prelude to Union*, 103, 108. See also Jacqueline Hill, *Dublin Civic Politics and Irish Protestant Patriotism 1660–1840* (Oxford: Clarendon Press, 1997).

[37] Kelly, *Prelude to Union*, 131.

[38] *The Letters of Josiah Wedgwood*, ed. Katherine Eufemia Farrar, 3 vols. (Manchester: E. J. Morten, 1906), 3: 9–10, 15–16.

[39] *Letters of Josiah Wedgwood*, 3: 23, 28.

twenty.[40] To what remained the second proposition – which had specified
that Ireland grant funds for imperial expense – was added the stipulation
that these funds would be allocated to military expenditure. This was
a bold proposal given long-held sensitivities concerning standing armies
and was opposed as such by Sheridan and others (*Speeches*, I: 159–61).
The amendment was exceeded in both ambition and controversy by the
new fourth proposition, which demanded that the Irish Commons ratify
all trade laws passed at Westminster. Irish opposition became instantly
more vocal, as Irish legislative independence was clearly compromised
merely to appease British merchants anxious to secure their own privileges.
In this context, Sheridan had a difficult hand to play. He was not unsym-
pathetic to Irish interests; indeed, he supported measures beneficial to the
nation of his birth. He would have been acutely aware, however, that his
Staffordshire constituents were not minded to be so generous, not least
when he presented petitions on their behalf.[41] Sheridan spoke several times
during April and May and through June and July. On each occasion, he
defended both Irish legislative independence and the interests of the
British manufacturers. Sheridan supported the Manchester petitioners
when Pitt dismissed their claims. To substantiate his position, he added
that 'he had spent part of the summer in Lancashire, and had been
a witness to the infinite pains the manufacturers had taken to keep their
numerous workmen quiet, and to preserve the peace of the country'
(*Speeches*, 1: 149). On 24 May, he reiterated his opinion that, as originally
conceived, the propositions would be 'serviceable' to Ireland and that he
was mindful that 'something must be done' for that nation; but he was
equally attuned to the needs of northern manufacturers.[42] This doubled
position was hard to maintain. Animated and encouraged by the petitioners, the Foxites were fierce opponents of Pitt's propositions, regarding
them as a danger to British trade, while also treating them as a threat to
Irish legislative independence. To this end, they encouraged protest from
British merchants, as well making claims to defend Ireland. There was
some opportunism in this doubled response, notoriously when Fox
claimed to be a leading Irish patriot, having previously expressed an
appetite for Irish revenue. Sheridan's complicated and perhaps contradictory position was by this measure more consistent and more creditable
than that of many of his colleagues.[43]

---

[40] Kelly, *Prelude to Union*, 133–37.
[41] See *Journal of the House of Commons*, 56 vols. (London: HSO, 1802), 40: 1006, 1009; and *The Times*,
      24 May 1785.
[42] *Morning Herald*, 25 May 1785.   [43] Kelly, *Prelude to Union*, 142–44.

Although the Foxites concentrated on the threat to Irish legislative independence, Sheridan maintained a more independent path, paying careful attention to Ireland's trade. His attention to Ireland and to mercantile politics confirms not only the depth but also the breadth of his allegiance. Sheridan's most celebrated contribution to the debate came on 30 May, when he disputed both the amended second and the new fourth propositions. On the subject of the latter, he sensed a deeper conspiracy on Pitt's part: 'the true spring and incentive to this artful and complicated business', he suggested, 'lurked in this fourth proposition; the tendency of which was of a piece with their whole system of government' (*Speeches*, I: 170). True, the Irish parliament might debate British legislation before acceding to it, but this was small comfort. Sheridan reflected that if he were a 'member of the Irish parliament', he would not waste time debating these points as 'where fetters were to be worn, it is a wretched ambition to contend for the distinction of fastening our own shackles' (*Speeches*, I: 164). But even if the matter were viewed solely as a commercial arrangement, Ireland was expected to sacrifice too much. The new propositions, he explained, revealed that markets were not, in the end, to be opened to Ireland, but rather to please commercial interests in Britain, Irish manufacturers were to be squeezed out of the West Indies, Africa and Asia. Ireland was to lose all traffic and commerce with the rest of the world in exchange for little; it was nothing 'less than a direct fraud, cheat, and robbery'. Ireland, he claimed, was to 'surrender her now-acknowledged right of . . . legislation' in return for demeaning and restricted access to British markets. These efforts were merely to reassure English manufacturers, manufacturers whose petitions Pitt had treated with disdain (*Speeches*, I: 173–5). Sheridan's highly effective assault on the fourth proposition was printed in Dublin as *The Legislative Independence of Ireland Vindicated*.[44] The publication was an enormous success, and the speech was widely read. By late June, the *Morning Herald* could report from Dublin that 'Mr Sheridan's speech is in every man's hand, and has been read in most of the public schools, where it has also been given to the boys to study.'[45] By coincidence, or design, the 30 May was the final day of the theatrical season. Drury Lane commemorated the event with a Sheridan double bill: *The School for Scandal* followed by *The Critic*, a potent and provocative pairing.

---

[44] *The Legislative Independence of Ireland Vindicated: in a Speech of Mr. Sheridan's on the Irish Propositions, in the British House of Commons. To which is annexed an Authentic Copy of the Twenty Resolutions, on the Irish Commercial Intercourse* (Dublin: P. Cooney, 1785).

[45] *Morning Herald*, 30 June 1785.

Although the speech on 30 May was the high-water mark of Sheridan's engagement with the Irish propositions, he spoke again throughout June and July. Sheridan's correspondence from this period underscores the strength and complexities of his bifurcated commitments – equally his exasperation with Irish affairs and with Irish politicians in particular. His letters to Stratford Canning and Charles Sheridan are noticeably tart, seemingly the work of someone harried and hustled, but supremely confident in his own judgement. Charles Sheridan supported Pitt's proposals and had advocated trade concessions, hoping to secure amity between Britain and Ireland. So far he agreed with his brother. However, Charles Sheridan was willing to accept the fourth proposition, a case he made in his pamphlet *Free Thoughts on the Present Crisis*.[46] Sheridan's response was to execrate his brother as a 'Castle Tory' and to express the hope that if the propositions passed the Irish Commons that he might never hear the name of Ireland again (*Letters*, 1: 164–5). To Canning, he despaired that the Irish parliament would sacrifice its hard-won independence for short-term gain: 'they mean', he wrote on 26 July, 'to cajole Paddy out of his notions of an independent Legislature and persuade him that a parcel of fine words on the subject … are the same thing' (*Letters*, 1: 164). Sheridan's letters disclose a wary attitude to Irish politics. His use of 'Paddy' suggests, in Elizabeth Sheridan's phrasing, a distance from 'that country', indeed those people. Ireland, he implies, is not sufficiently robust in its opposition to Pitt, his measures or his rhetoric. In this context, the name 'Manchester' united several competing ideas in Sheridan's mind: active resistance to Ireland's commercial interests, on the one hand, but an equally committed intransigence to Pitt which the Foxites could exploit. Dublin could not be trusted so far. Manchester denominated a point of tension. It gave a name to English self-interest, yet it opened a clear path of party political opportunity. Fox would be cheered in the streets of Manchester when he visited the town in the late summer of 1785. It was an awareness of Manchester's status as the fulcrum of the Irish propositions debates that prompted Sheridan to insert it into his masterpiece.[47] Although Sheridan might merely have wanted to make a snide remark, perhaps to amuse Frances

[46] Charles Francis Sheridan, *Free Thoughts upon the Present Crisis in which are stated the Fundamental Principles upon which alone Ireland can or ought to agree to any Final Settlements with Great Britain* (Dublin: n.p., 1785). See also Kelly, *Prelude to Union*, 82–83, 159; and Livesey, 'Free Trade and Empire', 121, 126.
[47] Kelly, *Prelude to Union*, 199.

Crewe, the reference resonates more widely, ensuring that the insertion remediates, in O'Quinn's terms, a topical reference casting the picture scene in a more uncertain light.[48]

It is not difficult to see how the insertion of 'Manchester' underlined concerns about empire and nationhood, trade and belonging, to anyone reading the manuscript at Crewe Hall. It would have resonated equally during any theatrical performance, especially to members of London's merchant or Irish communities. The introduction of Manchester is transformative, adding uncertainty. When Charles refers to the 'Mayor of Manchester', something specific is indicated: an interchangeable person, one of a kind, has been replaced by a more pointed reference. Unlike the comment about the Blunt brothers, which preceded it, it not a waft in a general direction, but a distinct recollection:

CHARLES SURFACE: Here's a Jolly Fellow – I don't know what Relation – But he
    was Mayor of Manchester, take him at eight pounds.
SIR OLIVER: No, no – six will do for the Mayor.
CHARLES SURFACE: Come make it Guineas and I'll throw in the two Alderman
    there into the Bargain –
SIR OLIVER: They're mine. (*DW*, I: 406)

The dialogue subsequent to the altered line gains an additional charge from the reference. The business of the scene, already ambiguous, resonates differently. Whereas Sir Oliver has previously accepted any price, his response to this more uncertain figure is to haggle. The dialogue now accentuates barter and concession: a price needs to be paid for, and implicitly to, the 'Mayor of Manchester'. The Mayor has his price and Sir Oliver must pay it. The economy of the picture scene is altered. The Mayor once the subject of an insouciant shrug – 'I don't know what Relation' – now seems both a reference and a rebuke. The Mayor of Manchester has a negotiable value. Loyalties are traded, discarded and a bargain taken. Once the deal is clinched, Charles asks his sidekick, Careless, to 'knock down the Mayor and Alderman', before expressing a desire to 'deal wholesale' and have Sir Oliver take 'the Rest of the Family in the Lump'.

Something curious has occurred. But what, precisely? Jean Baudrillard's analysis of the slender semiotics and slight economies of art auctions proves instructive in this context. Auctions, he argues, are not about the establishment of worth; they do not even establish exchange value. Quite the

---

[48] O'Quinn, *Entertaining Crisis*, 65–67.

reverse: they are a fiction of that process, an economy of the sign in which the signifiers of wealth are purchased for their own sake. Arts auctions do not mark or convey value or wealth; they destroy it, burying money in an object that is only truly valuable semiotically. They are a *potlatch* – a ritual process that marks the end of exchange and ensures the destruction of value. It is though the auction as *potlatch* that excessive wealth is put beyond use.[49] There is something of that appetite to lose value, though not face, at stake in *The School for Scandal*. Charles's pictures, unfashionable and 'Aukward' as they are, are not worth the money Sir Oliver pays for them. Neither is Charles. He is a spendthrift, a waster of time and wine. By rescuing him, Sir Oliver exchanges the wealth of empire, of the East specifically, to pay for his sentimental reintegration into his long-abandoned family. His purchases, combined with Charles's limited act of remembrance, ensure that his portrait will hang in the family house with all the old aunts and their kind. But beyond the dubious flurry of the auction, unions are not so easily forged; something, or rather somebody, must give way. This is arguably the lesson of the scene, indeed of the play. Relationships are manipulative, exploitative masquerades. The pain of this process is more exquisitely felt by those possessed of (or possessed by) more than one set of loyalties. The Sheridans were quintessentially that sort of family, and they knew it. Charles Surface and Careless make this sorry fact clear when they select the Surface family's lineage as their auctioneer's gavel. The names are tellingly familiar to anyone cognisant of Sheridan's own descent: 'What parchment have we here [*takes down a roll*] *Richard Heir to Thomas* – our genealogy in full! ... now you may knock down my Ancestors with their own Pedigree' (*DW*, I: 405).

If the familial is to be discarded, what else must be taken 'in the Lump'? It is significant in the wider context of the play, and Sheridan's attitude to empire, that the East Company, Sir Oliver's erstwhile employers, occupied a crucial and contested place in the Irish propositions; indeed, part of the uncertainty generated by the propositions focused on the status of the Company and its goods. Sheridan certainly complained that Irish trade would lose the lucrative Indian market (*Speeches*, I: 174). Some Irish politicians expected that as trade was freed, Ireland would be able to conduct its commerce with Asia openly, including the re-export of colonial goods and supplies to the colonies. Irish expectations relied upon a confederate understanding of empire, one that had not been imagined

---

[49] Jean Baudrillard, *For a Critique of the Political Economy of the Sign*, trans. Charles Levin (St. Louis: Telos Press, 1981).

by Pitt, who, on the contrary, wished to see Ireland bound more tightly to Britain.[50] With a sharper eye for Pitt's designs than many of his compatriots, Sheridan understood the importance of both imports and exports from Asia and argued passionately that Irish trade should not suffer restriction.[51] Beyond even these concerns, Sheridan resisted any encroachment on Ireland's legislative independence, a protective attitude that was further demonstrated in the Union debates in 1799 and 1800. When this greater imperial dimension is registered, the revised *The School for Scandal* is freighted with the anxieties of imperial commerce and migrated identities.[52] Throughout *School for Scandal,* relations are noted but eschewed: 'our genealogy' might appear 'in full' but it is half cast adrift and half clutched in desperation. Sheridan's necessarily doubled position, though it could be performed superbly, was never without difficulty, compromise or doubt. The play and its Mancunian mayor rehearse Sheridan's position, caught between the Foxites and their allies and his Irish identity. It is the oscillation between the display and disguise of this triangulation that makes the *School for Scandal* such a fantastic and poignant play.

---

[50] See Kelly, *Prelude to Union*, 148; and Livesey, 'Free Trade and Empire', 123–4.

[51] *Morning Herald*, 24 May 1785; and *Morning Post*, 24 May 1785.

[52] See Mita Choudhury, 'Sheridan, Garrick, and a Colonial Gesture: *The School for Scandal* on the Calcutta Stage', *Theatre Journal* 46 (1994): 303–21; and O'Quinn, *Entertaining Crisis*, 186–233.

CHAPTER 6

Sydney Owenson, Alicia Sheridan Le Fanu and the Domestic Stage of Post-Union Politics

Colleen Taylor

On her first trip to London in 1807, Sydney Owenson made her way to an elite dinner party at Lady Cork's in New Burlington Street, where she immediately faced reproach. Catching her at the door, the host reprimanded Owenson for not bringing her harp along, scolding, 'You are a fool, child, don't you know your own interests!'[1] Lady Cork had invited Owenson not as a guest, but as a pseudo-performer – an actress meant to play out her freshly published novel's eponymous role of 'Wild Irish Girl', complete with harp, Irish melodies and the periodical Irish language phrase. The wording of this exchange, when Lady Cork calls Owenson a 'fool', is particularly suggestive in the London setting. Throughout the eighteenth century, the London stage saw many Irishmen turned to fools by Stage Irishisms – characters like the Irish 'Teague', announcing 'arrah honeys' and 'Bajesus' – so that the Irish blunderer was a long-time staple character by the time Owenson showed up on Lady Cork's doorstep. Somewhat paradoxically, Lady Cork names Owenson a fool for *not* bringing that Irish act along to the party, where her parlour room would serve as an unofficial stage for Owenson's newly popular Irish character: the charming, wistful and wild Irish girl Glorvina. Throughout the rest of her London tour and those following, Owenson played her heroine Glorvina wherever she could, donning her red Gaelic mantle for added dramatic effect and, as we will see, for subtextual political meanings. After the Rebellion of 1798 and the Act of Union, the underlying meanings of Owenson's Irish act were arguably too inflammatory for the public stage, but they could find expression underneath an 'unthreatening' feminine costume in an ostensibly neutral domestic scene like a parlour room. Owenson recognised the national and feminist potentials of drawing

---

[1] Sydney Owenson, *The Book of the Boudoir*, 2 vols. (London: Henry Colburn, 1829), 1: 103.

room performance – a subversive strategy her mentor Alicia Le Fanu would later put directly back on London's dramatic stage in 1812.

This chapter explores the connections between women's relegation to the domestic realm and their relationship to the national stage, using Owenson's Glorvina costume and Alicia Le Fanu's 1812 play *The Sons of Erin,* which I bring together here for their shared patriotic-feminist ideology. Sydney Owenson's Irish costume and Alicia Sheridan Le Fanu's play drew on tropes and plots employed by earlier male playwrights and actors in order to (re)stage Anglo-Irish relations in feminine and feminist terms. We typically think of Irish women's writing after the Act of Union exclusively in terms of the novel form, but plays written by women, although fewer in number, also proved significant.[2] I will argue that the post-Union era's Irish fashions, like the Irish theatre, became frameworks through which women could rehearse their politics and engage in the cultural exchange between London and Dublin at the turn of the nineteenth century. Owenson's party performances as the red-cloaked 'wild Irish girl' and Le Fanu's London play apply domestic tools like women's dress and parlour room conversation to a public, political endeavour. Together, the two dramatists reveal the national discourse and the gendered discourse around women to be mutually inextricable in the years following the Union.

Owenson's Glorvina Costume

After *The Wild Irish Girl* took Ireland and England by storm in 1806, Owenson quickly became what Mary Campbell terms 'a public persona of Irishness'.[3] William Hepworth Dixon, the author's biographer, explains that up until her marriage and adoption of the title Lady Morgan in 1812, Owenson and her heroine Glorvina were indistinguishable in the popular mindset.[4] Male admirers, in particular, loved the fantasy of the fairylike Glorvina, a role she played right back to them.[5] In *The Wild Irish Girl,*

---

[2] English publishers complained of being inundated with Irish novels by female authors in the first three decades of the nineteenth century. Claire Connolly notes 114 Irish novels published between 1800 and 1829, most of which were written by women. See Claire Connolly, *A Cultural History of the Irish Novel* (New York: Cambridge University Press, 2012) and Rolf and Magda Loeber, 'Literary Absentees: Irish Women Authors in Nineteenth-Century England' in *The Irish Novel in the Nineteenth Century: Facts and Fictions,* ed. Jacqueline Belanger (Dublin: Four Courts Press, 2005).
[3] Mary Campbell, *Lady Morgan: The Life and Times of Sydney Owenson* (London: Pandora, 1988), 103.
[4] Sydney Owenson, *Lady Morgan's Memoirs: Autobiography, Diaries, and Correspondence,* ed. W. Hepworth Dixon, 2 vols. (London: W. H. Allen, 1863), I: 277.
[5] Campbell, *Lady Morgan,* 98.

Glorvina first appears to Horatio, and to readers, dressed in her scarlet cloak, a descendent of the early modern Gaelic mantle, complete with the Irish bodkin or pin: 'From the shoulder fell a mantle of scarlet silk, fastened at the neck with the silver bodkin, while the fine turned head was enveloped in a veil of point lace.'[6] From this moment, Glorvina's mantle becomes a moniker of her appearance in the novel, a signature Owenson adopted for her own public wardrobe. In the decade following the publication of *The Wild Irish Girl*, the writer's typical dress was a white muslin frock with a flower at her bosom paired with her red Gaelic cloak. Campbell explains that Owenson's routine donning of her red cloak, perhaps more than anything else, 'add[ed] to her fame' wherever she went.[7] Owenson's costume in London undoubtedly points to her deft self-marketing skills, as Campbell, Claire Connolly, Julie Donovan and others have suggested, but it also signifies much more than a marketing ploy for celebrity.[8] The cloak represents a carefully dressed theatrical and historical reference, which, I will argue, Owenson designed for her own patriotic and proto-feminist message.

Helen Burke has traced the mantle's resonances for English theatre-going audiences over the course of the eighteenth century. Sir Robert Howard's *The Committee* put the mantle on the London stage in 1662, when his poor, Irish 'shrouded figure', the popular character Teague, meets his future employer, Careless. Burke explains that throughout the eighteenth century and into the nineteenth, Teague's 'blanket', or mantle, became a tag for the Stage Irishman in England – an outward signifier of that loveable Irish fool character trope, who is loyal to his English master but nothing more than 'a poor simple fellow' and comic relief.[9] In almost every portrait of Teague from the eighteenth century, depicted by actors such as John Moody (1776) and Edward Anthony

---

[6] Sydney Owenson, *The Wild Irish Girl*, ed. Kathryn Kirkpatrick (Oxford: Oxford University Press, 1999), 48. Joseph Cooper Walker's 'Essay on Irish Dress' – quoted extensively by Owenson – describes the premodern Gaelic mantle as a long 'cloak' or 'shawl' with a hood, worn by Irish noblemen and made of elegant silk 'fringed with gold or silver lace, [decorated] with elegant and costly ornaments' (80). The most famous English images of the mantle from the period are John Derricke's *Image of Irelande* (1581), which depict the Irish chieftains in the long cloaks. The bodkin, meaning 'little dagger', was used as both a weapon and a pin in the same era. See Walker's 'Essay on Irish Dress' and Mary Campbell's *Lady Morgan*.
[7] Campbell, *Lady Morgan*, 111, 72.
[8] Campbell, *Lady Morgan*, 86, 100, 114; Claire Connolly, '"I accuse Miss Owenson": The Wild Irish Girl as Media Event', *Colby Quarterly* 36.2 (2000): 98–115; 104–5; Julie Donovan, *Sydney Owenson, Lady Morgan and the Politics of Style* (Bethesda: Maunsel & Company, 2009), 60.
[9] Helen Burke, 'Integrated as Outsiders: Teague's Blanket and the Irish Immigrant "Problem" in Early Modern Britain', *Éire-Ireland* 46.2 (2011): 20–42; 34.

Rock (1797), he is portrayed in the signature blanket/mantle in which he first appears, poor and begging, until his future English employer Careless saves him from destitution.[10] Teague's mantle had cultural currency in London throughout the eighteenth century: Burke argues its prevalence as a popular image assuaged English anxieties over the Irish immigrant problem by presenting a warm and harmless version of a cloak that had once signified Irish otherness. In the sixteenth century, Edmund Spenser associated the mantle with Irish barbarity, writing that the homeless, animalistic Irish used their mantles as shelter when wandering or as a disguise for thievery.[11] When Howard's Teague appeared on the London stage, he helped domesticate that Irish threat for London eyes.

Sydney Owenson could not have missed the prevalence and cultural currency of Teague's mantle. She had grown up in the theatre world: her father, Robert Owenson, was a famed Irish actor and established a short-lived national theatre on Fishamble Street.[12] What's more, *The Committee*'s Teague was one of her father's famous roles in his acting career, second to another popular Stage Irish character, Major O'Flaherty in Richard Cumberland's *The West Indian,* for which Owenson was known long after his retirement from the stage. In her memoirs, Owenson praises her father's acting in a patriotic sense, recounting that 'Cumberland and Sheridan thanked [him] for redeeming their creations from caricature'.[13] As this esteem in her father's atypical Irish characterisation evinces, Owenson sought to resist, even challenge, the typical Stage Irish Teague that London audiences had grown to recognise over the past one hundred years. She was not alone in this: earlier playwrights like Thomas Sheridan and Charles Macklin had made significant steps in countering the Stage Irishman with more complex characters, such as Captain O'Blunder and Sir Callaghan

---

[10] Ibid., 21–24.

[11] Edmund Spenser, *View of the Present State of Irelande*, ed. W. L. Renwick (Oxford: Clarendon Press, 1970).

[12] Owenson's sister, Lady Olivia Clarke, also followed in their father's footsteps and briefly dipped into the dramatic world. Her play, *The Irishwoman*, was put on in Dublin's Crow Street Theatre in 1818 and played for three months. The play marks Clarke's only public literary endeavour. Although she was always overshadowed by her famous sister, *The Irishwoman* represents a significant political and dramatic effort: its prologue and epilogue (written by Charles Morgan) lobbies for Catholic Emancipation by appealing to the patriotism of women in the audience. See *The Irishwoman* (London: H. Colburn, 1819).

[13] Owenson, *Memoirs,* 1: 59. This suggests that a consideration of Robert Owenson might be useful in assessing the opposing perspectives of Davis (Chapter 2) and Cox Jensen (Chapter 3) on John Johnstone in this volume.

O'Brallaghan.[14] For a fashionable and literary young woman like Owenson, then, the mantle – Teague's most famous tag – became the perfect surface on which to re-signify Irishness in London. Owenson cleverly played it 'au simple' when she arrived in London as a young author, but even a foolish Stage Irish Teague is never wholly 'simple', particularly when played by patriots like the Owensons, and especially when dressed in a mantle.[15]

In the later years of her life, Owenson admitted that Glorvina's costume of mantle and bodkin was only tolerated in elite English and Ascendancy social circles, like Lady Cork's gathering of 'princes, ambassadors, dukes and duchesses', because it was a 'period of relaxation' in Irish affairs following the Union.[16] Her memoirs imply the Glorvina routine acquiesced to English and Anglo-Irish expectations about wild yet unthreatening Irishness. Nevertheless, her costume also boldly repackaged the mantle before English eyes while also re-signifying its subtext. In *The Wild Irish Girl*, Owenson correlates Glorvina's mantle with the tragic dispossession of her father, the Prince of Inismore. A local peasant explains that during the 'wars of Queen Elizabeth', one of the Prince's ancestors 'had a castle and a great tract of land on the borders, of which he was deprived, as the story runs, because he would neither cut his *glibbs* . . . nor shorten his shirt'.[17] In a subsequent footnote, Owenson cites a law ratified in 1616 whereby anyone who 'appeared in Irish robes or mantles should be punished by fine and imprisonment'.[18] As the novel suggests, the English tried to erase the mantle signifier of Irish identity to bolster their claims on Irish territory. Owenson, on the other hand, very publicly redesigned Teague's coarse blanket into Glorvina's elegant, feminine mantle before some of the most elite and powerful eyes in England, transforming an item that had previously connoted poverty and ignorance into a refined and modestly seductive form of traditional Irish dress.

Owenson's familiarity with both the historical suppression of Irish dress and with the popular culture surrounding Teague's image enables us to

---

[14] Sheridan's *The Brave Irishman* and Macklin's *Love à la Mode* counterweigh standard eighteenth-century Stage Irish stereotypes. See Helen Burke, *Riotous Performances: The Struggle for Hegemony in the Irish Theater* (Notre Dame, IN: University of Notre Dame Press, 2003), 252–55, 286–87.

[15] Campbell, *Lady Morgan,* 86.

[16] Owenson, *Book of the Boudoir,* 1: 3, 68. In *Book of the Boudoir,* Owenson cynically writes that despite their enthusiasm for Glorvina, most of those Ascendancy women would have sooner let Owenson perish in the streets from 'want or infamy' than 'stretched forth a finger to save her from either' (68).

[17] Glibbes were an Irish style of wearing hair long at the front of the head, banned in 1616 for its 'otherness' in an attempt to conform the Irish to English fashion. Owenson, *The Wild Irish Girl,* 37–38.

[18] Ibid., 38.

read her Stage Irish performances in London in terms of political subtext. In contrast to Teague's mantle, which, as Helen Burke argues, ideologues English stereotypes about unskilled Irish labourers, Owenson's appearance as the 'wild Irish girl' at English parties destabilised the established relations between London audience and Irish comic actor. For example, in 1829, Owenson published her account of that night at Lady Cork's in a collection of memoirs entitled *The Book of the Boudoir*. She satirises the party scene, depicting her English observers as the fool figures for a change. Owenson details Lady Cork's obsessions with Glorvina's Irish performance, rehashing some of the Lady's words and manner:

> Lord Erskine, this is the 'Wild Irish girl', whom you were so anxious to know. I assure you, she talks quite as well as she writes. Now, my dear, do tell my Lord Erskine some of those Irish stories, you told us the other evening. . . . Mrs. Abington says you would make a famous actress, and she does indeed! You must play the short-armed orator with her; she will be here by and by. This is the Duchess of St. A–, she has your 'Wild Irish Girl' by heart.[19]

The quote captures the infatuation of a babbling Lady Cork and her followers, their failure (whether conscious or not) to recognise Owenson's deeper, critical messages in *The Wild Irish Girl*. It is worth noting that the *Book of the Boudoir,* published in 1829, directly engages with Catholic Emancipation, which Owenson references in her address 'To the Reader':

> I have written 'from my youth, up,' under the influence of one and all-pervading cause, Ireland and its wrongs. . . . But the day is now fast approaching when all that is Irish will fall into its natural position. . . . Among the multitudinous effects of Catholic emancipation, I do not hesitate to predict a change in the character of Irish authorship.[20]

In writing to those in favour of Catholic Emancipation, Owenson can retroactively unveil – perhaps even reconstruct – her mantle routine as a political manoeuvre. Looking back at her costume with a new framework in 1829 – a more appropriate time for explicit expressions of Irish nationalism – Owenson illustrates how putting on the Irish act at Lady Cork's party enabled her to use English popular response for her own patriotic gain. Her account of that night destabilises the hierarchised, imperial space of the English drawing room by staging a politicised spectacle in London's inner domestic circle. That Owenson used her costume as clever Irish

---

[19] Owenson, *Book of the Boudoir,* 1: 107.   [20] Ibid., iv.

disguise for her anti-imperial message arguably harbours a patriotic allu-sion to the Irish literary tradition as well. Joseph Cooper Walker's 'Essay on Irish Dress', which Owenson quotes extensively in *The Wild Irish Girl*, references the ancient tactic of Irish women using the mantle as disguise, and thus enabling acts of heroism.[21]

In re-dressing Teague's blanket, Owenson also re-dresses misogynistic depictions of Irish women in English writing. The early modern English mindset associated the Irish mantle with 'lascivious female sexuality', a belief that lasted well into the seventeenth, even the eighteenth, century.[22] Spenser, John Derricke and other writers propagated the idea that Irish women, naked underneath their 'sluttish Mantells', were barbaric and suspect, and this idea persisted into Owenson's period.[23] For instance, a *Times* article on 'The Irish Cloak' in 1825, paraphrases Spenser's descrip-tion of the mantle as one that still applies to the current dress among natives in Ireland. Interestingly, the author of that article refuses to reprint Spenser's discussion of Irish women's mantles, which it says is 'nothing less than scandal'.[24] Perhaps this addendum, refusing to repeat the 'scandalous' ideas proposed by Spenser, suggests that Owenson-as-Glorvina had been successful in recasting prejudice about the 'sluttish mantel' into the accep-table social mores of the proper Enlightened lady – a lady who wears English muslin underneath her Irish mantle, and who is desirable in her modesty, just like Glorvina. More importantly, in both her novel and her social performance, Owenson refashions the image of the subservient Irish subject associated with the Stage Irish character. The scenes of Horatio prostrating himself at the hem of Glorvina's mantle that recur in *The Wild Irish Girl* gain subversive poignancy in light of the mantle's history. The English gentleman who 'fell at [Glorvina's] feet kissing the hem of her robe' reorders the colonial hierarchy surrounding the mantle in both Spenser's and Howard's writings.[25] In Owenson's text, the mantle becomes a site of English respect – perhaps even deference – for Irish culture, as well as a site of masculine, British deference to Irish femininity.

The greatest design of Owenson's mantle costume was a commercial one. As Owenson became 'the very embodiment of "the Irish look"',

[21] For example, the 'beautiful Irish romance' where Princess Favarla sneaks Carval O'Daly out of prison using her mantle as a cover. Joseph Cooper Walker, *An historical essay on the dress of the ancient and modern Irish: addressed to the right Honourable Earl of Charlemont. To which is subjoined, a memoir on the armour and weapons of the Irish* (Dublin: George Grierson, 1788), 54.
[22] John R. Ziegler, 'Irish Mantles, English Nationalism: Apparel and National Identity in Early Modern English and Irish Texts', *Journal for Early Modern Cultural Studies* 13.1 (2013): 73–95, 79.
[23] Ibid., 61.   [24] *The Times*, 22 September 1825.   [25] Owenson, *The Wild Irish Girl*, 164.

English and Anglo-Irish socialites became eager to emulate it.[26] While *The Wild Irish Girl* continued to appear in papers and libraries, and while Owenson circulated among the elite in London and Dublin, flirting and charming the upper classes, a consumer demand for Glorvina cloaks developed. The Dublin company Brush and Sons began to manufacture the Glorvina costume such as described in *The Wild Irish Girl,* and English and Anglo-Irish ladies were buying the bodkin ornaments and cloaks in spades.[27] The demand induced drapers in Dublin to manufacture the Glorvina cloaks, and advertisements for these modern-day mantles appeared across the city.[28] The eminent Duchess of Bedford, wife of the Lord Lieutenant of Ireland, whose daughter-in-law later was a close friend of Queen Victoria,[29] became English patron of the Glorvina look, pushing the fabrics and jewels onto the ladies in the vice-regal court in Dublin. Together, Owenson and the duchess had been so successful in their commercial endeavour that when Percy Shelley took his young wife Harriet to Ireland, she 'immediately bought a red cloak – à la Glorvina'.[30] Whereas English rule had forced the Irish people to disrobe their mantles, Owenson had hoodwinked the upper echelons of English and Anglo-Irish society into desiring and elevating the native Irish look, making fashionable what was once considered the primitive signifier of the colonised other. What's more, whereas the London stage had seized cultural control of Teague's mantle a century prior, turning it into the docile image of a subservient Irish servant and simple fool, Owenson used her own costume to regain control of the item's symbolism and cultural currency, refashioning the coarse mantle into an elegant cloak desired and emulated by English women.

Owenson's dramatic efforts reached their apotheosis back in her native Dublin on 11 March 1807 for a special performance of the comic opera *The First Attempt, or The Whim of the Moment.* Riding on the coattails of her newfound celebrity, Owenson had agreed to write the libretto for Thomas Cooke's score of *The First Attempt,* which she hastily composed. Critically speaking, the show had no more than a respectable run;[31] however, it did have a remarkable 'Author's Night' on 11 March, a week after

---

[26] Claire Connolly, 'I accuse Miss Owenson', 110.   [27] Ibid., 105.
[28] Campbell, *Lady Morgan,* 72.
[29] Anna Maria Russell married Frances Russell, eldest son of John Russell, 6th Duke of Bedford and Lord Lieutenant of Ireland 1806–7.
[30] Campbell, *Lady Morgan,* 124.
[31] John Greene tells us that comic operas were the third most popular dramatic genre to be produced in Dublin throughout the eighteenth century. Acknowledging the difficulty in measuring popularity, he nevertheless describes a 'respectable run' in Dublin theatres as about ten to fifteen performances.

opening on 4 March 1807.[32] What made the 11 March performance so special was the fashion show it witnessed: the ladies in attendance at the Theatre Royal followed the lead of the Duchess of Bedford and Owenson herself and wore the manufactured Glorvina bodkins that that had become a popular commodity among fans of *The Wild Irish Girl*.[33] Owenson would later recall the thrill of looking up to the vice-regal box to see 'The Duchess of Bedford and all the ladies of her circle w[earing] the Irish bodkin'.[34] That night, Owenson took her Glorvina performance outside the private sphere and, with the duchess, led a decidedly public, explicitly theatrical Irish fashion show, putting her Gaelic dress and the patriotic message it contained on bright display.

Reviews of *The First Attempt* imply the real show on 11 March happened offstage, in the audience. The *Freeman's Journal* praised the evening's agenda yet carefully omitted any commentary on the quality of the opera itself. The *Journal* likely avoided assessment of lyrical merit as a courtesy to Owenson, who had joked about the show's poor quality in her letters.[35] Rather than review the opera, the *Freeman's Journal* reviewed the audience of *The First Attempt* instead:

> Miss Owenson's night was one of the most overflowing and brilliant audiences we ever recollect to have witnessed. Their Graces the Lord Lieutenant and the Duchess of Bedford, honoured the theatre with their presence – an honour we believe conferred upon no author in this kingdom since the days of the Duke and Duchess of Rutland.[36]

This glowing review presents the crowd at the Theatre Royal as a type of performance in and of itself, celebrating the social turn-out instead of musical success, praising the 'overflowing and brilliant audiences' as an

---

It is worth noting, however, that it was rare for Dublin theatres to put on new works, like *The Whim of the Moment*, that had not already been established in London. After this initial debut in March, the opera was reprised in May of the same year as an afterpiece to *The West Indian* at the Theatre Royal (*Freeman's Journal*, 15 May 1807). See *The Dublin Stage 1720–1745: A Calendar of Plays, Entertainments, and Afterpieces*, ed. John C. Greene and Gladys L. H. Clark (Bethlehem: Lehigh University Press, 1993), 72; *Theatre in Dublin, 1745–1820: A History*, ed. John C. Greene, 2 vols. (Bethlehem: Lehigh University Press, 2011), 2: 330–33; and, *Theatre in Dublin, 1745–1820: A Calendar of Performances*, ed. John C. Greene, 6 vols. (Bethlehem: Lehigh University Press, 2011), 5: 3563–65, 3579.

[32] According to William Fitzpatrick, the 'Author's Night' on 11 March 1807 was so well attended because word got out that Owenson had paid from her own pocket to hire the Theatre Royal. Her supporters packed the house that night to show their financial support for Owenson's career. William John Fitzpatrick, *Lady Morgan; Her Career, Literary and Personal, with a Glimpse of Her Friends, and a Word to Her Calumniators* (London: C. J. Skeet, 1860), 132.

[33] George Patson, *Little Memoirs of the Nineteenth Century* (London: Grant Richards, 1902), 119.

[34] Fitzpatrick, *Lady Morgan; Her Career, Literary and Personal*, 133.

[35] Campbell, *Lady Morgan*, 77.   [36] *Freeman's Journal*, 13 March 1807.

unparalleled dramatic achievement. The review even goes so far as to dub the night the 'most illustrious' in the history of Irish theatre – a tall achievement for a poorly and hastily composed opera. Clearly the offstage demonstration, featuring the Lady Lieutenant and all her friends wearing Glorvina bodkins, made so strong an impact that it muffled Owenson's nonsensical lyrics. That the *Freeman's Journal* renamed *The Whim of the Moment* 'Miss Owenson's night' speaks volumes to us now: it was the collective assertion of female agency, not the opera, that left an impact on the Dublin theatre.

The resonance of this fashionable display is even more suggestive in light of the Irish performance that *did* take place onstage at the Theatre Royal. Owenson wrote a minor Stage Irish character and accompanying ballad for her father (the only Irish reference in the score), which occurred in the middle of the two-act opera. As explained in the published text, Robert Owenson played the 'facetious' role of an 'Irish servant'.[37] In other words, he took to the stage as a variation on Teague, the most famous Irish servant in eighteenth-century theatre and a character for which he had been known earlier in his career. The ballad Robert Owenson sang is part ridiculous stereotype, part national praise and completely out of sync with the rest of the opera, which takes place in Spain and involves primarily Spanish and Italian characters. The first verse of the Irish song reads like nothing more than a drinking song. The second verse, however, appears more candid in parts, such as the line: 'And as for myself, by this twig in my hand,/For old Ireland I'll fight while I'm able to stand.'[38] As a whole, the song comes across like Robert Owenson's reprise as Howard's Teague, but it may also signify his daughter's self-conscious effort to demonstrate the weakened currency of this Irish stereotype, made ridiculous in the wake of *The Wild Irish Girl*'s patriotic achievements.[39] On 13 March 1807, editors at the *Freeman's Journal* included a letter to the editor from 'M.T.' that expressed dissatisfaction with the 'vulgar expressions' of Robert Owenson's Stage Irish character, yet assured Miss Owenson 'The Wild Irish Girl is not forgotten'.[40] Perhaps unconsciously, this commentary documents

---

[37] *The First Attempt, or The Whim of the Moment: a Comic Opera in Two Acts* 'Performing with unbounded applause at the Theatre Royal Dublin, Written by Miss Owenson, the Music Composed by Thomas Cooke' (London: Powers Music House and Westmoreland St. Dublin, 1807), 1.

[38] Ibid., 27.

[39] A letter from Robert Owenson to his daughter implies he first suggested the inclusion of this Stage Irish role as a way to draw a crowd. As I argue here, however, the 'Wild Irish Girl' was the real attraction for audiences. Owenson, *Memoirs*, 1: 317–18.

[40] *Freeman's Journal*, 13 March 1807.

Owenson's successful negation of the Stage Irish stereotypes via her new, more resonant typecast: the refined 'wild Irish girl'.

As a first-time playwright, Owenson wielded control of Stage Irishism.[41] Glorvina's Irish costume and its assortment of English and Anglo-Irish patrons outperformed Teague that night at the Theatre Royal, drowned out the words of his ballad and the stereotypes Ascendancy audiences might find in them. Like her father, Owenson saw the theatre as a patriotic space, as well as a place where fashion could exude a national message. Her recollections of nights spent at the National Music Hall in Dublin in the late eighteenth century insinuate Owenson saw symbolic power in the combination of fashionable display and theatrical venue: 'The audience [at the Music Hall] was as national as the performance . . . and the boxes exhibited a show of beauty and fashion, such as Ireland above all other countries could produce.'[42] On 11 March 1807, Owenson succeeded in recreating a similar memory for a new, post-Union Ireland: that same kind of national audience with an unparalleled 'show of beauty and fashion'. Owenson's run as Glorvina in her parlour room performances had successfully persuaded Dublin's female community – both English and Irish attendees – to put on the Irish look and replace Teague's blanket with Glorvina's mantle, figuratively and literally. Le Fanu, we will see, went on to urge a similar response among the women of London when she put Owenson's offstage tactics directly back on the London stage.

Le Fanu's Stage Irish Feminist

Unlike Sydney Owenson, Alicia Sheridan Le Fanu was accustomed to a life backstage. The sister of Richard Brinsley Sheridan, she spent most of her career behind the scenes of the Irish theatre, despite having a famous dramatist for a brother and the actor-manager of Dublin's Smock Alley for a father. After years of holding private plays in the drawing room of the Le Fanu house on Cuffe Street in Dublin, Alicia finally worked her way up to the public stage, with the debut of her five-act comedy *The Sons of Erin, or Modern Sentiment* in April 1812 at the Lyceum Theatre, in affiliation with the Drury Lane company.[43] Although her literary career technically began

---

[41] Owenson had one other stint as a playwright later in her career, when she published a collection of three short plays, *Dramatic Scenes from Real Life*, in 1833. The plays include *Manor Sackville, The Easter Recess* and *Temper*, none of which were staged.

[42] Owenson, *Memoirs*, 1: 24.

[43] Anna M. Fitzer, '"Feeling and sense beyond all seeming": Private Lines, Public Relations, and the Performances of the Le Fanu Circle', *Nineteenth Century Theatre and Film* 38.2 (2011): 26–37; 28, 32.

after Sydney Owenson's, Le Fanu served as a mentor and friend to the younger author, encouraging her public endeavours. When Owenson was still trying to publish her first novel, *St. Clair*, they exchanged correspondence, and Le Fanu helped introduce Owenson to Dublin society. Their letters discuss the Irish national tradition, the songs of the bards, O'Carolan, Ossian and the work of Charlotte Brooke's *Reliques of Irish Poetry*.[44] In fact, Le Fanu encouraged Owenson to go to London, writing, 'I make no doubt that your work will succeed: going yourself to London is certainly the best security for justice being done you.'[45] Owenson later described Le Fanu as 'vice-Queen' of the Dublin Bluestockings circle – 'vice' only because the highest title was customarily reserved for the provost's wife. Anne Fitzer explains that Owenson saw Le Fanu as a Dublin counterpart to the 'Queen of the Blues', Elizabeth Montagu.[46] Le Fanu, unsurprisingly, was also an enthusiastic patron of the Glorvina fashion items. Because of the longevity of Le Fanu's experience with Irish drama, and her senior role as mentor to Owenson, the patriotic philosophy expressed in *The Sons of Erin* can be read as both precursor and response to the politicised fashion show produced by Owenson's Glorvina costume in 1807. Between the seemingly trivial, romantic lines of Le Fanu's comedy is a serious, targeted message that chimed with Owenson's: that educated, politicised Irish women had power to influence the state of the Union beyond the stage doors.

The plot of Le Fanu's *The Sons of Erin* is not particularly original, which was one of the common critiques in 1812. On paper, it looks like nothing more than a variation of her brother's one-act play *St. Patrick's Day* (1775), where the hero disguises his nationality so as to trick his way into the English domestic circle and marry his English lover. Similarly, in *The Sons of Erin,* the hero, Fitz Edward, enlists the help of his cousin, a widow named Lady Ann Lovel, to win the acceptance of his new in-laws, the English naval family, the Rivers. Le Fanu's play can be read as a feminised revision of *St. Patrick's Day,* in which a strong, female lead serves as the wily, charming Irish character that fools the prejudiced English upper class, much like Owenson herself did in London. Lady Ann teaches Fitz Edward

---

Critics have overlooked this play, erroneously suggesting it was unsuccessful. The contrary was the case: the play was popular, staged multiple times over three years, and appeared in regional theatres as well as the Lyceum, such as Hull and Exeter and Bath. I would like to thank David O'Shaughnessy for bringing the actual success of Le Fanu's play and the Larpent manuscript (discussed later) to my attention.

[44] Percy Fitzgerald, *The Lives of the Sheridans*, 2 vols. (London: R. Bentley, 1886), 1: 418.

[45] Ibid., 420.   [46] Fitzer, 'Feeling and Sense', 37.

to dress himself as an Englishman and enter the Rivers's family circle undercover. The play unravels English prejudice against the Irish when the Rivers family is inevitably charmed by their son-in-law's disguise. Unlike her brother, however, Le Fanu attached a more sombre, politicised preamble to her play. In it, she identifies her hero Fitz Edward as a new character type on the London stage, what she dubs 'the Irish gentleman' – a foil and alternative to the blundering Stage Irishman that appeared on so many other English stages at the time. She writes, 'The Principal object of the Author in the following Comedy, was to do away any lingering prejudice that may still exist in England against the people of Ireland: this she has endeavoured to effect, by drawing a character she believes new to the Stage, that of an *Irish Gentleman*.'[47] Whereas Owenson chose the subversive route, Le Fanu directly and publicly complicates dramatic renderings of Irishness by presenting her play as an effort to counter the Teague figure – or, at least, present an Irish gentleman alongside him.

Despite Le Fanu's lofty claims, *The Sons of Erin* does feature a Teague type, the comic servant Patrick O'Shee, who was played by John Henry Johnstone, the most famous Irish actor on the London stage in the late eighteenth century, known principally for his rendition of Teague in *The Committee*.[48] The key difference between Patrick and Howard's Teague, however, is that Patrick is a loyal servant to an *Irish* gentleman, Fitz Edward, and to an explicitly Gaelic ancestry. Le Fanu alludes to patriotic sentiments when Pat corrects the English landlady Mrs Furbish who calls him Mr Shee instead of Mr O'Shee, saying, 'If you please, Madam; I had the O in my family before your first ancestor was born.'[49] Here, Patrick voices a belief promoted by late eighteenth-century Irish antiquarians like Charles O'Conor and Joseph Cooper Walker, albeit for comic purposes. He alludes to the longevity of the Gaelic lineage in Ireland, which antiquarian writing like O'Conor's claims to be much older and more dignified than the English Saxon tradition.[50] Although, in part, Patrick represents the stereotype of Irish bull and blunder, he also, like his master, the Irish gentleman Fitz Edward, offers a revision of the

---

[47] Alicia Sheridan Le Fanu, *The Sons of Erin, or Modern Sentiment: A Comedy, in Five Acts Performed at the Lyceum Theatre*, 3rd edition (London: J. Ridgeway, 1812), iii.
[48] Burke, 'Integrated as Outsiders', 21.   [49] Le Fanu, *The Sons of Erin*, 27–28.
[50] O'Conor argued for the Milesian origin of Irish ancestry – a culture Irish antiquarians believed to be distinct and separate from the Greco-Roman. He emphasised that the pre-Christian Irish developed key aspects of civilisation, such as writing and parliamentary democracy, and promoted the Irish Celts as the most influential and civilised society in the pre-Christian world. See essays by Luke Gibbons and John Wrynn in *Charles O'Conor of Ballinagare, 1710–91: Life and Works*, ed. Luke Gibbons and Kieran O'Conor (Dublin: Four Courts Press, 2015).

standard Teague by displaying loyalty to an Irish national past and scholarly tradition. The strong relations between these two characters, although
divided by class and education, represent an idea of Irish social cohesion,
allegorically demonstrating Le Fanu's political ethos of religious tolerance
and Irish-self governance.

What is most important about Le Fanu's play, however, is not this new
revision of the Stage Irish (gentle)man, but the feminist character Lady
Ann Lovel.[51] As it turns out, most of the reviews and audiences responded
more favourably to Lady Ann than to Fitz Edward anyway.[52] Lady Ann
became the distinguishing feature of *The Sons of Erin* in London, and she is
also the character that links Le Fanu with Owenson's patriotism-by-Irish-
costume. Lady Ann's own nationality in the play comes across as ambiguous: she runs the social circles in London, is revered and respected by
everyone, including the anti-Irish Rivers family, and yet she clearly has
Irish connections. At one stage, Pat, impressed by Lady Ann's authority,
reasons that she 'must be an Irishwoman'.[53] Reviews suggest Lady Ann's
character was played Irish in some productions, but the play text never
designates her as such.[54] Whatever her birth, her character represents
outright feminism and allegorical Irish nationalism.

In her first scene on the stage, Lady Ann declares never to relinquish the
social independence her premature widowhood had given her under the law.
She says, 'I have not the least inclination to part with my dearly-prized liberty;
I hate control; and when that submissive animal, a lover, is changed into that
lordly one, a husband, adieu to all the delights of life.'[55] Considering the post-
Union context, this line carries allegorical weight, albeit in jest. Several decades
prior, Le Fanu's sister, Elizabeth Sheridan, made a similar allegorical connection in her novel *The Triumph of Prudence over Passion,* published in 1781, in
which the heroine's decision not to marry the man who loves her symbolises
a deliberate disavowal of a union with Great Britain. Frequently throughout
the novel, the protagonist Louisa Mortimer expresses both her Irish patriotism
and her suspicion of marriage with nationally symbolic comments like,
'I never had a high idea of matrimonial felicity' and 'Providence designed
me for a single life'.[56] Likewise, Lady Ann's aversion to marital law addresses an

51 Lady Ann is foiled by a Miss Rivers, who is an exaggerated, stereotypical pseudo-feminist type.
52 *The Scourge, or, Monthly Expositor of Imposture and Folly* ([London], 1811–12), 507.
53 Le Fanu, *Sons of Erin,* 29.
54 *Universal Magazine of Knowledge and Pleasure* 2: 17 (London: J. Hinton, 1812), 321.
55 Le Fanu, *Sons of Erin,* 32.
56 Elizabeth Sheridan, *The Triumph of Prudence Over Passion*, ed. Aileen Douglas and Ian
  Campbell Ross (Dublin: Four Courts Press, 2011), 72.

analogous critique of Britain's legislative control over Ireland within the
Union. The dialogue's open reflection on the legal confines of marriage
imbues Lady Ann's feminist profession with patriotic allegory when a direct
critique of the Union was not permissible on the London stage. Before its
premiere in 1812, Le Fanu's manuscript was subject to edits by the Examiner of
Plays. The Examiner excised a speech made by Captain Rivers, which casts
doubt on the Union and which never found its way back into the printed
version.[57] This speech originally came after Lady Ann boasts to the Captain
that Mr Melville (Fitz Edward in disguise) chose an assistantship to
Miss Rivers over a 'lucrative situation under Government in Ireland'.
Captain Rivers replies, 'Nay, that is hardly a compliment. Mr. Melville
would perhaps have hardly worried his Sea Sickness before he would find
himself [superseded?] by a new secretary to a new Lord Lieutenant.'[58] Here, Le
Fanu makes a loaded joke about the failure of England to maintain any sort of
legislative order and consistency in Ireland, even after the Union. Similarly,
Irish feminist Lady Ann refuses to let any man or any marital bond control her
freedom in the play's domestic plot.

Lady Ann's most critical moment onstage, however, comes earlier in Act
II, when she performs a satirical parlour room version of the Act of Union.
Sanctioning Fitz Edward's new disguise as an Englishman, she says, 'And
now your name, of my own authority, and without an Act of Parliament,
I change to Melville; and your country [to England].'[59] With Lady Ann's
guidance, Fitz Edward proceeds to act the part of the English gentleman
and convince his in-laws to support his own union with their daughter.
Lady Ann's rechristening of Fitz Edward as Melville marks another anti-
Unionist joke: her line mocks the 'legality' of the Act of Union when she
farcically anglicises him 'without an Act of Parliament'. In this scene, Le
Fanu transforms the woman's parlour room into a public, political fantasy
that exposes the Union's legality as mere fabrication. Le Fanu need not
have worried about the Examiner's edits: her critique of the Union still
carried, thinly veiled under domestic language. What's more, this scene
reverses the gendered social paradigm by awarding a woman legal authority
over a man's identity and position. With her background as a Bluestocking
and her own experience holding plays in her Dublin drawing room, Le

---

[57] The printed version skips this short speech by the Captain, jumping from Lady Ann's line to Fitz
Edward's which says 'Though I have no objection to going to Ireland; which, after all, I believe to be
a tolerable country, yet at present I certainly should prefer a situation in your family, Sir' (II: 37).
[58] Alicia Le Fanu, *Prejudice; or, Modern Sentiment*. Larpent Manuscript, LA 1714, fol. 26v, Huntington
Library.
[59] Le Fanu, *Sons of Erin*, 34.

Fanu was well rehearsed in transforming a domestic setting into a dramatic, political stage – something she acknowledges in her preface to the play's Boston edition, when she writes that she hopes the play will be as well received 'in the domestic circle, as it has been already on the public scene'.[60] In the wake of the Union, when any official, political spaces in Ireland had been disqualified by the erasure of an Irish governing body, private spaces were forced to become political platforms for Irish national ideas. When Lady Ann performs her satiric Act of Union, *The Sons of Erin* directly acknowledges this change. We might also consider the subversive power in provoking an English audience to laugh at a pantomime of the Act of Union, when the British Parliament was frantically fighting to keep that Union secure outside the theatre doors.[61]

Finally, Lady Ann Lovel gets the last word in *The Sons of Erin*, and her epilogue raises serious and explicitly politicised consequences for its audience. In her parting verse, Lady Ann places the weight of political responsibility and cultural tolerance on her English audience, specifically the women. She says: 'The Sons of Erin shall protest themselves;/They must find favour in *the ladies'* eyes,/Which still rain influence and judge the prize.' She then concludes by saying her heart 'Rests for complete content its hopes on you'.[62] These words deliberately place the onus on English ladies to combat prejudice against the Irish in London, where they 'rain influence' (note the pun), inscribing the female community with power to influence public, political affairs, even from within their domestic conscription. In the spirit of her charismatic character Lady Ann Lovel, Le Fanu openly calls upon women to be advocates for tolerance and allies of the Irish cause. In doing so, she carries the ethos behind the assembly of Glorvina costumes at the Theatre Royal over to an English theatrical context, urging a female movement of participatory political performance. Le Fanu rhetorically activates in London what Owenson visually effected in Dublin: that is, a plea for the Irish national cause, conceptualised through a feminist model.

It should come as no surprise that Alicia Le Fanu's political assertions ruffled some feathers in London's literary circles. Reviewers at *The Satirist*, the *Universal Magazine*, the *Critical Review* and the *Theatrical Review* did

---

[60] Mrs. Lefanu. *The Sons of Erin, or Modern Sentiment: A Comedy in Five Acts, as performed at the Boston Theatre* (Boston: Thomas Wells, 1812), v.

[61] English politicians experienced almost constant alarm at Union's instability, evinced by Parliament's 114 commissions and 60 committees sitting on Irish issues between 1810 and 1833. See Kevin Whelan, *Acts of Union: The Causes, Contexts, and Consequences of the Act of Union* (Dublin: Four Courts, 2001).

[62] Le Fanu, *Sons of Erin* (London), 101.

not appreciate the Irish lady's depiction of English men and women. Several reviews went so far as to call Le Fanu's play a 'libel on [English] national character'.[63] Most significantly, the *Universal Magazine* expressed unease at declarations 'coming from the pen of an Irish lady and put into the mouth of an English[man]'.[64] In light of this, Lady Ann Lovel's speech about control becomes even more evocative. Lady Ann's authority, her ability to permeate different national and gendered spaces, realises the conservative English critic's worst nightmare: that is, an Irish woman who speaks on behalf of English men, and perhaps even worse, a woman who dresses an Irishman in a convincing English disguise. Yet, despite this official censure, Le Fanu's skill for dialogue and comic disguise delighted London audiences. The public loved *The Sons of Erin* and praised it with rapturous applause night after night at the Lyceum, so that the play continued to be staged in London, as well as regional English theatres, for more than seven years, until 1819. It even went international, with a performance at the Boston Theatre in 1812.[65] On top of the applause, Le Fanu's play also achieved a twofold symbolic success. It merged the private parlour room discourse about romance, marriage and culture with the parliamentary one about Anglo-Irish politics. Likewise, it merged women's civil right to social and financial independence in British society with Ireland's own civil right to equality under the Union. That the masculinised circle of literary criticism took such offense to Le Fanu's comedy evinces her success in making the Irish*woman*, more so than the 'Irish gentleman', newly visible and authoritative on an English stage.

Conclusion

The night of 11 March 1807 was one of Robert Owenson's final performances. He stood on the stage of the Theatre Royal and sang a ridiculous Irish drinking song composed by his daughter. The retirement of this father figure of Irish drama, who had established the Dublin theatre on

---

[63] *The Satirist, or Monthly Meteor,* 10 (10 May 1812), 390.
[64] *Universal Magazine of Knowledge and Pleasure* (April 1812), 321.
[65] A performance of *The Sons of Erin* was staged at the Theatre Royal, Haymarket as late as May 1819. 'Theatre Royal, Haymarket, A Collection of Playbills from Haymarket Theatre, 1817–1821', *MS British Playbills, 1754–1882*, British Library, *Nineteenth Century Collections Online,* 169. *The Sons of Erin* was both printed and staged in Boston. Le Fanu wrote an advertisement for the American edition, in which she hopes that '*The Sons of Erin* may be received by their friends on the other side of the water, as cordially by the fireside.' Le Fanu plays to her expatriate audience and shows more open patriotism than in the London advertisement. Le Fanu, *The Sons of Erin, as performed at the Boston Theatre,* v.

Fishamble Street, also marked the waning end, particularly in the wake of the Union, of an era of institutionalised Irish national theatre led by Robert Owenson and the Sheridan family in the late eighteenth century. However, that same night in 1807 also marks a new beginning for Irish national performance. By inspiring her audience to dress up and act the part of Irish patriotism, Sydney Owenson transferred political agency onto the audience and designed a self-consciously anti-imperial fashion show. Supplanting her father as this powerful family's face and voice of Irish culture in both Dublin and London, Owenson represents a new order of female agency on the national stage. Five years after *The Whim of the Moment,* Le Fanu vocalised the philosophy behind Owenson's costume on the metropolitan stage, with the parting words of Lady Ann Lovel, who urged English women to be social allies for the Irish.

Donned in red mantles and blue stockings, Sydney Owenson and Alicia Le Fanu leave us with an important scene in the history of Irish drama. These two authors' utilisation of the public theatre reveals a creative affinity between mentor and mentee where feminism and patriotism coalesce. They also reveal a circuit of cultural transmission between Dublin and London, where women's plays and women's fashions converse transnationally about the state of the Union. In turn, women's playwriting sheds light on another oversight in the history of Irish drama: the echoes travelling between London's theatres and Dublin's halls – a trend worthy of further exploration. By inscribing a theatrical performance with appeals for female audience participation in extant social circles in London and Dublin, these two writers transformed the scene of British domesticity into an Irish political stage. Instead of laughing at the Irish act, as was so often the case with Robert Owenson, John Henry Johnstone and the wily Irish characters written by Brinsley Sheridan, English and Ascendancy audiences were invited to join in Irish national play, to laugh *with* rather than *at*, to repeat some of the play's lines in their own conversations and even get dressed up just like the actors. For Owenson and Le Fanu, women comprised the most important theatregoing populace in London and Dublin. In their theatres, whether domestic or public, whether London or Dublin based, women could find the tools of political performativity and the encouragement to speak out in political discourses that too often silenced them.

PART III

Enlightened Perspectives

CHAPTER 7

Civility, Patriotism and Performance: Cato *and the Irish History Play*

David O'Shaughnessy*

Recent scholarship has underscored history writing as central to the culture of the eighteenth century and as a key mode of Enlightenment thought and practice in both Britain and Ireland.[1] British elites, conscious of their own historiographical failings, looked uneasily on the French exemplar national histories which sparked a patriotic urging to match their Continental competitors.[2] Writ properly, history could also lead to a more rational patriotic attachment to one's own country, one enriched by a recognition of the achievements of other nations, in the spirit of Enlightenment.[3] The proper framing and writing of national history, understood in the main to aspire to rigorous neoclassical values, also conveyed that country's teleological progressiveness, its emergence from barbarity towards modernity, civilisation and associated institutional norms. The form and content of a well-written national history – encompassing *inter alia* a decorous tone, idealised characters, moral didacticism – mirrored each other, allowing a reader to assess their own civility as well as that of the country and its people in question. 'Enlightenment' is a term with a myriad of associated values; this chapter looks at history plays while keeping notions of patriotism and civilisation foremost in mind.

* My sincere thanks to Emily Anderson and David Taylor for their helpful comments on an earlier version of this chapter. This project has received funding from the European Union's 2020 research and innovation programme under the Marie Sklowdowska-Curie grant agreement No 745896.
[1] Noelle Gallagher, *Historical Literatures: Writing about the Past in England, 1660–1740* (Manchester: Manchester University Press, 2012); Ruth Mack, *Literary Historicity: Literature and Historical Experience in Eighteenth-Century Britain* (Stanford: Stanford University Press, 2009); and Karen O'Brien, *Narratives of Enlightenment: Cosmopolitan History from Voltaire to Gibbon* (Cambridge: Cambridge University Press, 1997). On Ireland and history writing, see Clare O'Halloran, *Golden Ages and Barbarous Nations: Antiquarian Debate and Cultural Politics in Ireland, c. 1750–1800* (Cork and Notre Dame, IN: Cork University Press and Notre Dame Press, 2005), and *Charles O'Conor of Ballinagare, 1710–91: Life and Works*, ed. Luke Gibbons and Kieran O'Conor (Dublin: Four Courts Press, 2015).
[2] Gallagher, *Historical Literatures*, 1–2.   [3] O'Brien, *Narratives of Enlightenment*, 15.

It is perhaps surprising then that history plays of the period have remained the poor cousins of comedy and tragedy, the two genres that remain the focus of critical attention.[4] This chapter argues for the greater relevance of the history play to our understanding of theatrical culture of the eighteenth century. That the first three plays refused a licence under the Stage Licensing Act were history plays should alert us to the significance of this neglected genre. That they were written, respectively, by an Irishman, a Scotsman, and an Englishman indicates the centrality of the history play to ideas of nationhood in the era of Enlightenment.[5] The affective force of historical drama, the genre's cultural capital as well as its capacity for political provocation, particularly in the wake of Joseph Addison's *Cato* (1713), makes this unsurprising. We would benefit then to bring history plays more into the conversation of eighteenth-century theatre, thus complicating the existing canon of British theatre, both synchronically and diachronically.

The chapter freely concedes that further work will be required in terms of theorising the history play, not least, for example, in terms of distinguishing it – to the extent that it can be – from tragedy. The Irish case study discussed here shows how consideration of the neglected history play can bear critical fruit; it provides the justification for the pursuit of such a broader study, a point I will return to in my conclusion. The Irish example is well chosen: as the Introduction to this volume details, historiography and patriotism are closely linked in Irish writing at a time when Irish writers and actors were in the ascendant in London. If theatre plays a part then in an Irish Enlightenment, we are obliged to consider how playwrights and actors treated the history play genre. And if, as Paddy Bullard and Michael Brown have argued, rhetoric is central to the discourse of Irish patriotism, then we must put Irish dramatists and actors' command or otherwise of verse tragedy under scrutiny.[6] As a rich site of discursive confluence of patriotism, rhetoric, and historiography, the history play demands our attention when considering the Irish

---

[4] Paulina Kewes has also lamented the sidelining of the history play's transformation of history writing from the sixteenth to eighteenth centuries. Paulina Kewes, 'History and Its Uses' in *The Uses of History in Early Modern England*, ed. Kewes (San Marino, CA: Huntington Library Press, 2006), 4–5. But see some recent work on Romantic period history plays in *Staging History 1780–1840*, ed. Michael Burden, Wendy Heller, Jonathan Hicks and Ellen Lockhard (Oxford: Bodleian Library, 2016).

[5] After Brooke's *Gustavus Vasa* (1739), James Thomson's *Edward and Eleonora* (1739) and William Paterson's *Arminius* (1739) were subsequently refused performance licences. We might also note, given our interest in Cato, that Arminius tells the story of a great German hero who resisted Caesar.

[6] See Introduction, 17–19.

Enlightenment. To pick up, for instance, Brown's oppositional threads of empiricism and rationality, we note they can coexist happily in the history play: Irish actors delivering complex speeches in verse challenge stereotypes of Irish bulls (evidence of ethnic civility) and Irish dramatists displaying mastery of a 'high' literary genre dispute notions of Irish cultural barbarism (evidence of rational thought). History plays were a potent political genre, capable of casting light on the present state of affairs and gesturing towards a different kind of future. For Irish writers, the genre had a particular attraction: not only could the force of historical resonance be brought to bear on a particular issue but the history play also provided a forum for a writer to display not only a collective ethnic claim to civility but individual flair and literary acumen as well. The history play that evoked patriot sentiment allowed the Irish to demonstrate their capacity for self-regulation and political autonomy in cadenced and rational speeches, trumpeting the values – liberty, love of country, reason, etc. – that Britain held dear. The history play also provided a clear generic leap away from the uncouth Stage Irishman such as Teague from Robert Howard's *The Committee* (1665), enhanced by the growing affective force of Irish actors working in London who became increasingly influential through the century. James Quin, Dennis Delane and Charles Macklin, as we shall see, were pivotal but so too were Catherine Clive and Margaret Woffington, amongst others mentioned in the Introduction to this volume.

Tracing Irish echoes of *Cato*, arguably the most important political play of the century, will be central to my argument. How Irish dramatists and actors responded to this idealised representation of British values is an illuminating barometer of their Enlightenment ambitions and the reception of those same ambitions. I have argued elsewhere that *Cato* was an important influence on Macklin's *The Man of the World* (1781) in an essay that made the case for Macklin as an Enlightenment figure.[7] Here, I wish to first deepen the Irish association with Addison's historical tragedy before working through three earlier examples of *Cato*-inflected Irish dramas: William Philips's *Hibernia Freed* (1722), Henry Brooke's *Gustavus Vasa* (1739) and Charles Macklin's *King Henry the VII. Or The Popish Impostor* (1746). Using *Cato* to connect these plays (and them to the later *The Man of the World*) helps us understand the importance of history plays to eighteenth-century dramatists eager to politicise their work. History

---

[7] David O'Shaughnessy, '"Bit, by some mad whig": Charles Macklin and the Theater of Irish Enlightenment', *Huntington Library Quarterly* 80.4 (2017): 559–84.

plays offered writers the capacity to present political critique as well as make intellectual claims through their deft command and re-presentation of historical narrative. Moreover, using the thread of *Cato* to make connections between history plays written over this period offers us a glimpse of an alternative Irish dramatic tradition that runs parallel to our usual interest, insofar as Irish playwrights are concerned, in comedies.

I

Cato was a touchstone for American patriotism, demonstrated by the famous performance staged by George Washington in Valley Forge for his beleaguered troops in 1778; that the play also proved a touchstone for Irish writers committed to political autonomy in the face of 'tyranny' should be unsurprising. The play's eponymous hero was particularly associated with Robert Molesworth (1656–1725), author of *An Account of Denmark* (1694), a seminal text in the Whig library. As we have noted, Molesworth was a major Whig figure of the period. Such was the strength of his reputation and his association with progressive Whiggism that he was also commonly assumed to be the author of *Cato's Letters* (1724), which, according to Blair Worden, was 'the principal depository of Republican ideas in the early eighteenth century'.[8] The provocative John Toland even produced election propaganda depicting Robert Molesworth as Cato.[9] The play certainly resonated among Irish patriots of the 1710s and 1720s.

Lisa Freeman's analysis of the play helps explain the attraction of the play for these Irish. *Cato*, she argues, could not project the 'glories of an idealized Rome' onto England without also bringing into view the 'less than ideal politics' of its rise and its subsequent fall from power. Freeman sums up, 'If Rome were taken as the analog through which to project the future glory of England not only as a nation but as a burgeoning empire, the burden of history inexorably required an awareness of that empire's

---

[8] Blair Worden, 'Republicanism and the Restoration, 1660-1683' in *Republicanism, Liberty, and Commercial Society, 1649–1776*, ed. David Wootton (Stanford, CA: Stanford University Press, 1994): 177. The essays in *Cato's Letters* were published in almanacs from 1721. As it happens, it was, in fact, another graduate of Trinity College Dublin, John Trenchard, who co-authored them with Thomas Gordon.

[9] Robert Molesworth, *An Account of Denmark, with Francogallia and Some Considerations for the Promoting of Agriculture and Employing the Poor*, Edited and with an Introduction by Justin Champion (Indianapolis: Liberty Fund, 2011), 17.

inevitable decline.'[10] Laura Rosenthal's useful reading of the play puts Juba's enlightened cosmopolitanism front and centre and allows, as Daniel O'Quinn puts it, 'a consistent critique of Cato's tragic iconicity', and he illustrates how 'certain audiences forgot about the tragedy of *Cato* to make "history" – that strange attempt to figure forth a past that makes a future for life'.[11] Irish patriots saw the possibilities of *Cato* re-presenting the Irish past to fashion future political agency. This re-presentation made claims of Celtic civility, honourable lineage and organised systems of governance that predated colonialism; the subsequent alleged slide into violence and ignorance being blamed on repeated invasions. Thus the plays considered in this chapter should be understood as emerging in dialogue with the historical revisionism of Irish writers from William Molyneux to Geoffrey Keating to Charles O'Conor, which also presented Ireland and the Irish as civilised before the debilitating destruction of invasion.[12] Just as *Cato*'s exploration of republican values takes place 'off-site' in North Africa, patriots present the treatment of Ireland as a proxy for the validity of Britain's imperial authority. Ultimately, as Rosenthal has deftly shown, to be Roman – that is, to adopt the ethical position of a virtuous Briton – 'demands the renegotiation of all other identity'.[13] Successful Irish appropriations of the play then could disrupt pejorative historical justifications for British direct rule in a powerful and readily understood manner: Irish writers could prove themselves 'Roman' on a very public stage by writing historical dramas, the force of their writing augmented by the rich panoply of Irish actors working in the London theatres.

Remarkably, this most English of British plays is an illuminating example of the forceful Irish thespian presence. After the death of Barton Booth, the original Cato, in 1733, the role had a decidedly Irish flavour. Dennis Delane and James Quin were the primary actors of the part for many years in London theatres. Quin, in particular, was dominant: he took the eponymous role for the first time on 18 January 1734 at Covent Garden and had three subsequent performances that season including on his benefit night. The following season he moved to Drury Lane where he

---

[10] Lisa A. Freeman, 'What's Love Got to Do with Addison's Cato', *Studies in English Literature, 1500-1900* 39.3 (1999): 463–82; 465.
[11] Laura J. Rosenthal, 'Juba's Roman Soul: Addison's *Cato* and Enlightenment Cosmopolitanism', *Studies in the Literary Imagination* 32.2 (1999): 64–75; and Daniel O'Quinn, 'Half-History, or The Function of *Cato* at the Present Time', *Eighteenth-Century Fiction* 27.3–4 (2015): 479–507; 486.
[12] See Introduction, 21–22.   [13] Rosenthal, 'Juba's Roman Soul', 70.

played the part eight times.[14] He continued as Cato at both major theatres
up until his retirement in 1751. At the same time, Dennis Delane also
played the part regularly at Goodman's Field, Drury Lane and Covent
Garden in the 1730s and 1740s. The two Irishmen dominated the role in
these decades: in the eighty-five performances of *Cato* documented in
the *London Stage* between 1732 and 1745, the pair played the Roman
hero on at least sixty-six of those occasions (some performances do not
have cast lists so it is likely the actual figure is slightly higher).[15] After
Quin's retirement, the play seems to have lost some favour with the
audiences and is performed much less often, but Irish actors continued
to appear nonetheless: Francis Gentleman in 1747 (1), Thomas Sheridan
in 1754–55 (2) and 1760 (2) and Henry Mossop in 1756–57 (4).
In October 1775, Richard Brinsley Sheridan could write to Thomas
Linley the Elder with pride that 'My father was astonishingly well
received on Saturday night in Cato.'[16] Irishness was imbricated in the
performance of Addison's play through these various acts of surrogation
from the 1730s through to the 1770s; the Irish actors playing Cato
embodied the values of Whiggish constitutionalism during the mid-
century for London audiences. James Quin even superintended the
famous performance of Cato by members of the royal family in 1748.
Jason Shaffer has argued that this royal performance was intended to
show the public that the 'requisite transmission of constitutional ideals
and cultural "Britishness" had taken place' within the German
Hanoverian family; if an Irishman was entrusted with ensuring the
success of this piece of royal propaganda, it is a powerful example of
how the stock of the Irish had risen as well as indicating Quin's
dominance of the role.[17]

   We will turn now to looking at how *Cato* materialised in the political
theatre of Irish dramatists. As the Introduction to this volume has suggested, the passage of the Declaratory Act in 1720 – an 'enslaving act' in

[14] It is ironic that one of these nights saw Charles Macklin kill Thomas Hallam in a backstage fight at
      Drury Lane over a wig, considering Macklin's interest in *Cato* and his aspirations to contribute to
      Enlightenment discourse.
[15] *The London Stage 1660–1800*, ed. Emmett L. Avery, Charles Beecher Hogan, William Van Lennep,
      Arthur Hawley Scouten and George Winchester Stone, 5 parts, 11 vols. (Carbondale, IL: Southern
      Illinois University Press, 1960–68), pt. 3.
[16] This was, the advertisement claimed, Sheridan's first appearance at Covent Garden in sixteen years.
      The Letters of Richard Brinsley Sheridan, ed. Cecil Price, 3 vols. (Oxford: Oxford University Press,
      1966), 1: 91.
[17] Jason Shaffer, '"Great Cato's Descendants": A Genealogy of Colonial Performance', *Theater Survey*
      44 (2003): 5–28.

Archbishop King's view – was particularly important in stoking up Irish oppositional politics.[18] Jonathan Swift's *Proposal for the Universal Use of Irish Manufacture*, first published in Dublin in 1720, is probably the best-known riposte to the Declaratory Act, the first in a series of acerbic pamphlets that would earn him his moniker as the father of Irish patriotism.[19] Helen Burke has already shown how Dublin's Smock Alley Theatre was a prominent site of resistance and how Swift and Sheridan encouraged theatre audiences to 'wear Irish stuff' in an act of retaliatory economic intent.[20] But responses also manifested themselves in London – Dermod O'Conor's translation of Keating's *Foras Feasa ar Éirinn* being a significant example (see Introduction, 21) – where the Irish were equally galvanised by the Declaratory Act. And theatre was also a crucial forum in London for such resistance.

Desmond Slowey rightly suggests that the Irish MP William Philips (d. 1734) has not been adequately recognised for his patriot drama *Hibernia Freed* (1722).[21] Philips was a Tory member of the Irish parliament between 1707 and 1711 and had previously had dramatic success in London and, notably, at Dublin's Smock Alley Theatre with *St Stephen's-Green; or, The Generous Lovers* (1699), the first significant play to feature a Dublin setting. The incendiary Declaratory Act prompted the return of his dramatic impulse after more than a twenty-year gap.

The plot recounts an Irish victory over tyrannous Danish invaders at an unspecified, but evidently pre-Norman, epoch. It was enthusiastically received by the Lincoln's Inn Field's audience. The reviewer for the *Freeholder's Journal* for 21 February 1722 expressed surprise at the rapturous reception: 'I never knew a Play so Clapped . . . till a Friend put me in Mind, that half the Audience were *Wild Irish*', perhaps an indication of an emboldened Irish presence in London in the wake of the passage of the Declaratory Act.[22] In his dedication, Philips asked 'for what is so noble as to free ones Country from Tyranny and Invasion?'[23] The play offers no simple equation of the English with the Danes, but there are certainly

[18] Cited in Burke, *Riotous Performances*, 59.
[19] See *Swift's Irish Writings: Selected Prose and Poetry*, ed. Carole Fabricant and Robert Mahony (Basingstoke: Palgrave, 2010).
[20] Ibid., 53–83. See Colleen Taylor (Chapter 6, this volume) on a later manifestation of the wearing of Irish 'stuff' as political gesture.
[21] Desmond Slowey, *The Radicalization of Irish Drama, 1600–1900* (Dublin: Irish Academic Press, 2008), 114.
[22] *London Stage*, 2:1, clxiv.
[23] William Philips, *Hibernia Freed, A Tragedy* (London: Printed for Jonah Bowyer, 1722). Further references will be cited in the text by page number.

veiled and pointed jibes made in the English direction. An early speech
from the play's King O'Brien sets the tone:

> Fertile *Hibernia!* Hospitable Land!
> Is not allow'd to feed her Native Sons,
> In vain they toil, and a-mid Plenty starve.
> The lazy *Dane* grows wanton with our Stores,
> Urges our Labour, and derides our Wants.   (9)

Anyone with even the faintest knowledge of Irish politics could not
have failed to pick up the references to trade, the issue identified by
Swift (and indeed Molyneux before him) that would remain at the heart
of Irish Protestant discontent for the rest of the century, right up to the
Act of Union, as the chapters in this volume by Jones (Chapter 5) and
Taylor (Chapter 6) testify.[24] Rather than rejecting the principle of
British rule, Philips asks for fair treatment, particularly in commercial
matters, as well as for internal political autonomy. The play's conclusion
simultaneously accepts the principle of British rule while challenging the
empire to live up to its supposed precepts: the final scene sees the
defeated Turgesius of Denmark deliver a dark prophecy that is subsequently turned on its head by Eugenius, bard and chief adviser to
O'Brien:

> TURGESIUS: But e'er I part, remember I foretell,
> Another Nation shall revenge my Death,
> And with successful Arms invade this Realm.
> . . .
>
> EUGENIUS: Another Nation shall indeed succeed,
> But different far in Manners from the *Dane*,
> (So Heav'n inspires and urges me to speak)
> Another Nation, famous through the World,
> For martial Deeds, for Strength and Skill in Arms,
> Belov'd and blest for their Humanity.
> . . .
>
> And mix their Blood with ours; one People grow,
> Polish our Manners, and improve our Minds.   (60–61)

This pointed conclusion underlines a central aspect of the Irish patriot
movement: the demand for political autonomy did not imply a separation
from Britain. Irish patriots largely insisted on Ireland as a separate

---

[24] For a useful treatment of the difficulties over trade, see the chapter on the eighteenth century in
Thomas Bartlett, *Ireland: A History* (Cambridge: Cambridge University Press, 2011).

kingdom – with all its associated institutional trimmings – but tied to Britain under the authority of the monarch; this would remain true right through the century.[25] In a drama where the Irish characters have displayed virtue, self-restraint and reason throughout, Eugenius's closing speech asks the audience to consider the appropriateness of the Declaratory Act, given what they have just witnessed.

Philips's forthright challenge to external regulation of the Irish people seems to have met with approval from the audience – judging by the newspaper report cited earlier at least – and it played for a respectable six nights in February, finishing off with a seventh performance on St Patrick's Day. The Irish characters of *Hibernia Freed* demonstrate time and time again their capacity for virtue, their privileging of reason, and their inherent civility. O'Brien bemoans the condition of 'Hibernia! Seat of Learning! School of Science!' (9) and declares 'Reason is our guide. . . . Reason directs us to the Choice of Good' (35). Slowey's analysis shows how the play details 'an ancient Irish society displaying both the neo-stoic virtues of the Enlightenment and a civilization equal to ancient Greece and Rome'.[26] But we may be more specific, it seems, given the prominence of Molesworth among 1720s London Whigs. The emphasis laid on reason in the play is particularly pronounced and, juxtaposed against the venal Danes, makes clear that Phillips is aligning his drama with Molesworth's *Account of Denmark* and thus investing the Irish with those values of liberty and reason lauded in that text. *Hibernia Freed* was staged at a moment in London when the origins of the Irish nation were being replotted in a new history, the national character of its people was being reimagined on and offstage, and when vocal patriot arguments were being made as to Ireland's right to economic and political self-determination in all sorts of forums. It would be rather surprising if elements of Addison's tragedy, the most well-known play about political freedom and resistance, were not found in Philips's play.

Hibernia Freed echoes many elements of *Cato*. That O'Brien's son is named Lucius, the name of a loyal senator to Cato, is immediately striking, but there are other echoes of the play such as Irish warrior Herimon's celebration of his sons' martial deaths: 'Five Sons I once cou'd boast, and in their Death/I Glory still. For you, for Liberty/They fell' (13); his daughter Agnes's rebuke of O'Connor's lovemaking: 'And hast thou Leisure to

---

[25] Stephen Small, *Political Thought in Ireland 1776–1798* (Oxford: Oxford University Press, 2012). For a later example of this tradition with a theatrical connection, see playwright Leonard MacNally's *The Claims of Ireland* (London: J. Johnson, 1782).

[26] Slowey, *Radicalization of Irish Drama*, 113.

reflect on Love?/Just on the verge of Death; nay worse, our Lives/
Depending on the Favour of the Danes' (15) invokes Marcia's slap down
of Lucius: 'wouldst thou have me sink away/In pleasing dreams, and lose
myself in love,/When every moment Cato's life's at stake?'[27] Throughout
the play, Turgesius's 'wild ambition' or 'vain ambition' is castigated just as
Caesar's ambition is repeatedly assaulted in *Cato*, right from the
prologue.[28] Speaking more generally, there is a disciplined martial virtue
as well as a chaste self-restraint in sexual matters in the Irish that
aligns them with the republican Romans of *Cato* rather than the popish
subservience of Catholic Rome. This capacity for principled and courageous self-regulation distinguishes them from the lustful, savagely violent
and power-hungry invaders of the play.

But there are some substantive variations in Philips's drama, particularly
in his rejection of Cato's suicide, a nodal point of critical importance.
Rosenthal has shown how Cato should be understood as an extreme rather
than an exemplar.[29] *Hibernia Freed*, despite its generic nomination as
a tragedy, shies away from any act of self-destruction by the Irish
characters.[30] Evidently, the prospect of presenting a London audience
with an Irish king prepared to kill himself before political subjugation
was far too hardnosed a position and one that would not be commensurate
with the general tenor of Irish patriotism. Indeed, at one point O'Brien
advocates a pragmatic acceptance of the situation that is far removed from
both Cato's rigid defiance and the traditional characterisation of the Irish
being prone to frenzied violence:

> The Loss of Empire and the Loss of Pow'r
> We may support, while Reason is our guide.
> Better be subject to the *Danes*, than as
> This *Dane*, to ev'ry Passion be a Slave.   (35)

These lines are rather extraordinary in their apparent acquiescence to
servitude. Yet for Philips, despite the undoubted strength of his feelings
on the inequities of the Declaratory Act and its reaffirmation of economic

---

[27] Joseph Addison, *Cato: A Tragedy and Selected Essays*, ed. Christine Dunn Henderson and Mark
   E. Yellin (Indianapolis: Liberty Fund, 2011), I.vi:11–13. Further references will be cited in the text by
   act, scene and line number.
[28] See 'wild ambition well deserves its woe' (Prologue, 12); Portius to Marcus 'Ye gods, what havoc does
   ambition make/Among your works!' (I.i.11–12); Sempronius bemoans the 'bars to his ambition'
   presented by Cato (I.ii.55); and Cato cries 'Oh curst ambition!' (IV.iv.104).
[29] Rosenthal, 'Juba's Roman soul', 65–66.
[30] The tragedy, it would appear by the play's satisfying conclusion for the Irish, is displaced offstage to
   the current political and economic woes of Ireland.

and political subjugation, it was more important to signal an ethnic disdain for untrammelled violence. There is a dignity to O'Brien in these lines which express his Enlightenment preference for individual and rational self-discipline and a sense that national pride cannot countenance such moral degradation. Enlightenment, it seems, is a process that requires patience and a willingness to embrace indignities for the greater scheme. Irish civility must be presented and maintained above all other considerations.

2

If in 1739 James Quin had actually played the title role of *Gustavus Vasa* as was intended by Henry Brooke, the connection with *Cato* would have been made more obvious.[31] Brooke claimed that British values of liberty and love of country motivated *Gustavus Vasa*, a claim that did not prevent it from becoming the first play to be refused a licence under the Stage Licensing Act (1737). Commentators such as L. W. Conolly and Herbert Wright are agreed that the play, in particular the venal courtier Trollio, is a blatant attack on Walpole and his corrupt premiership.[32] However, the influence of *Cato* on Brooke has not been fully acknowledged. Gustavus, after all, in a nod to Molesworth, was resisting Danish invaders and we know that Brooke, a friend of Swift, later imagined himself as a Cato figure in retirement. When Brooke had returned to Ireland, a visitor found these carefully transcribed lines – handwritten 'in imitation of print' – from *Cato* in Brooke's house:

> Let me advise thee to retreat by times
> To thy paternal seat, the Sabine field,
> Where the great censor toil'd with his own hands,
> And all our frugal ancestors were blest
> In humble virtues, and a rural life.
> There live retir'd, pray for the peace of Rome,
> Content thyself to be obscurely good.[33]

Turning to the play itself, Gustavus Vasa's love of country and willingness to make personal sacrifice make the play's debt to *Cato* quite clear. Brooke's preface – an indignant protest against the decision of the refusal to licence

---

[31] Herbert Wright, 'Henry Brooke's "Gustavus Vasa"', *Modern Language Review* 14 (1919): 173–82; 177.

[32] L. W. Conolly, *The Censorship of English Drama, 1737–1824* (San Marino: Huntington Library Press, 1976), 54–56; and Wright, 'Henry Brooke's "Gustavus Vasa"', 176.

[33] C. H. Wilson, *Brookiana*, 2 vols. (London: Richard Philips, 1804), 2: 83.

the drama – makes much of the play's championing of patriotism and personal freedom: 'By *Personal Freedom* I mean that State resulting from *Virtue*; or *Reason* ruling in the Breast superior to Appetite and Passion.'[34] The prologue even makes explicit references to Caesar:

> Such, such, of old, the first-born Natives were,
> Who breath'd the Vertues of *Britannia's* Air,
> Their Realm, when mighty *Caesar* vainly sought;
> For mightier Freedom against Caesar fought,
> And rudely drove the fam'd Invader Home,
> To tyrannize o'er polish'd —— venal *Rome*.   (Prologue, n.p.)

Other themes found in *Cato* are also present. The implication that love 'Degrades the Hero, and makes Cowards valiant' (20) echoes *Cato*'s scepticism towards romantic love and its debilitating effect on patriotic virtue. Cristina, the daughter of the usurper, recounts how she was offered up to Gustavus by way of appeasement, but he turned her down. Like *Cato*, Brooke's play is scathing of personal ambition; Cristina observes:

> What's all the gaudy Glitter of a Crown?
> What, but the glaring Meteor of Ambition
> That leads a Wretch benighted in his Errors,
> Points to the Gulph, and shines upon Destruction.   (25)

At the close of the play, Cristina's sublimation of personal desire to paternal duty brings both Lucia and Marcia from *Cato* to mind. The debt to Addison is quite clear, but the play also demonstrates how the discourses of Irish patriotism and English Whiggism could overlap in productive ways. Drawing on *Cato*, Brooke was able to make clear his adherence to those British values of liberty and personal freedom while also suggesting that the case of Ireland demanded that those values should also be equally applicable to Protestant Ireland. That Brooke set his opening scene, where Swedish nobles meet to outline the necessity of their patriotic revolution and where Gustavus reveals himself to them, in a copper mine leaves his political intentions in little doubt. The charge led by his friend Jonathan Swift on the Wood's ha'pence affair – concerning the feared introduction of debased copper currency into Ireland – is explicitly alluded to here. The pamphlets composed by Swift in 1724 attacking this British policy were even signed M. B. Drapier, Marcus Brutus being one of the

---

[34] Henry Brooke, *Gustavus Vasa, The Deliverer of His Country, A Tragedy* (London: Printed for J. Buck, 1739). Further references will be cited in the text by page number.

anti-tyrannical republicans who assassinated Caesar and who, like Cato, later committed suicide.

Critics understood his Irish patriot intentions. One commentator produced a vitriolic scene-by-scene hatchet job of the play and repeatedly brought up its Irish traits, wondering of the scene in the copper mines whether it was to have been painted by 'Patrick Mac ma-hone', mocking another scene 'By my Shoul that was charmin!' and suggesting that the author adopted some 'new coin'd *Irish* words that seem'd strangely expressive'.[35] The criticisms might be thought to attack the author's Irish nationality rather than any purported Irish patriot reading of the play itself, but the critic makes a comparison between the Dalecarlians – that is, the people of an 'off-site' Swedish region whom Gustavus Vasa stirs to action – and the 'Wild Irish'.[36] The critical scene in which Gustavus, through the force of his principled rhetoric, stirs them to action is labelled 'dull Hibernian Stuff' and hence suggests that Gustavus's speeches exhorting love of country were read as offering a critique of colonial rule of Ireland.[37] The Dalecarlians are described in terms evoking primitivist accounts of Celtic purity:

> A Race of hardy, northern Sons he led,
> Guiltless of Courts, untainted, and unread,
> Whose inborn Spirit spurn'd th'ignoble Fee,
> Whose Hands scorn'd Bondage, for their Hearts were free.
>
> (Prologue, n.p.)

Recently returned to London after a stint of eight years in Ireland, Brooke was an outside observer, keen to reform the centre of governance. *Gustavus Vasa* places itself within the *Cato* tradition with Brooke suggesting his Irishness is an asset, capable of highlighting the fall from idealist grace of British politics. It is an apposite coincidence – but likely no more – that Brooke's letter of protest regarding the prohibition of his play appeared on 17 March 1737 in the *Daily Post*.[38] Publishing his letter on St Patrick's Day may have appeared to be a calculated gesture to align the play with Irish patriotism; certainly it left itself open to be

---

[35] *The Country Correspondent: Humbly addres'd to Gustavus Vasa, Esq* (London: Printed for R. Swan, 1739), 13, 19, 21.

[36] Ibid., 23.   [37] Ibid., 28.

[38] Indignant, Brooke explained how William Chetwynd, the examiner, had not only declined to issue a licence but had also refused to explain his decision. 'The Author', concluded Brooke, 'apprehending that he is greatly aggriev'd, in order to repair the Damages he hath sustain'd, proposes to print the said Play by Subscription, on Royal Paper, at Five Shillings each Copy, and humbly hopes the Encouragement of every impartial Lover of Virtue and Liberty', *Daily Post*, 17 March 1737.

understood in that way. When the play was performed in Dublin in 1742 as *The Patriot* – the city not being subject to the Stage Licensing Act – it was received with considerable applause as it was read as an attack on British rule.[39]

3

We turn now to our final example, Charles Macklin's *King Henry the VII. Or The Popish Impostor* (1746).[40] Macklin wrote *Henry VII* partly as a public declaration of loyalty to the Protestant Hanoverian regime: that much seems self-evident. Although Ireland itself was sufficiently docile that Dublin Castle could send troops to Scotland, the proximity of Jacobite forces – which came within 130 miles of London in 1745 – made for anxious times in the capital for the Irish, as noted by Ian Gilmour.[41] As an Irishman who struggled with mockery of his Donegal accent, as a convict found guilty of manslaughter in a high-profile case in 1734, and as an actor who had terrified theatregoers with his snarling Shylock, it is fair comment to say that Macklin had more cause to be concerned than others.[42] Moreover, he had only recently returned to the stage in December 1744 after a well-publicised feud with David Garrick that had left him isolated from his fellow actors and with a further reputation for dispute.[43] Perhaps a need for some good publicity was what fuelled the hasty six-week composition of his tragedy about Perkin Warbeck, the rebellious fifteenth-century Pretender. Staged on 18 January 1746 at Drury Lane, the play's prologue – delivered by Macklin himself in character as the Scottish noble Huntley – made a clear statement on his loyalties:

> When Popish Rage, & Persecution blaz'd
> And Britons bled on Altars Rome had rais'd;
> When Matrons saw their Sons in Flames expire

---

[39] Helen Burke, *Riotous Performances*, 122–23.

[40] Charles Macklin, *King Henry the VII. Or The Popish Impostor* (London: Printed for R. Francklin et al., 1746). Further references will be to the Larpent manuscript, titled *The Alternative, Tyranny or Liberty*, by folio number. Huntington Library, Larpent MSS, LA 55.

[41] Ian Gilmour, *Riot, Risings and Revolution* (London: Hutchinson, 1992), 118. Irish Catholics, of course, had long been associated with the nefarious Jacobite agenda, stretching back in recent memory to the Popish Plot of the late 1670s. Pamphlets citing supposed examples of Irish barbarism and violence in the 1641 Rebellion also emerged at this time. See, for example, *Popery and Slavery Display'd* (London: C. Corbett et al., 1745); *The Bloody Cruelties of the Papists against the Protestants* (London: J. Lewis, 1745), and *A Brief Account of the Methods used to Propagate Popery* (London: J. Oldcastle, 1746).

[42] See Emily Anderson, 'Celebrity Shylock', *PMLA* 126.4 (2011): 935–49; 940–42.

[43] See William W. Appleton, *Charles Macklin: An Actor's Life* (Cambridge, MA: Harvard University Press, 1960), 56–65.

And Husbands crackling in religious Fire,
Then Rome gave laws; our Kings & Council sway'd
While Briton mourn'd her Liberties betray'd.
But now she smiles, the Laws are all her own,
And rule alike the Cottage & the Throne.   (Prologue, n. f.)

However, it was a dismal failure. A gleeful Tobias Smollett jibed in *Roderick Random*, that the play 'by the strength of art, lingred till the third night, and then died in a deplorable manner'.[44] Susannah Cibber called it 'much below anything I ever yet saw'.[45] Consequently, it has received scant critical attention with Michael Wagoner producing the fullest account and explication of its failure to date.[46] On examination, however, the play's Larpent manuscript suggests a more complicated drama than previously acknowledged.

Despite Macklin's apparent ringing endorsement of the Hanover regime, the manuscript is marked in various places with small 'x's in a manner consistent with other emendations probably made by Thomas Odell, then deputy examiner. Looking at these interventions collectively, we observe that the lines marked for omission chiefly pertain to Huntley, the virtuous noble played by Macklin, and they refer to matters of kingly governance. One example will give a flavour of what excited Odell's attention: this is Huntley on the respect – determinedly equivocal, it seems – due to monarchical authority:

> The People's Interest,
> In free Nations is blended & Coequal
> With ye Kings, & he who separates or
> Over values either is the Traitor
> ...   when defil'd
> By Tyranny & PriestCraft, [majesty] becomes
> A Magazine of Vengeance, & all our
> Veneration turns to Contempt & Wrath.[47]   (f.45 r)

---

44 Tobias Smollett, *The Adventures of Roderick Random*, ed. O. M. Brack with an introduction and notes by James G. Basker, Paul-Gabriel Boucé and Nicole A. Seary (Athens, GA, and London: University of Georgia Press, 2012), 332. Smollett, a sufficiently brave Scottish nationalist to publish sympathetic poetry regarding Culloden in 1746, was presumably provoked to the jibe by Macklin's depiction of his countrymen.

45 Cibber to Garrick, cited in Appleton, 76.

46 Michael M. Wagoner, 'The "Merry" Tragedy of *Henry VII* as written by "Charles Macklin, Comedian"', *New Theatre Quarterly* 31.4 (2015): 372–80. Wagoner suggests that the dissonance between Macklin's reputation as a comic actor and the play's serious tone provoked the harsh audience reaction.

47 Other examples of passages marked unfit for representation include Huntley observing that 'Council void of Freedom may flatter and/Mislead but never can assist' (f.7r); 'I see Majesty – Deluded Majesty,/Hem'd in by a Band of crawling Parasites' (f.7v); 'the Interest at Court now/Is who bids most' (f.10r); and, 'gracious Sir, let Reason School/Y^r Youthful distemper'd Heat & Sound Judgm^t' (f.44r).

Macklin certainly extols the excellence of Protestant liberty in opposition
to the slavish obedience associated with Catholicism, but he is also keen to
offer a broad and constructive critique of British political life. His
Whiggish references to countering mendacious courtiers, his criticism of
the stagnancy of the body politic, and, his demarcation of the limits of
kingly authority that irked Odell are important elements, I have elsewhere
argued, that help facilitate a reading of Macklin's later and more successful
comedies as considered political commentary rather than surly ethnic
ripostes to prejudice.[48] While one could argue that the examiner's interventions are as much a reflection of the then political volatility as any intent
of overt political intervention on Macklin's part, the censored lines have an
explicitly patriot flavour and alert us to its resonance with *Hibernia Freed*
and *Gustavus Vasa*.

Macklin's play has strong whiffs of Whiggery with the play's determined
critique of 'ambition' and great men; an abhorrence of corrupt courtiers; and,
tellingly, a marked insistence on the virtue of commerce throughout – the play
ends with Henry declaring 'Let Faction cease, Commerce & freedom smile/
The World can't Conquer then, this War-proof Isle' (f.58 r). Building on
Brooke, trade and commerce are put front and centre of a play that underlines
how Whiggish principles and Irish patriotism overlap in powerful ways that
would persist through the rest of the century. There are also distinct echoes of
Cato; however, as I have previously documented these, I shall eschew working
through them in favour of building a larger argument.[49]

The Introduction to this volume placed Macklin as the heartbeat of the
Irish theatrical Enlightenment with his performance as Shylock at
a particularly potent moment for the London Irish theatrical world, sig-
nifying all sorts of possibilities for Irish success in the sphere of culture.
As I work towards a conclusion here, I want to show how his only history
play – despite its undoubted commercial failure – reveals an intellectual
and political ambition that strengthens Macklin's case to be considered as
the pivotal figure within Irish circles in the 1740s. By this mid-century
point, London has more Irish playwrights emboldened by growing patriotic sentiment, increasing numbers of middle-class Irish migrants, a more
pronounced Irish acting presence in the theatres, all in a city where there
was a growing culture of tolerance on the part of the English, particularly as
Scottophobia spread. Macklin's play, I will argue in what follows, is also an
act of emboldened Irish historical revisionism that evidences a third layer

---

[48] O'Shaughnessy, 'Bit, by some mad whig'.   [49] Ibid., 580–81.

of political ideology on top of the profession of Hanoverian loyalty and his proclamation of Whiggish values.

Henry the VII is a reworking of John Ford's *Perkin Warbeck* (1634). Although Ford's play was described by T.S. Eliot as 'almost flawless', the eighteenth century took a dimmer view, there being no record of its performance in the theatrical calendar.[50] Macklin's decision to go with a reworking of this play then seems immediately bold and ambitious, another attempt to restore a play to the canon as he had with *The Merchant of Venice*. Moreover, it offered a more sober response to the rebellion than the jeering of Cibber's *The Non-Juror* or Fielding's *The Old Debauchees*. By comparing Ford's and Macklin's versions of the Perkin Warbeck story, we can advance this argument. First, however, a brief sketch of the history dramatised in both plays is necessary.

Lambert Simnel (*b.* 1476/7–*d. after* 1534) was an earlier pretender to the throne in the late 1480s. The full story of his attempt to take the crown need not detain us long, suffice to say that the city of Dublin and various Irish supporters such as the Earl of Kildare, disaffected by Henry II's reign, gave significant support to Simnel's claim to be the heir of George, Duke of Clarence. Indeed, Simnel was actually crowned king of England in 1487 in Christ Church Cathedral in Dublin, prompting Henry to scoff that the Irish were so foolish that they would someday crown an ape. A subsequent invasion of England, supported by German mercenaries and four thousand Irish troops, ended in dismal failure in 1487. Simnel entered Henry's service as a scullion and later a falconer; he was considered useful propaganda and was once supposed to have been presented to Irish lords on a visit to court to remind them of their past foolishness.

A few years later, Perkin Warbeck was also recruited to the Yorkist cause while he was visiting Ireland. In 1491, he was persuaded by Fryon/Frion, a Burgundian diplomat and spy; the former mayor of Cork, John Atwater; and others to adopt the guise of Richard, second son of Edward IV and one of the princes in the tower. After his time in Cork, Warbeck gained some support in France, Vienna and England before an attempt to invade England in 1495 ended disastrously without even disembarkation. His flotilla moved on to Ireland where he tried unsuccessfully to take

---

[50] *Perkin Warbeck* in John Ford, *'Tis Pity She's A Whore and Other Plays*, ed. Marion Lomax (Oxford and New York: Oxford World's Classics, 1995), xxi. Further references will be cited in the text by act, scene and line number.

Waterford before finding succour at the court of King James IV
of Scotland. James married him to Katherine Gordon, Earl of Huntley,
as a demonstration of support. An invasion of England found few allies
south of the border and Ireland remained quiet under the now obedient
Earl of Kildare. Rebels in Cornwall offered significant assistance, but the
game was up by 1498 and his execution followed a year later. Apparently,
there were no more openings in the royal kitchen.

In Ford's play, the opening scene has Lord Chamberlain Stanley insist to
Henry that the memory of Simnel and others – including the Earl of
Kildare – would be enough to deter conspirators as they were 'Most
spectacles of ruin, some of mercy – ' (I.i.95). Throughout his play are
pejorative references to 'th'superstitious Irish' (I.iii.39). When Henry sus-
pects that 'Some Irish heads work in this mine of treason', Clifford responds:

> Not any of the best; your fortune
> Hath dulled their spleens. Never had counterfeit
> Such a confused rabble of lost bankrupts
> For counsellors; first, Heron, a broken mercer,
> Then John A-Water, sometimes Mayor of Cork
> Sketon, a tailor, and a scrivener
> Called Astley.   (I.iii.55–61)

Later, Frion tricks the foolish Irish contingent into making an 'Irish
hubbub' (II.iii.165) at the wedding, provoking them by suggesting the
Scots would take all the glory if they did not perform. The wedding
masque stage direction – *Enter at one door four Scotch Antics, accordingly
habited; enter at another four wild Irish in trousers, long-haired, and accordingly habited* – gives us both a clear indication of the visual comic force of
the Other offered by the Celts as well as Ford's easy and uncritical conflation of Irish and Scots. After the Irish leave the wedding, Frion complains
of having to deal with their idiocy:

> O, the toil
> Of humouring this abject scum of mankind!
> Muddy brained peasants!   (II.iii. 176–78)

In Ford's tragedy, Ireland features throughout as a source of dissent,
rebellion, barbarism, and stupidity. The character John A-Waters is very
much a Stage Irishman, uttering nonsensical Irish bulls to Henry after he is
caught, and he is easily manipulated by the wily Frion. Ireland is associated
with both Simnel and Warbeck and the casual association with Scotland
offers it little in terms of distinguishing itself from this other Celtic nation.

As one might imagine, the Irish were very keen to distinguish themselves from Scotland after 1745.[51] Just as Ireland had remained pacified in 1715, this was also true in 1745. And if we look at Macklin's play, this is borne out very clearly. There is no John A-Waters or any Irish character in the play which is fixedly targeted at Scottish perfidy. The opening scene has characters Frion and Sevez (his priestly master conspirator) meet in Holyrood Palace. Thus the story starts in Scotland and the Irish episodes with Simnel and Warbeck are cut from the story. And the lines between Ireland and Scotland are drawn early: Sevez notes the fact that their forces 'Abound in Scottish blood/Ready to be drain'd against England's peace' before asking 'But how/Stands Ireland? What Hopes from thence?' (f.1v). Frion responds:

> None
> Th'Apostate Slaves are fall'n off from Rome
> And firmly fixt in the Usurper's Cause
> Kildare Clanrikard with many others
> On whom we built Absolute assurance.
> Have at their own Charge arm'd their Friends & followers,
> And joind the English General Poinings–   (ff.1 v-2 r)

Ford's traitorous Kildare has now become a loyal supporter aligned seamlessly with English military forces at his own expense, his awkward historic treason expunged from the record. Moreover, Frion goes on to point out at length the extent of English treason; the danger from within is offered as being deeply problematic.

Paddy Bullard has argued that an emphasis on public speaking and oratory distinguishes Irish approaches to rhetoric in the eighteenth century. Molesworth, Swift, Berkeley and others all worried about a perceived failure of civic eloquence, and Bullard offers Sheridan's 'Hibernian Academy', a 1757 initiative which proposed a patriot educational system based on elocution as a response to such concerns.[52] But the history play tradition traced here of Philips, Brooke and Macklin might also be seen as 'praxis as response' that demonstrated the capacity of the Irish to fashion and articulate an Irish political future in harmony with British values whilst also demanding a moderate degree of autonomy. In Macklin's *Henry the VII*, the alliance of Poinings with Kildare signals the acceptance

---

[51] Charles O'Conor would continue to make this point (on Irish pacifity vs Scottish aggression in 1745) in the London press of the early 1760s. O'Shaughnessy, 'Bit, by some mad whig', 569.

[52] Paddy Bullard, 'Rhetoric and Eloquence: The Language of Persuasion' in *The Oxford Handbook of British Philosophy in the Eighteenth Century*, ed. James Harris (Oxford: Oxford University Press, 2013), 89.

of British norms, while the implications of Huntley's Catoesque rhetoric, the character written and played by Macklin, are that Britain should clean its own political Augean stable and extend its much vaunted 'liberty' to the Irish. While Philips and Brooke look to the ancient past and the European Other to frame their allegories, Macklin's insistence on tackling relatively recent British history – and limiting the historical distance between audience and object of historical enquiry – represents a heightened assertiveness in the Irish position, one that was emerging in an equally bold Irish historiography of the mid-century led by leading Irish Catholic intellectual Charles O'Conor, a historiography that was keen to advance beyond Keating.[53] We might also reflect that the cast of Macklin's drama included Macklin, Margaret Woffington, Dennis Delane and William Havard, providing a telling synecdoche for the collective affective force of Irish actors during the long eighteenth century in London which could be capitalised upon by dramatists.

Henry the VII may have been a failure, but it is an illuminating drama that opens an alternative perspective on the eighteenth-century Irish theatrical tradition, too often reduced to comedies. There is value in looking beyond *She Stoops to Conquer* and *The School for Scandal* to thicken our understanding of the Irish contribution to London's cultural life as well as our understanding of how the political and theatrical worlds interacted. Historical drama is a form of re-enactment: Mark Salber Phillips has defended re-enactment's affective tendencies on the ground that affect itself has cognitive implications.[54] It is a participatory mode of historical enquiry in which spectators, ultimately, have something of an ethical imperative to measure, assess and judge. In an age of sympathy, the collective Irish investment in historical enquiry, both on stage and off, speaks to a growing assurance on their part; increased tolerance on the part of their English audience; and, most tellingly, a determination on the part of the Irish diaspora to signal their cultural assimilation as well as their capacity to advance understanding and knowledge.

Irish dramatists such as Macklin saw historical drama as the mechanism by which they could connect themselves to an extant literary tradition, announce themselves as serious participants in political debate and make

---

[53] Other notable revisionists include John Curry and Sylvester O'Halloran. See O'Halloran, *Golden Ages and Barbarous Nations* and *Charles O'Conor of Ballinagare*, ed. Gibbons and O'Conor.

[54] Mark Salber Phillips, 'Introduction: Rethinking Historical Distance' in *Rethinking Historical Distance*, ed. Mark Salber Phillips, Barbara Caine and Julia Adeney Thomas (Basingstoke: Palgrave, 2013), 12.

explicit the rich contribution Irish writers could make to British intellectual life. A new genealogy of Irish theatre of the eighteenth century would include, for instance, William Havard's *King Charles I* (1737), Elizabeth Griffith's *Theodorick, King of Denmark* (1752), Robert Jephson's *Braganza* (1775), Leonard MacNally's *Robin Hood* (1784), Thomas Stratford's *Lord Russell* (1784), not to mention history plays produced by John O'Keeffe, Frederick Pilon, James Sheridan Knowles and Arthur Murphy to name but a few. What would happen, for instance, if we looked at Oliver Goldsmith's little-known oratorio *The Captivity* (1763) as a history play and read this story of resistance to Egyptian tyranny by a landless Jewish people through the lens of an Irish historiography which often drew comparisons between the Irish and Jewish peoples? How might this perspective alter our sense of his politics? Equally, how would our sense of his canon shift?

Collectively, these various plays represent an important facet of eighteenth-century Irish patriotism: the determination of a people to tell their own history with a view to achieving political autonomy. These interconnected history plays and their engagement with political thought bolster the idea that, as Ian McBride has suggested, theatre is one of the unexamined institutional structures of the Irish Enlightenment.[55]

The Goldsmith example shows the necessity of fully theorising the genre to advance critical discussion, and not just for Irish writers. When we start to look, we can see that many writers of the century wrote or attempted to write history plays: James Miller and John Hoadly (*Mahomet* [*the Impostor*], 1744), Samuel Johnson (*Irene*, 1749), William Whitehead (*The Roman Father*, 1750), Richard Cumberland, *The Banishment of Cicero* (1761), William Blake (*King Edward the Third*, 1783), Ann Yearsley (*Earl Goodwin*, 1789), William Godwin (*St Dunstan*, 1790), Samuel Taylor Coleridge (*The Fall of Robespierre,* 1794), Frances Burney (*Edwy and Elgiva*, 1795) and Percy Shelley (*Charles I,* 1822). Even from this brief selection, we can make some initial generalisations that provoke enticing questions: why do so many writers try to write a history play as their first dramatic venture in the supposed age of comedy? Why is there such a high degree of failure and incompleteness? And why was the history play genre so politically contentious (as well as

[55] Ian McBride, 'The Edge of Enlightenment: Ireland and Scotland in the Eighteenth Century', *Modern Intellectual History* 10 (2013): 135–51; 147–48.

the first three plays prohibited, many later history plays were refused licences)? These are worthwhile questions for the theatre historian. Paine's famous rebuke of Burke – that he should remember he was writing history, not plays – is not simply a reprimand for his florid style; Paine betrays his anxiety regarding Burke harnessing the affective and intellectual force of the history play, the neglected genre of the Georgian London stage.

CHAPTER 8

From Ireland to Peru: Arthur Murphy's (Anti)-Imperial Dramaturgy

Bridget Orr

Late Georgian tragedies are now at best damned with faint praise, although Felicity Nussbaum has recently made a persuasive case that serious plays such as Arthur Murphy's *Zenobia* (1767) were culturally important as vehicles for star performers including Sarah Siddons and Mrs Yates, functioning as powerful generators of enjoyable affects.[1] The arc of critical reception for Murphy's *The Grecian Daughter* (1770) as well as *Zenobia* certainly bears out Nussbaum's contention for the last decade of the eighteenth century, as by 1795 almost every critic referred to the former play as 'pantomime', notwithstanding Mrs Siddons's capacity to render the experience of watching the play 'sublime'.[2] But this belated contempt for Murphy's tragedies belies the fact that much of the initial response to his serious plays was enthusiastic, somewhat surprisingly given his personal political notoriety at the time of their first production. Frequently, if not uniformly, setting aside hostility to his history as propagandist for Henry Fox and then George III's highly unpopular adviser, Lord Bute, a range of contemporary commentators identified Murphy's skill in characterisation and the generation of heightened situations as the engines of successful tragic dramaturgy.[3]

The appeal of Murphy's serious plays was not just a question of his formal competence, however. In addition to his command of character and fable, the Irish playwright's tragedies were informed by his complex and ambivalent perspective on imperial expansion, a deeply sensitive awareness of the political, religious and cultural conflict engendered by colonial aggression and resistance that resonates with the multiple allegiances of

---

[1] Felicity A. Nussbaum, 'The Unaccountable Pleasure of Eighteenth-Century Tragedy', *PMLA* 129.4 (2014): 688–707.

[2] Howard Hunter Dunbar, *The Dramatic Career of Arthur Murphy* (New York and London: Modern Language Association of America and Oxford University Press, 1946), 221.

[3] For summary accounts of the contemporary reception of *The Orphan of China, Zenobia, The Grecian Daughter* and *Alzuma*, see Dunbar, 73–75, 194–97, 220–23 and 207 respectively.

Richard Brinsley Sheridan discussed by Robert Jones (Chapter 5). His choice of tragic topics was Drydenic in scope, ranging in location quite literally 'from China to Peru' as Johnson put it in *The Vanity of Human Wishes,* and he explored a wide variety of scenarios of imperial conquest, generally from the perspective of the losers. Such figures included Han patriots defeated by the Tartars and Zenobia, the heroic *femme forte* who fought against Rome.[4]

It seems likely that Murphy's interest in dramatising the effects of regime change in imperial contexts was shaped by the fact that he composed his tragedies during or in the wake of the Seven Years' War, often described as the first truly global conflict. With campaigns in South Asia, the Caribbean and North America as well as Europe, the war was indeed imperial in scope, and Britain emerged from the struggle in a newly dominant position.[5] As we shall see in more detail later, Murphy himself linked his composition of *Alzuma* (1773) to the contemporaneous conflict with the Spanish imperial state. Unlike Macklin *Henry the VII,* discussed by David O'Shaughnessy (Chapter 7), he followed theatrical precedent by avoiding the depiction of episodes from Britain's own colonial past, instead availing himself of the extensive repertoire of dramatic and narrative representations of imperial conflict familiar to him from ancient sources. Strikingly, however, this learned classicist, famed for having known the *Aeneid* by heart at school, went beyond Greek and Roman history to draw on subjects from the much less familiar but equally venerable civilisations of China and Peru.

Dramatic engagement aside, Murphy's own role in the Seven Years' War was that of publicist for the hated Bute, who had wrested control of government from the much more popular Pitt. Bute spent much of 1762 and the first months of the next year negotiating peace with France along somewhat less punitive terms than those desired by the commercial and financial interests who supported Pitt. Tobias Smollett's *The Briton* tried but failed signally to soften public opinion towards Bute's peace policy and in June 1762, Murphy took up the cudgels, using a new journal called *The Auditor* to attack Pitt and generate enthusiasm for peace on Tory

---

[4] For a recent analysis of Zenobia's role in Roman imperial culture, see I-Chun Wang, 'Zenobia as Spectacle: Captive Queen in Art and Literature', *Journal of Comparative Literature and Aesthetics* 36 (2013): 75–85.

[5] For an overview, see Brendan Simms, *Three Victories and a Defeat: The Rise and Fall of the First British Empire, 1714–1783* (New York: Basic Books, 2008). See also *The Culture of the Seven Years' War: Empire, Identity, and the Arts in the Eighteenth-Century Atlantic World,* ed. Frans De Bruyn and Shaun Regan (Toronto: University of Toronto Press, 2014).

terms. Murphy was no more successful than Smollett, and his theatrical career suffered as a result of his unpopular political journalism. Wilkes and Churchill, who, like the rest of Bute's enemies, were strongly hostile to returning Havana in exchange for Florida, made the most effective attack on him.[6] In December 1762, aware of the strength of feeling on this topic, Murphy published an anonymous letter he had received purporting to come from one 'Viator', claiming that Florida was a desirable colony whose rich peat or turf resources could form a useful trade with those Caribbean colonies in need of fuel.[7] Almost immediately, attacks on the absurdity of the claims came raining down, not just from the predictably hostile Whiggish *St. James's Chronicle* but from *The Chronicle* and even the more conservative *Gentleman's Magazine*. The concluding blow came, unsurprisingly, from No. 35 of *The North Briton*, likely source of the spurious letter from 'Viator'. Beginning by mocking Murphy's credulity in arguing for the '*commercial advantages ... of the Florida Turf*, that fine, rich vein of trade, just opened by our AUDITOR, to give, as he says, *comfortable fires* to our cold, frozen *West-Indian* islands', the paper amplifies the joke by linking Murphy's enthusiasm for the 'Peet Trade' to his ethnicity.[8] 'This wonderful genius, the AUDITOR', we are reminded, emerged 'from his native bog of Allen', and as an Irishman, it is suggested he would 'be ready to bargain for his dear *natale solum*, and would not more scruple to *sell his country* than to sell himself' (*NB,* 228). Turf, land, territory, nation – each homologous entity is rendered vendible by the slavish, mercenary and treacherous Irish, *The North Briton* suggests. The attack climaxes in a suggestion that Murphy would find congenial company among the Floridians because 'it is well-known that *Florida* has been chiefly peopled by *convicts* from *New-Spain*' (*NB,* 228). Thus 'our disciple of *St Omer's* ... would surpass in perfidy and fraud the most refined Jesuit, who is *tolerated* in these new conquests – possibly to read mass to this good *Irish Catholic*' (*NB,* 229). Concluding with a dig at Murphy's theatrical career, *The North Briton* sneers, 'If no untimely end prevents the dullest *play-wright* of our times, he may then at last present us with a woeful *Tragedy*, both new and *interesting*, but drawn not from fable and invention, but founded on his own real adventures, and *hair-breadth escapes*' (*NB,* 229).

---

[6] On this bizarre episode, and its negative consequences for Murphy's reputation, see Conrad M. Brunström and Declan Kavanagh, 'Arthur Murphy and Florida Peat: "The Gray's Inn Journal" and versions of the Author', *Eighteenth-Century Ireland/ Iris an dá chultúr* 27 (2012): 123–41.
[7] *The Auditor* (June 1762), 153–54.   [8] *The North Briton* 35 (July 1762), 228.

   Ironically, the last offensive comment is richly suggestive, notwithstanding its reiteration of a much-repeated accusation of plagiarism. Like many
if not most of his peers, Murphy certainly rifled other texts in search of
usable scenarios; in his prologue to *Zenobia*, he used an aggressively
patriotic nautical metaphor to justify, indeed glorify, his literary
plundering:

> Yet think not that we mean to mock the eye
> With pilfer'd colours of a foreign dye.
> Not to translate our bard his pen doth dip;
> He takes a play, as Britons take a ship;
> They heave her down; – with many a sturdy stroke,
> Repair her well, and build with Heart of Oak.
> To ev'ry breeze set Britain's streamers free,
> *New-man* her, and away again to sea.[9]

Despite the aggressive rhetoric of maritime appropriation invoked here,
however, Murphy showed a distinct preference for theatrical vehicles that
voiced the suffering and protests of those victimised by national and
imperial conflicts, frequently shifting towards or expanding a specifically
feminine perspective on war. Contemporary critics often commented on
the Sophoclean and Aeschylean echoes in his texts, unsurprising from
a writer steeped in the Western classics. But Murphy did not rearticulate
the scenarios he adapted as facile patriotism along the lines suggested in the
prologue to *Zenobia*: he did in fact use them, as *The North Briton* suggested
sardonically, to articulate 'his own real adventures', as a Catholic Irishman
making his way in a strange and hostile metropolis. Forced to abandon the
devotional affiliation he inherited from his adored mother, Murphy's
dramaturgy suggests an unresolved ambivalence over the religious, political
and subjective abjuration enjoined by colonial domination and a strong
degree of identification with those on the defeated side of imperial conflict.
   After his father's death at sea when he was a child, Murphy's education
at the Jesuit College at St Omer was sponsored by his aunt, with whom he
lived in Boulogne before commencing his studies. When he returned to
London after completing his schooling, a period in which he distinguished
himself and which he later described as 'the happiest in my life', his faith
was attacked brutally by his uncle, who had charge of establishing him in
business. The former called Catholicism 'a mean, beggarly, blackguard
religion', but although 'my Mother desired me not to mind his violent
advice ... my brother, who was educated at Westminster school, spoke

---

[9] Arthur Murphy, *Zenobia, A Tragedy* (London: W. Griffin, 1768), n.p.

strongly in support of my uncle's opinion, and he never gave up the point till he succeeded to his utmost wish.'[10] His older sibling shared Murphy's literary and theatrical interests so it is unsurprising that his persistent but amiable suasion appears to have led to the younger brother's conversion to an undemonstrative Anglicanism. In considering *Alzuma*'s treatment of the issue, however, it is worth bearing in mind that Murphy was deeply and persistently attached to his mother, who retained her faith. On the other hand, his uncle, who disinherited him after Murphy refused to travel from Cork to Jamaica to take up another clerical post, embodied a bigoted form of Protestantism, a dictatorial attitude to his dependents and a contempt for a career outside commerce. A decade later, the social heft of his uncle's prejudice would be confirmed by the pejorative characterisations of Murphy's nationality and education not just in *The Auditor* but also by Charles Churchill in *The Rosciad*, in which he characterised Murphy as a latter-day Shadwell: 'Bred at *St Omer's* to the shuffling trade,/The hopeful youth a Jesuit might have made,/With various readings stor'd his empty skull/Learn'd without sense, and venerably dull.'[11] It is suggestive that in referring bitterly to the journalistic work of his youth, Murphy cited the example of Sir Richard Steele, who also suffered from xenophobic attacks focused on his Anglo-Irish origins.[12]

Despite the libels, like Steele, Murphy remained loyal to his original affiliations, most conspicuously by taking a prominent role in opposing the anti-Catholic Gordon riots of 1780. He also openly saluted Pope's adherence to Catholicism, devoting one letter in the *Gray's Inn Journal* to publishing an epistle from Pope to Racine, in which the former responded to French perceptions of the *Essay on Man* as deistic by declaring his devotion to the doctrines of Paschal and the Archbishop of Combray and his detestation of Spinoza and Leibnitz.[13] In general, however, *The Gray's Inn Journal* suggests that Murphy was a serious advocate of toleration. In Letter 84 of the *Journal*, Murphy uses an oriental tale to argue against attempts at religious conversion, using a divine messenger to

[10] Jesse Foot, *The Life of the Late Arthur Murphy Esq.* (London: Printed for J. Faulder, 1811).
[11] Charles Churchill, *The Rosciad*, 6th edition (London: Printed for the author and sold by W. Flexney, 1766), 29. There was also an extended attack on Murphy in the anonymous *The Murphiad. A Mock Heroic Poem by* 'Philim Mocolloch' (London: J. Williams, 1761). This poem focused on Murphy's supposed birth in the bog of Allen and the goddess of mud's prophecies as to his future in the theatre, emphasising his Irish birth, his 'popish zeal' (18) and his pretentions to classical learning – 'Grecian rules' (13).
[12] For Murphy's sense of grievance over the effects of his journalism on his literary reputation, see the Preface to *The Collected Works of Arthur Murphy*, 7 vols. (London: Printed for T. Cadell, 1786), 1: xii.
[13] Arthur Murphy, *The Gray's Inn Journal*, 2 vols. (Dublin: William Sleater, 1756), 2: Letter 69, 96–100.

instruct an ambitious proselytiser that 'it will better behove thee to pay submission to the established Forms of Worship of thy Country, than to disturb the Peace of the faithful' pointing out that the result of throwing off 'settled Forms of Devotion' is to see those unmoored from their traditional beliefs as 'immersed in all manner of vicious Practices. Uncontrouled they invade each other's Rights; they make War to satisfy their Ambition'.[14] His support of toleration extended to the Jewish Naturalization Bill (1753) and for that he was mocked by *The North Briton* (*NB*, 141). Acutely aware of the violence of religious bigotry and racism from his own familial and professional experiences of anti-Catholic and anti-Irish prejudice, Murphy became a forceful proponent of tolerance, that most critical Enlightenment virtue, not just in his periodical writing but also in his dramaturgy.[15]

Black Legendry, Noble Savages and Indigenous Critique

Although not the most successful, Murphy's own favourite among his serious plays was *Alzuma*, and it is in that text that his subjective ambivalence over colonialism and his political critique of empire is most vivid.[16] In the long eighteenth century, British playwrights and spectators presumed that plays about Latin America would reiterate the black legend of Spanish conquest, whose dramatisation stretches from Dryden's *Indian Emperor* (performed in 1667) to Richard Brinsley Sheridan's *Pizarro* (1799) more than a century later.[17] The black legend represented the Spanish conquest of the new world as an exceptionally brutal process, as the indigenous population was slaughtered, enslaved and forcibly converted

---

[14] Ibid., Letter 84, 181–85.

[15] For further discussion of toleration in a London Irish context, see Jim Davis, Chapter 2, this volume, on John Johnstone.

[16] See John Pike Emery, *Arthur Murphy: An Eminent English Dramatist of the Eighteenth Century* (Philadelphia: University of Pennsylvania Press, 1946), 110.

[17] Most of the commentary on the literary dimensions of the black legend focuses on the Renaissance, rather than the eighteenth century. See William S. Maltby, *The Black Legend in England: The Development of Anti-Spanish Sentiment, 1558–1660* (Durham, NC: Duke University Press, 1971) and *Rereading the Black Legend: The Discourses of Religious and Racial Difference in the Renaissance Empires*, ed. Margaret Rich Greer, Walter D. Mignolo and Maureen Quilligan (Chicago: University of Chicago Press, 2007). Classic essays on noble savagery appear in *The Wild Man Within: An Image in Western Thought from the Renaissance to Romanticism*, ed. Edward J. Dudley and Maximillian E. Novak (Pittsburgh: University of Pittsburgh Press, 1973). See also Anthony Pagden, *European Encounters with the New World: From Renaissance to Romanticism* (New Haven: Yale University Press, 1993). In Terry Jay Ellingson, *The Myth of the Noble Savage* (Berkeley: University of California Press, 2001), the author argues that the figure disappears during most of the seventeenth and eighteenth centuries.

by hypocritical, fanatical and avaricious priests and soldiers. Theatrical performances were the primary means of communicating the legend to a wide band of the public, and were often produced during times of conflict with Spain. Although encoding critiques of European colonisation, religious intolerance, social relations and institutions, black legendry has generally been seen as a form of colonial discourse, alibiing (Protestant, liberal, commercial) British imperialism, a form presumed superior to the Spanish 'cross-and-booty' model.[18] But not all plays about the Spanish invasion of the Andes can be reduced to iterations of the same myth. Revisiting its pre-texts reveals that *Alzuma*, like other black legend texts, was shaped by, rather than simply ventriloquising, indigenous critiques of empire.

In a revisionary discussion of the noble savage, Robert Stam and Ella Shohat argue that far from being a pure projection of European fantasies, ventriloquising European critiques of their own cultures, dialogues spoken by New World natives and Western interlocutors constitute a 'discourse of radical indigeneity'.[19] Stam and Shohat argue that from the Renaissance on, encounters with Amerindians were the catalyst which enabled Europeans to articulate the questioning of monarchy, of hierarchical society and of empire which we associate with Enlightenment and out of which, via Marxism and liberalism, anti-colonialism *tout court* emerged.

This argument is provocative in the context of eighteenth-century stagings of New World societies, opening up the question of the extent to which theatrical re-enactments of early conflicts with European colonisers were created by 'native' perspectives – in Murphy's case, a viewpoint of Irish as well as Indian indigeneity. Most scholarship on the literature of early modern empire written within a postcolonial framework has assumed that representations of imperial expansion were governed entirely by European perspectives. From this standpoint, such non-Western 'sources' as have been recognised as contributing to depictions of colonial encounter have been treated as discursive raw material, a resource shaped and exploited by the coloniser, whether on the ground or back in the metropolis. Thus Doris L. Garraway suggests that the speech of noble savages is always projection or mimicry, a ventriloquism of European ideas with no grounding in indigenous Amerindian or Pacific thought or culture.[20]

[18] For a discussion of the competing imperial modes as they were dramatised in the Restoration, see Bridget Orr, *Empire on the English Stage, 1660–1714* (Cambridge: Cambridge University Press, 2001).
[19] Robert Stam and Ella Shohat, 'Whence and Whither Postcolonial Theory?' *New Literary History* 43.2 (2012): 371–90; 376.
[20] Doris L. Garraway, 'Of Speaking Natives and Hybrid Philosophers: Lahontan, Diderot, and the French Enlightenment Critique of Colonialism' in *The Postcolonial Enlightenment: Eighteenth-*

Shohat and Stam are not alone, however, in arguing that non-European discourses actually shaped early modern perceptions of non-Western societies, colonial encounters and Europeans' understandings of their own cultures. Major accounts of non-Western origins of Enlightenment culture include Ros Ballaster's *Fabulous Orients* (2008) and Srinivas Aravamudan's *Enlightenment Orientalism* (2012), which have tracked the importance of *The Thousand and One Nights* in particular, as it informed the development of eighteenth-century European fiction.[21] Chi-Ming Yang's *Performing China* (2011) and Eugenia Zuroski Jenkins's *A Taste for China* (2013) both explore British eighteenth-century dependence on East Asian material and literary culture, using Murphy's *The Orphan of China* as a prime example.[22] Perhaps the most striking argument for the power of a non-European discourse over European representation comes from Wendy Belcher's *Abyssinia's Samuel Johnson* (2013). Belcher argues that when he translated Pere Lobo's *Voyage to Abyssinia* in 1733, Johnson became possessed by Habesha thought – an energumen, or discourse of the other – and that Abyssinian belief moulded thereafter much of his literary production, including *Irene* (1749) and *Rasselas* (1759).[23]

Murphy's *Alzuma* is thus by no means the only play for which one can make the case that 'energumen' is actively articulated in the text and performance. Gordon Sayre has demonstrated that Dryden's *The Indian Emperor* (1667) – whose eponymous protagonist Montezuma is often cited as an early example of noble savagery – needs to be understood as, at the least, a hybrid text, shaped as much by Aztec perspectives as by those of Europeans.[24] Another example is John Dennis's *Liberty Asserted*, first successfully performed in 1704. This play dramatises First Nation responses to Anglo-French colonial rivalry in North America and was written after Dennis probably met Lahontan, author of the *New Voyages*

Century Colonialism and Postcolonial Theory, ed. Daniel Carey and Lynn Festa (Oxford: Oxford University Press, 2009), 207–39.

[21] See Ros Ballaster, *Fabulous Orients: Fictions of the East in Europe, 1662–1785* (New York: Oxford University Press, 2008) and Srinivas Aravamudan, *Enlightenment Orientalism: Resisting the Rise of the Novel* (Chicago: University of Chicago Press, 2012).

[22] Chi-ming Yang, *Performing China: Virtue, Commerce and Orientalism* (Baltimore: Johns Hopkins University Press, 2011) and Eugenia Zuroski Jenkins, *A Taste for China: English Subjectivity and the Prehistory of Orientalism* (New York: Oxford University Press, 2013).

[23] Wendy L. Belcher, *Abyssinia's Samuel Johnson: Ethiopian Thought in the Making of an English Author* (Oxford and New York: Oxford University Press, 2013).

[24] See Gordon Sayre, '*Les Sauvages Americains*': *Representations of Native Americans in French and English Colonial Literature* (Durham: University of North Carolina Press, 1997) and *The Indian Chief as Tragic Hero: Native Resistance and the Literature of America, from Moctezuma to Tecumseh* (Durham: University of North Carolina Press, 2005).

to North America, published in English in London in 1703.[25] The playwright certainly read Lahontan's text which includes the *locus classicus* of noble savage discourse, the Dialogue with Adario: *Liberty Asserted* not only uses vocabulary from the *New Voyages'* glossary and incorporates customs reported there but also reproduces many of the political and religious views voiced by the brilliant Iroquois debater Kondiaronk.

Garcilaso de La Vega and Incan History

Murphy's *Alzuma* is thus by no means the first of such texts, being preceded by Aaron Hill's *Alzira* (based on Voltaire's *Alzire* [1736]) which appears some thirty years earlier in 1744. In all three plays, the Peruvians demonstrate great natural virtue and intelligence, certainly supportive of the plays' shared tolerationist argument but equally consonant with, and arguably derived from their New World sources, the chief of whom was Garcilaso de la Vega, known as 'El Inca' and the most authoritative source on Peruvian civilisation in the eighteenth century. With his work translated into several European languages from the original Spanish, Garcilaso became known to Anglophone readers through the translation of the *Royal Commentaries* published by Paul Rycaut in 1688.[26] Garcilaso was a *mestizo*, the child of a union between the daughter of the Inca princess (palla) Ocllo Chimpu and a Spanish conquistador, Sebastian Garcilaso de La Vega. Although he goes on to stress that his work is constituted by previous histories by Spanish writers, the author is emphatic that his indigenous perspective places him in an authoritative position, able to judge and correct the earlier colonial accounts. He explains that he was raised an Indian for twenty years and that he learned his nation's history from his family and as an eyewitness. Thus he asserts that 'those stories ... which in my youth I received from the relation of my mother and my uncles ... will certainly be more

[25] One index of Dennis's inclusion of First Nation discourse is his use of language derived from the brief glossary of Huron and Iroquois vocabulary provided by Lahontan at the end of his second volume. See Louis Armand de Lorn d'Acre, Baron de Lahontan, *New Voyages to North America: Containing an Account of the Several Nations of that Vast Continent; their Customs, Commerce and Ways of Navigation*, 2 vols. (London: Printed for H. Bonwicke, T. Goodwin, M. Wotton, B. Tooke and S. Manship, 1703): 2.

[26] Benjamin Bissell, *The American Indian in English Literature* (New Haven: Yale University Press, 1925). Bissell speculates that the eighteenth-century popularity of the *Royal Commentaries* stemmed from the ease with which El Inca could be construed as a deist recording the operations of natural law (18–33).

authentick and satisfactory than any account we can receive from other Authors.'[27]

Assertions of Incan civility, consonant with deist beliefs in a general human capacity for Enlightenment rendered the *Commentaries* attractive material to Temple, Voltaire, Algarotti and others.[28] What I want to underline here, however, is that the *Commentaries*' repeated invocation of female lament is reflected in the eighteenth-century plays set in Peru – *Alzire, Alzira* and Murphy's *Alzuma*. All these texts have plots structured by Garcilaso's account of the crucial role of exploitative sexual alliances in enabling the Spanish conquest, a topic scarcely mentioned by other sources such as Augustin de Zarate.[29] Enlightenment dramas about the conquest of Peru extrapolate the *Royal Commentaries*' record of elite female resistance to marriage with Spaniards and highlight protests made by Indian women as the Spaniards sought to eradicate all male descendants of the Incas – including their own *mestizo* sons – as they appropriated the bodies and properties of the female heirs to Andean lands. Commenting on the early years of the Conquest, Garcilaso remarks that initially, the families of women who bore children by Spaniards welcomed the affiliation but rapidly changed their attitude after they were massacred at the hands of the Spanish puppet Atahualpa (491). He further records that the most vociferous denunciation of the Spanish came from Incan women who objected to being forcibly married to Spaniards for their estates and who protested the imprisonment and murder of their *mestizo* sons (491, 865).

Garcilaso's text remains controversial, with commentators noting the difficulties generated by an attempt to combine a celebration of Incan history with the Spanish Conquest; some critics see the text as an apology for the Conquest, others as highly critical of the process.[30] Certainly *The Royal Commentaries* – particularly by contrast with Augustin de Zarate's *History of the Discovery and Conquest of the Province of Peru*, the other source used by dramatists – is notably Incacentric. He begins by

[27] Garcilaso de La Vega, *Royal Commentaries of Peru*, ed. Paul Rycaut (London: Jacob Tonson, 1688), 11. All other quotations will be from this edition and will be cited in the text by page number.

[28] Richard A. Brooks, 'Voltaire and Garcilaso de la Vega' in *Studies on Voltaire and the Eighteenth Century*, ed. Theodore Besterman, 30 (Geneva: Institut et Musée Voltaire, 1964): 189–204.

[29] Augustin de Zarate, *The Discovery and Conquest of Peru*, trans. and ed. J. M. Cohen (Harmondsworth: Penguin Books, 1968).

[30] See Margarita Zamora, *Language, Authority and Indigenous History in the Commentarios reales de los Incas* (Cambridge: Cambridge University Press, 1988); Barbara Fuchs, *Mimesis and Empire: The New World, Islam and English Identities* (Cambridge: Cambridge University Press, 2001), 72–85 and Aurora Fiengo-Varn, 'Reconciling the Divided Self: Inca Garcilaso de la Vega's *Royal Commentaries* and His Platonic View of the Conquest of Peru', *Revisita de Filología y Lingüística de Universidad de Costa Rica* 29.1 (2003): 119–27.

describing pre-contact Peru and ends his account of the Conquest not with the final establishment of royal authority, like Zarate, but with the death of the first Inca. His text is shaped to emphasise both the technological sophistication of Inca civilisation and the rationality of their religious beliefs. Published in Lisbon, *The Royal Commentaries* necessarily conformed to both ideological and rhetorical conventions of its scene of production. But rather than simply collaborating with the conquest, the *Commentaries* speak in the sometimes ironic, sometimes elegiac but always distinctive voice of an Incan elite who has had to come to terms with external power. In much of Garcilaso's text, and particularly in his reportage of female Indian protest, however, direct indictment of the Spaniards' strategic sexual predation, territorial appropriation and racially motivated filicide is voiced with startling directness.

Alzuma

Murphy's iteration of this narrative, his tragedy *Alzuma*, was written 'in the year 1762, [when] the British forces were then actually doing at the HAVANNAH, what ALZUMA prays for in the third act'. Towards the end of the Seven Years' War, which produced a high watermark of imperial hubris, hostilities were declared with Spain. The British rapidly achieved successes in the Caribbean and in the Pacific, taking Havana in August and Manila in October. It therefore seemed to Murphy an obvious time to dust down the black legend and recast 'the story of a people massacred because they abounded in gold-mines, and had not heard the important truths of the Christian religion, [which] seemed of all others the fittest for the English stage, as it tended in a strong degree to that pathetic distress, and that vigour of sentiment, which constitute the essential beauty of tragedy'.[31]

Like its predecessors, Dryden's *Indian Emperor* and Aaron Hill's *Alzira*, *Alzuma* was written at a time of New World military conflict with Spain, although it was not to be produced for another decade. Garrick was never enthusiastic about the play and with Murphy's contemporaneous notoriety over his work for Bute an added disincentive, *Alzuma* was set aside. Although Garrick paid £300 for the play, he remained unwilling to produce it, so Murphy bought back the rights and arranged for its performance at Covent Garden, where it appeared on 23 February 1773.[32]

---

[31] Arthur Murphy, *Alzuma, A Tragedy* (London: Printed for T. Lowndes, 1773). Advertisement, n. p. All quotations will be from this edition and will be cited in the text by act and page number.
[32] For details of the play's production history, see Emery, *Arthur Murphy*, 112–17.

The play is set in Cusco; at the opening, we learn that Alzuma, the son of the last Incan emperor, has been missing in Chile during the last decade of the Spanish invasion. His mother, zealous Christian convert Orazia, has married the Spanish Governor Pizarro who killed her husband, and Pizarro's son Don Carlos wants to marry Orazia's unconverted daughter Orellana. Orellana discovers that Alzuma is alive; as she tries to hold Carlos off, he becomes jealous of Alzuma, imagining him to be her lover. Eventually, after Alzuma is finally recognised by his mother, he falsely proclaims himself a convert and kills Pizarro – and by accident his mother – on the altar of the Christian church. The dying Orazia forgives her son, as does Don Carlos: won over by these examples of Christian virtue, Alzuma and Orellana suggest an openness to conversion.

Although Murphy stressed in his *Advertisement* that he did not follow Voltaire (the model for Hill), and the plot does diverge from *Alzire* and *Alzira,* this version of the end of Incan rule shares the focus they drew from Garcilaso de la Vega on the central role of Inca women in the Spanish conquest: intermarriage, concubinage and the eradication of Incan male nobles in securing Spanish land ownership and rule are the critical issues. *Alzuma* is even more feminocentric than *Alzira.* In Murphy's play, Orellana's father is dead and her mother has married his murderer, Pizarro. *Alzuma* is shaped to contrast Orazia's and Orellana's antithetical responses to the invaders: Orazia chooses conversion, cultural assimilation and marriage, while Orellana is a model of political, religious and sexual resistance. Although Alzuma is the eponymous hero, Orellana is the more compelling figure. Alzuma brings about the climax but for most of the play he is markedly impotent, helplessly imprisoned and saved from death only by the repeated interventions of his female relatives (an aspect of the plot drawn from De la Vega). In *Alzira,* Zamor represented a real challenge to the Spaniards, not just because he was a militarily threatening claimant to the throne but also because his alliance with Alzira would have guaranteed the sexual and political reproduction of the Inca regime. By making Alzuma the heroine's brother rather her lover, and eradicating her father from the text, Murphy's work radically reduces the agency of male indigenes. In *Alzira,* the friendship between Don Alvarez and Ezmont and their joint enthusiasm for their children's marriage created an impression of alliance and patriarchal mutuality: in *Alzuma,* indigenous patriarchy is already defeated and the chief Inca woman is already traduced.

The Prologue to *Alzuma* deftly charts the play's appeal to British sensibilities by condemning 'the bigot rage and avarice' of the

Conquistadors, appealing to the supposedly tolerant audience for a sympathetic hearing for the 'voice suppress'd' of 'the FEATHER'D CHIEFS'. While the latter may be 'in error blind', Bennett exhorted his audience 'Against the pow'r that would opinion bind,/Assert the freedom of the human mind', drawing a contrast with the 'fierce religious zeal' that produces 'dread calamities'. Throughout the Prologue, Murphy's own position oscillates; described at one point as an 'advent'er', implicitly comparing him to the Spanish, in the closing six lines he is aligned with the Indians, hoping the audience will demonstrate 'moderate principles' and 'toleration' as opposed to the 'persecuting spirit' of Rome.

The rhetorical fluidity of the authorial posture in the Prologue encapsulates Murphy's multiple allegiances; as an unenthusiastic convert from Catholicism, and an Irishman who sought professional success in the imperial capital, he had himself occupied the position both of supposed bigots and persecuted indigenes. While attempting to interpellate his audience as above all tolerant and merciful, *Alzuma*'s characteristic effect, noted by several critics, was that of horror: the nightmare of forced conversion, sexual predation and cultural genocide. In an early speech that encapsulates these horrors, Orellana describes a prophetic dream to her attendant Emira:

> Methought Pizarro
> With fury dragg'd me to the altar's foot;
> There urg'd imperious to renounce my gods,
> And wed Don Carlos; with apostate zeal
> My mother join'd her aid; – conspir'd against me;
> When, oh! Distracting sight! My brother, rushing
> To save a sister from the vile dishonor,
> Receiv'd Pizarro's dagger in his heart.
> The altar smoak'd with gore; – the cruel Spaniard
> Look'd a grim joy to see the only hope
> Of desolate Peru, – a Prince descended
> From a long race of Kings, ignobly fall
> And welter in his blood before him. (I.3)

But while Orellana does come under great pressure from her mother to marry 'the cruel Spaniard', the play actually concludes with the indigenous royalty alive, while viceroy Pizarro is dead and his fanatic son is dying. The play closes, however, with intimations that Carlos's last-minute renunciation of 'mistaken zeal' and consequent forgiveness of his father's death has finally convinced Orellana and Alzuma of the rectitude of

Christianity. Thus it is the erstwhile 'cruel Spaniard' who closes the play with a paean to toleration: 'Enlighten'd hence, ye rulers of each state/Learn to extinguish fierce religious hate' (V.70).

The contemporary response to *Alzuma* suggests that for portions of the audience at least, the anti-Spanish dimension of the text was itself a sign of prejudice: one reviewer inquired with obvious skepticism 'whether it be required in times of peace, that an odium should be cast on the Spanish for acts that have long been execrated among themselves'.[33] Dismissing the play with a familiar accusation of plagiarism, the *St. James's Chronicle* reworks the merchant-adventurer trope with venom:

> If Murphy steal his tasteless tragick Hash,
> Like Shakespeare's thief, he surely steals but Trash,
> Have we not late the Graecian seen him roam,
> Nor yet one grain of Attick salt bring home?
> And now the rich Peru the Bard will travel
> But what does he bring home? A load of gravel.[34]

Suggesting Murphy was persuasive in his overt aims, however, there was a good deal of agreement that the primary aim of the play was indeed the indictment of forced conversion: 'The question between the Spaniard and the American is, whether any man has a right to compel another to be of his opinions, or else to put him to the sword?'[35] There was also a degree of consensus on the elevated nature of Orellana's role in bearing this theme: 'The spirit of her character shows itself in a prayer to the Sun, which she concludes with a vow never to join the enemies of her country' (*Plan*, 27). Her mother is clearly seen as a negative contrast: 'Orazia, who was the wife of the last Peruvian emperor, and is now married to Pizarro, has embraced the Spaniard's religion and the cruelty of his principles' (*Plan*, 26). Another reviewer similarly stressed the contrast between Orellana and her mother: 'On the advance of Pizarro, Orazia, etc. candour and bigotry are strikingly contrasted, and the sentiments of Carlos, and the simplicity and firmness of Orellana, do honour to the Author.'[36]

Commendations of patriotic loyalty to inherited belief and religious toleration are familiar topoi in eighteenth-century discourse: what is

[33] *An Account of* Alzuma, *a new tragedy, now acting at Covent-Garden Theatre* in the *Universal Magazine of Knowledge and Pleasure* 52 (March 1773): 361.
[34] *St. James's Chronicle*, 6 March 1773.
[35] *Plan of the Tragedy of* Alzuma in the *Sentimental Magazine, or General Assemblage of Science, Taste and Entertainment* 5 (26–27 March 1775). Further references will be cited in the text by page number.
[36] 'Alzuma, A Tragedy *as performed at the Theatre Royal in Covent-Garden*' in the *Monthly Review* 48 (March 1773): 212–15.

striking here is their application to a play by an Irishman educated by the Jesuits. As is invariably the case, Murphy's decision to write a black legend play is caulked on the outbreak of hostilities with Spain in the New World. But just as *Alzuma*'s reiteration of De la Vega's anti-conquest discourse problematises a reading of the text in which 'noble savages' are simply mouthpieces for anti-Spanish propaganda, so too Murphy's own experience of the politics of conversion and the mid-century development of West British patriotism suggests the tragedy encodes a critique of 'bigotry' and colonialism that is more complex than first appears.

Murphy's shaping of *Alzuma* was surely informed by his own experience of the pressures to convert within a colonial society, but he was not alone in recognising the salience of the black legend in characterising the relationship between the English and the Irish. From the mid-century at least, comparisons between Ireland and Spain's New World colonies were being made in Irish patriot discourse. In *A Nineteenth Address to the Free-Citizens and Free-Holders of the City of Dublin* (1749), Charles Lucas, an enthusiastic country Whig thunders, 'I shew from the best authority that this nation has not been better treated by some of the ancient English governors than the Peruvians or Mexicans by the Spaniards.'[37] Lucas's application of the black legend to England's treatment of Ireland undoubtedly informed Henry Brooke's *Montezuma*, a revision of *The Indian Emperor* that presents the Conquest as an event in which indigenous agency – and competition and disarray – play a much more significant role than in Dryden's original text. In Brooke's version, the lust, avarice and cruelty of the Spaniards are less vividly depicted, while the internal conflict between Traxallans and Aztecs is highlighted. *Montezuma*'s alterations in plot and character provide a reading of the Conquest in which Spanish triumph seems much more contingent and much less certainly authorised by Providence, technology and civilisational superiority.

Brooke's play develops the Lucasian analogy between England and Spain in regard to Ireland by re-humanising the Mexicans, exorbitating their agency and complexity, arguing for patriotic unity in the face of oppression. Murphy's reworking of the trope also focuses on the colonised, those reckoning with invaders violently insistent on conversion. In a scenario which echoed his own personal history, *Alzuma* presents women as the bearers of traditional religion, sources of social as well as sexual reproduction. The affective and physical violence with which

---

[37] Charles Lucas, *A Nineteenth Address to the Free-Citizens and Free-Holders of the City of Dublin* (Dublin: James Esdall, 1749), 18.

conversion is associated through the figure of Don Carlos does relatively little to indict Catholicism specifically – as the reviewer points out, that was an ancient *canard*. But the tragedy does most severely condemn attempts to enforce religious uniformity in a subordinate territory, a policy still pursued to the detriment of Murphy's fellow compatriots and former co-religionists across the Irish Sea. The lesson would not have been lost on at least some of *Alzuma*'s spectators.

Murphy's reputation as a comic writer, less skilled than his brilliant compatriots Sheridan and Goldsmith but still highly successful, is secure. But his status as a tragic playwright who engaged with the central Enlightenment concerns of religious toleration and resistance to colonial oppression, requires recognition and further exploration. Lampooned as a Tory hack, Murphy was nonetheless the author of plays depicting struggles for religious and political liberty, of which *Alzuma* is only the most striking example. More than just superb vehicles for star actresses, Murphy's tragedies suggest that he deserves to be numbered among those who created Ireland's theatrical Enlightenment.

CHAPTER 9

The Provincial Commencement of James Field Stanfield

Declan McCormack

> A London engagement is generally considered by actors ... as the great prize in the lottery of their professional life. But this appears to us, who are not in the secret, to be rather the prose termination of their adventurous career: it is the provincial commencement that is the poetical and truly enviable part of it.[1]

Hazlitt wrote this romantic appraisal of a strolling player in 1817, the year after he published Thomas Holcroft's memoirs.[2] However, Holcroft did not write favourably about the years he had spent as a provincial actor, an experience that provided the material for his first novel *Alwyn: Or the Gentleman Comedian*.[3] The dismissal of provincial theatre as a second-rate place for vulgar amateurs is a recurrent trope in memoirs written by Georgian actors once they had acquired their 'London engagement'. Theatre historians have generally done little to dispel this notion. The bias towards London in eighteenth-century theatre historiography was highlighted by Jane Moody, who stressed the productive potential of paying greater attention to provincial theatre.[4] With the notable exceptions of Sybil Rosenfeld, Cecil Price and a handful of local historians writing the histories of specific town theatres or county circuits, the British provinces have been largely ignored and indeed continue to be so.[5] Frederick Burwick pointed out as recently as 2015 that 'No history of

---

[1] William Hazlitt, 'On Actors and Acting' in *Hazlitt on Theatre*, ed. Archer William and Robert Lowe (New York: Hill and Wang, 1957), 141–42.

[2] *Memoirs of the Late Thomas Holcroft*, ed. William Hazlitt, 3 vols. (London: Printed for Longman, Hurst, Rees, Orme and Brown, 1816).

[3] Thomas Holcroft, *Alwyn: Or the Gentleman Comedian*, 2 vols. (London: Printed for Fielding and Walker, 1780).

[4] Jane Moody, 'Dictating to the Empire' in *The Cambridge Companion to British Theatre 1730–1830*, ed. Jane Moody and Daniel O'Quinn (Cambridge: Cambridge University Press, 2007), 21.

[5] Sybil Rosenfeld, *The Georgian Theatre of Richmond, Yorkshire, and Its Circuit: Beverley, Harrogate, Kendal, Northallerton, Ulverston and Whitby* (London: Society for Theatre Research, 1984) and

the provincial companies of the 18th and 19th centuries has ever been written ... and of the minor circuits we know practically nothing at all.'[6]

There is also a gap in the historiography of the Irish diaspora to England in the eighteenth century.[7] However, new research on eighteenth-century London has highlighted the diversity of the diaspora experience. For example, Craig Bailey's *Irish London* used social network analysis and the linking of records belonging to approximately 1,000 law students, lawyers and merchants to build a prosopographic study of the London-Irish middle class.[8] As an obvious hub of sociability, the theatre is well suited to such research methods and promises rich pickings, especially when one considers the considerable presence of Irish thespians working in London during the period.[9] The Irish were also well represented in provincial theatre, and regional research has great potential to provide new insights, particularly when considered in the light of recent surveys of eighteenth-century Irish identity which attempt to place the nation and its people in an enlightened international context. The stated aim of Ian McBride's *Eighteenth-Century Ireland* is 'to write the history of Ireland from the outside in' and thereby position the country among its fellow European nations.[10] The subject of Enlightenment geographies is also central to Michael Brown's landmark *Irish Enlightenment,* which attempts to map Ireland's place in the Enlightenment by concentrating on the movement's public face.[11] Irish theatre studies have also been influenced by the spatial turn, leading to questions about the subaltern nature of Ireland and its diaspora. For example, Helen Burke specifically employed notions relating to periphery and centre in a study of Irish theatre which examined 'acts of colonial mimicry which subverted and estranged the dominant cultural script'.[12] Shifting from the general to the particular, Bridget Orr's

---

Cecil Price, *The English Theatre in Wales in the Eighteenth and Early Nineteenth Centuries* (Cardiff: University of Wales Press, 1948).

[6] Frederick Burwick, *British Drama of the Industrial Revolution* (Cambridge: Cambridge University Press, 2015), 1–2.

[7] See this volume's Introduction and David O'Shaughnessy, '"Tolerably Numerous": Recovering the London Irish of the Eighteenth Century', *Eighteenth-Century Life* 39.1 (2015): 1–13.

[8] Craig Bailey, *Irish London: Middle-Class Migration in the Global Eighteenth Century* (Liverpool: Liverpool University Press, 2013), 15.

[9] David O'Shaughnessy, '"Bit, by some mad whig": Charles Macklin and the Theater of Irish Enlightenment', *Huntington Library Quarterly* 80.4 (2017): 559–583.

[10] Ian McBride, *Eighteenth-Century Ireland: Isle of Slaves* (Dublin: Gill and Macmillan, 2009), 20.

[11] Michael Brown, *The Irish Enlightenment* (Boston, MA: Harvard University Press, 2016), 11.

[12] Helen Burke, 'Acting in the Periphery: The Irish Theatre' in *The Cambridge Companion to British Theatre,* ed. Moody and O'Quinn, 219.

examination of Richard Steele as an Anglo-Irish sentimental writer also explores a similar cluster of ideas related to colony, empire and identity.[13]

Most work on the Irish diaspora and the theatre in England has focused on London. Of course, the capital was an important centre of cultural production, but it was by no means the only one; by concentrating exclusively on the metropolis, one runs the risk of missing a whole range of contributors, networks of association and entire centres of production. To illustrate the potential of regional theatre research, this chapter presents an overview of James Field Stanfield, an Irish actor who spent his entire forty-year career performing in British provincial theatres. It is perhaps fitting that Stanfield should be a conduit into such relatively uncharted territory, because he was a pioneer who used his acting persona to bring his influence to bear on a number of key British institutions. He was the first common sailor to publish an account of the horrors of the Atlantic slave trade; about whom the maritime historian Marcus Rediker wrote: 'Few people in the eighteenth century were better equipped to capture the drama of the slave trade.'[14] His influence on abolition stems from a harrowing sea voyage in a slave ship across the Atlantic, which he later wrote about while employed as an actor performing in Yorkshire playhouses.[15] Stanfield said he knew the place where a man lost his moral compass and the exact location on the globe where that was to be found: 'Flogging did not commence with us till about the latitude 28. . . . It no sooner made its appearance, but it spread like a contagion.'[16] If, as Michael Brown suggests, 'the imperial aspect of the Irish Enlightenment might be better captured by seeing it as one venue in a broader Atlantic Enlightenment' then Stanfield's *Observations on a Guinea Voyage* might be understood to trace a critical path directly across that geographical imaginary.[17] More locally, Stanfield helped to establish the first subscription library in Sunderland, where he was 'a great man in freemasonry' according to his friend the Reverend James Tate.[18] Stanfield has also been recognised as the first person to write a full-length study of biography in

[13] Bridget Orr, 'Empire, Sentiment, and Theatre' in *The Oxford Handbook of the Georgian Theatre 1737–1832*, ed. Julia Swindells and David Francis Taylor (Oxford: Oxford University Press, 2014), 621–37.
[14] Marcus Rediker, *The Slave Ship: A Human History* (London: Penguin, 2007), 132.
[15] James Field Stanfield, *Observations on a Guinea Voyage, in a Series of Letters Addressed to the Rev. Thomas Clarkson* (London: Printed by James Phillips, 1788).
[16] Stanfield, *Observations*, 11.   [17] Brown, *Irish Enlightenment*, 5.
[18] Royal Museums Greenwich (RMG), STN COLLECTION: Uncatalogued, STN/6/3, Tate Letter to Clarkson (4 January 1832).

English.[19] Biography flourished in the eighteenth century and his call to
use it as a scientific tool to explore the self allies him with late Scottish
Enlightenment thinkers engaged in exploring the new science of the
mind.[20]

The acting profession made Stanfield highly itinerant, facilitating
a cosmopolitan ambition. He was in contact with a wide range of people
from different social orders, including Yorkshire reformers, Durham MPs,
and the Scottish Professoriat, with whom he associated while acting on
theatre circuits in the north. Where he did what he did is significant and
raises fundamental questions about where the periphery and centre were
actually located. 'Thinking geographically', says Charles Withers, 'illustrates that ideas do not "float free" but are "grounded" in particular sites
and social settings, the study of which can help explain the nature, mobility
and reach of the ideas themselves'.[21] This chapter falls into two parts.
A biography summarises Stanfield's known activities and identifies some
of his Irish acting associates and reform-minded friends. Then a second
section provides an overview of three areas of Enlightenment-forged
experience where he made significant contributions: freemasonry, abolition and the literature of improvement.

A Biographical Sketch

Stanfield was born in Dublin in 1749 to unknown parents.[22] In his youth,
he studied for the priesthood at one of the Catholic colleges in France, for
which no record has survived. This accounts for his command of Latin,
and it is where he developed a passion for the philosophy of Francis Bacon,
which was 'remarkable for its profoundness . . . and its zeal'.[23] He did not
baptise any of his ten children as Catholic, but he remained a religious man

[19] Felicity Nussbaum, 'Biography and Autobiography' in *The Cambridge History of Literary Criticism Vol. 4, The Eighteenth Century*, ed. H. B. Nisbet and Claude Rawson (Cambridge: Cambridge University Press, 1997), 303.
[20] James Field Stanfield, *An Essay on the Study and Composition of Biography* (Sunderland: Printed by George Garbutt, 1813).
[21] Charles W. J. Withers, 'Space, Geography and the Global French Enlightenment' in *The Cambridge Companion to the French Enlightenment*, ed. Daniel Brewer (Cambridge: Cambridge University Press, 2014), 215.
[22] The main source of biographical information about Stanfield comes from an incomplete manuscript written in the late nineteenth century by his grandson Field Stanfield. RMG, STN, Field Stanfield Memoir. Pieter van der Merwe drew from this and added further research for a PhD thesis which provides the most complete survey of Stanfield's life yet compiled, P. T. van der Merwe, 'The Life and Theatrical Career of Clarkson Stanfield 1793–1867', unpublished Ph.D thesis, University of Bristol (1979), 1–30.
[23] RMG, STN/6/4, Tate Letter to Clarkson (21 May 1832).

and encouraged piety in his children. In a letter to his son Clarkson, Stanfield advised him: 'Do not on any account neglect your duties to your God.'[24] After the seminary, Stanfield became a common mariner, travelling to many parts of Europe and North America before taking a final journey on a slave ship to the West Indies in 1776.[25] He then joined Joseph Younger's theatre company which was performing in Manchester. He started his acting career in good company as a playbill dated 19 March 1777 announced a joint benefit night for an unknown Sarah Siddons playing Hamlet alongside her twenty-year-old brother John Philip Kemble.[26] Also on stage with them were Elizabeth Inchbald and Elizabeth Farren. It was a unique provincial theatrical moment, as four of the biggest stars of late Georgian theatre performed together before any of them became famous. The Cork-born actress Elizabeth Farren, noted in a memoir that Stanfield had helped her financially at this difficult time, which she later repaid when 'the fortunes of the Farrens had attained to the ascending scale'.[27] This suggests that sharing the experience of being Irish in another country generated forms of mutual exchange, dependency and community, which could endure over long periods of time.

For the next ten years, Stanfield's activities are difficult to trace. There is no record of him performing in London, but he did spend time there in 1781 and was made a freemason in October at *Lodge Number 215*, which met at the One Bell Inn, Fleet Street.[28] At the end of that year, he performed at Lichfield with the Cheltenham Company of Comedians, managed by the Irish actor-manager James Boles Watson. Watson had taken over Roger Kemble's midlands company earlier in 1781.[29] Stanfield may have remained with this company for several years, as he was a witness to Watson's wedding in Cheltenham in October 1785.[30] The following week, Stanfield married the actress Mary Hoad in the town. He also claimed to have performed at the Bristol Theatre Royal.[31] Stanfield appeared at Bath during the 1782 to 1783 season for which playbills survive.[32]

[24] RMG, STN/2/5, James Field Stanfield letter to Clarkson (Sunderland, 15 June 1813). He named his son Clarkson after the abolitionist Reverend Thomas Clarkson.

[25] Stanfield, *Observations*, 21.   [26] W. J. Lawrence, *New York Dramatic Mirror* (8 July 1905), 3.

[27] *A Biographical Dictionary of Actors, Actresses, Musicians, Dancers, Managers & Other Stage Personnel in London, 1660–1800*, ed. Philip H. Highfill et al., 16 vols. (Carbondale: Southern Illinois University Press, 1993), 5: 161–62.

[28] Thomas Olman Todd, *The History of the Phoenix Lodge, No 94* (Sunderland: Printed by J. D. Todd, 1905), 67.

[29] Price, *English Theatre in Wales*, 76–81.   [30] Merwe, 'Clarkson Stanfield', 7.

[31] *Edinburgh Evening Courant*, 12 March 1814, Advert for composition and elocution class cited in Merwe, 'Clarkson Stanfield', 4 n5.

[32] Merwe, 'Clarkson Stanfield', 5.

In October 1786, he joined Tate Wilkinson's Yorkshire circuit and for the rest of his career performed only in the north, acting on circuits belonging to Joseph Austin and Charles Edward Whitlock, Stephen Kemble, Samuel Butler and James Cawdell.[33] There were several Irish actors in Wilkinson's company. Thomas William Betterton, the grandson of a Dublin sexton, had also arrived that season.[34] At Wilkinson's theatre at Hull, Eliza beth Farren performed the role of Patrick in John O'Keeffe's *The Poor Soldier* and another Irish actor, Fielding Wallis, appeared as Fitzroy.[35] Wallis was the son of the Protestant Rector of Boho and Templecare in County Fermanagh. He had abandoned his indenture to a Dublin bookseller and started his acting career at Ripon with Butler's company in 1773.[36]

Wallis and Stanfield were with Butler's company when he opened the new Richmond Theatre in September 1788, for which Stanfield provided the prologue.[37] James Tate wrote about meeting these two actors for the first time during this season: 'Mr Fielding Wallis and Mr. Stanfield had then been for many years acquainted and much attached to each other, both Irishmen, both brought up for different and higher pursuits, both on stage, and both Freemasons.'[38] Tate later became the headmaster of the Richmond School and married Wallis's actress daughter Margaret. He was a prolific letter writer and by marrying into an acting family, this correspondence provides a unique insight into provincial theatrical life in the period. Stanfield introduced Tate to George W. Meadley from Bishopwearmouth, a young man he had met after joining Cawdell's theatre company in 1789.[39] Stanfield, Tate and Meadley remained close friends; their letters reveal a mutual interest in reform and abolition, while also making Stanfield's movement and activities easier to trace.

In the 1790s, Stanfield held a 'principal situation' with Cawdell's company at the Scarborough theatre.[40] Playbills from other theatres also show that he was a versatile performer, playing secondary and principal roles in

[33] York Minster Library (YML), Playbills 1786–87. Hull, 31 October 1786.
[34] John C. Greene, *Theatre in Belfast 1736–1800* (Bethlehem: Lehigh University Press, 2000), 167–69.
[35] YML, Playbills 1786–87, Hull, 15 November 1786.   [36] Rosenfeld, *Richmond*, 3–5.
[37] L. P. Wenham, *James Tate* (Northallerton: North Yorkshire County Records Office, 1991), 26.
[38] RMG, STN/6/4, Tate Letter to Clarkson (21 May 1832).
[39] Although best known for writing the biography of William Paley who lived in Bishopwearmouth, Meadley also wrote a biography of Algernon Sidney, the Whig martyr. He also wrote a memoir of Ann Jebb, the wife of the radical reformer John Jebb, for the *Monthly Repository,* a British Unitarian periodical dedicated to rational dissent. He was working on a biography of Dissenter John Disney as well as John Hampton when he died at the age of 45.
[40] *Biographia Dramatica; or A Companion to the Playhouse*, ed. David Erskine Baker, Isaac Reed and Stephen Jones, 3 vols. (London: Printed for Longman et al., 1812), 1: 682.

tragedy and comedy. This is evident from a week in September 1801 when Stephen Kemble invited George Frederick Cooke to perform a different role every night at Newcastle's Theatre Royal.[41] Stanfield played significant secondary parts in thirteen pieces during this week. Of Stanfield's acting ability, Tate Wilkinson wrote that he 'was (and is) a performer of astonishing abilities as to quickness of study. Indeed I had instances, almost would be termed impossible, were they numerated. He ... has strong talents for poetry ... and that aided by marks of strong genius and good understanding'.[42] However, Wilkinson went on to mention a feature which probably had a negative impact on Stanfield's career: 'But nature has not been partial to him, for I think at a wager, even Tate Wilkinson (whom his friend Stephen Kemble has pronounced the ugliest man he ever saw) might, on ballot, stand a chance for an odd ball as being the handsomer of the two.'

Between 1798 and 1806, Stanfield ran his own company in partnership with the Scottish actor George Graham. Their company occasionally provided assistance to Stephen Kemble's circuit in the north-east and Borders areas. In 1781, Graham had moved with John Philip Kemble from Edinburgh to Dublin's Theatre Royal, where he had an affair with the actress Mary O'Keeffe (*née* Heaphy), prompting her husband, John O'Keeffe, to move to London where he found fame as a playwright.[43] Mrs O'Keeffe, along with two daughters fathered by Graham, Fanny and Charlotte, acted regularly with Stanfield and his children for more than twenty years. Stanfield's daughter Mary attended Mrs O'Keeffe's wake at Dalkeith in 1812 and described her death in a letter to her brother Clarkson, which provides a reminder of the conditions actors typically lived in during the period:

> My dear Brother she died without a groan they all slept together when they waked in the morning they found her dead by their side. O my dear Brother think what they suffer'd but she is now at rest. I must write to my father he will be very sorry at her death.[44]

Stanfield finished his career in Scotland and performed opposite John Philip Kemble in the actor's final visit to Glasgow in 1817. He passed his last days living near Clarkson in London's Lambeth, where he died in 1824.

---

[41] Newcastle Central Library, Theatre Royal Playbills, 1801.

[42] Tate Wilkinson, *The Wandering Patentee*, 4 vols. (York, 1795), 3: 22.

[43] *Theatre in Dublin, 1745–1820: A Calendar of Performances*, ed. John C. Greene, 6 vols. (Bethlehem: Lehigh University Press, 2011), 3: 1206.

[44] RMG, STN/2/3, Letter from Mary Stanfield to Clarkson, January 1813.

Almost fifty years later, a correspondent wrote to the *Manchester Times* that Stanfield's 'representation of Irish character and of such characters as Sir Peter Teazle, Jobson Fag, and many others, were considered very good and far above mediocrity, and his abilities for both writing and singing comic songs rendered him a useful performer'.[45] Contemporary local reviews are rare, but one from the *Kelso Mail* confirms this regarding an Irish character part: 'We must not, however, omit to mention our old acquaintance, Mr Stanfield, who performed the character of *Dennis Brulgruddery* [a character from George Colman's *John Bull* (1803)], a kind hearted, blundering Irishman, with considerable humour.'[46] Stanfield's Irish stage-persona appears to have been in the line of middle-class Irishmen. Two Irish songs written by him have survived, 'Poor Patrick O'Neal; or, the Irishman's Description of a Man of War' to the tune of 'Sheela-na guira' and 'The Wedding of Ballyporeen'.[47]

A Freemason on the Northern Stage

Recent research has explored the Irish dimension of London's eighteenth-century world of freemasonry.[48] Margaret C. Jacob has highlighted the provincial expansion away from the metropolis of late eighteenth-century freemasonry, stressing that 'modern civil society was invented during the Enlightenment in the new enclaves of sociability of which freemasonry was the most avowedly constitutional and aggressively civic.'[49] Theatre played an important part in this process and many actors were freemasons. Tate Wilkinson's 1787 season at Hull gives the first indication of the role played by Stanfield. The playbill for his first benefit with the company announced that 'at the desire of several of the brethren Brother Stanfield will give his masonic song'.[50] Freemasonry also featured two weeks later at a benefit for Mr and Mrs Mills when *The Man of the World* was performed 'by desire of the two ancient and honourable societies of free and accepted masons' after which Stanfield and four other male members of the cast sang *Hail Glorious*

---

[45] *Manchester Times*, 29 June 1867.
[46] Woodhorn Museum and Northumberland Archives, *Kelso Mail*, 3 February 1808.
[47] For 'Patrick O'Neal', see *Freemasons' Magazine: Or General and Complete Library*, 4 (London, 1795), 346–47 and for 'The Wedding of Ballyporeen', see Thomas Meadows, *Thespian Gleanings* (Ulverston: Printed by George Ashburner, 1805), 107–9.
[48] Ric Berman, 'The London Irish and the Antients Grand Lodge', *Eighteenth-Century Life* 39.1 (2015): 103–30.
[49] Margaret C. Jacob, *Living the Enlightenment: Freemasonry and Politics in Eighteenth-Century Europe* (New York: Oxford University Press, 1991), 15.
[50] YML, Playbills 1786–87, Hull, 10 January 1787.

Masonry.[51] Brother John Mills died shortly after and Stanfield wrote a fourteen-verse gothic elegy commemorating his fellow actor-mason, which was published in the *Freemasons' Magazine.*[52] Wilkinson mentioned the actor's death in his autobiography, although somewhat more pithily: 'Mills died of a decline and dropsy at Hull' and his wife not long afterwards married the actor John Fawcett.[53]

Stanfield wrote a number of songs celebrating the self-fashioning and improvement through excellence to which freemasonry aspired.[54] These were sung at lodge meetings between rituals and in theatres at masonic bespeaks, which were a regular feature of each theatrical season on all the circuits. Stanfield's benefits were often supported by the local lodge belonging to the town in which he was performing.[55] His poems and songs were published in the first English periodical dedicated to free-masonry, *The Freemasons' Magazine: Or General and Complete Library,* which ran from 1793 to 1798. At least fifteen examples from the magazine show how Stanfield used his theatrical identity to help publicly associate the values of freemasonry with the stage. In an early edition, the editor personally thanked him for contributing to its success, writing that Stanfield's 'exertions have raised the *Freemasons' Magazine* to a degree of credit with the Fraternity, that, at so early a period, was scarcely to have been hoped for'.[56] Stanfield also helped to associate British freemasonry with abolition. In April 1795, the editor published one of his anti-slavery poems 'Written on the Coast of Africa in the year 1776'.[57] He also announced that he would not publish poems in support of slavery.[58] The magazine had by this time won the official approval of the Grand Lodge, which suggests that despite freemasonry's stated apolitical status, the institution was expressing a public position regarding slavery via the publication.[59] Stanfield mentioned his masonic writing in a letter to Tate, while also revealing that his interest in print culture and political debate had manifested itself in the foundation of Sunderland's subscription library: 'My scribbling, for this last year, has been chiefly laid out in the

---

[51] YML, Playbills 1786–87, Hull, 24 January 1787.   [52] *Freemasons' Magazine,* 4: 274–75.
[53] Wilkinson, *Wandering Patentee,* 3: 53.
[54] See Andreas Önnerfors, '"Perfection by Progressive Excellence": An Initial Analysis of the Freemasons' Magazine 1793–1798' in *Researching British Freemasonry, 1717–2017,* ed. Andreas Önnerfors and Róbert Péter (Sheffield: University of Sheffield, 2010), 159–80.
[55] British Library, Play Books 270, 'For the Benefit of Mr and Mrs Stanfield By Desire of the Northumberland Lodge of Freemasons' (Alnwick, 20 Jan 1808) cited in Merwe, 'Clarkson Stanfield', 6 n1: The Sea Captains Lodge supported Stanfield's Benefit at which 'Secrets Worth Knowing' was performed at Sunderland in December 1811. Palatine Lodge No. 97 *Record Book,* 119.
[56] *Freemasons' Magazine,* 3: iii.   [57] Ibid., 4: 273–74.   [58] Ibid., 3: ii.   [59] Ibid., 2: 245.

Freemasons' Magazine to which I have been a constant contributor. . . .
I have been the means of establishing a Library in this place which promises
fair. We have also a debate once a month tolerably attended and carried on,
at least by some, above mediocrity.'[60] The initial meeting for the library
was held in Stanfield's house and he was the secretary for the first year. This
institution would later become Sunderland's Literary and Philosophical
Society.

Another public way that Stanfield used his actor's persona to promote
freemasonry was through masonic spectacle. Highly theatrical events
combining procession, costume, ceremony and ritual were designed to
extend freemasonry's status as an institution and attract the public to the
craft. Stanfield choreographed what was probably the largest example of
this in the north in the eighteenth century, when he acted as Marshal of
Ceremonies for the opening of the Wearmouth Bridge on 9 August 1796
and 'upwards of 50,000 persons' gathered on the banks of the River Wear
to witness the event.[61] The bridge was a local masonic initiative, largely
funded by MP for Durham Rowland Burdon, who was Grand Master of
the *Sea Captains Lodge* where Stanfield acted as secretary.[62] Burdon shared
copyright of the bridge with two Sunderland freemasons, the financial
controller, Michael Scarth, and the engineer, George Wilson. Stanfield
later appeared in theatres celebrating the bridge with elaborate scenogra-
phy that showed '*Ships* in full sail, *Boats* and *Keels* in natural motion on the
River Wear, and passing under the *Arch* of that *Stupendous Fabric*'.[63] This
civic improvement, then the largest single-span iron bridge in the world,
helped transform Sunderland into a major industrial centre.

A Forgotten Hero of the Abolition Movement

If Enlightenment is understood to be a shift of focus from the divine to the
human, then the struggle for the recognition of human rights must be
considered one of its key dramas. Adam Hochschild argues that the Society
for the Abolition of the Slave Trade carried out the first modern human
rights campaign by drawing attention to the society's innovative use of the
press release, the campaign badge and its attempt to by-pass Parliament

[60] Wenham, *James Tate*, 66–67.
[61] William Nesfield, *An Oration, Delivered at the Opening of the Iron Bridge at Wearmouth* (Stockton: Printed for Christopher and Jennett, 1796), 42.
[62] Palatine Lodge, *Palatine Lodge Minute Book, 1794–1795. Sea Captains Lodge* was later renamed *Palatine Lodge*.
[63] Durham University Special Collections (DUSC), C18/20 ACF 286, Durham Theatre Advert.

through mass boycott.[64] Stanfield's role in this activity is confirmed by an undated broadsheet entitled *Slave Trade* which he wrote calling for the boycott of slave-produced sugar.[65] His activism evidently made a powerful impression on the youthful James Tate who described their first encounter in 1788 in a letter to Meadley:

> In a happy hour was I admitted to the acquaintance of my much beloved and ever honoured friend Mr. Stanfield, and the high esteem with which I regard him as a genuine philosopher, a noble spirited man and an actively benevolent Citizen of the World, afforded me sufficient inducement to wish for something more than a nominal acquaintance with one who ranks amongst his friends and of consequence amongst the friends of mankind.[66]

Tate's reference to Stanfield as a 'Citizen of the World' relates to a series of letters that Stanfield had published in 1788 and for which, more recently, he has been described as an unsung hero of the abolition movement.[67] When the Reverend Thomas Clarkson famously went to Bristol and Liverpool in 1787 to seek out first-hand evidence from sailors about the slave trade, it was Stanfield's testimony that the newly formed society chose to print. Three thousand copies of Stanfield's *Observations on a Guinea Voyage, in a Series of Letters Addressed to the Rev. Thomas Clarkson* appeared in their first printed collection the following year. This was a graphic record of Stanfield's experiences in the slave trade, which included his recruitment in Liverpool, his voyage to West Africa, his work inland at a slaving factory and his voyage on a slave ship from modern-day Benin to the West Indies. Acknowledging that Stanfield was the first common sailor to write about the horrors of slavery, Rediker dedicated a chapter of his book *The Slave Ship* to this account which 'was in many ways more detailed, more gruesome, and, in a word, more dramatic, than anything that had yet appeared in print by May 1788'.[68] Stanfield's outspokenness was courageous. According to Emma Christopher, an estimated 300,000 to 350,000 common sailors were engaged in the slave trade between 1750 and 1807, but accounts of their experiences are extremely rare.[69] Tate Wilkinson may have been alluding to this when describing Stanfield as 'bred a sailor … and is

---

[64] Adam Hochschild, *Bury the Chains* (London: Macmillan, 2005), 1–8.
[65] The printed broadsheet held at DUSC was tentatively identified by Rediker as authored by Stanfield on the basis of initials: *Slave Ship,* 134 n10. This can now be confirmed as the original manuscript in Stanfield's hand is in the Lancaster Maritime Museum, LANLM.1986.171.
[66] Wenham, *James Tate,* 191–92.   [67] Rediker, *Slave Ship,* 132.   [68] Ibid., 154.
[69] Emma Christopher, *Slave Ship Sailors and their Captive Cargoes, 1730–1807* (Cambridge: Cambridge University Press, 2010), 9.

what a good English tar should be, a man of bravery'.[70] He clearly
intended his published account to be a form of legal testimony as he
swore an affidavit to its veracity. Shortly after its publication, the leading
abolitionist Reverend James Ramsay referred to it in support of his own
arguments to counter the pro-slavery lobby, specifically when stressing
the need to reduce the numbers of slaves shipped per voyage.[71]

Stanfield identified himself on the *Observations* title page as 'a mariner
in the African Slave Trade', and he stressed this subaltern status as
a common sailor throughout the series of letters. His account emphasised the hardships experienced by sailors working in the slave trade; in
the sixth letter, he stated that the suffering of his fellow mariners was an
important motivating factor for his writing: 'The unabating cruelty,
exercised upon seamen in the Slave Trade, first prompted me to give
in my mite of information to the cause.'[72] Rediker has described the
ship as 'an early precursor of the factory' in which sailors were assembled
and enclosed as wage labourers, thereby initiating 'a process by which
labour was carefully coordinated and synchronized'.[73] As well as bringing the dreadful experience of the slaves to public attention, through his
concentration on mariners' work, harsh punishments and high death
rates, Stanfield's record has been recognised by maritime scholars as also
acting as a critique of labour conditions. Stephen D. Behrendt considers
Stanfield to be an early agitator for workers' rights who may have
influenced MPs to amend the Dolben Act of 1788, which set limits on
the number of slaves that British vessels could carry.[74] Stanfield
described the deleterious effect of poor sleeping conditions on the
crew in some detail and the 1789 amendment to the Dolben Act defined
contractual terms between captain and crew stipulating that sailors
receive regular daily provisions and that at least half the crew be
provided sleeping accommodation below deck.

In offering the British a constructive critique of their imperial ambitions, Stanfield could be read as belonging to a tradition of other Irish
writers and early abolitionists, including Oliver Goldsmith and Edmund

[70] Wilkinson, *Wandering Patentee*, 3: 22.
[71] James Ramsay, *Objections to the Abolition of the Slave Trade with Answers* (London: James Phillips, 1788), 71.
[72] Stanfield, *Observations,* 30.
[73] Marcus Rediker, *Between the Devil and the Deep Blue Sea* (Cambridge and New York: Cambridge University Press, 1989), 290, cited in Christopher, *Captive Cargoes,* 9.
[74] Stephen D. Behrendt, 'Crew Mortality in the Atlantic Slave Trade' in *Routes to Slavery: Direction, Ethnicity and Mortality in the Atlantic Slave Trade,* ed. David Eltis and David Richardson (London: Routledge, 2006), 63.

Burke.[75] Tate's description of Stanfield evokes Goldsmith's *The Citizen of the World*, a series of epistolary observations by an imagined Chinese visitor which offered a moral critique of English manners and life.[76] However, apart from the severity of the subject matter and lack of satire, Stanfield differs from Goldsmith because his description is not presented in a distanced, fictionalised form. Rather, he experienced the nation's darkest secrets first-hand as a subaltern and then described them in gruesome detail to his superiors. With regard to such imperial critique, Sean Moore has highlighted the liminal status of the Irish, arguing that they were both agent and object, the 'colonized, dialectical "Others" helping to define the enlightenened subject'.[77] In this context, Stanfield's autobiographical description of his experience on board a slave ship could be considered a precise embodiment of Moore's notion of agent and object. Stanfield himself is the subject of his own critique; as he reveals, he and his fellow common mariners are not simply the oppressors of the slaves but also victims of the trade.

A year after *Observations*, Stanfield published *The Guinea Voyage*, a verse-form version of his experience.[78] This was described in the *Gentleman's Magazine*, with a nod to his profession, as an 'addition to the stage machinery of the abolition of the slave trade'.[79] Stanfield's local celebrity as an actor allowed him to gain entrance to gentry houses where he promoted this work. This is apparent from a surviving letter to Sir Charles Hotham, a member of the East Yorkshire gentry, who Stanfield reminds: 'You honoured me at S. Dalton, with reading a little work of mine on the Slave Trade.' While seeking his patronage, Stanfield informs Hotham of the purchasers of his new book: 'The Gentlemen of the Committee for the Abolition take 200. Friends at Bath and Cheltenham about 100 and about 100 more are named among connections here.'[80] This shows that Stanfield's experience as an itinerant actor had helped him to extend his influence to different areas of the nation. At the moment of

[75] See Michael Griffin, *Enlightenment in Ruins: The Geographies of Oliver Goldsmith* (Lewisburg: Bucknell University Press, 2013), 4–10 and Luke Gibbons, *Edmund Burke and Ireland: Aesthetics, Politics, and the Colonial Sublime* (Cambridge: Cambridge University Press, 2003), 147–80.
[76] Oliver Goldsmith, *The Citizen of the World* in *The Collected Works of Oliver Goldsmith*, ed. Arthur Friedman, 5 vols. (Oxford: Clarendon Press, 1966), 2.
[77] Sean D. Moore, 'Introduction: Ireland and Enlightenment', *Eighteenth-Century Studies*, 45 (2012): 345–54; 347, cited in Brown, *Irish Enlightenment*, 5 n28.
[78] James Field Stanfield, *The Guinea Voyage, A Poem in Three Books* (London: James Phillips, 1789).
[79] *Gentleman's Magazine*, 59 (1789), 933.
[80] Hull History Centre, UDDHO/4/23/54 Letter from Stanfield to Sir Charles Hotham, Darlington, 20 June 1789.

writing, he was with Cawdell's company performing at Darlington. The 'connections here' presumably refers to people he had met while working with Wilkinson, Butler and Cawdell, the managers whose circuits covered a substantial area of north-east England. Evidently, his acting experience earlier in the decade in Cheltenham and Bath had also led to a substantial number of potential readers. It is unclear whether by 'friends' Stanfield literally means Quaker contacts. It is possible that his relationship with John Boles Watson in Cheltenham brought him into contact with Quakers, as Watson had been born to Quaker parents at Cashel in County Tipperary. Despite the fact that he was an actor, Stanfield certainly enjoyed good standing with the Quakers. Evidence of this appears in a letter written seventeen years later when Meadley had suggested publishing a second edition of the *Guinea Voyage*; Stanfield, who was then in Edinburgh, 'consulted several, and especially among the benevolently – persevering society of Quakers in this part of the country, who all seem to concur in the friendly opinion of Mr. Meadley'.[81]

Of the many poets who wrote about the slave trade, 'only Stanfield, Thomas Boulton, Thomas Branagan, and Captain John Marjoribanks had actually made a slaving voyage.'[82] The *Guinea Voyage* deserves to be better known, not least as the poem allowed his abolitionist passion full vent. In the *Observations*, Stanfield wrote that on the subject of the treatment of slaves, 'no pen, no abilities, can give more than a very faint resemblance of the horrid situation.'[83] However, in poetic form, he made a more explicit attempt to convey the horrors experienced by slaves, warning readers from the outset that he intended to blast like a 'black *Tornado*' through their minds. For this task, he considered genteel sensibility to be utterly inadequate, noting that 'No spicy zephyrs borne on wings of love,/No gentle pinions, fanning spring-tide air,/ Should give one image, or be mentioned here.'[84] A contemporary critic for the *Monthly Review* remarked that Stanfield 'dwells on every minute circumstance in this tale of cruelty, and obliges us to witness every pang of complicated misery'.[85] It was precisely this immediacy that Stanfield sought to convey and which he believed would bring about a necessary change. As he wrote in his *Observations*: 'One *real* view – one MINUTE absolutely spent in the slave rooms on the middle passage, would do

---

[81] Wenham, *James Tate*, 254. Stanfield letter to James Tate, Musselburgh, East Lothian, Scotland, 16 November 1806.
[82] Rediker, *Slave Ship*, 134 n8.   [83] Stanfield, *Observations*, 30.   [84] Stanfield, *Guinea Voyage*, 2.
[85] As cited in Rediker's *Slave Ship*, 154.

more for the cause of humanity, than the pen of a *Robertson*, or the whole collective eloquence of the British senate.'[86]

However, Stanfield did also manage to bring this immediacy directly to members of the British senate. Through the theatre and his activities within freemasonry, he had come to know several members of Parliament. In 1790, he was Junior Warden at the masonic initiation ceremony for Roland Burdon at Sunderland's *Phoenix Lodge*.[87] Two years later, Burdon delivered a petition against the slave trade to Parliament, signed by 181 of the 'principal inhabitants' of Stockton-upon-Tees.[88] Stanfield's personal intimacy with another Durham MP, William Henry Lambton, led him to write a biographical piece for the *Freemasons' Magazine* for which he sought Meadley's advice.[89] Perhaps most notably, Stanfield dedicated his 1807 republication of *The Guinea Voyage* and *Observations* to Sir Ralph Milbanke, Durham Provincial Grand Master and also MP for Durham, who, as Stanfield points out, seconded the successful Abolition of the Slave Trade Act.[90] Both the *Sea Captains* and the *Phoenix Lodge* minute books contain records of their joint attendance at lodge meetings and masonic theatre bespeaks. The first record dates from 1791, shortly before Milbanke supported Wilberforce's unsuccessful 1792 bill. The next year, twenty members of the *Sea Captains Lodge* gathered with twelve visitors including Milbanke and the actors Stanfield, Graham and Cawdell, who then proceeded to the theatre for the performance of Francis Gentleman's *The Modish Wife; or, The True Born Tar* (1774) and Elizabeth Inchbald's *Appearance is Against Them* (1785).[91] Milbanke also became president of the Sunderland Subscription Library where Stanfield was a lifelong honorary member. Their close friendship is evident in an 1809 letter from Meadley to Stanfield: 'Sir Ralph Milbanke had been enquiring your address a few days before I received your favour ... desiring me to say that he will write you in a few days, and therefore begs that if you leave Portobello, you will leave directions to have his letter forwarded to you elsewhere.' That year, at the

---

[86] Stanfield, *Observations*, 30. The Scottish Presbyterian Reverend William Robertson was an abolitionist.

[87] Tyne and Wear Archive, Sunderland *Phoenix Lodge* Minute Book, S.MAS 9/1/1, 169 (11 March 1790).

[88] John Brewster, *The Parochial History and Antiquities of Stockton-upon-Tees* (Stockton, 1796), 158.

[89] DUSC, AD MS 1028, Letter from Meadley to Stanfield.

[90] James Field Stanfield, *The Guinea Voyage, A Poem in Three Books to which are added Observations on a Voyage to the Coast of Africa in a series of letters to Thomas Clarkson*, 2nd edition (Edinburgh, 1807). Dedication.

[91] Palatine Lodge, *Minute Book*, 29–30.

age of sixty, Stanfield had just found a new 'situation' in Scotland while Meadley was in Sunderland helping him sell the second edition of *The Guinea Voyage*. Meadley told him that 'Thomas Clarkson was here lately, though the "Friends" kept him all to themselves. I understand however that he promised to exert himself to forward the sale of your book.' Meadley revealed that Stanfield also used the theatre for this activism: 'I hope … your new engagement will help the sale of your poem – and the poem contributes to fill the Houses at your Benefits at Glasgow and Aberdeen.' As he was then acting in Scotland, Meadley also suggested that Stanfield's friend Professor Dugald Stewart would be able to assist: 'Mr Stewart's interest would be highly useful to you, with the Professors at both places, which I hope you will not fail to procure.'[92] This suggestion was to prove rather fruitful.

An Improving Character

Stanfield's relationship with the Scottish Professoriat relates to a third aspect of his theatrical persona which has a bearing on the mapping of the theatrical strand of the Irish Enlightenment. Stanfield started work on *An Essay on the Study and Composition of Biography* in 1795 and eventually published it in Sunderland in 1813, after attending Dr Playfair's lectures on the philosopher Francis Bacon's *Organum Novum* in Glasgow and befriending Professor Dugald Stewart in Edinburgh, with whom he had sought an introduction from his friend James Tate. Tate was a leading classicist who collaborated on publications with Edinburgh University's professor of Greek, Andrew Dalzell.[93] A letter from Tate to Stewart written in 1807 asked him to consider a new translation of Bacon's *Organum Novum* 'to suit the present exigencies of science'. Tate informs Stewart that his interest in Bacon derived from their 'common friend … Mr Stanfield; who early in life impregnated my mind with an almost romantic attachment to the *Organum Novum* and the *Instauratio Magna*'.[94] A surviving letter from 1795 records Stanfield asking Tate, 'Have you ever thought more of the translation of the *Novum Organum*? I wish I had weight enough to urge you to what would be a benefaction to mankind.'[95] Playfair appears on Stanfield's list of subscribers for his *Essay* and Stewart took two copies.

---

[92] RMG, STN /101/7, Meadley letter to Stanfield (Portobello, 8 October 1809).
[93] Wenham, *James Tate*, 177.   [94] Ibid., 255.   [95] Ibid., 67.

As Stanfield's *Essay* is the first full-length study of biography in English, the work has attracted some academic interest. It was brought to critical attention by both Richard Altnick and Joseph Reed in 1966.[96] Reed's pioneering *English Biography in the Early Nineteenth Century* included a chapter 'Higher Criticism: Stanfield and Carlyle' in which he noted that Stanfield 'consistently introduces vital questions of biographical art'.[97] More recently, in the context of Scottish Enlightenment, Elizabeth Manning has drawn attention to Stanfield's efforts to encourage a systematic philosophical approach to the analysis of character.[98] The *Essay on Biography* has also come to the attention of life-writing scholars such as Jane Darcy, who noted that the book 'is evidence of an ongoing discourse about biography's potential to explore the science of mind'.[99] Darcy doubts the work's influence, commenting that 'despite Stanfield's Edinburgh connections ... the only lengthy treatment it received was in the evangelical *Eclectic Review*.'[100] This fourteen-page review was not positive and described the composition as 'ineffective, in a very strange degree'.[101] However, lengthy reviews did appear in at least two other major publications, the *Critical Review* and the *Monthly Review*.[102] Where the *Eclectic Review* failed to follow Stanfield's logic, the *Monthly Review* was generally favourable, stating that the work 'abounds with delicate and original observations on the use which may be made of the documents of biography'.[103] Stanfield's obituarists and others generally agreed that it was for his *Essay on Biography* that he would be remembered.[104] Darcy has called for attempts to 'trace the influence of the Scottish Enlightenment notions of "philosophical biography" written on inductive principles'.[105] Whether or not Stanfield's work ultimately

---

[96] Richard D. Altick, *Lives and Letters: A History of Literary Biography in England and America* (London: Alfred A. Knopf, 1966), 184–85; Joseph W. Reed, *English Biography in the Early Nineteenth Century, 1801–1838* (New Haven: Yale University, 1966), 66–82.

[97] Reed, *Biography*, 68.

[98] Susan Manning, 'Historical Characters: Biography, the Science of Man, and Romantic Fiction' in *Character, Self, and Sociability in the Scottish Enlightenment*, ed. Thomas Ahnert and Susan Manning (Basingstoke: Palgrave Macmillan, 2011), 233.

[99] Jane Darcy, *Melancholy and Literary Biography, 1640–1816* (Basingstoke: Palgrave, 2013), 209.

[100] Darcy, *Literary Biography*, 209.

[101] *Critical Essays Contributed to The Eclectic Review by John Foster*, ed. J. E. Ryland, 5 vols. (London, 1856), 2: 193–205, 202.

[102] *Critical Review* 4.6 (December 1813), 592–98; *Monthly Review* 74 (May–August 1814), 356–66.

[103] *Monthly Review* (May–August 1814), 363.

[104] Eneas Mackenzie and Marvin Ross, *An Historical, Topographical, and Descriptive View of the County Palatine of Durham*, 2 vols (Newcastle, 1834), 1: 305n1.

[105] Jane Darcy, 'Contesting Literary Biography in the Romantic Period: The Foreshadowing of Psychological Biography', *Literature Compass*, 5.2 (2008): 292–309; 294.

influenced his contemporaries, it is significant that he was the first person who explicitly attempted to apply inductive reasoning in questions of philosophical biography, and research into the circumstances of this attempt has potential to provide new insight.

Stanfield argued that biography had two purposes. Firstly, he stated it must 'offer examples to practical observation and improvement' for which 'moral illustration' was required.[106] Classical sources litter the text, and his identity as an actor steeped in the art of rhetoric is frequently recognisable. An example of this can be found in his description of Plutarch's writing:

> That *calling to*, (as the painters term it) of his animated pictures, which not only places before our eyes the very transaction in all its interest and bearings, but, absolutely, by a sensitive kind of violence, compels us into the actual situation of the scene, and fills us with every sentiment, purpose, and passion, which impel and agitate the bosom of the actor.[107]

This is highly reminiscent of Quintilianus' lessons in oratory 'whereby things absent are presented to our imagination with such extreme vividness that they seem actually to be before our very eyes'.[108] Stanfield also makes repeated references to Cicero's *On Oratory*. This recognition of the value of rhetoric associates Stanfield with the Irish actor and writer Thomas Sheridan. Sheridan's elocutionary movement specifically sought to combine rhetoric, acting, civic action and moral development for the improvement of character.[109] According to Michael Brown, such a positive attitude towards rhetoric was a distinctly Irish characteristic. He notes that this 'Irish school of oratory' was developed in opposition to an English discourse which 'rejected the value of rhetoric' considering it 'a system of deceit and pretence' and that this sceptical approach dated back 'at least as far as the works of Thomas Hobbes, with his concern for plain style and clear speaking'.[110] In making such material his point of reference, Stanfield was also in the company of far more famous contemporaries who had produced fictional work that explored related ideas in early examples of *bildungsroman*. Thomas Holcroft's *Alwyn: Or the Gentleman Comedian* and Goethe's *Wilhelm Meister's Apprenticeship* are stories of moral improvement featuring protagonists who are travelling players in the provinces. These actor-characters undergo personal development as their authors

---

[106] Stanfield, *Essay*, 145.   [107] Ibid., 127.
[108] Quintilianus, *Institutio Oratoria*, 6.2.29–30 cited in Joseph Roach, *The Player's Passion, Studies in the Science of Acting* (Newark: University of Delaware Press, 1985), 24.
[109] Paul Goring, *The Rhetoric of Sensibility in Eighteenth-Century Culture* (Cambridge: Cambridge University Press, 2005), 91–141.
[110] Brown, *Irish Enlightenment*, 172.

intentionally link theatrical experience with character formation.[111] As a thespian, Stanfield appears to have been similarly drawn to ideas related to character formation, but he approached the subject of self in an entirely different manner.

Stanfield's stated second purpose of biography gives us a sense of his innovation. 'Biography' he argued, served 'to obtain a deeper insight into the principles of the human mind'.[112] To pursue this, he drew from Francis Bacon, 'the great master, by whose institutes this treatise has attempted to apply the science of induction to moral and intellectual operations'.[113] As a methodology in imitation of Bacon, Stanfield drew up synoptical tables which contained examples of character observation.[114] He recommended that the subject to be studied for biography should be compared to similar tables previously drawn up by the 'biologist'.[115] The *Critical Review* found this notion too difficult to accept, stating that 'our worthy author talks as if it were about as easy to resolve that curious compound, "the whole character" into its elementary ingredients, and then to shake them together again, as if it is to decompose any chemical substance, and afterwards restore it to its pristine form, by a synthetic operation.'[116] This criticism summarises the challenge that Stanfield faced when attempting to apply the scientific method to questions of self at this moment in time. Darcy has noted 'the struggle, in this pre-Freudian period, to articulate the need for psychological insight'.[117] This struggle was also apparent in the *Eclectic Review*, when the reviewer described Stanfield's 'ludicrous' suggestion that the biographer 'go back to the very birth of his hero, and to any recorded or reported circumstances which, even before that event, might have made impressions on his incipient existence tending to determine his future character'.[118]

To some post-Freudian minds, this may not seem ludicrous at all. Similarly, the *Monthly Review* questioned the relevance of Stanfield's advice to observe a subject's childhood closely but acknowledged that 'perhaps men are too inattentive to the early indications and permanent

---

[111] For a study of Holcroft's *Manthorn the Enthusiast* (1779) and *Alwyn: Or the Gentleman Comedian* (1780), see Rick Incorvati, 'Developmental Stages: Thomas Holcroft's Early Fiction, Elocutionary Rhetoric, and the Function of the Theater in the Progress of Character' in *Re-Viewing Thomas Holcroft, 1745–1809: Essays on His Works and Life*, ed. A. A. Markley and Miriam L. Wallace (Farnham: Ashgate, 2012), 17–30.
[112] Stanfield, *Essay*, 145.   [113] Ibid., xv.   [114] Ibid., 89.
[115] Stanfield was possibly the first writer to use the word 'biology' and 'biologist' in English, but in the sense of one who writes biography scientifically. See ibid., 88.
[116] *Critical Review*, 598.   [117] Darcy, 'Contesting Literary Biography', 293.
[118] *Eclectic Review*, ed. Ryland, 200.

impressions of bent to which this age is liable'.[119] In its summary, the
Critical Review concluded that 'there are many good remarks in this essay;
but as a whole, it is prolix and tedious. In this respect it bears a close
resemblance to some of the productions of the German literati.'[120] Again,
with hindsight, it is perhaps a resemblance to the German literati that
might warrant further consideration.

In his essay *On Actors and Acting*, Hazlitt suggested that when on stage in
performance, actors show how human beings are shaped by circumstance
and we, the audience, 'see ourselves at second hand'.[121] He was also
acknowledging that, to some degree, we are all actors shaped by the
circumstances of our lives. Stanfield was evidently interested in this idea
and lived up to it as an ideal in his own life. Hazlitt also suggested that
outside of the playhouse, an actor was something of a changeling, an empty
vessel waiting to be filled up by character when performing on stage.
However, the example of Stanfield shows that provincial actors could be
far more than mere puppets that became animated in the playhouse when
propelled by the latest offering from the London intelligentsia. Some were
active agents in the wider community, bringing their actor personas to bear
on subjects important to their public and themselves.

Stanfield may have been a relatively poor, Irish travelling player, scraping a living in the north of England, but that did not make him a marginal
figure. Rather, he was a well-educated, middling-sort Irishman, striving to
influence his community and bring about improvement in his public. His
network of associates shows that he engaged with influential and powerful
individuals at the forefront of local and national socio-political development and that he played an important role in several of the most important
contemporary civic expressions of Enlightenment culture. As a Catholic,
although probably lapsed, he is a rather rare figure with regard to Irish
Enlightenment, and there is a mercurial element to his identity. He was
associated with the Scottish Enlightenment but was not a convert to the
moderate Presbyterianism by which it is frequently identified. He may
have been attracted to the rigour of Francis Bacon's philosophy, but his
masonic hymns to reason and science are highly gothic in style and his
comic songs are filled with Gaelic improbability and exaggeration. What
may appear to be contradictory characteristics could be understood as
features of contending currents of thought then vying for consensus.
Stanfield was living in the age of Enlightenment and was a product of his
time. Furthermore, he is just one Irish actor who worked in the provinces

---

[119] *Monthly Review,* 364.   [120] *Critical Review,* 598.   [121] Hazlitt, 'On Actors', 133.

in the eighteenth century. Who knows how many more Irish actors were similarly immersed in their locales, helping to shape local and even global mentalities? Certainly, in the case of James Field Stanfield, rather than performing as an obscure extra on the national stage, it transpires that this forgotten Irish provincial actor may have actually played a rather significant supporting role.

CHAPTER 10

Worlding the Village: John O'Keeffe's 'Excentric' Pastorals

Helen Burke

When the five-act pastoral comedy *Wild Oats: Or the Strolling Gentlemen* opened at Covent Garden Theatre in April 1791, its author was not identified, but reviewers for the London press confidently attributed the play to the Dublin-born playwright John O'Keeffe, on the basis of what they termed its 'eccentricity': 'The characteristic of this play is eccentricity, and the author, after the manner of the O'Keeffean School has, without scruple, made free with probability', *The Diary; or, Woodfall's Register* wrote.[1] The reviewer for the *Evening Mail* reached a similar conclusion. This 'excentric piece' has all the 'Tricks' of O'Keeffe, 'its reputed father', this critic wrote, adding that if he was laying this 'bantling' (or foundling) at this playwright's doorstep it was because he has 'sown more dramatic WILD OATS than any of his contemporaries'.[2] O'Keeffe's dramatic deviancy in this instance is treated with a patronising tolerance but, on other occasions, his perceived disregard for the rules of the drama and the norms of probability elicited a more hostile response. This is apparent, for instance, in reviewers' different reactions two years later to *The World in a Village*, O'Keeffe's next five-act pastoral comedy. While acknowledging that this play was 'full of eccentricity', the reviewer for the *Public Advertiser* praised this comedy for offering 'several strong strokes of satire' in addition to 'pointed observations, moral lessons, and well enforced appeals to the heart and head'.[3] The writer for the *World*, however, condemned this play for many of the same traits. Distinguishing himself from those who are content to accept the 'shallow offerings of a *bastard* Muse', this reviewer described the 'sentiment' in this play as 'grossly misapplied' and the plot as 'miserably interweaved and horribly perverted', its five acts being composed merely of 'scenes of endless irregularity and extravagance [which

---

[1] *The Diary; or, Woodfall's Register*, 18 April 1791.   [2] *Evening Mail*, 15 April 1791.
[3] *Public Advertiser*, 25 November 1793.

are], sometimes foreign to the subject and nearly always foreign to nature and sense'.[4]

In the analysis that follows, I will be focusing on those elements in O'Keeffe's pastoral drama that generated this charge of 'excentricity', illegitimacy and 'foreignness' in the effort not only to restore the complexity and critical edge that his contemporaries recognised in his writing but also to situate these pastoral productions within a dramatic tradition of vernacular cosmopolitanism, one that in his case had its roots in native Irish culture and the culture of the Irish Enlightenment. 'Vernacular cosmopolitanism' is one of several terms coined by postcolonial scholars, anthropologists and sociologists over the past two decades to describe that different form of global consciousness that evolves in populations that travel not from a position of wealth and privilege but rather out of some compulsion or necessity.[5] This necessity could arise from war, invasion and conquest, or, as was the case for O'Keeffe and countless others from the eighteenth century onward, it could result from the unequal economic development that followed such events. Most crucially, and in contradistinction to its older philosophical variant, the cosmopolitanism that emerges from this more coerced form of travel does not entail the abandonment of culturally specific loyalties or practices. Instead, as Kwame Anthony Appiah notes, this less-privileged class of migrants takes its roots and memories with them,[6] thus generating a variety of different paths to cosmopolitanism and those values of tolerance, inclusivity and openness to other cultures that remain its defining tenets. 'Like nations', as Bruce Robbins observes, 'cosmopolitanisms are now plural and particular.'[7]

O'Keeffe's 'excentric' pastoral comedies, I will suggest, are a product of this more ambivalently positioned kind of cosmopolitan consciousness, his productions, in this instance, registering the crossing over into mainstream British drama of a body of stories, experiences and survival strategies that came out of the culture of the Irish Catholic dispossessed.[8] Because they

---

[4] *The World*, 25 November 1793.

[5] For an account of the development of this concept, see Pnina Werbner, 'Introduction: Towards a New Cosmopolitan Anthropology', in *Anthropology and the New Cosmopolitanism* (Oxford and New York: Berg, 2008), 1–29. Other terms used to describe this consciousness include 'rooted cosmopolitanism', 'demotic cosmopolitanism', 'discrepant cosmopolitanism' and 'cosmopolitan patriotism'.

[6] Kwame Anthony Appiah, 'Cosmopolitan Patriots', *Critical Inquiry* 23 (1997): 617–39; 618.

[7] Bruce Robbins, 'Introduction Part 1: Actual Existing Cosmopolitanisms' in *Cosmopolitics: Thinking and Feeling Beyond the Nation*, ed. Pheng Cheah and Bruce Robbins (Minneapolis: Minneapolis University Press, 1998), 2.

[8] David O'Shaughnessy's discussion of how Irish writers appropriated *Cato* (Chapter 7, this volume) also shows how this ambivalence generates productive generic modification.

had no political voice, and because their culture, religion and language were proscribed by the state, Irish Catholics were in many ways outsiders in their own country for much of the century; they knew the experience of exile without ever having to travel. We have been 'proscribed as aliens … for 75 years past', Charles O'Conor, the historian, antiquarian and founding member of the Catholic Committee, wrote to his friend John Curry in 1778, and he repeated that notion on other occasions as he reflected back on the years since the passage of penal laws.[9] O'Keeffe's family, which had lost its lands for its support of the Jacobite cause, felt similarly alienated, and it generated in them that same kind of backward glance, that experience of 'living here and remembering/desiring another place', which, as James Clifford notes, is characteristic of diasporic communities.[10] When he was a boy, the playwright later recalled, his father, 'with pride not unmixed with dejection' led him over the 'tracts of fine lands, once the property of his ancestors' in Knock-Drin, near Edenderry, and he added that his mother 'had much the same remark to make of *her* family losses in the county of Wexford' (*Recollections*, 1:8).

However, from mid-century on, Catholic writers, following O'Conor, Curry and other leaders in the newly founded Catholic Committee, began appropriating and reworking Irish Enlightenment discourses and practices to intervene in public debates about the status of Irish Catholics. And, as he was growing up in Ireland, O'Keeffe would have also learned those reinvention skills – strategies and practices that were at their core both mimetic and performative. As Michael Brown has recently noted, confessional issues were the central preoccupation of Irish Enlightenment literati leading these writers to engage in an extended debate over 'which faiths or faith were sufficiently civil as to be permitted to publicly engage in religious, social and political discourse'.[11] From the late 1740s onwards, O'Conor, Curry and others entered this debate on behalf of Irish Catholics, drawing on some of the same Enlightenment discourses, methods, and practices as their Protestant counterparts. Pleas to incoming administrations for the redress of Catholic grievances, for instance, were couched in sentimental 'addresses' and public performances that emphasised the Catholic community's suffering, loyalty and deference towards

---

[9] Charles O'Conor to John Curry, 23 October 1778, in *The Letters of Charles O'Conor of Belanagare,* ed. Catherine Coogan Ward and Robert E. Ward, 2 vols. (Ann Arbor, Michigan: University Microfilms, 1980), 2: 129. See also 2: 127 and 2: 143.
[10] James Clifford, 'Diasporas', *Cultural Anthropology* 9 (1994): 302–38; 311. Future references will be included in the text.
[11] Michael Brown, *The Irish Enlightenment* (Cambridge, MA: Harvard University Press, 2016), 11.

existing institutions, and through such emotional and well-publicised appeals (these addresses and performances were usually noted by Irish newspapers), Catholic leaders sought to exploit the culture of sentiment and sensibility that, as Brown has noted, was a central component of the Irish as well as the English Enlightenment.[12] At other times, however, Catholic literati adopted a more muscular stance, staging the defence of their community on more rationalist and empirical grounds. Often using a liberal Protestant guise, for instance, O'Conor and Curry entered paper wars to counter opponents who resurrected time-worn arguments about Catholic duplicity and native Irish savagery; to the same end, they engaged in antiquarian research and revisionist history writing.[13] Like the kind of feminist mimicry that the performance theorist Elin Diamond describes, their genre of imitation effectively "'split what it double(d),'" displacing the authority and authenticity of the original"[14] – in this case, the authority and authenticity of the sectarian state.

O'Keeffe used a similarly subversive form of mimicry to make a name for himself as an actor in Ireland,[15] and he brought this repertoire of mimetic survival strategies with him when, at the age of thirty-three, he emigrated and began writing full time for London's demanding and competitive entertainment business. Like the other enterprising migrants that Craig Bailey describes in his groundbreaking book *Irish London: Middle-class Migration in the Global Eighteenth Century*, O'Keeffe was drawn to the great city at the heart of empire by the opportunities it opened up for further wealth creation and social advancement, and he never lost sight of those goals even after suffering an eye infection that, shortly after he settled in England, left him in a state of near blindness (*Recollections*, 1: 386; 2: 84–88). With the aid of an amanuensis, he continued to write for two of London's patent houses, Covent Garden and the Haymarket, often labouring to the point of illness to turn out the two or

---

[12] Brown, *Irish Enlightenment*, 307–457. Such emotional displays of loyalism by Catholics were also particularly common during the period of the American Revolutionary War (see Helen Burke, 'The Catholic Questions, Print Media, and John O'Keeffe's The Poor Soldier [1783]', *Eighteenth-Century Fiction* 27.3–4 (2015)): 419–48.

[13] For a discussion of this Catholic counteroffensive, see Clare O'Halloran, *Golden Ages and Barbarous Nations; Antiquarian Debate and Cultural Politics in Ireland, c. 1750–1800* (Notre Dame and Cork: University of Notre Dame Press and Cork University Press, 2004); Hilary Larkin, 'Writing in an Enlightenment Age? Charles O'Conor and the Philosophes', in *Charles O'Conor of Ballinagare, 1710–91: Life and Works* (Dublin: Four Courts Press, 2015), 97–115; and Luke Gibbons, '"A Foot in Both Camps": Charles O'Conor, Print Culture and the Counter-public Sphere', in *Charles O'Conor of Ballinagare*, 116–32.

[14] Elin Diamond, *Unmaking Mimesis: Essays on Feminism and Theatre* (London: Routledge, 1997), vi.

[15] See Burke, 'Eighteenth-Century Theatrical Touring', 129–35.

three new pieces that these playhouses needed each season to add variety
and novelty to their evening's entertainments. With no less assiduity, he
cultivated those who had the power to influence his career, whether it was
the managers and audiences that he needed to please to get his plays
produced or the wealthy patrons that he needed to sanction a dedication
or to subscribe to the printed collections of his works (*Recollections*, 2:23;
1:400; 2:10). But as we know from his self-representations in his
Recollections, O'Keeffe also continued to identify with what he termed
the 'Old Milesian' (i.e. native Irish and Catholic) segment of the Irish
diaspora (1:89); in pastoral comedy, a genre that has always had the capacity
to be oppositional even while sounding entirely conventional, he found
a vehicle for representing the discrepant knowledge of empire and modernity that came out of that diasporic experience. As Raymond Williams first
noted, in Virgil's seminal pastoral *The Eclogues*, we hear not only from
Tityrus the happy shepherd who sings songs in praise of his mistress and his
benevolent Roman patron but also from Meliboeus, the goatherd who,
reflecting the reality of rural life in the Italy of Virgil's own day, has been
evicted by the Roman army and now faces the prospect of exile in far-off
lands. The inclusion of this second perspective, moreover, adds
a transnational component to this pastoral since the space that
Meliboeus contemplates now stretches, as he tells us, 'from bone-dry
Africa' to 'Britain – that place cut off at the world's end'.[16] O'Keeffe's
later pastoral comedies have a similar spatial, tonal and political complexity. The kind of 'light careless laughter' that would induce William Hazlitt
(with scant regard for Irish sensibilities) to dub O'Keeffe 'our English
Moliere' is most often found in his earliest pastoral comedies.[17] But in
his later works, a more critical Meliboeus strain of commentary frequently
undercuts this humour; in these dramas, the themes of loss, dispossession
and exclusion predominate, even as the Milesian story itself becomes
increasingly deterritorialised. Being uprooted and set adrift in the world
is no longer represented as an exclusively Irish experience; instead, it is
depicted as one of the paradigmatic stories of modernity itself. In the
remainder of this chapter, I focus on selected examples from this playwright's extensive body of work that track this movement from the local
and culturally specific to the global and the parabolic. As we will see, this
broadening of horizons did not require a jettisoning of the past; it entailed

---

[16] Raymond Williams, *The Country and the City* (New York: Oxford University Press, 1973), 16–17.
[17] William Hazlitt, *Lectures on the English Comic Writers* (London, 1819), 339. Hazlitt made these
remarks after seeing a revival of *The Agreeable Surprise*, one of O'Keeffe's earliest successes in the
pastoral genre on the London stage.

rather a repeated return to, and reworking of, that pastoral space that this playwright used to represent his homeland in his first and most optimistic Irish pastoral – a space that was shadowed by the Irish 'Big House'.

From Patriotism to Vernacular Cosmopolitanism: O'Keeffe's Irish 'Big House' Pastorals

As O'Keeffe tells us, this first Irish pastoral drama, *The Shamrock,* was written to honour the Illustrious Order of the Knights of Saint Patrick, an organisation that had been installed with great pomp and circumstance at Dublin Castle on 17 March 1783 (*Recollections* 2: 49). Since this order had been created to bolster Dublin Castle's influence in the wake of the legislative victory of 1782, the play might seem, on the face of it, to be a loyalist production, but as David O'Shaughnessy has persuasively argued, it is better read as a 'polite but assertive Irish patriot response' to this power play by the administration.[18] This way of reading this play can also be supported by looking at the ways the Installation was represented on the Dublin stage just prior to this London production. In February and March of 1783, the Dublin stage enthusiastically previewed and then commemorated the Installation of the Knights of St Patrick in various kinds of afterpieces, but it did so by incorporating these celebrations into the kind of culturally syncretic patriot drama that, as I have argued elsewhere, was prevalent in the Irish theatre in the 1770s and early 1780s.[19] The advertisements for the preview of the Installation that was staged at Dublin's Crow Street on 27 February 1783, for example, explicitly acknowledged this drama's debt to *The Fairy Prince,* the impeccably loyalist masque that George Colman Senior had written for Covent Garden to commemorate an induction into the Order of the Garter at Windsor Castle in 1771; like this piece, too, the Crow Street masque promised 'scenery, transparencies [and] dresses … by capital artists'. In place of the fairies, nymphs and sylvan characters of Colman's piece, however, the Crow Street Installation featured the Genius of Ireland, Bards, and Druids (one of which was played by the bilingual Irish singer Robert Owenson); it showed its Irish patriot allegiance and its commitment to the cause of Irish economic independence by advertising that all the dresses in the show would be of 'Irish Manufacture'.[20]

---

[18] David O'Shaughnessy, "'Rip'ning Buds in Freedom's field": Staging Irish Improvement in the 1780s', *Journal for Eighteenth-Century Studies* 38.4 (2015): 541–54.

[19] See Helen Burke, *Riotous Performances: The Struggle for Hegemony in the Irish Theatre, 1712–1784* (Notre Dame: University of Notre Dame Press, 2003), 241–80.

[20] *Theatre in Dublin, 1745–1820: A Calendar of Performances*, ed. John C. Greene, 6 vols. (Bethlehem: Lehigh University Press, 2011), 3: 2149.

O'Keeffe's *Shamrock,* which was performed at Covent Garden on 7 April 1783, was another patriot reworking in this Installation dramatic genre, one that testifies to the two-way crossings in music, art and culture that shaped Irish diasporic drama. Like Colman's masque and the Crow Street afterpiece, O'Keeffe's pastoral drama has a fairy host, though in *The Shamrock,* the ruler of these otherworldly creatures is the King of the Leprechauns and Thomas Arne's music has been replaced by melodies drawn from Turlough O'Carolan and the indigenous Irish musical tradition. In setting his play near Carton House, the County Kildare seat of William Fitzgerald, the Duke of Leinster, and in depicting that surrounding countryside as 'Beautiful',[21] O'Keeffe was also drawing on an Irish pastoral tradition that he knew well from his own training and early experience in the visual arts. During his youthful summers as a strolling actor in Ireland, O'Keeffe had supplemented his income by doing many similarly flattering landscape drawings for Irish estate owners, and he would most likely have been familiar with the idyllic 'views' of Carton that Ireland's best-known landscape artist Thomas Roberts had painted and exhibited in Dublin in the mid-1770s.[22]

In this case, however, the idealised depiction of Carton and, by extension of its owner, amounted to more than mere flattery of a wealthy patron. The Duke of Leinster was not only the foremost Irish noble in the recently established Knights of St Patrick, but he was also a leader who had gained widespread popularity in Catholic Ireland for his parliamentary support of the cause of Catholic relief.[23] In addition, he was colonel of the radical-leaning Dublin Volunteers, a military organisation that the playwright himself and his young son had joined in the late 1770s after it began admitting Catholics into its ranks. As O'Keeffe's daughter later noted, her father 'gloried' in being part of this organisation, a pride that he publicly expressed in 1780, when dressed, in a Volunteer uniform, he

---

[21] *The Shamrock, or, Anniversary of St. Patrick* (1782), Huntington Library, Larpent MS, 620, f. 1.
[22] O'Keeffe describes doing four such landscape 'views' in the Belfast area for 'the pride and pleasure' of Lord Donegal, and he mentions doing two others in Kilkenny, each with Ormond Castle in the background, for the proprietor of the Kilkenny newspaper (*Recollections* 1: 133; 201–2; 208–9). For a discussion of Roberts's landscape paintings, see Julian Walton, 'Et in Arcadia Ego', *Irish Arts Review* 26 (2009): 90–93; and William Laffan and Brendan Rooney, *Thomas Roberts: Landscape and Patronage in Eighteenth-Century Ireland* (Churchill House, Kerry: Churchill House Press, 2009).
[23] For Fitzgerald's role in the Knights of St Patrick, see William Monck Mason, *The History and Antiquities of the Collegiate and Cathedral Church of St Patrick* (Dublin: Printed by W. Folds, 1820), 450. For Fitzgerald's support of the 1778 Catholic Relief bill and his popularity with the Dublin crowd, see Maurice R. O'Connell, *Irish Politics and Social Conflict in the Age of the American Revolution* (Philadelphia: University of Pennsylvania Press, 1965), 121; and Burke, *Riotous Performances,* 269.

sang his own song in praise of that military force on the Crow Street stage.[24] The 'beautiful country' that *The Shamrock* depicts, too, can be read as a vision of the imagined nation that O'Keeffe and many other of his co-religionists were hoping was coming into being under the kind of benign and religiously inclusive leadership that Fitzgerald represented. In that imagined world, the quarrels of two pairs of temperamentally mismatched lovers, complicated by the scheming of clownish villagers, are the only sources of conflict, and those quarrels are ultimately resolved by the spells of the King of Leprechauns, a figure who, like the inhabitant of the nearby 'Big House', presides with benevolence over this Irish arcadia.[25]

By late 1783, however, it had become impossible to sustain this optimistic vision. Over the summer and early autumn of that year, the Volunteers and the Patriot Party in Ireland began to split over the question of granting further concessions to Catholics, and those tensions spilled over into the London press, reactivating a debate on what could be called the character question behind the Catholic Question: namely, could Irish Catholics ever be trusted with the full rights of citizenship, including, and perhaps most controversially, the right to bear arms? For a commentator in the *Whitehall Evening Post*, writing in late October 1783, the argument was a resounding 'no', or, at least when it came to the common people. 'From the more enlightened, there would be no danger to apprehend', this correspondent wrote, 'but the lower orders are mere machines, puppets moved by the all-directing hand of the juggling Priest, who would instigate a murder to enjoy the authority of pronouncing Absolution'.[26] For O'Keeffe who, unusually for an Irish playwright, remained a Catholic even after settling in England, this rhetoric would have been deeply disturbing; to respond, he rewrote *The Shamrock*, relying this time on strategies and arguments borrowed from the Catholic political movement described earlier. With that change, his pastoral drama also begins to take a more transnational

---

[24] Adelaide O'Keeffe, 'Memoir', in *O'Keeffe's Legacy to his Daughter, being the Poetical Works of the Late John O'Keeffe, Esq.* (London: G. Whittaker, 1834), xxii; *Recollections,* 1: 260; Burke, *Riotous Performances,* 272–73.

[25] It seems likely that Carton House was represented in the scenic backdrop of this play. Pat, for instance, refers to the 'Duke's house' as being 'yonder' (*The Shamrock,* f.10), while the scenic description for *The Poor Soldier* (which almost certainly used the same backdrop) opens with a country scene with 'a large Mansion at some distance', and two smaller structures, 'a small House' and 'a Cottage' near the front of the stage (*The Poor Soldier* in *The Plays of John O'Keeffe,* ed. Frederick Link, 4 vols. (New York and London: Garland, 1981), 2: 295). All subsequent references to O'Keeffe's plays are to this edition and will be cited by play title, volume, and page number in the text.

[26] *Whitehall Evening Post,* 30 October–1 November 1783. For more on the press reaction, see Burke, 'The Catholic Question', 434–37.

turn, effecting that linking of the culturally specific to the universal that is characteristic of vernacular cosmopolitanism.

The Poor Soldier, which opened in November 1783, retains the same Carton setting and the same traditional Irish music as *The Shamrock,* and it kept the two characters whose antics had provided so much of the latter play's broader humour: the worldly minded parish priest, Father Luke, and Derby, a country trickster character played by John Edwin, an actor and singer whose great comedic talents O'Keeffe would rely on throughout his career. The story of the two principal lovers in this pastoral, however, is substantially rewritten in this second version. Pat, the carefree rakish lad of *The Shamrock,* is now recast as Patrick, the destitute infantry man who is returning to Carton, his native village after being wounded while serving on the British side in the American colonies, and Norah is the devoted lover who has stayed true to her soldier boy despite pressures from her guardian, Father Luke, and a wealthy suitor, Captain Fitzroy, a visitor in nearby Carton House. In fashioning a story about this poor soldier's suffering and heroism during the American war – we later discover that Patrick acquired his wounds by rescuing on the battlefield the very officer who is now his rival – O'Keeffe was also responding to those who argued that the Irish lower orders could not be trusted to bear arms. And as Irish Catholic leaders had done with their addresses to government since the mid-century, he sought to generate sympathy for the Irish common people by emphasising the loyalty and distress of his emblematic Irish hero. In Mrs Kennedy, the actress who played Patrick as a breeches role, he also found a performer who was ideally suited to generating this kind of affective response.[27] Margaret Kennedy, *née* Doyle, was an Irish-born actress who had achieved fame on the London stage not only for her skill in performing breeches roles but also for the rare quality of her singing voice, an instrument that one contemporary described as the 'finest counter-tenor ever heard'.[28] She would have been particularly effective, then, in generating sympathy with her rendition of the melancholy songs that Patrick sings early in the play as, under the mistaken belief that Norah has been unfaithful, he once again contemplates going into exile (*The Poor Soldier,* 2: 295). And for those who were familiar with the Irish musical tradition, the female body that would have been 'ghosted' in such performances

---

[27] Between 1783 and 1789, Kennedy or other women played this Irish soldier character no fewer than ninety-eight times on the London stage. See Dror Wahrman, *The Making of the Modern Self: Identity and Culture in Eighteenth-Century England* (New Haven: Yale University Press, 2006), 51.

[28] William Thomas Parke, *Musical Memoirs,* 2 vols. (London: Henry Colburn and Richard Bentley, 1830), 1: 27.

would have added an additional layer of pathos to her performance. 'A Rose tree full in bearing', for instance, the song that Patrick sings at the end of Act I, is set to an Irish tune that is known, among its many other titles, as 'Móirín ní Chuileannáin', one of the female names that Jacobite poets used for Ireland.[29]

But in making the case for the disenfranchised Irish Catholic, *The Poor Soldier* also drew on some of the Enlightenment principles that Catholic apologists like O'Conor were using in their arguments to counter prejudice, and this universalising rhetoric transformed the story of this poor Irishman into a more far-reaching populist fable, one that, as the record shows, had appeal on both sides of the Atlantic. The play received at least 165 performances in London alone prior to 1800, and it was widely reprinted and performed in the provinces, Ireland and America.[30] O'Keeffe began to lay the groundwork for the transnational appeal of his drama in the enlightened principles that Captain Fitzroy enunciates as he rejects Father Luke's suggestion that Norah's religion or her nationality might constitute an obstacle to his plan of marrying her. 'I am incapable of an illiberal prejudice for not having breath'd the same air with me, or for worshiping the same Deity in another manner', Fitzroy tells the priest, and he goes on to add 'we are the common children of one parent, and the honest man who thinks with moral rectitude and acts according to his thought, is my countryman let him be born where he will' (*The Poor Soldier*, 1: 273). In expressing such sentiments, Fitzroy advances principles of religious and cultural tolerance that were gaining currency across the Atlantic world, but what this officer still has to learn, and what the play teaches at its most parabolic level through the story of Patrick's heroism, is that this 'honest man who thinks with moral rectitude' can come from the lowest and most disenfranchised segment of the population. As Appiah has noted, one of the ethical obligations that stems from the notion of cosmopolitanism is that 'we take seriously the value not just of human life but of particular human lives.'[31] *The Poor Soldier* makes such a demand in relation to the type of human life Patrick represents – one that has been deemed 'poor' or lacking because of religion, ethnicity and social status.

[29] Francis O'Neil, *Irish Folk Music: A Fascinating Hobby* (Chicago: Regan Printing House, 1910), 130; Máirín Nic Eoin, 'Sovereignty and Politics, *c.* 1300–1900', in *The Field Day Anthology of Irish Writing: Irish Women's Writing and Traditions*, ed. Angela Bourke et al., 2 vols. (Cork: Cork University Press, 2002), 1: 274.

[30] Link, *Plays of John O'Keeffe*, 1: xxxiii.

[31] Kwame Anthony Appiah, *Cosmopolitanism: Ethics in a World of Strangers* (New York and London: Norton, 2006), xv.

The obligations that are attendant on recognising the value of such life are likewise dramatised by the social and material rewards that this soldier receives at the play's conclusion; after the Captain recognises what he calls the 'superior merit' of the poor soldier (*The Poor Soldier*, 1: 310), he relinquishes his claim on Norah and promises Patrick an officer's commission.

On two other occasions, in *The Prisoner at Large*, a two-act farce that he wrote in 1788, and *The Wicklow Mountains*, a musical drama that he wrote in 1796,[32] O'Keeffe used the pastoral genre to intervene in debates about Ireland and its people; in these two plays, he placed a further strain on the pastoral comic form by attempting to use it to rehabilitate an even more controversial type of poor Irishman: the 'Whiteboy'. This term was first used in conjunction with the agrarian agitators who appeared nightly in the southern Irish countryside in the early 1760s, but it was subsequently applied to other Irish agrarian rebel groups, including the Rightboys in the mid-1780s and the Defenders in the 1790s.[33] The strangeness of O'Keeffe's later pastoral plays, however, did not come solely from his attempt to deal with this problematic subject matter; it also came from the fact that the Irish landscape of these dramas, like the landscapes drawn by so many later Irish playwrights, is also a memoryscape, a site for representing and creatively reconfiguring an experience of exile and loss.[34] The result in each case is a palimpsestic dramatic text that operates on different temporal, spatial and symbolic registers and that speaks to the concerns of all those, including the playwright himself, who are 'at large' in the world because of what Stuart Hall, in his discussion of vernacular cosmopolitanism, terms 'the disjunctures of modern globalization'.[35] *The Prisoner at Large* can serve to illustrate this kind excentricity, one generated from the attempt to reconnect what this global modernity has pulled apart.

Like *The Poor Soldier*, *The Prisoner at Large* is again set in the vicinity of an Irish 'Big House' and, as in the earlier play, too, a returning migrant is

---

[32] *The Wicklow Mountains* first appeared as a five-act main piece entitled *The Lad of the Hills,* in the spring of 1796; the following season, it was cut to two acts and renamed *The Wicklow Mountains.* A three-act version of this play with the latter title was included in the authorised *Dramatic Works of John O'Keeffe,* 4 vols. (London, 1798).

[33] For the continuities as well as the differences between these various agrarian secret organisations, see James S. Donnelly Jr., 'The Rightboy Movement 1785-8', *Studia Hibernica* 17/18 (1977/1978): 120–202.

[34] See, for example, Nicholas Grene's discussion of the plays of Tom Murphy and Brian Friel in 'Some Versions of Pastoral', *The Politics of Irish Drama* (Cambridge University Press, 1999), 194–218.

[35] Stuart Hall, 'Cosmopolitanism, Globalisation and Diaspora' in *Anthropology and the New Cosmopolitanism*, 347.

its central character. The returnee this time, however, is not a poor peasant but an Irish peer, Lord Esmond, who, having been imprisoned for debt for ten years in a Paris jail, is now temporarily 'at large' on his own Irish estate in the company of his French jailor (*The Prisoner at Large*, 2: 3,6). As one reviewer noted, this plot was drawn in part from the real-life escapades of Lord Massereene, an Irish peer with estates in Antrim who had attracted the attention of the press four months earlier when he had attempted to escape from a Paris jail where he had been imprisoned for more than seventeen years for refusing to pay his debts.[36] Though he did not allude to this incident or mention Massereene by name, O'Keeffe referenced an event in this lord's earlier history when he discussed the origin of this play in his *Recollections*. When he was in Antrim in the late 1760s, O'Keeffe wrote, an innkeeper told him how he and other tenants in the area were refusing to pay their rent to some Frenchmen who were holding their Irish landlord prisoner in Paris; this incident, the playwright went on to say, gave him the idea for *The Prisoner at Large*, a play that also features a tenant rent strike and a French agent who (with the cooperation of an Irish middleman) is trying to cheat an imprisoned Irish lord out of his estate (*Recollections*, 1: 199–200). As at least some of O'Keeffe's contemporaries would have known, that anecdote connected the play to Massereene; historical records show that there was such a disturbance in Antrim in 1769 after this lord (from his Paris jail) rashly sent two Frenchmen to Ireland to manage his property.[37]

In *The Prisoner at Large*, however, O'Keeffe shifts the location of the play's troubled estate from Antrim to the countryside around the Lake of Killarney (2: 9), a setting that, in the authorised print version of this play, is described as being 'in the West of Ireland'.[38] In so doing, O'Keeffe began the Irish dramatic tradition of using an indeterminate Irish western space to comment on Ireland and its people – a commentary that, in this case, also took its meaning from the heated public discussion that followed the outbreak of the Rightboy disturbances in the south of Ireland in 1785. These disturbances went on for three years; during that period, Richard Woodward, the Bishop of Cloyne, and his supporters in Ireland flooded the English-speaking world with publications that suggested that this

---

[36] *Public Advertiser*, 4 July 1788. For an account of the events behind Massereene's imprisonment, see A. P. W. Malcomson, 'Election Politics in the Borough of Antrim, 1750-1800', *Irish Historical Studies* 17 (March 1970): 32–57; 35–36. For press coverage of his attempted escape, see, for instance, the *Edinburgh Magazine* 7 (March 1778), 28.

[37] Malcomson, 'Election Politics', 37–38.

[38] See 'Dramatic Personae', *The Prisoner at Large* in *The Plays of John O'Keeffe*, 2: n.p.

agrarian unrest was the prelude to a new Irish Catholic uprising, one that, they argued, promised to revive all the gothic horrors of the 1641 Irish rebellion. Catholic writers and their liberal Protestant supporters attempted to counter these charges with their own pamphlets and letters. But as is evident from one such response, the lengthy *Defence* which O'Keeffe's old Cork friend, Father Arthur O'Leary, published in Dublin and London in 1787, spokesmen for the Catholic community remained deeply worried about the effect of these attacks on public opinion at home and abroad.[39] The widespread dissemination of the prints of Woodward and his supporters, O'Leary wrote, was leading foreign nations to believe that Ireland was in a 'state of barbarism and rebellion', and he added, it was turning 'Irish Catholics, in particular [into] objects of detestation all over Great-Britain'.[40]

The Prisoner at Large, then, could be read as another attempt to refute this image, albeit while seeking to obscure its political engagement by drawing on the Massereene lore. There is only one explicit reference to an Irish agrarian insurgency in this play, and that is made by a female servant in Lord Esmond's house who is alarmed at the decision of a fellow-servant, Muns, to open the door of this mansion at night to a stranger (in this case the plainly dressed lord himself). 'The deuce! Were you mad . . . ?' she asks, 'He may be a white boy' (*The Prisoner at Large,* 2: 16). That comment, slight as it is, suggests something of the terror generated in Irish big houses by the nightly ridings of 'Captain Right' and his followers, and it gives an additional layer of meaning both to the tenant rent strike on the Esmond estate and the spectre that haunts its manor house (a ghostly female figure, we learn early in the play, is appearing nightly in the bedroom of the lord's dead mother). The Whiteboys took on a similar ghostly female appearance in their nightly ridings through the Irish countryside, dressing themselves in white smocks and casting themselves as the children of Queen Sive, a sovereignty figure from Irish popular culture. And, as Luke Gibbons has pointed out in his analysis of the discourse of the sublime in eighteenth-century descriptions of Killarney, those appearances also generated a fear that 'straddled the boundary between the imaginary and the real'.[41]

---

[39] For an account of this paper war, see James Kelly, 'Inter-Denominational Relations and Religious Toleration in Late Eighteenth-Century Ireland: The "Paper War" of 1786–88', *Eighteenth-Century Ireland: Iris an dá chultúr* 3 (1988): 39–67.

[40] *A Defence of the Conduct and Writings of the Rev. Arthur O'Leary, during the Late Disturbances in Munster, with a Full Justification of the Irish Catholics and an Account of the Risings of the White-Boys, Written by Himself: in Answer to the False Accusations of Theophilus and the Ill-Grounded Insinuations of the Right Reverend Doctor Woodward, Lord Bishop of Cloyne* (London, 1787), 53.

[41] Luke Gibbons, 'Topographies of Terror: Killarney and the Politics of the Sublime', *The South Atlantic Quarterly* 95 (1996): 23–44; 38.

The plot device that excited the loudest charges of improbability from the critics – namely the conceit of imagining that Lord Esmond would be allowed out of his jail by his Parisian jailer[42] – is, then, the mechanism that O'Keeffe used to deflate such fears; to that end, he merged the pastoral with another emerging genre of writing that reflected on the Irish countryside and its people: Irish tourist literature. By the second half of the century, Killarney had become famous as much for the pleasures of the beautiful as the terrors of the sublime; as the audience is reminded by the comical boasting of the servant, Muns, in this play, genteel visitors were now coming to that location to enjoy those wild beauties. 'They may talk of fine views, and vistos, and beauties of nature', Muns states, 'but 'tis to hear the divine echoes of my horn that brings the gentlefolks all the way from Cork and even Dublin down here to the lake of Killarney' (2:9). As Joep Leerssen notes, this new type of tourist also tended to displace the blame for the unrest in the Irish countryside from the peasantry (whom they viewed as part of its untouched nature) to the middlemen who managed Irish estates in the absence of their owners;[43] it is that more forgiving perspective that the London audience was encouraged to adopt in this play as it followed Lord Esmond in his 'ramble' (2: 22) through his Killarney estate. The disguised lord's encounters with Jack Connor, the tenant famer who is leading the rent strike, for example, show this peasant leader to be hospitable, good natured, and loyal to his old master (all attributes that Arthur Young, for instance, attributed to the Irish 'common people' in *A Tour in Ireland* [1780]),[44] while Old Dowdle, Lord Esmond's steward, is shown, by contrast, to have all the tyrannical and grasping traits of the stereotypical middleman. When Esmond finally gains access to his own house, the audience discovers too that this play's 'ghost' is none other than Esmond's own lover, Adelaide, who sleepwalks in his dead mother's clothes as she mourns his rumoured death. After this lord regains control of his estate and is united with his lady, this spectre, like the gothic spectre of a peasant rebellion more generally, disappears. The politics of this resolution, it should be noted, is also nicely ambiguous. There are undoubtedly Jacobite undertones to an ending that suggests, as this one does, that peace

---

[42] *The Morning Chronicle and London Advertiser*, 3 July 1788, called this conceit 'highly improbable' and a 'daring defect', while also characterising the whole play as 'the most *laughable* nonsense' ever witnessed.

[43] Joep Leerssen, *Mere Irish and Fíor Ghael: Studies in the Idea of Irish Nationality, Its Development and Literary Expression Prior to the Nineteenth Century* (Notre Dame and Cork: Cork University Press and Field Day, 1986), 72–81.

[44] See Leerssen, *Mere Irish,* 79–80.

in Ireland depends on the restoration of its old landowning class, but as Karen J. Harvey and Kevin B. Pry have argued, this conclusion also resonates with Irish Protestant patriot beliefs about absentee landlordism. Esmond is echoing an oft-repeated patriot sentiment, they note, in his last hortatory speech when he suggest that instead of travelling, 'our nobility' should 'stay at home and spend their fortunes amongst their honest tenants, who support their splendor'.[45]

In assessing the meaning of this play, however, it is important to note that this last speech ends not with these remarks about the nobility but with this restored lord's promise to extend to others the hospitality that he received when he was seen only as a 'stranger in distress' (*The Prisoner at Large*, 2: 35). The inclusion of that motif in this play, it could be argued, has its origin in a different, less culturally specific kind of history – one that drew from the playwright's own experience of being 'at large' in the world. To unpack this dimension of this play, it is useful to look at a poem which O'Keeffe claims he wrote during his first visit to London at the age of fifteen but which he evidently thought sufficiently important to cite in full in his *Recollections* some sixty-four years later. This poem was inspired by a young English friend's refusal to include the patronymic 'O' in O'Keeffe's name, but, as it reveals, that humiliation caused the young boy to reflect more broadly on the Irish diaspora and the reception afforded 'old Milesians' (like himself) in their various countries of settlement. While the old Irish were received 'like brothers' and as 'men of some account' in Spain, France and Germany, O'Keeffe relates, they suffered a bleaker fate in England. 'Huff'd at great men's doors/By porters and by pages', they fell behind their English counterparts and were forced to accept the most demeaning kinds of work.

Lord Esmond, who, at the beginning of this play, is in sight of his own great house but without shelter for the night because, as he laments, he is no longer 'master of one foot of land' is another figure for this marginalised 'Old Milesian'; indeed, at an earlier point in the play as other characters discuss his travels across Europe, he is compared to a 'wild goose' (*The Prisoner at Large*, 2: 6,3). But this play does not only focus on the plight of this dispossessed nobleman; it also shows the abuse suffered by Muns and his fellow-servant, Tooten, at the hands of their new master, Old Dowdle. By telling their story alongside Esmond's, O'Keeffe expands the ethical horizon of his drama, giving its message about the importance

---

[45] Karen J. Harvey and Kevin B. Pry, 'John O'Keeffe as an Irish Playwright within the Theatrical, Social, and Economic Context of His Time', *Éire-Ireland* 22 (1987): 19–43; 33–37.

of offering hospitality to distressed strangers, a resonance beyond its strictly Irish diasporic context. Played by John Edwin, Muns at first view would seem to be a reprise of Darby, the good-natured country clown role that this actor played in *The Shamrock* and in *The Poor Soldier*. Accompanied by Tooten (described in the play as a 'black' or 'black-a-moor' [2: 9,15]), he initially provides much of the music and 'good cheer' (2: 10) that could be expected in a comic afterpiece. However, when Old Dowdle discovers that this entertainment is being provided for a tryst between Jack Connor and his daughter, the merriment comes to a rapid end. The black servant is beaten simply for having the audacity to sit down at the steward's table (2: 15), and shortly afterwards, Muns himself is turned out of the house without his wages for the crime of letting a 'strange man' (2: 20) (Lord Esmond) into the house. There is no further reference to Tooten in the play, but when we meet Muns again in the opening scene in the play's second act, he is in as abject a condition as his old master. Hungry and tired with his horn around his neck and his box under his arm, he is also tramping the road as he goes in search of new shelter and new employment.

The form of inclusiveness that this play endorsed in its conclusion under the name of 'hospitality' (2: 25) then extends to these displaced and abused servants, figures who, it could be said, stand in for all those who lost their place or who suffered violence in the new eighteenth-century world order. In the very last line of the play, Esmond also advocates this kind of outreach and inclusiveness, even as he raises Muns to the position of household steward. With this honest servant as his new keeper, he states, he will offer 'a welcome to the kind friend, social neighbour, and, above all, the stranger in distress' (2: 35). Implicit in this description is the recognition of a set of moral obligations that go beyond those defined by the ties of kith, kin and nation, and this ethical horizon, we could say, is ex-centric in its cosmopolitism.

The 'Worlding' of the English Village

Until the very end of his career, O'Keeffe continued to experiment with ways to express his uniquely vernacular form of cosmopolitanism. Two five-act pastoral comedies from the 1790s can serve to illustrate his most mature efforts in this regard: *The World in a Village* (1793) and *Wild Oats: Or the Strolling Gentlemen* (1795), which continues to be revived to the present day. These two plays differ greatly in mood and tone, but, as we will see, through their importation into pastoral drama of the Irish migrant experience they each effect a 'worlding'[46] of the English village.

The play that explicitly thematises its globalising intent in its title – *The World in a Village* – was performed just as Britain entered the war with revolutionary France. As Frederick Link has noted, it reflects the country's preoccupation with naval power during that period.[47] The male romantic leads, Charles Willows and William Bellevue, are both returning sailors, as are the two sea captains, one Dutch, the other Irish, who accompany these English sailors on their (separate) journeys back to their native village. The story which O'Keeffe weaves around this Irish seaman, Captain Mullinahack, and his daughter, Louisa (the play's two only Irish characters), may also have been designed to address the suspicions about Irish strangers which were always heightened when Britain went to war with France. Indeed, O'Keeffe had personal reasons for this concern: his daughter Adelaide and son Tottenham both attended school in France until the outbreak of the French Revolution. As the playwright noted in his *Recollections*, he often had to intervene in squabbles with his neighbours after Tottenham returned to England because of the latter's adoption of 'high Parisian court-fashion' and his son's near-inability to speak English (2: 147). In his play, O'Keeffe addresses and attempts to counter this kind of Francophobia through his representation of these Irish characters. Captain Mullinahack, the play concedes, was an officer in the French navy, but after the outbreak of the war, the Irishman notes, he abandoned that service out of loyalty to 'George my belov'd king and Ireland my honour'd country' (4: 61–62). The virtue of this Irish family is further established by the character of Mullinahack's devoted daughter, Louisa, a figure who has some of the distressed gentility and sensibility that Edmund Burke and other anti-Jacobin writers attributed to the aristocratic female victims of the French Revolution.[48] When we meet this Irish woman in the opening scene of the play, for instance, she is leaving her lodgings and preparing, as she puts it, to 'unlady' (4: 3) herself as she goes out in search of employment, having exhausting all her savings on setting up a school for the village poor.

These French-Irish refugees, however, are only two of the estranged and alienated characters who make up the 'world' of this emblematic English

---

[46] For the notion of 'worlding' literature, see, for example, Homi K. Bhabha, *The Location of Culture* (London and New York: Routledge, 1994), 12.

[47] Link, *The Plays of John O'Keeffe*, 1: liii.

[48] Claudia Johnson, *Equivocal Beings: Politics, Gender, and Sentimentality in the 1790s* (Chicago: University of Chicago Press, 1995), 2–6.

village. In telling the stories of impoverished and marginalised English characters alongside his Irish ones, O'Keeffe again revised and expanded the story of dispossession that he brought with him from Ireland. Like *The Prisoner at Large*, *The World in a Village* features a rural community that has been upended by the ascendancy of a new gentry, here represented by Allbut, a clerk who has cheated the widow of his former employer (a wealthy brewer) out of her business. Like the middleman of the earlier Irish play, this clerk is also now in possession of this play's great house (here an 'elegant Villa'), while its former owner, the widow, has sunk to being 'a poor pauper in [a] hovel' (*The World in a Village*, 4: 23,13). Much of the play's laughter, then, is directed at the literary pretension of this social upstart and his wife who, along with the village barber-turned-doctor, make up the new gentry in this community.[49] But these satirical scenes are juxtaposed with others that dramatise this new elite's refusal to share their prosperity with anyone below them in the social ladder, and the insistence of that motif – which is again actualised through the symbol of a big house's closed door – complicates what might otherwise seem to be a conservative if not a reactionary response to upward mobility.

This motif of the closed door is first introduced verbally into this play when we hear of a poor woman and her children being turned away from the house by Mrs Allbut, even as, ironically, that lady studies a poem on the merits of sensibility (*The World in a Village* 4: 9–10). In a reprise of the Muns trope in *The Prisoner at Large*, a servant within the Allbut house (William Bellevue's sister, Maria) is then fired and shut out of the Allbut house for admitting and giving some relief to its previous owner, the poor widow, and William himself and Captain Mullinhack meet with similarly inhospitable treatment when they arrive at the door. Not only are the native Irish excluded from the prosperity enjoyed by those at the top of the English social order, these scenes suggest, but so are many other domestic groups – poor women and children, servants, returning veterans, and old widows. The scenes that are built around this play's second sailor character, Charles, further develops this social critique while also providing a meta-theatrical commentary on the jolly 'old England' genre of pastoral that O'Keeffe himself had helped promote earlier in his career. The audience first encounters Charles in *The World in a Village* just as he is re-entering his native village after a long absence, and as he looks around with delight

---

[49] In the contemporary press, this satire was also interpreted as a satire against Hester Thrale Piozzi and her brewer husband (see *The Morning Post*, 27 November 1793). Like Mrs Allbut, Mrs Piozzi was a poet, and like her dramatic counterpart, too, she had 'travelled all over Italy in the first circles of fashion' (*The World in a Village*, 4: 11).

at this familiar landscape, he regales his companion, the Dutch captain, with accounts of the warm reception that he now expects to receive. 'Ah no place like old England', he boasts, 'not a house that won't fling open its doors to me; not a table without a plate, or a parlour without a nail for my hat! Bells rung! bonfires, I warrant!' (*The World in a Village*, 4: 17). These expectations about the hospitable nature of 'old England' would also have been set by scenes like the one that opened O'Keeffe's own highly success-ful 1781 pastoral comedy, *The Agreeable Surprise*. This opening scene shows that play's landlord, Sir Felix Friendly, sharing his table with a penniless captain and dispensing beer to his merrymaking tenants, all the while expounding on why he believes 'little England' is preferable to all the gardens and fountains of France or the palaces of Italy (*The Agreeable Surprise*, 1: 16). The 'remarkably beautiful'[50] scenic backdrop which the painter Michael Angelo Rooker created for this opening scene would also have served to reinforce this bucolic image. Rooker, an accomplished landscape painter, was known for his nostalgically sentimental representa-tions of English country life.

The social interactions that Charles observes after his return home in *The World in a Village*, however, provide an ironic commentary on this idealising rural vision. This sailor has no sooner made his remarks praising 'old England' when he sees the village doctor chasing away some sick villagers because they are too poor to pay him (*The World in a Village* 4: 17–18), and Charles himself soon comes in for the same treatment from other wealthier villagers (the Allbuts among them) who look at him with 'strangeness' and contempt because of his ragged clothing (4: 20,36). The question Charles poses after observing this contemptuous treatment – 'Is this our village?' (4: 18) – continues to hang over the ending of the play, too, even as it works to resolve the social inequities that it has exposed. This play's happy resolution, which is largely enabled by the disclosure that Charles has, in fact, acquired enormous wealth in the Far East, merely raises the spectre of a new form of injustice as Allbut himself sardonically notes when he states that this sailor has been 'ransacking abroad' and has made his fortune 'by cutting Rajahs throats and running off with their coats' (4: 56).

In his 1791 play, *Wild Oats or the Strolling Gentlemen*, O'Keeffe also raises the issue of the relationship of the colonies to the centre; but in this play, by contrast, he stresses the generative potential of this contact. These two contrasting visions, we could say, speak to that ambivalence that is

---

[50] *The Morning Chronicle and London Advertiser*, 5 September 1781.

always at the core of the diasporic consciousness, one that as Clifford notes 'lives loss and hope as a defining tension'.[51] *Wild Oats* is set in and around the manor house of Lady Amaranth in Hampshire, in the south of England, and it follows the adventures of a strolling player, Jack Rover, who has been barnstorming in the surrounding countryside with his companion, Harry Thunder. In Rover, more clearly than in any other of his characters, O'Keeffe was continuing that tradition of self-representation in London-Irish dramatic writing that George Farquhar began when he made Roebuck, a gentleman with a similar 'wild roving temper' the hero of his first play, *Love and a Bottle*; for O'Keeffe, as for Farquhar, this construct allowed the playwright to reflect on a liminal moment in his early life – the moment when he, like Farquhar, was moving from acting to writing, and from Ireland to England. Between 1766 and 1780, as noted earlier, Jack Keeffe (as he was then known) was, like his dramatic hero, Jack Rover, a 'strolling gentleman', performing not only with Dublin theatre companies but also with the itinerant theatrical companies that crisscrossed the Irish countryside each summer. In the summer of 1778, however, three years before he finally settled in England, O'Keeffe brought the stand-up comic act that had made him famous all over Ireland – 'Tony Lumpkin's Rambles' – to Portsmouth, a town that was then abuzz with dignitaries, including George III who came to inspect its naval base in preparation for war with the American colonies. Presumably to gather the needed information for the Portsmouth version of his act, the young O'Keeffe spent much of his free time during that summer rambling through the surrounding countryside where, as we know from his *Recollections* (1: 366–83), he shared meals with retired naval officers and kindly country people. The naval characters and friendly country folk whom Rover encounters over the course of this this play – the retired sea captain, Sir George Thunder, and his faithful old boatswain, John Dory, for example, or the farmer's goodhearted children, Sim and Jane – are arguably based on the memory of those encounters. Like so many of O'Keeffe's works, this play is woven, in part, out of his own life story.

At the end of *Wild Oats,* however, we learn that O'Keeffe's actor hero is not, in fact, Irish. He has arrived in England instead from colonial India and now, in the guise of a 'forlorn stroller', he is searching for the parents and the identity that he lost in the fog of the Hyder Ally wars (*Wild Oats,* 3:10,85). That backstory, coupled with this character's habit of quotation – Rover repeatedly responds to other characters by citing lines from Shakespeare and

---

[51] Clifford, 'Diasporas', 312.

other plays that were part of the eighteenth-century dramatic repertoire –
also gives his character a significance beyond the autobiographical. Rover
stands more broadly, it could be argued, for the new kind of colonial
immigrant that Britain had produced through its imperial adventuring,
demonstrating both the estranging as well as the generative effect of that
kind of subject's engagement with the dominant language and culture.
In an essay in which he argues that minority and migrant populations in
present-day Britain should be described as vernacular cosmopolitans, the
Indian-born critic Homi Bhabha stresses this creative potential, even as he
notes the inequality inherent in this population's engagement with the
dominant culture. Compelled 'to make a tryst with cultural translation as
an act of survival', he notes, 'vernacular cosmopolitans are forced in many
cases to insert their threatened and repressed histories between the lines of
dominant cultural practice', but, he adds, the crossing over of practices
and performance that are created in 'such cramped conditions of creativity' also produces something new and interesting – aesthetic and ethical
values that do not belong exclusively to any one culture but are mean-
ingful to both.[52] That the borrowings and dramatic crossing in *Wild Oats*
exemplify this kind of creativity can be seen, for example, early in the play
when Rover first confronts Farmer Gammon, one of the play's villains.
This affluent farmer, we learn, is threatening to evict two poor cottagers,
Mr Banks and his sister, who live on Lady Amaranth's estate because the
sister, Amelia Banks, has refused his marriage offer (*Wild Oats*, 3:13–24).
As in O'Keeffe's Irish pastorals, this oppression is associated with the
ascendancy into positions of power of a mercenary breed of 'new men';
Farmer Gammon, we discover, is in an alliance with the Quaker estate
agent, Ephraim Smooth, who, having converted Lady Amaranth to his
puritan ways, is now exercising control over her house, her land and her
tenants (*Wild Oats,* 3: 4–6, 13). But as this scene also shows, in this case,
English dramatic literature and, more particularly, the language of
Shakespeare's *King Lear*, provides Rover, and by extension the type of
colonial migrant he represents, a new and compelling way of telling his
story while also speaking out against injustice. As Rover is trying to escape
a 'pelting shower' by seeking shelter in Farmer Gammon's house, for
instance, he mutters 'Poor Tom's a cold' (3: 17), and when the farmer
refuses him entry, he subsequently uses Lear's denunciation of Goneril to

[52] Homi Bhabha, 'The Vernacular Cosmopolitan' in *Voices of the Crossing; The impact of Britain on Writers from Asia, the Caribbean and Africa*, ed. Ferdinand Dennis and Naseem Khan (London: Serpent's Tail, 2000), 139–40.

reign down curses on the uncharitable Gammon's head. Kneeling on the stage in a manner that recalls the medieval beggar's curse, Rover calls out:

> Hear, Nature, dear goddess, hear! If ever you designed to make his corn-fields fruitful, change thy purpose; that, from the blighted ear no grain may fall to fat his *stubble goose* – and, when to town he drives his hogs, so like himself, oh, let him feel the soaking rain, then may he curse his crime too late, and know how sharper than a serpent's tooth 'tis. (*Wild Oats*, 3:17)

At one level, this cobbling together of eighteenth-century and Shakespearean speech is funny, and audiences in the theatre would have been encouraged to laugh by Rover's own next self-deflationary line: 'Damme, but I'm spouting in the rain all this time' (3: 17). But the comic effect that this speech produces is also not unlike that produced by the macaronic verse of contemporary Gaelic poets and, like their code-switching too, this meshing of languages has a socially disruptive effect, upsetting cultural hierarchies and creating new unexpected linguistic and social conjunctures. In this case, it links the 'forlorn stroller' of this play and, by extension, the whole history of colonial diaspora that this character evokes to the poor bare-forked wanderers and madmen who populate the landscape of Shakespeare's greatest tragedy, and it brings Lear's powerful outcry against a merciless social order to bear on the new world order that was turning such subjects into homeless migrants.

To attribute this kind of meshing of languages, genres and cultures to a vernacular cosmopolitan consciousness, we could say in conclusion, is also to expand the chronological boundary of the new, non-national theatrical historiography that has emerged in recent years as critics have begun to study the impact of diasporic and immigrant populations on mainstream metropolitan drama. Such studies tend for the most part to focus on present-day theatrical productions as Una Chaudhuri does, for instance, in her recent theoretically rich essay on the contemporary American stage. As playwrights and performers from newly arrived migrant groups make their way into the US theatre, Chaudhuri notes, they rework existing dramatic traditions to accommodate their hybridised identities and their cross-cultural experiences; in so doing, they, too, generate a 'macaronic' form of drama – performances that challenge what counts as verisimilitude in mainstream bourgeois drama even as they unsettle the national 'community effect' that theatre has historically worked to produce.[53] O'Keeffe's 'dramatic Wild Oats', it could be said, represent an

---

[53] Una Chaudhuri, 'Theatre and Cosmopolitanism: New Stories, Old Stages' in *Cosmopolitan Geographies: New Locations in Literature and Culture*, ed. Vinay Dharwadker (New York and London: Routledge, 2001), 184, 175.

early stage in the construction of this ideologically complex and challenging kind of theatre. This migrant playwright's unorthodox pastoral productions proleptically configure the dramatic productions of the thousands of other playwrights – from Ireland, India and elsewhere on the globe – who, in the centuries ahead, would appropriate and estrange existing conventions and genres as they wove their new stories and their new characters into mainstream metropolitan plays, rendering that drama 'excentrically' cosmopolitan.

Select Bibliography

Primary Sources

Adolphus, John. *Memoirs of John Bannister, Comedian*, 2 vols. London: Richard Bentley, 1839.

Baker, David Erskine . *Biographia Dramatica; or, A Companion to the Playhouse*, 2 vols. London: Longman et al., 1812.

The Companion to the Play-house: Or, An Historical Account of All the Dramatic Writers (and Their Works) that Have Appeared in Great Britain and Ireland, from the Commencement of Our Theatrical Exhibitions, Down to the Present Year 1764, 2 vols. London: Printed for T. Becket and P. A. Dehondt, 1764.

Boaden, James. *The Life of Mr Jordan including Original Private Correspondence and Numerous Anecdotes of her Contemporaries*, 2 vols. London: Edward Bull, 1831.

Bourke, Angela, Siobhán Kilfeather, Maria Luddy, Margaret Mac Curtain, Geraldine Meaney, Máirín Ní Dhonnachadha, Mary O'Dowd and Clair Wills, eds. *The Field Day Anthology of Irish Writing: Irish Women's Writing and Traditions*, 2 vols [vols 4 and 5]. Cork: Cork University Press, 2002.

Brooke, Henry. *Gustavus Vasa, The Deliverer of His Country*. London, J. Buck, 1739.

Busby, Thomas. *Concert Room and Orchestra Anecdotes of Music and Musicians, Ancient and Modern*, 3 vols. London: Clementi and Co, 1825.

Cooke, William. *Memoirs of Charles Macklin, Comedian: With the Dramatic Characters, Manners, Anecdotes & c. of the Age in Which He Lived*. London: J. Asperne, 1806.

Danchin, Pierre, ed. *The Prologues and Epilogues of the Eighteenth Century: A Complete Edition*, 6 vols. Nancy: Presses universitaires de Nancy, 1990–1994.

Deane, Seamus, gen. ed., *The Field Day Anthology of Irish Writing*, 3 vols. Cork: Cork University Press, 1991.

Edgeworth, Richard Lovell and Maria Edgeworth. *Essay on Irish Bulls*. New York: Printed by J. Swaine, 1803.

Garrick, David. *The Letters of David Garrick*, ed. David Mason Little, George M. Kahrl and Phoebe de K. Wilson, 3 vols. Cambridge, MA: Harvard University Press, 1963.

The Plays of David Garrick, ed. Harry William Pedicord and Fredrick Louis Bergmann, 7 vols. Carbondale, IL: Southern Illinois University Press, 1980.

[Gentleman, Francis] 'Sir Nicholas Nipclose'. *The Theatres: A Poetical Dissection*. London: Printed for John Bell and C. Etherington, 1772.

Goldsmith, Oliver. *The Collected Works of Oliver Goldsmith*, ed. Arthur Friedman, 5 vols. Oxford: Clarendon Press, 1966.

The Letters of Oliver Goldsmith, ed. Michael Griffin and David O'Shaughnessy. Cambridge: Cambridge University Press, 2018.

Greene, John C., ed. *Theatre in Dublin, 1745–1820: A Calendar of Performances*, 6 vols. Bethlehem, PA: Lehigh University Press, 2011.

Greene, John C., and Gladys Clark, eds. *The Dublin Stage 1720–1745: A Calendar of Plays, Entertainments, and Afterpieces*. Bethlehem, PA: Lehigh University Press, 1993.

Highfill Jr, Philip, A. Burnim Kalman and Edward A. Langhans, eds. *A Biographical Dictionary of Actors, Actresses, Dancers, Managers and Other Stage Personnel in London, 1660–1800*, 16 vols. Carbondale and Edwardsville: Southern Illinois University Press, 1973–93.

Hunt, Leigh. *Critical Essays on the Performers of the London Theatres*. London: Printed by and for John Hunt, 1807.

Keating, Geoffrey. *The General History of Ireland ... Collected by the Learned Jeoffrey Keating, D.D.*, trans. and ed. Dermod O'Connor. London: Printed by J. Bettenham, 1723.

Kelly, Hugh. *Thespis: Or a Critical Examination into the Merits of All the Principal Performers Belonging to Drury-Lane Theatre*. London: Printed for G. Kearsley, 1766–67.

Kelly, Michael. *Reminiscences of Michael Kelly*, ed. Roger Fiske. London: Oxford University Press, 1975.

Kirkman, James Thomas. *Memoirs of the Life of Charles Macklin, Esq.*, 2 vols. London: Printed for Lackington, Allen and Co., 1799.

Le Fanu, Alicia Sheridan. *The Sons of Erin, or Modern Sentiment: A Comedy, in Five Acts Performed at the Lyceum Theatre*, 3rd edn. London: J. Ridgeway, 1812.

Macklin, Charles. *Four Comedies by Charles Macklin*, ed. J. O. Bartley. London: Sidgwick and Jackson, 1968.

MacNally, Leonard. *The Claims of Ireland*. London: J. Johnson, 1782.

Macready, William. *Macready's Reminiscences, and Selections from His Diaries and Letters*, ed. Frederick Pollock. New York: Harper and Brothers, 1875.

Mathews, Anne. *Anecdotes of Actors: With Other Desultory Recollections*. London: T. C. Newby, 1844.

Molesworth, Robert. *An Account of Denmark, With Francogallia and Some Considerations for the Promoting of Agriculture and Employing the Poor*, ed. Justin Champion. Indianapolis, IN: Liberty Fund, 2011.

Moore, Thomas. *Memoirs of the Life of the Right Honourable Richard Brinsley Sheridan*, 2 vols. London: Longman, Hurst, Rees, Orme, Brown and Green, 1825.

The Murphiad. A Mock Heroic Poem by 'Philim Mocolloch'. London: J. Williams, 1761.

Murphy, Arthur. *The Collected Works of Arthur Murphy*, 7 vols. London: Printed for T. Cadell, 1786.

The Gray's Inn Journal, 2 vols. Dublin: William Sleater, 1756.

The Life of David Garrick, Esq., 2 vols. London: J. Wright, 1801.

O'Conor, Charles. *The Letters of Charles O'Conor of Belanagare*, ed. Robert E. Ward, John F. Wrynn and Catherine Coogan Ward. Washington, DC: Catholic University Press, 1988.

The Letters of Charles O'Conor of Belanagare, ed. Catherine Coogan Ward and Robert E. Ward, 2 vols. Ann Arbor, MI: University Microfilms, 1980.

O'Hara, Kane. *Midas: An English Burletta*. London: G. Kearsley et al., 1764.

O'Keeffe, Adelaide, ed. *Recollections of the Life of John O'Keeffe: Written by Himself*, 2 vols. London: H. Colburn, 1826.

O'Keeffe, John. *The Dramatic Works of John O'Keeffe Esq.* in Four Volumes, ed. Frederick M. Link. New York: Garland, 1981.

Owenson, Sydney. *The Book of the Boudoir*, 2 vols. London: Henry Colburn, 1829.

The First Attempt, or the Whim of the Moment: a Comic Opera in Two Acts 'Performing with unbounded applause at the Theatre Royal Dublin, Written by Miss Owenson, the Music Composed by Thomas Cooke'. London: Powers Music House and Westmoreland St. Dublin, 1807.

Lady Morgan's Memoirs: Autobiography, Diaries, and Correspondence, ed. W. Hepworth Dixon. London: W. H. Allen, 1863. In *British and Irish Women's Letters and Diaries: 1500–1950* [https://bwld.alexanderstreet.com]

The Wild Irish Girl, ed. Kathryn Kirkpatrick. Oxford and New York: Oxford University Press, 1999.

Oxberry, William. *Oxberry's Dramatic Biography and Histrionic Anecdotes*, ed. Catherine Oxberry, 5 vols. London: George Virtue, 1825–26.

Parke, William T. *Musical Memoirs; Comprising an Account of the General State of Music in England*, 2 vols. London: Henry Colburn and Richard Bentley, 1830.

Sheridan, Elizabeth. *Betsy Sheridan's Journal: Letters from Sheridan's Sister 1784–1786 & 1788–1790*, ed. William Le Fanu. London: Eyre & Spottiswoode, 1960.

The Triumph of Prudence Over Passion, ed. Aileen Douglas and Ian Campbell Ross. Dublin: Four Courts Press, 2011.

Sheridan, Richard Brinsley. *The Dramatic Works of Richard Brinsley Sheridan* ed. Cecil Price, 2 vols. Oxford: Clarendon Press, 1973.

Letters of Richard Brinsley Sheridan, ed. Cecil Price, 3 vols. Oxford: Clarendon Press, 1966.

Speeches of the Late Right Honourable Richard Brinsley Sheridan: Several Corrected by Himself and Edited by a Constitutional Friend, 5 vols. London: Patrick Martin, 1816.

Works of the Late Right Honourable Richard Brinsley Sheridan, ed. Thomas Moore, 2 vols. London: John Murray, 1821.

Stanfield, James Field . *The Guinea Voyage, A Poem in Three Books*. London: James Phillips, 1789.

The Guinea Voyage, A Poem in Three Books to which are added Observations on a Voyage to the Coast of Africa in a series of letters to Thomas Clarkson, 2nd edition. Edinburgh, 1807.

Observations on a Guinea Voyage, in a Series of Letters Addressed to the Rev. Thomas Clarkson. London: Printed by James Phillips, 1788.

Swift, Jonathan. *Swift's Irish Writings: Selected Prose and Poetry*, ed. Carole Fabricant and Robert Mahony. Basingstoke: Palgrave, 2010.

'Theatre Royal, Haymarket, A Collection of Playbills from Haymarket Theatre, 1817–1821', *MS British Playbills, 1754–1882*, British Library, *Nineteenth Century Collections Online*.

Theatrical Biography, or Memoirs of the Principal Performers of the Three Theatres Royal, 2 vols. Dublin: Printed for H. Saunders et al., 1772.

The Thespian Dictionary or Dramatic Biography of the Present Age. London: James Cundee, 1805.

Taylor, John. *Records of My Life*, 2 vols. London: Edward Bull, 1832.

White, Harry and B. Boydell, eds. *The Encyclopaedia of Music in Ireland*, 2 vols. Dublin: University College Dublin Press, 2013.

Wilson, C. H. *Brookiana*, 2 vols. London: Richard Philips, 1804.

Winston, James. *Drury Lane Journal: Selections from James Winston's Diaries, 1819–1827*, ed. Alfred L. Nelson and Gilbert B. Cross. London: Society for Theatre Research, 1974.

Secondary Sources

Anderson, Emily. 'Celebrity Shylock'. *PMLA* 126.4 (2011): 935–49.

Appleton, William W. *Charles Macklin: An Actor's Life*. Boston, MA: Harvard University Press, 1960.

Bailey, Craig. *Irish London: Middle-Class Migration in the Global Eighteenth Century*. Liverpool: Liverpool University Press, 2013.

Bartlett, Thomas. *Ireland: A History*. Cambridge: Cambridge University Press, 2011.

Bartley, J. O. *Teague, Shenkin and Sawney: Being an Historical Study of the Earliest Irish, Welsh, and Scottish Characters in English Plays*. Cork: Cork University Press, 1954.

Brown, Michael. *The Irish Enlightenment*. Cambridge, MA: Harvard University Press, 2016.

Brunström, Conrad. *Thomas Sheridan's Career and Influence: An Actor in Earnest*. Lewisburg, PA: Bucknell University Press, 2011.

Brunström, Conrad M. and Declan Kavanagh. 'Arthur Murphy and Florida Peat: "The Gray's Inn Journal" and versions of the Author'. *Eighteenth-Century Ireland/Iris an dá chultúr* 27 (2012): 123–41.

Bullard, Paddy. *Edmund Burke and the Art of Rhetoric*. Cambridge: Cambridge University Press, 2011.

Burden, Michael. *The English Theatre Masque 1690–1800*, 2 vols. PhD diss., University of Edinburgh, 1991.

Burke, Helen. 'Acting in the Periphery: The Irish Theatre'. In *The Cambridge Companion to British Theatre, 1730–1830*, ed. Jane Moody and Daniel O'Quinn. Cambridge: Cambridge University Press, 2007, 219–31.

'The Catholic Question, Print Media, and John O'Keeffe's *The Poor Soldier* (1783)'. *Eighteenth-Century Fiction* 27.3–4 (2015): 419–48.

'Country Matters: Irish "Waggery" and the Irish and British Theatrical Traditions'. In *Players, Playwrights, Playhouses: Investigating Performance, 1660–1800*, ed. Michael Cordner and Peter Holland. Basingstoke: Palgrave Macmillan, 2007, 213–28.

'Crossing Acts: Irish Drama from George Farquhar to Thomas Sheridan'. In *A Companion to Irish Literature*, ed. Julia M. Wright, 2 vols. 1: 125–42. Oxford: Wiley-Blackwell, 2010.

'Integrated as Outsiders: Teague's Blanket and the Irish Immigrant "Problem" in Early Modern Britain'. *Éire-Ireland* 46.2 (2011): 20–42.

'The Revolutionary Prelude: The Dublin Stage in the Late 1770s and Early 1780s'. *Eighteenth-Century Life* 22.3 (1998): 7–18.

Riotous Performances: The Struggle for Hegemony in the Irish Theater, 1712–1784 (Notre Dame, IN: University of Notre Dame Press, 2003.

Burke, Richard and Ian McBride, eds. *The Princeton History of Modern Ireland*. Princeton: Princeton University Press, 2016.

Campbell, Mary. *Lady Morgan: The Life and Times of Sydney Owenson*. London: Pandora, 1988.

Carey, Daniel and Lynn Festa, eds. *The Postcolonial Enlightenment: Eighteenth-Century Colonialism and Postcolonial Theory*. Oxford University Press, 2009.

Cave, Richard Allen. 'Staging the Irishman'. In *Acts of Supremacy: The British Empire and the Stage, 1790–1930*, ed. J. S. Bratton, Richard Allen Cave, Breandan Gregory, Michael Pickering and Heidi J. Holder. Manchester: Manchester University Press, 1991, 62–128.

Chandler, James. 'A Discipline in Shifting Perspectives: Why We Need Irish Studies'. *Field Day Review* 2 (2006): 19–40.

Choudhury, Mita. 'Sheridan, Garrick, and a Colonial Gesture: *The School for Scandal* on the Calcutta Stage'. *Theatre Journal* 46 (1994): 303–21.

Clark, Peter. *British Clubs and Societies 1580–1800: The Origins of an Associational World*. Oxford: Oxford University Press, 2000.

Clarke, Norma. *Brothers of the Quill: Oliver Goldsmith in Grub Street*. Cambridge, MA: Harvard University Press, 2016.

Connolly, Claire. *A Cultural History of the Irish Novel*. Cambridge and New York: Cambridge University Press, 2012.

'"I accuse Miss Owenson": The Wild Irish Girl as Media Event'. *Colby Quarterly*, 36.2 (2000), 98–115.

Conolly, L. W. *The Censorship of English Drama, 1737–1824*. San Marino, CA: Huntington Library Press, 1976.

De Bruyn, Frans and Shaun Regan, eds. *The Culture of the Seven Years' War: Empire, Identity, and the Arts in the Eighteenth-Century Atlantic World*. Toronto: University of Toronto Press, 2014.

DeRochi, Jack E. and Daniel J. Ennis, eds. *Richard Brinsley Sheridan: The Impresario in Political and Cultural Context*. Lewisburg: Bucknell University Press, 2013.

Donohue, Frank. '"Avoiding the Cooler Tribunal of the Study": Richard Brinsley Sheridan's Writer's Block and Late Eighteenth-Century Print Culture'. *ELH* 68 (2001): 831–56.

Donohue, Joseph. 'Burletta and the Early Nineteenth-Century English Theatre'. *Nineteenth Century Theatre Research* 1 (1973): 29–51.

Donovan, Julie. *Sydney Owenson, Lady Morgan and the Politics of Style*. Bethesda, MD: Maunsel & Company, 2009.

Dunbar, Howard Hunter. *The Dramatic Career of Arthur Murphy*. New York and London: Modern Language Association of America and Oxford University Press, 1946.

Edelstein, Dan. *The Enlightenment: A Genealogy*. Chicago: University of Chicago Press, 2010.

Emery, John Pike. *Arthur Murphy: An Eminent English Dramatist of the Eighteenth Century*. Philadelphia: University of Pennsylvania Press, 1946.

Fiske, Roger. *English Theatre Music in the Eighteenth Century*. Oxford: Clarendon Press, 1986.

Fitzer, Anna M. '"Feeling and sense beyond all seeming": Private Lines, Public Relations, and the Performances of the Le Fanu Circle', *Nineteenth Century Theatre and Film* 38.2 (2011): 26–37.

 'Relating a Life: Alicia LeFanu's Memoirs of the Life and Writings of Mrs Frances Sheridan'. *Women's Writing* 15.3 (2008): 32–54.

 'Revealing Influence: The Forgotten Daughters of Frances Sheridan'. *Women's Writing* 20 (2013): 64–81.

Fitzgerald, Percy. *The Lives of the Sheridans*, 2 vols. London: R. Bentley, 1886.

Fitzpatrick, William John. *Lady Morgan; Her Career, Literary and Personal, with a Glimpse of Her Friends, and a Word to Her Calumniators*. London: C. J. Skeet, 1860.

Flynn, Christopher. 'Challenging Englishness from the Racial Margins: William Macready's *Irishman in London; Or; The Happy African*'. *Irish Studies Review* 16.2 (2008): 159–72.

Foot, Jesse. *The Life of the late Arthur Murphy Esq*. London: Printed for J. Faulder, 1811.

Gallagher, Noelle. *Historical Literatures: Writing about the Past in England, 1660–1740*. Manchester: Manchester University Press, 2012.

Gargett, Graham and Geraldine Sheridan, eds. *Ireland and the French Enlightenment, 1700–1800*. Basingstoke: Palgrave, 1999.

Gibbons, Luke. *Edmund Burke and Ireland: Aesthetics, Politics, and the Colonial Sublime*. Cambridge: Cambridge University Press, 2003.

Gibbons, Luke and Kieran O'Conor, eds. *Charles O'Conor of Ballinagare, 1710–91: Life and Works*. Dublin: Four Courts Press, 2015.

Goring, Paul. '"John Bull, Pit, Box, and Gallery, Said No!": Charles Macklin and the Limits of Ethnic Resistance on the Eighteenth-Century London Stage'. *Representations* 79.1 (2002): 63–81.

Griffin, Michael. *Enlightenment in Ruins: The Geographies of Oliver Goldsmith*. Lewisburg: Bucknell University Press, 2013.

Harvey, Karen J. and Kevin B. Pry. 'John O'Keeffe as an Irish Playwright within the Theatrical, Social, and Economic Context of His Time'. *Éire-Ireland* 22 (1987): 19–43.

Harris, James, ed. *The Oxford Handbook of British Philosophy in the Eighteenth Century*. Oxford University Press, 2013.

Hayton, David. 'From Barbarian to Burlesque: English Images of the Irish c. 1660-1750'. *Irish Economic and Social History* 15 (1988): 5–31.

Higgins, Padhraig. *A Nation of Politicians: Gender, Patriotism, and Political Culture in Late Eighteenth-Century Ireland*. Madison: University of Wisconsin Press, 2010.

Hill, Jacqueline. *Dublin Civic Politics and Irish Protestant Patriotism 1660–1840*. Oxford: Clarendon Press, 1997.

Jones, Robert W. 'Texts, Tools and Things: An Approach to Manuscripts of Richard Brinsley Sheridan's *The School for Scandal*'. *Review of English Studies* 66 (2015): 723–43.

Kanter, Douglas. *The Making of British Unionism, 1740–1848: Politics, Government, and the Anglo-Irish Constitutional Relationship*. Dublin: Four Courts, 2009.

Kelly, James. *Prelude to Union: Anglo-Irish Politics in the 1780s*. Cork: Cork University Press, 1992.

and Martyn J. Powell, eds. *Clubs and Societies in Eighteenth-Century Ireland*. Dublin: Four Courts Press, 2010.

Kennedy, Máire. *French Books in Eighteenth-Century Ireland*. Oxford: Voltaire Foundation, 2001.

Klein, Axel. 'Stage-Irish, or the National in Irish Opera, 1780–1925'. *Opera Quarterly* 21 (2005): 27–67.

Langan, Celeste. 'Scotch Drink & Irish Harps: Mediations of the National Air'. In *The Figure of Music in Nineteenth-Century British Poetry*, ed. Phyllis Weliver. Aldershot: Ashgate, 2005, 25–49.

Lawrenson, Sonja. 'Frances Sheridan, "The History of Nourjahad" and the Sultan of Smock Alley'. *Eighteenth-Century Ireland* 26 (2011): 24–50.

Leerssen, Joep. *Mere Irish and Fíor Ghael: Studies in the Idea of Irish Nationality, Its Development and Literary Expression Prior to the*

Nineteenth Century. Notre Dame, IN and Cork: Cork University Press and Field Day, 1986.

Livesey, James. 'Free trade and Empire in the Anglo-Irish Commercial Propositions of 1785'. *Journal of British Studies* 52 (2013): 103–27.

Maxwell, Margaret F. 'Olympus at Billingsgate: The Burlettas of Kane O'Hara'. *Educational Theatre Journal* 15/2 (1963): 130–35.

McBride, Ian. 'The Edge of Enlightenment: Ireland and Scotland in the Eighteenth Century'. *Modern Intellectual History* 10 (2013): 135–51.

  Eighteenth-Century Ireland: Isle of Slaves. Dublin: Gill and Macmillan, 2009.

Mee, Jon. *Conversable Worlds: Literature, Contention, and Community, 1762 to 1830* . Oxford: Oxford University Press, 2011.

Moody, Jane and Daniel O'Quinn, eds. *The Cambridge Companion to British Theatre, 1730–1830*. Cambridge: Cambridge University Press, 2007.

Moore, Sean D., ed. 'Ireland and Enlightenment'. Special issue, *Eighteenth-Century Studies*, 45 (2012).

Morash, Christopher. *A History of Irish Theatre, 1601–2000*. Cambridge and New York: Cambridge University Press, 2002.

Morwood, James and David Crane, eds. *Sheridan Studies*. Cambridge: Cambridge University Press, 1995.

Nussbaum, Felicity. *Rival Queens: Actresses, Performance, and the Eighteenth-Century British Theater*. Philadelphia: University of Pennsylvania Press, 2010.

O'Brien, Karen. *Narratives of Enlightenment: Cosmopolitan History from Voltaire to Gibbon*. Cambridge: Cambridge University Press, 1997.

Ó Catháin, Diarmuid. 'Dermot O'Connor, Translator of Keating'. *Eighteenth-Century Ireland/Iris an Dá Chultúr* 2 (1987): 67–87.

O'Dowd, Mary. *A History of Women in Ireland, 1500–1800*. Harlow: Pearson Longman, 2005.

O'Halloran, Clare. *Golden Ages and Barbarous Nations; Antiquarian Debate and Cultural Politics in Ireland, c. 1750–1800*. Notre Dame and Cork: University of Notre Dame Press and Cork University Press, 2004.

Oliver, Kathleen M. 'Frances Sheridan's Faulkland, the Silenced, Emasculated, Ideal, Male'. *SEL* 43 (2003): 683–700.

O'Quinn, Daniel. *Staging Governance: Theatrical Imperialism in London 1770–1800*. Baltimore, MD: Johns Hopkins University Press, 2005.

O'Quinn, Daniel and Gillian Russell, eds. 'Georgian Theatre in an Information Age: Media, Performance, Sociability'. Special issue, *Eighteenth-Century Fiction* 27.3–4 (2015).

Orr, Bridget. *Empire on the English Stage, 1660–1714*. Cambridge: Cambridge University Press, 2001.

O'Shaughnessy, David . '"Bit, by some mad whig": Charles Macklin and the Theater of Irish Enlightenment'. *Huntington Library Quarterly* 80.4 (2017): 559–84.

  'Networks of Aspiration: The London Irish of the Eighteenth Century'. Special issue, *Eighteenth-Century Life* 39.1 (2015).

"'Rip'ning Buds in Freedom's Field": Staging Irish Improvement in the 1780s'. *Journal of Eighteenth-Century Studies* 38.4 (2015): 541–54.

O'Toole, Fintan. *A Traitor's Kiss: The Life of Richard Brinsley Sheridan*. London: Granta, 1998.

Parry, Sir Edmund Abbott. *Charles Macklin*. New York: Longmans, Green, and Co., 1891.

Powell, Martyn J. 'Charles James Fox and Ireland'. *Irish Historical Studies* 33 (2002): 169–90.

Prendergast, Amy. *Literary Salons across Britain and Ireland in the Long Eighteenth Century*. Basingstoke: Palgrave, 2015.

Ragussis, Michael. 'Jews and Other "Outlandish Englishmen": Ethnic Performance and the Invention of British Identity under the Georges'. *Critical Inquiry* 26 (2000): 773–97.

   Theatrical Nation: Jews and Other Outlandish Englishmen in Georgian Britain. Philadelphia: University of Pennsylvania Press, 2010.

Richards, Jeffrey H. *Drama, Theatre, and Identity in the American New Republic*. Cambridge: Cambridge University Press, 2005.

Robbins, Caroline. *The Eighteenth-Century Commonwealthman*. Cambridge, MA: Harvard University Press, 1959.

Rosenfeld, Sybil. *Foreign Theatrical Companies in Great Britain in the 17th and 18th Centuries*. London: Society for Theatre Research, 1955.

Rosenthal, Laura J. 'Juba's Roman Soul: Addison's *Cato* and Enlightenment Cosmopolitanism'. *Studies in the Literary Imagination* 32 (1999): 64–75.

Russell, Gillian. *Women, Sociability and Theatre in Georgian London*. Cambridge: Cambridge University Press, 2007.

Sadie, Stanley. *The New Grove Dictionary of Opera*, 4 vols. London: Macmillan, 1992.

Schellenberg, Betty A. 'Frances Sheridan Reads John Home: Placing *Sidney Bidulph* in the Republic of Letters'. *Eighteenth-Century Fiction* 13 (2001): 561–77.

Schweitzer, David R. 'The Failure of William Pitt's Irish Trade Propositions'. *Parliamentary History* 3 (1984): 129–45.

Siskin, Clifford and William Warner, eds. *This Is Enlightenment*. Chicago: University of Chicago Press, 2012.

Slowey, Desmond. *The Radicalization of Irish Drama 1600–1900: The Rise and Fall of Ascendancy Theatre*. Dublin: Irish Academic Press, 2008.

Small, Stephen. *Political Thought in Ireland 1776–1798: Republicanism, Patriotism, and Radicalism*. Oxford: Oxford University Press, 2012.

Spenser, Edmund. *View of the Present State of Irelande*, ed. W. L. Renwick. Oxford: Clarendon Press, 1970.

Swindells, Julia and David Francis Taylor, eds. *The Oxford Handbook of the Georgian Theatre, 1737–1832*. Oxford: Oxford University Press, 2014.

Taylor, David Francis. *Theatres of Opposition: Empire, Revolution, and Richard Brinsley Sheridan*. Oxford: Oxford University Press, 2012.

Truninger, Annelise. *Paddy and the Paycock: A Study of the Stage Irishman from Shakespeare to O'Casey.* Bern: Francke, 1976.

Wagoner, Michael M. 'The "Merry" Tragedy of *Henry VII* as written by "Charles Macklin, Comedian"'. *New Theatre Quarterly* 31.4 (2015): 372–80.

Walsh, T. J. *Opera in Dublin 1705–1797: The Social Scene.* Dublin: A. Figgis, 1973.

Werkmeister, Lucyle. *A Newspaper History of England 1792–1793.* Lincoln: University of Nebraska Press, 1967.

Whelan, Kevin. *Acts of Union: The Causes, Contexts, and Consequences of the Act of Union.* Dublin: Four Courts, 2001.

Wiesenthal, Christine S. 'Representation and Experimentation in the Mayor Comedies of Richard Brinsley Sheridan'. *Eighteenth-Century Studies* 25 (1992): 309–30.

Withers, Charles W. J. *Placing the Enlightenment: Thinking Geographically about the Age of Reason.* Chicago: University of Chicago Press, 2007.

Wood, Gillen D'Arcy. *Romanticism and Music Culture in Britain, 1770–1840: Virtue and Virtuosity.* Cambridge: Cambridge University Press, 2010.

Wright, Herbert. 'Henry Brooke's "Gustavus Vasa"'. *Modern Language Review* 14 (1919): 173–82.

Wyn-Jones, David. *Music in Eighteenth-Century Britain.* Aldershot: Ashgate, 2000.

Index